Salt

in Their Veins

Salt
in Their Veins

Conversations with Coastal Mainers

By Charlie Wing

Camden, Maine

Down East Books

An imprint of Globe Pequot, the trade division of
The Rowman & Littlefield Publishing Group, Inc.
4501 Forbes Blvd., Ste. 200
Lanham, MD 20706
www.rowman.com

Distributed by NATIONAL BOOK NETWORK

British Library Cataloguing in Publication Information available

Library of Congress Cataloging-in-Publication Data Is Available

ISBN: 978-1-68475-081-8 (paperback)
ISBN: 978-1-68475-082-5 (ebook)

∞™ The paper used in this publication meets the minimum requirements of
American National Standard for Information Sciences—Permanence of Paper
for Printed Library Materials, ANSI/NISO Z39.48-1992

*Dedicated to the memory of my grandfather,
Clarence Goddard, for passing me the salt.*

CONTENTS

Down East—Bucksport to Eastport

Acknowledgments
Credits

"The cure for anything is salt water: sweat, tears, or the sea."
—*Isak Dinesen*

INTRODUCTION

In the dim glow of a summer evening in 1945, a six-year old boy stood at the end of a wharf and slowly poured salt from a five-pound bag into the ocean below. Except for the surroundings and the boy's bare feet, he might have been an altar boy in a ceremony of the Catholic Church. The thin, weathered man standing close by his side spoke, "All of us who take our living from the sea must give back to the sea. If we care for the sea, it will provide for us."

The old man was my grandfather, Clarence Goddard, and I was that small boy. The ritual took place on grandfather's wharf on Dingley Island, in Harpswell, Maine.

Clarence and his brother Howard owned Goddard Bros. Ice. They harvested and sold ice to Portuguese schooners headed for the Grand Banks They also lobstered, built boats, maintained wharfs and floats for summer folk, kept chickens, two cows, pigs, a horse, and a garden, and somehow found time to father ten children between them. The industrious Goddard brothers were not unlike thousands of other men along the long, rugged coast of Maine.

From left: grandfather Clarence, great-uncle Howard, and great-grandfather, Frank Goddard pose at the farm on Dingley Island, Harpswell, Maine in 1914.

The Goddard Brothers' ice house. The double walls were 12 inches apart, and the gap was filled with sawdust insulation. Ice blocks slid down to the wharf on the rails in the foreground.

Harvesting the ice. The two men at left were poling ice blocks in an open channel. The huge blocks were then pulled up the ramp on a horse-powered conveyor.

After the ice blocks were weighed, grandfather Clarence and uncle Chester [Howard's son] used pikes to slide the blocks to the fishing schooner in the background.

A typical fishing schooner being loaded. Many Portuguese vessels loaded ice at Maine coastal ice houses before heading out to fish Georges Bank or the Grand Banks.

Great-uncle Howard delivering his day's catch to Watson's General Store in nearby Cundys Harbor. Howard and Clarence each hauled sixty traps by hand within a half mile of home.

Clarence's seven children aboard "Joker," the family's one-lunger-powered Hampton. They are dressed up, probably for the occasional 25-mile shopping trip to Portland. It was quicker to go by boat than by automobile.

The Town of Harpswell, Maine, consists of dozens of islands and three peninsulas that jut like long, arthritic fingers twelve miles into Casco Bay. The town is not unlike nearly 100 others that comprise a broad swath of rocky Maine coastline that stretches some 220 miles from Portland to Eastport.

Diners at Cook's Lobster House on Bailey Island can look across Harpswell Sound to Harpswell Neck and see people on the other shore. The distance is a mere half mile by water, yet twenty-seven miles by land. Imagine, if you will, making the trip by horse and carriage. What is now a forty-minute drive was an all-day journey at the time Harpswell was incorporated 250 years ago.

Surviving in these coastal Maine peninsula and island communities required a combination of industriousness, flexibility, and self-sufficiency, coupled with a willingness to pull together in a tight-knit community. The majority of the early settlers were ideally suited to the challenge: poor but tough, hardworking Scotch, Irish, and English peasants, lured by the promise of freedom and, better yet, free land.

Pull together they did. They created their own peninsula and island worlds. Even today, after most of the United States has turned to full-time professionals for every aspect of government: town manager, tax collector, fire chief, code enforcer, animal control officer, and police chief, many of these communities still rely almost exclusively on volunteers. Every year, during spring thaw, the residents gather in the town hall or local school for town meeting, a forum for socializing over sandwiches, cookies, and coffee (proceeds to benefit the cause of the day);vigorous debate; colorful displays of down east humor; and voting on 100 or more items of town business.

The social structures in these towns are so complete and satisfying that few young people leave. Of those who venture beyond the next town, most eventually return, having found the wider world wanting. It is not unusual to find that ten percent or more of a town's inhabitants share the same surname, and many of their family homes have been passed down through six or more generations.

This feeling of place and destiny is instilled at an early age. One foggy morning I was drinking coffee on my boat while anchored in New Harbor, on Pemaquid Peninsula. A young boy rowing a skiff appeared out of the fog and noticed my shipboard cat. Fascinated by the cat, he began circling the boat, calling out to the cat.

"Would you like to come aboard?" I asked.

"Shoah [sure]," he answered. Expertly cleating his skiff's bow line, he climbed aboard in flannel shirt, torn denim jeans and muddy clamdigger boots.

"Where do you live?" I asked.

"Right heah in New Haaba."

"How old are you?"

"Nine."

"So what do you want to be when you grow up?"

That gave him pause. He seemed puzzled by the concept either of growing up or of wishing to be something he wasn't already. After pondering my question, he finally stated, "Lobsterman. Already got twelve traps."

"Wouldn't you like to travel, to see the world?" I asked.

"Why should I?"—this time without a second's deliberation. "We got a movie theater right up to Damariscotta." [Damariscotta lies at the head of the bay, a distance of twelve miles.]

When a village is too small to support an eatery, the hub of the social network is often the post office. In these microcosms, the postmistress is the equivalent of the Google search engine—a vast repository of town history, facts, and goings-on. Another true story, told to me by a native of Phippsburg, will illustrate the importance of this key position.

John had been watching for a worrisome letter from the IRS. As the weeks passed, he became more and more concerned. Finally he broached the subject with the postmistress, "Dottie, I've been expecting a letter from the IRS...."

"Why John, didn't you find it? It looked real important, so I put it under the telephone in your kitchen."

Down East Mainers are, to put it mildly, not fond of larger forms of government, either state or federal. They are naturally taciturn, as if words are too precious to spare. If you ever wish to hear more than an "ayah" or "naow," just ask them how they feel about any aspect of government.

They don't decry the need for regulations. They simply prefer to define and enforce their own rules—rules tailored to the needs of their immediate communities. A prime example is law enforcement, particularly as it applies to fisheries. Few of the hundred or more small Maine fishing communities have police departments. They don't need them, as the following story demonstrates.

Not too many years ago the lobstermen in one community suspected a poacher in their midst. Rather than calling in the County Sheriff or the Maine Marine Patrol, they waited for the sort of foggy day favored by poachers, then staked out the shore in the area he was thought to be working. It wasn't long before he was spotted in a small skiff hauling up a trap not his own. The marine radio signal went out, and the designated enforcer roared out of the fog in his forty-foot lobsterboat and ran the skiff over. The skiff splintered and sank, leaving the poacher floundering and shouting, "Help, I can't swim!"

Drowning being considered excessive punishment for the crime of poaching, the man was pulled up with his arms over the boat's gunwale. Then, without judge or jury [for they would have been unqualified to judge the heinousness of the crime], justice was rendered: the poacher's arms were broken with blows of an oar and the man unceremoniously dumped onto the nearest dock. The poacher has never been seen in the area again. And it is likely he never poached again.

Rather than lawless, these fishing communities are, in fact, among the most crime-free areas in the nation. For example, the 2006 FBI-reported property crime rate in Phippsburg was 4/1,000 residents versus the national average of 34/1,000. Every resident of these communities knows every other, or at least a brother or a cousin, and everybody knows the rules. Break the rules and you will be punished or banished—no police, fancy lawyers, judge or jail required. These are people who have long ago lost the keys to their front doors. These are people who leave the key to their pickup in the ash tray, just in case a neighbor has a bonafide need to borrow it.

Other lobstermen may not have been as explicit as my grandfather in passing on the conservation ethic, but they were conservationists before the word existed. Long before fisheries committees and state and federal regulations, Maine lobstermen agreed among themselves to take only lobsters above and below certain size limits. The lower limit was to allow the lobsters to reach breeding age; the upper to preserve the larger, more prolific breeding females. In addition they instituted voluntary notching of the tails of any egg-bearing female caught. Like tattoos, the notches were for life, and notched females were never to be kept. While the rest of the world has been clear-cutting forests, extracting every barrel of oil, and catching every haddock in the sea, the Maine lobsterman has been tending his farm. To the astonishment of government regulators, the annual lobster catch continues to grow.

Hear the word, "Maine" and three images probably come to mind: LL Bean, moose, and lobstering. The Maine lobsterman has become the iconic symbol of the Maine coast: hard working, rugged, honest, independent, the cowboy of the coast. But behind every lobsterman stands a sternman...a bait dealer, a diesel mechanic, a boatbuilder, a pastor, an auto mechanic, a fuel oil dealer, a general store owner, a road commissioner, the teachers of his children, and myriad other vital members of the community. And yes, there's usually a postmistress too.

Like barnacles on a tidal ledge, these closely-knit communities cling to the edge of the sea. They have salt in their veins, and the Maine coast is their ecosystem. Here are some of their stories.

NOTE
People born in another state, no matter how well intentioned, no matter how generous with either money or time spent on volunteer committees, are forever relegated to the status "from away."

A much-loved woman, brought to Maine from Massachusetts at the age of two, was bestowed upon her death at age ninety-two the highest compliment possible for a person "from away." Chiselled into her headstone are the words:

Mable Smith
b. 1868 – d. 1960
Almost one of us

During the writing of this book I encountered a few people from away who had similarly lived among the natives for sixty, seventy, even ninety years. I found them so "almost one of us" that I chose to include several of their stories as well.

SOUTH COAST
Cape Elizabeth to Brunswick

PHINEAS SPRAGUE

Portland Yacht Services
Portland
Age 61

Munjoy Hill, Portland, with the Portland Company and
Portland Yacht Services in the foreground.

The Portland Company is a sprawling, nineteenth-century complex of brick buildings on ten acres of Portland waterfront. Before closing its manufacturing doors in 1978, the company had built 628 locomotives and 160 ships. Among the present occupants are a narrow guage railroad museum and Portland Yacht Services, owned and managed by Phineas Sprague, Jr., and his wife, Joanna.

Joanna told me to meet "Phin" outside the entrance door at 10a.m.. When I arrived the marine complex was buzzing, and I wondered how I would distinguish Phin from the other boatyard workers.

I didn't wonder long. A head taller than the rest, with a neatly-trimmed white beard and old-fashioned wire-rimmed glasses, Phineas Sprague reminded me of photos of famous early geologists I'd seen in a book. Who did he remind me of: Charles Darwin, Louis Agassiz, John Wesley Powell?

Phin led me up two flights of ancient creaking wooden stairs to a barn-like wooden office overlooking the complex. "This is where I come to think," he said.

I regarded his gentle, genial, intelligent visage. It felt like I was about receive a lecture on geology. Instead, I dove right in.

Phineas Sprague

Phineas—now there's an old name.

That's right. There have been fourteen Phineases since Spragues have been in New England.

There has been a male child named Phineas in every generation?

Not quite every generation, but for a long while it has been the first son in every generation. My son is Phineas, my father is Phineas, my grandfather was Phineas. The Sprague family came over in 1629 on a boat named the "Lion's Whelp."

Actually, two Sprague families came over in the 1620s. One of them we are not related to. That was the Sprague Electric family. They had a governor of Rhode Island.

My branch of the family stayed in the area around Malden, Massachusetts. They were a shipping family and ran vessels up and down the coast.

When it was favorable to get an education, in the early 1800s, one of my relatives got a degree in geology. He ended up doing a lot of the early work in the Mesabi Range [the largest iron-ore deposit in the U.S., located in Minnesota]. Then he went to West Virginia and took a look at the bituminous coal down there. He came back to his dad and said, "Hey, look around. They've cut all the trees in New England. We're going to have a fuel crisis."

The Spragues were forward looking.

Yes. If you remember, the cities were growing rapidly, and they were having a difficult time bringing in firewood.

I remember pictures of Maine coastal towns where there wouldn't be a single large tree standing!

That's right. Because his dad was chartering vessels, he said let's get into the coal business. So they helped set up the coal terminals in Newport News, Virginia, and ran coal mines in West Virginia. Then they brought coal up to New England to replace the wood they were running out of.

Portland became a big coal port.

Right. Coal replaced wood before oil became plentiful enough to be a dependable source of energy. The Sprague family had coal pockets [large structures for storing coal] in most of the towns in New England and largely controlled the distribution.

The Sprague family had a monopoly on coal distribution in New England?

We had a good position, a very good position, and until WWII we had a ship's agent company called Sprague Steamship. They operated about sixty percent of the Liberty Ships. I basically grew up in that family.

I imagine that, in spite of your family's wealth, you didn't think of your childhood as being at all special.

You are right. My great grandfather, a thirty-third degree Mason and a wonderful person, bought a large piece of property during the period of the rusticators [wealthy early-twentieth-century vacationers from the big cities] in about 1906. At that time the cities were really nasty. They were unhealthy places to be in the summer, even Boston and Portland. If you had the money, you got out.

He came up from Boston and bought land in Cape Elizabeth and Prouts Neck. He actually put a hotel in Prouts Neck, the Black Point Inn. My great grandmother ran it, and he bought the land that became Ram Island Farm in Cape Elizabeth to supply fresh produce to the Inn.

He had great vision for the future. In a letter to his son he wrote, "Some day aero machines will land in Portland, the railroad will come to Portland, and this property faces South and West and has adequate water on it. In the future it will be an important place, not too far from Boston."

Were there any other visionaries in the family? I think it was visionary for you to buy this property. [The Portland Company: formerly a steel fabricating company situated on ten acres of the Portland Waterfront.] As I recall it was just an ugly abandoned locomotive factory.

We don't know whether we own it or it owns us! It's a big property. It has a lot of potential. Great-grandfather would have said, "Someday this property will...." It depends on how much pain you want to take because, believe me, it's painful.

Business is very difficult in a state that doesn't understand that the creation of equity is the source of the income for the government. The progressive cultural battle is self-defeating because they end up not having the revenue needed to do their programs. I think they have their hearts in the right place, but they don't know how to run the checkbooks.

In business school you learn that a great plan poorly executed is no better than a poor plan poorly executed. There is a cultural foundation for successful businesses. It's the environment that people work under that is the foundation for success.

You have grown up with that philosophy.

Actually, I have not grown up with it. Great-grandfather was the hard worker, but grandfather, being born into a family with wealth, was very spoiled. He didn't work very hard at all. That happens a lot: one generation builds and the next generation consumes. If the consuming generation consumes too much, that is the end of the family fortune. You can't build a business with a playboy attitude.

Building a business means being really considerate of the people working with you. They are your assets, your tools. And building a business is not about power; it's about getting the right answer.

So great grandfather was a sound businessman, but grandfather was somewhat of a playboy. How about your father?

My dad got hurt by HIS dad. He was damaged.

Did you observe this growing up?

I observed it, but I was really more interested in geology. Dad went to Bowdoin with the head of the Geology Department at Syracuse, Gary Boone. When I was thirteen I went up to the woods with Gary as his field assistant. Instead of hanging around

Prouts Neck and attending parties, I was out in the woods making piles of mosquito bodies while Gary was looking at the rocks. By the time I was a junior in college, I was a principal mapper for the State of Maine.

When I was sixteen, my grandfather sent me down on my vacation into the coal mines in West Virginia. At that point we were the largest exporter of coal in the United States. One time I'd go to Newport News, and I'd stay with somebody in the company, and they'd teach me about how you could identify the quality of the coal in a big cargo. The next time I would go Beckley, West Virginia, and I would stay with a wonderful man who was the troubleshooter. At 5:30 in the morning there would be a phone call. The miners were striking; the feds had come in to close the mine; a tipple would be broken.

I'd be down in the mines with him. There'd be a meeting, and he'd say, "Phin, keep your hands in your pockets and your mouth shut so they won't know how stupid you are. I'll tell you what happened after the meeting, but observe and keep your ears open."

This was as valuable as what you learned in college.

Absolutely! I got to see the hopelessness of trying to run a business where the organizational behavior is flawed. Safety in the coal mines was basically controlled by the unions. The company had no control. Miners wouldn't wear their masks because wearing a mask marked you as a wimp. They would be drilling into the overburden, which is usually sandstone, and they'd get silicosis [a lung disease caused by inhalation of mineral dust].

And the company would be blamed?

Of course. Down in the mine I'd see this young guy with a hollow drill bit, and he wouldn't be wearing his mask. I'd go up to him and say, "What the hell are you thinking?" They were so interested in not being wimps that they wouldn't wear their masks.

We see this in our industry, too [Phin operates a boatbuilding and repair company, Portland Yacht Services] with volatile boatbuilding chemicals. Then I'd go to the same person's house for a picnic on the weekend, and there would be his dad with a tube up his nose attached to an oxygen bottle. It just blew me away. I'm a sixteen-year old kid wondering, "What is wrong with this picture? How come our family can't solve this problem?"

The union participated in this because, if you fired him, they'd just pick up the next guy on the bench, and the next guy on the bench would be the same, so there was a pervasive antisafety, antipersonal care organizational behavior. That was one of the things that hit me in the head. All my life I've been trying to deal with that. It's not only safety consciousness, it's organizational behavior consciousness.

What an organization needs is trust, and you get trust by establishing what is the acceptable norm, not by imposing something on someone. Not only follow the rules, but follow the rules because that is what you think is right. Everyone, the management and the workers, all have to internalize the rules.

I can't go out and count the number of screws somebody is buying for a particular job. I have to trust that they will think it out and buy the right number of screws. If in the middle of winter we are having a storm, and we have to go out and check the jackstands under the boats, I have to trust that the guy is actually going to do it and do it right. The primary responsibility of the boss is to establish the ethic.

Is being the coach of the team a good analogy?

Absolutely. You can't do the batting or the fielding. You have to give them your best guidance, and when they leave they are going to turn what you have taught them into action. I still have this in my mind, seeing the dad with the tube up his nose.

My grandfather sold the company while I was in college. It had been C.H. Sprague, and it turned into Sprague Energy. Basically, my grandfather was unable to perpetuate his legacy. There were serious challenges he was not equipped to deal with.

Do you think you could have handled those challenges today?

Who knows?

Would you have tried?

I would have been willing to try. I was the last Sprague employee of the Sprague Energy Company. I went down into the mines while I was at college and said goodbye to the miners.

The people who bought the company didn't want any more Spragues around. I was lost. Everything I had planned to do was suddenly gone. There weren't any jobs in geology in Maine at the time. So I bought an old schooner and sailed around the world.

Whoa! We are way ahead of where I wanted to be. I'd like to hear about your childhood. Let's go back to your connection with the ocean, your first memory of the sea.

We were living in Rhode Island, and every weekend we would come back to Ram Island Farm. We also had a place up at Sugarloaf, so we'd ski in the winter and come to the farm in the summer.

I used to live in the horse barn, 600 feet from the house. The horse barn was "where it was at." Even when I was six I lived in the horse barn. We played in the hay, and we were out in the fields when they were doing the mowing and baling. The farm is a saltwater farm, and it has lovely beaches.

Suddenly one day I became allergic to hay, to horses, to cats, to cows, to about everything around a barn. My eyes would puff up, and my nose would run, so I could no longer go into the barn.

A friend of my grandfather's, Joe Barlow, had a sixteen-foot skiff on the beach so he could get out to his bigger boat. But it turned out to be too heavy to drag up and down the beach, so he gave it to me.

How old were you when he gave you the boat?

Six. I would be out on the water at eight in the morning when the dew had come off the grass, and I'd be in the southwest wind [the prevailing daytime wind direction along the coast in summer] all day, which kept me free of all the land pollen.

There was Richmond Island and Little Ram Island, and the Spurwink River. It was a large protected area.

My grandfather had a deal with one of the lobstermen, Stan Doughty, that he could have a lobster shack on the river with the condition he would keep an eye on me. Stan would be out there lobstering while I was out trying to get myself in trouble.

Did you ever get to go on Mr. Doughty's lobsterboat?

Yeah, every time he rescued me! [laughs]. I used to have a little aluminum Grumman canoe, and when it blew northwest [off the shore], you had to paddle from the bow, and it was pretty scary for a little kid. Stan would be out there, and I'd be sitting there crying because I'd see the land receding.

Stan would come up and stand off a little bit and watch me paddling like hell. He'd come over and he'd say, "Well, young Mr. Sprague, are you looking for a bus?" [we both laugh] He was just a wonderful man. Like having another father.

Another time I went over onto Little Ram Island in the Grumman canoe. I was too little to pull it far up the beach. I used to collect the eggs from the sea gulls and put them in the incubator at the farm, so I'd have a pet seagull all summer. So I was out collecting seagull eggs, and the canoe took off. Here I am, frantic. How am I going to dig myself out of this hole? Around the corner comes Stan with the canoe in tow, and Stan says, "You lookin' for somethin' young Mr. Sprague?" He had a wonderful sense of humor.

Earlier you said you bought this old schooner and sailed around the world—by yourself?

I had three partners. We bought it together. I paid for the majority of it, but Dad wanted me to gather up some friends. In retrospect I probably wouldn't do that again.

Was the schooner in good shape? Was it capable of going around the world?

It was ok. There are two parts to being seaworthy. One is the captain; the other is the boat. We had no interest in going around the Horn [Cape Horn, the tip of South America, which is the Mt. Everest of circumnavigation]. I had been following Irving Johnson in *National Geographic* for years. He was my hero, and he would go around the world in eighteen months. We had this feeling that

Phin Sprague at the helm.

we could sail around the world in short order. It turned out not to be true. It took us almost four years.

We got into a bad storm right off the bat. We didn't leave until December. We got in a big storm between Newport and the Chesapeake. When the wind came around northeast, we were doing fifteen knots toward the Chesapeake. We were in a real hurry to get in. But we folded the boat around a watertight bulkhead that was put in to satisfy the Coast Guard. It busted five or six planks on that bulkhead.

I didn't even know it had happened. We dropped the boat off a wave, and it wasn't until we hauled the boat in Lantana, Florida, to fix a leak that we discovered the broken planks. But that is where I met Joanna. She was a nurse at the hospital. I met her on Lantana Beach.

We had a waterbed on the boat. We could fill it with water and tow it to the schooner if we ever ran out of water and couldn't get into a dock.

One day it was blowing like hell, and it was a weekend so there was no work going on, so Pierre and went down to Lantana Beach. We blew this water bed up, and we were sliding in on the waves in our green LL Bean shorts and Topsiders. Three girls came over and wanted to play. We'd throw them up on top of the water bed, and it would scoot in on the waves. After a while they asked where we lived and who we were.

I said, "I'm Phineas," and they looked at me like I had two heads. Then my buddy, Pierre, who had this mane of a blond beard, said, "And I'm Pierre." They go, "Sure you are!" And then we told them we were sailing around the world. "RIGHT!"

They thought they were going to catch us in our lie, so they said, "So where's your boat? We want to see your boat." The boat was up on the hard at Lantana Boatyard, and of course it was even more impressive out of water. We drove into the boatyard and pointed, "There it is." They were speechless.

After that Joanna let me use her car. She worked the night shift, and I'd pick her up after work, and we'd go out. We spent a month just enjoying each other. Then we sailed away.

Without Joanna?

Without Joanna. It was hard but we were sailing around the world. Who knew what was going to happen. The first stop after that was Isabella, where Columbus landed. We got in there, our first foreign port, and there was no band! There wasn't even a parade to meet us at the dock!

This wasn't exactly what my friends had imagined. They thought we were doing something really special, like nobody had ever done before, and nobody had paid any attention.

The next port was Kingston, Jamaica. The customs guy said, "Do you have any weapons?" I said, "Absolutely." He said, "Son, are you sure?" And I said again, "Absolutely, I've got a twenty-two and a thirty-eight." He said, "You are under arrest."

We had a hell of a time. This was the seventies when the natives had killed business executives on the golf courses. If you were British and had a single bullet, it was life in prison. They were trying to decide whether, because I had declared them, I had a right to have them on the boat. What saved me was my declaring them. If they had searched the boat and found them, I would have been in deep trouble. We finally left Jamaica for the Panama Canal. I did my first celestial fix, and we hadn't had much sun.

How far off were you?

Let's just say we got there. We found it. Then on the way into Panama we lost oil pressure on the main engine. Our so-called "engineer" had neglected to check the oil level. He was designated engineer only because he seemed the most engine-oriented in our group. We got into Panama with nineteen pounds of oil pressure in our Ford-Lehman diesel [normal pressure is about fifty pounds].

At that point we were way behind schedule, and we had had a really tough time getting to Panama. Many crews break up in Panama. Ours broke up. People have in their head an anticipation of what it is like to be sailing that doesn't match with the reality. The fantasy is that you will always be on a beam reach with two-foot waves. The reality is quite different. The guys looked at the swells coming in on the Pacific side, and they decided they didn't want to go any farther.

The swells were eight feet high, and you knew that, somewhere out there, those waves had started as forty-foot waves.

One of the guys was planning to get married, and this was messing up his life. Another said, "We were supposed to do this for eighteen months, and here we are almost a year into it, and we've only gotten to Panama. Also, I don't think they trusted the boat. So they packed up on me.

I decided I was going to somehow pull it back together again. I called Joanna, and I said, "How'd you like to sail to the Marquesas [islands in French Polynesia about 4,000 nautical miles from Panama]?" She showed up with a couple of bikinis and a pair of sunglasses and said, "Where are the Marquesas?"

The first thing she did was figure out what stores we had for the trip across the Pacific. She went through every compartment on the boat, and if she didn't know what something was she drew a little picture and said, "We have three of these."

You were probably thinking, "We could have used this on the way down here!"

She was a miracle. She's very detailed oriented. She's the one who pulls it all together here at Portland Yacht Services. Joanna and I got engaged in Tahiti.

How many crew did you have for the rest of the trip?

Seven. We had three watches of two people where one of the people shift out every two hours. But an unanticipated problem soon developed. My friends and I had attended Harvard, a very liberal school, so there was this philosophy, "Why can't I be Captain for a day?" If you are truly going to be progressive, when someone says, "Why can't I be Captain for a day?" you say, "Gosh, I don't know. OK, you can be Captain for today."

Think about this. Seven young people on the boat. I'm titular Captain, but this is a little microcosm of organizational behavior. It wasn't long before I learned that, as Captain, you can delegate someone to be responsible for something, but in the final analysis you are responsible. That was an important lesson.

The other question was how do you get people to live and work together positively? We decided we needed rules. That created "lawyers." So if you had a rule for a particular thing, this is what you were supposed to do. Well then we wouldn't be sure whether the rule applied to a particular situation, and maybe we needed a new rule. It became so complicated that it just didn't work.

Joanna and I eventually said, "We're glad to have you on board. This is our home. If Joanna's happy, you are safe, so pay attention to Joanna." And we said, "The rules of the boat are that every one behave like a lady and a gentleman. If you don't know what a lady or a gentleman would do, ask. If you don't act like a lady or a gentleman, we'll put you off on a buoy."

All of our problems miraculously went away.

Let me guess: this is the way you run Portland Yacht Services.

I hope so.

You are sixty-one now. How many more years are you going to run this company?

Well, life does things to you. You don't really control life. I have thirty employees who depend on me to figure out a way to keep their houses over their heads and their kids in school. It's not fun.

But aren't you hoping that, somehow, you will be able to taper off from that responsibility?

Great-grandfather wrote a letter to grandfather, saying that, at fifty-five, you should pick your understudy, and then leave, allowing them room to grow into the responsibility.

Do you have an understudy?

We have understudies, plural. Our legacy will be the organization we leave behind.

Are you already allowing your understudies to make company decisions?

That's why I have the time to sit here and talk to you.

CHARLIE POOLE
Warfinger, Union Wharf
Portland
Age 55

Charlie Poole, Wharfinger of Portland's Union Wharf.

"Wharfinger"—*the keeper or owner of a wharf. The wharfinger takes custody of and is responsible for goods delivered to the wharf.*

Not just anyone can be the wharfinger of Portland's Union Wharf, built in 1793. Charlie Poole, a patrician Yankee, is obviously proud of his position—not vain, but in awe of the responsibility now his.

We are sitting in his office overlooking the bustling activity on the famous wharf below.

Do you have a first memory of the ocean?

I was about four. We lived out at Cape Elizabeth and we had some boats on moorings. I would sit at the beach all day long and yell out to one of the rowboats, "Hey rowboat, hey rowboat, I want to row the rowboat!"

I rowed at boarding school and college, then coached rowing and founded a rowing club in Yarmouth. I still row nearly every morning. I plan to row until the day I can't climb in and out of a boat. I guess I was serious when I talked to that rowboat!

My wife kids me because I judge the success of my day by how many things I can cram in, and one of those things is usually a row, a sail, or a swim—all in the ocean.

How did you become involved with Union Wharf?

My father's mother was Marjorie Shurtleff. The Shurtleffs were some of the early owners of Union Wharf. The Proprietors of Union Wharf, was founded in 1793 by 25 shareholders. I can show you the incorporation document from 1793. It says that in February, 1793, the 25 shareholders *"agreed to build a wharf on a piece of flatts, at the bottom of Union Street in Portland..."*

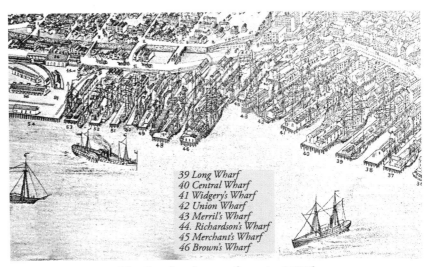

39 Long Wharf
40 Central Wharf
41 Widgery's Wharf
42 Union Wharf
43 Merril's Wharf
44. Richardson's Wharf
45 Merchant's Wharf
46 Brown's Wharf

The Portland waterfront in 1876.

If memory serves me, Union Wharf is mentioned in stories about the War of 1812 battle between the British *Boxer* and the American *Enterprise*.

Memory serves you right. It's all described in this book [hands me a little book, *The History of Union Wharf*].

The American *Enterprise* defeated the British *Boxer* off Monhegan [an island 40 miles from Portland]. Both of the captains were highly respected and beloved by their crews, and both were killed in the battle. The *Boxer* lost all of her masts, so *Enterprise* towed her in to Union Wharf.

An elaborate double funeral was held for the two captains at the Second Parish Meeting House right up on Middle Street. During the funeral all of the local businesses closed, and every ship in the harbor lowered its flag. The two captains are still buried side-by-side at Eastern Cemetery.

The graves of the commanders of Enterprise and Boxer, Eastern Cemetery, Portland, Maine.

Henry Wadsworth Longfellow, was there. He was only six at the time, and it must have made quite an impression because he wrote about it in one of his poems.

[I looked it up and quote it here. From the poem *My Lost Youth*.]

> *I remember the sea-fight far away*
> *How it thundered o'er the tide!*
> *And the dead captains, as they lay*
> *In their graves, o'erlooking the tranquil bay*
> *Where they in battle died.*

As time went on, the ownership of the shares changed hands, and in 1858 the name Shurtleff first appears in the list of shareholders. In 1902 the W.H. Shurtleff Company was incorporated here on the wharf. The company's primary business was importing and distributing salt. Salt was hugely important back then because refrigeration had yet to be invented, and salting meat and fish was the least expensive way to preserve it.

The company owned a sailing schooner that used to bring salt in from Italy, Spain, and the Bahamas. There were a number of grades of salt, from "extra fina" to "kurkutch [coarse]," but most of it was fisheries salt, for drying fish and preserving lobster bait, things like that. It was a profitable business, and over time, the Shurtleffs bought out the other wharf business owners.

My grandfather, Parker Poole, Sr., married William Shurtleff's daughter, Marjorie, in 1920. When William got sick, Parker took over running the business and became president of the Shurtleff Company at William's death. By the 1960s the Poole family controlled all of the shares in Union Wharf. It had taken 167 years, from 1793 until 1960, to get all of the shares into one family.

Tell me about this word, "wharfinger."

My dad always said it was a British word, meaning the manager or overseer of the wharf or pier. To his dying day he was proud to be the Union Wharf wharfinger, a position of responsibility. He put it on his business card and, as you can see [hands over a card], I put it on my card, too.

Can anyone who owns a wharf be called a wharfinger, even if the wharf is a dinky little thing in front of a cottage?

I think for you to be considered a true wharfinger, your wharf has to be run as a commercial business. Most wharfingers maintain an office on the wharf from which to handle wharf business.

How big is Union Wharf?

Union Wharf is about 1,100 feet long [two-tenths of a mile]. It used to be 2,200 feet long, but when the city built Commercial Street, it split the wharf in half. It's also 220 feet wide, so it covers about four acres.

At the periphery of wharfs I always see wood pilings, but most, if not all, of them are rotted away to virtually nothing where the tide goes up and down. What the hell is holding these wharfs up?

That would be Widgery Wharf, next door—a totally pile-supported wharf. Union Wharf is a solid-fill pier, which is fortunate. There is a granite crib around the perimeter, which is filled with rocks and dirt. Outside of the granite crib you have a pile-supported wood deck—an apron or skirt of wood. As those pilings rot, we replace them. We are replacing the last section of pilings since I joined the company.

What does it cost to replace a pile?

Oh, with the barge time, and the cost of the piling itself, and the pull time for the old piling, about a thousand bucks. You could have a couple grand in one piling.

Wow. You must have hundreds of pilings!

Thousands. Maintenance is a huge expense. Well-meaning people say, "Gee, we want to preserve the working waterfront and the fishing boats. We want Union Wharf to stay marine," and then the fisheries die. We've been fortunate to diversify our tenant base so that we are not totally dependent on fishery-related tenants. The fisheries have died; in fact, we have no fishing boats at all.

Union Wharf today.

We have spent millions of dollars on tearing things down and building new buildings. We just put a new water line down the length of the wharf. The old one used to freeze and blow out. We went to a new molecular plastic type that could freeze solid and not blow apart.

So you have a long-range vision for the wharf.

If you look down the wharf, there are only two buildings that are older than 1990.

What are some of the businesses located on Union Wharf?

Cozy Harbor Seafood has their lobster business here and a shrimp business in the winter. CVS Lobster does lobster and bait. Portland Pilots bring in the large oil tankers. Maine Lobster Direct does very high end air-freighting of lobsters around the world. Portland Trap builds lobster traps.

MSRC, Marine Spill Response Corporation, was created after the Exxon Valdez spill. The U.S. government went to the oil industry—Exxon, Mobile, Texaco, and so on—and said, "You will equip yourself for a worst-case oil spill, or we'll do it for you." Faced with that, the oil companies said, "We'll do it." That was the Oil Pollution Act of 1990.

The oil companies put up the money to create sixteen oil spill response sites around the U.S.. We are the most Northeast. We cover Maine, New Hampshire, Massachusetts, all the way down to Long Island. The next one is down in New Jersey.

We have a barge, this large vessel at the end of the wharf, and a bunch of smaller boats on trailers for fast response.

In addition, we own Brown Ship Chandlery, and Brown Ship has a dba [doing business as] Custom Float Services. We started the float business to keep our guys busy when the oil slowed at the pipeline.

We also run a whole float parts department: marine-grade lumber and all the hardware so the customer can build a float themselves. We have a design team; we have a CAD designer.

I created Custom Floats because Brown Ship needed more steady revenue. We weren't getting it out of the oil tankers, and we had talented people I didn't want to lose, so off we went. We built one float, and quickly one became two, and two became four, and....We cover the whole coast, from Canada to the Mid-Atlantic states.

It appears that your secret to success is being able to adapt.

We do know how to survive. The wharf has been here since 1793. There is a saying, "The first generation builds it; the second generation grows it; the third generation kills it." We've already beaten the odds. We feel we are stewards in time. Now that my dad has passed on, it is my time to have a go at it. Hopefully one of my kids will be here when I go.

When I came to work in the business, all my dad said was, "Charlie, let's run the place." He never said as much, but I know he was excited to see the pier, not only continue on, but renew and grow.

He ran it for sixty years, and I am now on year twenty-six. I had no business experience when I came in, but we've grown the business. The best feeling is to have started something—my idea—from scratch. We took an idea and grew a business. It was like growing a garden. Plant a seed and watch it grow.

Of course, you had a base. It wasn't like your kids were going to starve. You could afford to start small. When you start small and make a mistake, it's a small mistake.

This economy is challenging, but we have great people, flexible people, so we are able to swell and shrink with the economy. With the float company we had to buy some tools, but we didn't have to hire any more people, and we didn't have to build a building, and we didn't have to take on debt.

Are your children as excited as you about the business?

I want my kids to run someone else's submarine first, then they can come back, if they want, to run this one.

Of the three, the youngest is the most likely. After a year at Trinity he came home and said, "I think I need to go to the Coast Guard or the Naval Academy." He starts at Annapolis at 0700 hours, July 1. After 4 years of college, he'll owe them another 5 years. He's working here right now; he's the most likely to come back some day and say, "Dad, the time has come."

Do you think the coast of Maine is so different from the rest of the United States?

The first word that pops into my head is "tradition." I think native Mainers hang on very strongly to their tradition and the fact that they are from Maine. Of the six children in my family, all but one are still here in Maine. It's like the sign you see when you enter Maine: "Maine—the way life should be." Why live somewhere else?

I always say it this way: here's Portland; go five hours to the south; how many millions of people are you going to go by? Now go five hours the other way; how many people are you going to see? My daughter and I went skiing in Idaho. Absolutely incredible, the best skiing I've ever done! The skiing was just perfect every day. But when we were at the airport, surrounded by mountains, we looked at each other and both said, "We need the ocean."

Maine is broken into such diverse areas. South of Portland you have the beaches. Then, starting here in Portland, all the way to Canada, you have the rocky coast of Maine with its thousands of islands. Then drive just an hour north and you are in the mountains. Drive from here to Eastport, and it's like passing through three European countries.

We have problems in terms of jobs and what it costs to live, but it's a tradeoff. Which do you want: a lot of money or a life? What we have in Maine is a life—a good life.

I'm always telling my brother, "When you get up in the morning and put your feet on ground, whether it's at home or at work, it has to feel good. If it doesn't feel right, change it."

I live in Yarmouth, twelve miles from work. How many places can you bike 10 miles to work in the state's largest city? My wife says I measure my day by how many things I can cram in. Here I can go for a row, ride my bike to work, go for a sail or a swim, and still get a day's work done.

Do you have any concerns about the future of Maine?

Yes. I run a business. I have to generate income; I have to meet payroll; I have to pay expenses; and I can only borrow so much money before I start paying it back. Now you can't tell me running a state isn't like running a business. You can't be all things to all people. You can only spend what you take in, no matter how many things people want.

I think Portland, Maine, will always remain a viable deepwater port. We have a lot to offer the world in terms of coming and going by sea, whether it's oil, cargo, people. But we have a major issue that needs to be tackled—dredging. It's expensive. We need government help, if not financial help, then to at least to get out of the way.

If the problem isn't solved, the harbor will become useless. Here is a company that has been in business since 1793. We have been able to do the wharf maintenance to remain viable, but something else is critical to our continued existence—the water depth alongside. If we can't land a vessel safely at all tides, people will go elsewhere. The single biggest issue with this harbor is dredging. It's expensive, and there is the problem of how to dispose of the fill. We as a state, as a region, need to solve this problem.

Chellie Pingree, several business people, the City of Portland, the City of South Portland, are all focussing on a CAD cell [contained aquatic disposal cell]. The CAD cell is very big in Massachusetts, Rhode Island, and Long Island Sound. A CAD cell is a football-sized—260 feet by 442 feet—trench that you fill with the contaminated dredged material. The material taken out of the trench is clean fill that can be dumped out at sea. We hope to be dredged in 2011—800,000 cubic yards. The company that dredges Portland harbor could also dredge around the wharfs, other harbors, the Royal River. Economy of scale.

The other issue is that we allow the uses of the waterfront to change with the times. It makes no sense to zone the waterfront for fisheries if there are no fish. Even if fishing comes back in 30 years, the wharf owners can't just sit on their hands on that assumption. If wharfs can't be used, they will deteriorate.

In 1993 we had the first zoning referendum, which went a long way in moving us toward more flexible zoning. I and all of the other wharf owners, from the State Pier to the International Terminal, minus one, have gotten together and are in the final draft of an even more flexible ordinance. It's not opening the waterfront up to condos, to residential; it is trying to take what we have and make it commercially viable. I am all for fishing, but we have a fish pier that was designed to accommodate the needs of the fisheries. If the fish come back, supply and demand will create homes for the fishing boats.

We now have a 50/50 mix of marine and non-marine uses. We would be the poster child of what we are trying to accomplish. I think my dad would have approved. Right before I came on board, he started tearing the old buildings down and building new. He had a long-range vision. I think that is what we all need.

TIM SAMPLE
Maine Humorist
Portland
Age 60

Tim Sample, purveyor of Down East humor

You have probably seen and heard Tim Sample even if you have never been to Maine. He produced and appeared in more than 100 "Post- cards from Maine" for the Emmy Award-winning TV Show, "CBS News Sunday Morning."

Few Mainers would dispute that Tim is Maine's Humorist Laureate. Given his considerable fame, I thought it would be difficult to secure an in-depth interview. His gracious response blew me away. With me as the sole audience in his recording studio, he delivered not only an hour of laughter, but a scholarly lecture on the origins and nature of Maine humor.

Are you really a Maine native?

I was born in the county [Aroostook County, which is so large its residents refer to it simply as "the county"], but we moved down to the coast when I was five.

My mom, Leah Graham, was from Brooklin, on the coast. My birth father was from Castine. They met at what was then Castine Normal School [teacher college], which later became Maine Maritime Academy. They married when they were young, and then WWII came along, and he went into the Navy.

After the war my parents were living in Limestone, and things weren't going well. My mother never liked living in the middle of nowhere, so they divorced. She moved back down to the coast. There may have been a little something going on before the divorce, who knows? It's lost in the mists of time. You didn't get to know, and you don't want to know. Anyway, she was getting a divorce, and Frank Sample, who owned Sample's Shipyard in Boothbay, was getting a divorce, and they got married in '57. Frank adopted all three of us kids to add to his three kids, and my mother and Frank had another kid, Link, who's running for the legislature now and whose politics are somewhere to the right of Attila the Hun's. Link thinks Rush Limbaugh is a pinko-liberal.

Were you expected to help out at the shipyard?

Every one of us worked at the shipyard. I joke now that I didn't have any choice but to become a Maine humorist because of growing up at that shipyard. Frank Sample taught us the value of work. We all worked a couple hours a day, cleaning up the docks. We had time cards and got fifty cents an hour, but that gave us the idea of how the world worked. I was nine when I started working at the yard.

What was it like working at the shipyard?

Well, there were guys working there, old guys in their eighties, who were born in the latter decades of the 19th century. They would spin oakum and tell stories and smoke pipes, and they had this thick, old-time accent. I was mesmerized.

I have just realized what it was that fascinated me. There had been a lot of chaos in my early childhood: we lived here; then we lived there; first my name was this; then it was that. Suddenly I'm with these old guys, and they had a certain quality that was appealing.

Something happened that shows what that quality was. I was nine years old, and there were three of these old guys sitting on the dock. I ran up to them and blurted out, "There's a car on fire down on Townsend Avenue!" The three old guys just sat there and said NOTHING for about three minutes. They just stared out at the harbor. Finally one turned to the others and said, "Wasn't theah a caa on faa back in twenty-six?" One of the others said, "Why ayah, and didn't it burn right down to the groun'?"

They had seen it all before. Their blood pressure didn't go up. They telegraphed this idea that it has all happened before, and it will all happen again.

These old guys told endless stories. One time there were squid coming into the harbor. We'd never had squid, and suddenly we had big schools of squid. Now, as an adult, I understand that these things happen in cycles, but I didn't know that then. The old guys would talk, "Oh, yas, we remembah, back then, I don't know, '93 or '94, I dunno, but they was menhaden, menhaden. They was all ovah heah, hahbah was full of 'em. You could walk across the hahbah on them menhaden!" Of course I knew they were outa their friggin' minds. There weren't no fish you could walk on across no harbor.

Then along came the '80s and the pogy invasion. JUST like what those guys had said! There were marine biologists on television, "Oh, this happens about every ninety years. Back in the '90s they were called by their official name, "menhaden." Those old men DID know what they were talking about! They HAD seen this all before!

Did you ever go fishing?

At sixteen I worked for Arnold Rogers as sternman on a lobster-boat going out of East Boothbay. Get up at four in the morning, shovel bait and this and that. Arnold Rogers was one of those classic lobstermen—a simple, modest man who knew how to do what he did. He couldn't explain it, but he knew how everything worked. If you wanted the nuance of why the rope is coiled this way, and why you hold your knife that way, and why this is done this way, he couldn't necessarily give you a verbal explanation. The bottom line was that if you didn't do it that way bad things might happen, like somebody might die. This is how this pragmatic way of doing things evolved.

And it's not just the fishermen who are this way. I was twenty-five years old and living in Palmyra, Maine. I'd been living for a year and a half in a little cabin with no plumbing. That, by the way, is romantic for about fifteen minutes.

I had this idea. Cianbro [Maine's largest construction company] was right next door in Pittsfield. You could rent a crane. I had this little sixteen by twenty frame building. I decided I could build a foundation along side of it, get a crane to come out, pick it up and put it on the foundation, build onto the back, put the plumbing in. Perfectly good idea. I checked it out. You could get a crane for a day for $250.

Well, there was this guy named Royce Semple. He's no longer with us, but he was a backhoe guy. Every little town has a backhoe guy, a guy who has a couple of beat-up old dump trucks, a 4-wheel drive pickup with no tailgate, and a backhoe. He'll grade; he'll dig a ditch; he'll dig your foundation. Most of these guys dropped out of grade school. They have no education, but they know how to do what they do.

So I call up Royce. I was about twenty-five, Royce was about forty-five, but he looked about sixty-five. Missing most of his teeth. Just beat to shit. Rode hard, and put away wet. He had this way of talkin' like he was gargling gravel. He used to call me up at five o'clock in the morning. I'd say, "Yes, Royce?" He'd say, "Long's you're not in the grave."

Anyway, I call Royce up and I tell him what my idea is. I'm all excited because I'm going to have a real house with a foundation and plumbing, quite exciting. I says, "Now Royce, I see these houses around here, and the friggin' house is way the hell up here. There's two or three feet of foundation stickin' up. I don't want that. I want a nice house like you see in the magazines with just a little foundation showin'.

Royce said, "Well, you can do that if you want, but I think you ought to put her up here like this [indicates about four feet off the ground]." I said, "Roy, for god sakes, why …?"

Well, we went back and forth like this, and every time I mentioned it he'd say, "Well you can do what you want, but I think you ought to …" Finally I said, "Royce, I'm the guy paying for this. Put her down there like she's supposed to look."

Well, Royce built the thing, we moved the cabin over, and built on the back. Jesus, didn't she look shahp! Still looks shahp. Went through the winter, pipes didn't freeze, easy to heat, everything fine.

I had my graphic arts studio down in the basement. I came home one day in April, and the friggin' basement had three feet of water in it. I almost got electrocuted. I went down and grabbed hold of my drawing table.

Jesus, I was some pissed off! I had a sump pump, but the sump pump had failed, or whatever. Well, what Royce had been trying to tell me was I should put the foundation above the water table, and that he would grade the ground back up around it. It would look the way I wanted, and it wouldn't flood in the spring. But he didn't have the verbal skills to put it into words.

What you were supposed to do is simply trust him, and it would come out right. Just leave it the fuck alone and - it - will - be - ok. This a Maine ethic. It's a way of doing things. You should just trust the natives because they know how things work.

Why do you think Maine has a mystique for people from away?

I do have a few thoughts on that. There are only two or three states in the U.S. that have that kind of mystique. Alaska is one. Part of it is being remote, but another part of it is the pragmatism required to function under difficult circumstances.

Mainers have a distinct dialect because they are geographically cut off. If you were to draw a map of the forty-eight contiguous states and draw circles and arrows indicating commerce and social development over the first 200 years, a lot of those arrows would come up to Boston and go right back down again and swirl around, leaving little pockets of relatively untouched culture. The result is that you have these islands and peninsulas where families persist in isolation for many generations.

Another thing is that Maine is near the bottom of the economic ladder. However, a little known fact about Maine is that it has the highest number of millionaires per capita. Right alongside the natives you have the retired CEOs, the celebrities, and the artists. What has developed over a couple of centuries is this symbiotic relationship between the natives and the wealthy people from away—not your average tourist, but the Rockefellers, the Martha Stewarts, the John Travoltas.

There's a great story from the turn of the century, the era when the rusticators from New York and Philadelphia owned summer cottages, which in Bar Harbor meant fifteen bathrooms. They would have a decades-long relationship with a caretaker, sometimes a family of caretakers. Maybe the wife would cook, the kids would mow the lawn, and the man would do the carpentry. But there was this long term understanding.

Typically what would happen is the family would arrive on the train from Philadelphia on the 4th of July weekend. The caretaker would pick them up in the old flivver at the station and drive them to the "cottage." There was an inherent mutual respect about this relationship. It wasn't condescending at all.

So now it's 1923 or something, and the old man dies, and the family thinks about selling the place. But the young daughter, who's never had much interest but has inherited this place, decides to spend the summer. She's twenty-something. She comes up by herself to get the place opened up. She shows up at the train station with bags and bags of luggage. The old caretaker lugs her luggage. They don't really know one another, but there is this long family relationship, so he packs her up and they head down to the cottage. He turns to her and says, "Nice day, ain't it?" She looks at him like he's a bug on the sidewalk, and she says, "I pay you to do work on my cottage. I do NOT pay you for conversation."

Well, not a word is said. He paints the boat, puts the boat overboard, does whatever needs to be done. At the end of the summer, Labor Day, he takes her back to the station and presents an itemized bill for what he has done.

She goes over the bill with a fine-toothed comb to make sure she isn't being cheated. There is lawn mowing: so much, carpentry: so much, this and that. At the bottom there is a $20 charge with no indication what it is for. She gets into high dudgeon and says, "What, may I ask, is that $20 charge?" He says, "That, dear, is for sass. I don't often take it, but when I do, I charge for it."

There is another more recent story going around, and it will still be going around in 100 years. Like all these things, I have no idea where it originated. The story goes that Martha Stewart was down in Southwest Harbor, Northeast Harbor, wherever the hell she goes down there. She pulls up to the local store in a limousine, and she's in a giant rush. Some big deal is going down, tens of millions of dollars, and her telephone is out, and she has to use the telephone outside the store. But there's a line. Three or four people are ahead of her in line.

There's an old duffer, about eighty-five, there's a couple of people ahead of him, and someone's yacking on the phone. Martha comes up and says in a loud voice, "Excuse me, I have to get in there. I have to use that phone. This is very important!" The old duffer turns to her and says, "Uh, madam, nobody cuts the line here. Everybody has to get in line."

She says, "Don't you know who I am? I am Martha Stewart. These people can wait, but this has to happen in the next five minutes." He looks at her and he says, "I understand that, madam Let me introduce myself. I'm John D. Rockefeller."

Rockefeller represents the top of the heap, but he knows the rules. He's been living here. his family donated Acadia National Park. Martha Stewart represents the new generation of wealthy, which will have to learn the old ways, how it works.

That's the thing in a nutshell. You can come from anywhere, you can be anybody, and I really don't care about your race, creed or religion. Do we have racists? Yes, we do. Do we have anti-semites? Yes, but by and large you are ok being anybody you want to be—as long as you observe one cardinal rule. That rule is that you don't think that being from away makes you better than the local people.

David Rockefeller, the younger—about five or six years ago I get this call from his secretary, "Mr. Rockefeller is having a get together at the Seal Harbor compound, and he'd like to have you entertain. I said we could probably work something out. Of course there was no question about the money. We set it up, and she said, "When we get closer to the date David would like to talk to you about how everything goes." I said, "Fine."

A couple of weeks before the event she sets up a phone conference, and I talk to him. David said [in a New York accent], "We are so happy you can come. We have a few people coming. The Secretary of the Interior will be there, and the president of this, and the president of that... I was just wondering if... You can say no if you don't...."

"What is it?" I said. "Well, you know, and I don't mean to tell you how to..." I said, "David, what is it?" "You can say no if you..." "I know I can say no. So what is it?" "I just wondered if I could get up on stage and just do a little something with you." He wanted to perform with me. So we did this little thing about "native" and "from away" and goofed around. Everybody loved it, and he loved it. We had a great time, a lovely evening.

Somewhere in one of these file cabinets I have a great handwritten letter from him, "Gee Tim, it was so fantastic. Out of the park home run. We had a wonderful time. Thanks so much for coming, blah, blah, blah. All my best, David Rockefeller. PS: When you are in town, please come and see me."

The address on the stationery was 1 Rockefeller Center. I mean, what the hell, that is Maine. That's not Utah; that's not Nebraska; that is a whole different thing. It is woven into our sense of ourselves. It's woven into our culture, and it's very appealing. It's a recipe for a very specific place.

Do you do a lot of these stand-up story-telling events?

I've been fortunate to be able to have a full-time career as a story teller. I've never had a day job.

Nowadays I get calls strictly because I don't do off-color material. I don't even understand what comedy is any more. Not only is it vulgar, it's mean, it's nasty. Whatever goes, I guess, but that's not the way I do it.

Anyway, I get a call from the XYZ Corporation. They're having their annual banquet at the Samoset [resort in Rockland] or down in Boston at the Ritz Carlton. Somebody on the board of directors is a fan of mine, and they want me do my Maine thing. They don't know too much about what I do, so after a bit they get nervous. They want to know what I'm going to be doing. I say, "I'm going to do what I do. I'm going to get up there, and I'm going tell Maine stories."

Years ago I learned you have to read the audience. All the time I see these CEOs plodding through some six-page thing they wrote in the hotel room. It isn't going anywhere, and people's eyes are glazed over, but they plod on.

What I've learned is that, whatever I'd planned, if that line that got a laugh last night is not working, I've got to shit-can that and do something else. You've got to read your audience, and you've got to work with them.

So I do this thing I call a hand-holding meeting, a conference call with the CEO and the CFO and the this and that. They make all kinds of suggestions like, "Well, Fred's a good golfer. You ought to make fun of his golf game." They try to write the monologue for me. I don't say much. I just take a few notes. I say, "If you want someone to roast and humiliate Fred, you've got the wrong guy. I don't make fun of people. I don't pick out some weakness in their character and embarrass them. But tell me more about Fred."

What I know, and they don't really know, is that if they'd leave me alone and put me in front of a microphone, at the end of the dinner everybody will have had a good laugh. I know how to do that. Like Royce Semple, I don't know how to explain how I know how to do that, but I've been doing it for years, and it works. That's the Maine ethic. It's the same with the lobsterman and the backhoe man.

Do you have any common themes for your Maine humor?

Over the years one of my main subjects is the issue of native versus from away. We have this beautiful state, a very tough economy, and tough weather. Life in Maine is a hardscrabble existence. But people can come from all over the world; they can buy the land; they can sail the coast. They can have it all, but the one thing we hold out, the one thing that gives us a leg up, is you can do anything you want, but you will never be a native. We have developed a whole culture about that, and it galls people, it irritates people. But we do it gently. We kind of joke about it.

People from away will come in and think they can sell us something. If you wanted to start a new religion, five or six hours on a street corner in Los Angeles and you'd have a dozen converts. Six months later you'd have two or three churches. In the State of Maine, if you want to start a new religion, about five years later they might come to your church supper if the chowder was any good.

Maine people don't go for the quick fix. Don't come in here, flim-flamming like a carpet bagger, saying we're going to bring all these jobs. Understand, we've heard this before. You're not the first one to come through here saying, "Don't do it your way; do it our way."

On the other hand, if something actually works, we are pragmatic. If you've got a different way of making a lobster trap and it works, if it's lighter and more durable, and if it fishes better, we're all for it. We are all about Yankee ingenuity.

What do you think of Maine's representation in Washington?

Oh, God yes! Look at, from this teeny tiny state, the people Maine has sent into national politics: Margaret Chase Smith, Ed Muskie, George Mitchell, Bill Cohen, Olympia Snowe, Susan Collins, people on both sides of the aisle. What characterizes all these Maine politicians? They are pragmatic, they're goal oriented, they are open-minded, they are intelligent, and they want to get something done. Our attitude is, "Don't tell me; show me. How does this thing work? What goes on here? Don't give me the theory; show me how it works.

What do you think of the Internet?

Quite honestly a lot of this is hoopla and horse shit. I say to people, "When you have to get something done in the next twenty minutes, a better number of options would be three or four, not 3,984. As the world gets more complex and confusing, there is a lot of appeal in a community and culture with a direct connection to the past, where we have a sense of who we are based on threads that go back in time.

I do a workshop for middle-school kids called "Story Telling in the Oral Tradition." I talk about how the oral tradition is the oldest one. It has the same elements as the print version: an author, an editor, and a publisher. But what happens in the oral tradition is that every single one of us who participates in the discourse of the community, whether we know it or not, and most of us have no idea, we wear those hats. We tell that story, and what we are doing without realizing it is submitting a manuscript to the oral-tradition publishing house. If it's no good, then no one cares about it, and it's not repeated. But if it is good, someone will repeat it, slightly edited perhaps, and it will be republished, over and over. If you learn how to read it, it's like an archeological dig. It's a message in a bottle from our forebears, and it tells us something about what their values were.

I use the examples of William Shakespeare's farces. These are centuries old. Think of the things that have changed since Shakespeare wrote "Much Ado About Nothing." Those plays still have laugh lines in them. Why? Because the architecture of the humor is that of human nature. Those are the nuts and bolts: insecurity, pomposity, avarice, sexual innuendo, or discomfort. Those things haven't changed, so if somebody in Maine was laughing at a story in 1820, 1920, and today, let's see what that's about.

I don't think it's an accident that the two strongest tap roots of humorous story telling in Maine are logging and fishing: difficult, back-breaking, dangerous, life-threatening work out of which comes some of the most enduring humor.

What we have is powerfully funny stories coming from really tragic and brutal situations. If there is a message, I think it is that one of the most dangerous things you can do in a difficult situation is to take yourself too seriously. We don't use humor in Maine as a way of escaping reality. We use humor as a lubricant to grease right through the middle of the most difficult things.

My mother is eighty-seven. Last summer we were talking about how the recession was the worst since the Great Depression. She grew up on the coast of Maine during the Great Depression. I said, "What did people say back then?" She said, "The depression wouldn't be so bad if it weren't coming right on the heels of such hard times." That is Maine humor in a nut shell. It doesn't pretend anything. It doesn't go away. It goes right through the middle of it.

After I do a performance someone usually asks, "Is this a true story?" What I always say is, "The story that I just told you, if it's one from the oral tradition, if it's something that's been around for 200 years, that story is more true than any of the facts that went into its construction. It has had the stamp and approval of successive generations. It's been honed; it's been developed; and it has been passed on as a living document of the values of all the people it passed through. This is resonating and living like a folk song. It is a truth about who we are, and it reflects and amplifies and educates along the way.

One of the great drawing cards of the State of Maine, why there is a mystique, why there is that appeal, is that people have to want to be here. They come here, and they find out that they don't have everything they had, the deli around the corner and a few other things. If you've been here a long time, you are here because you want to be here. You are not here because you have to be here.

WALTER GREENE

Legendary Builder and Racer of Multihull Sailboats
Yarmouth
Age 65

After interviewing other boatbuilders and sailors I asked, "Is there any-one else I should talk to?" The answer was usually, "Walter Greene." One added, "He is still looking for a better shape for a wheel than round."

There is no sign on Route 1, or anywhere else, pointing the way to Greene Marine, but as the natives say, "You'll know it when you get there." A half mile down a pot-holed dirt road I am surrounded by chaos: several large sheds apparently constructed entirely from salvaged materi-als, a dozen large monohull, catamaran, and trimaran hulls scattered about as if deposited by an extra-high tide, and a yellow school bus long ago converted into a crane for raising sailboat masts.

Behind a hinged sheet of plywood, hand-lettered "Office," I am con-fronted with a huge trimaran, looking for all the world like a gigantic, prehistoric pterodactyl. Under the looming trimaran, a man festooned in glass fibers and epoxy resin works on a small catamaran. I have found the legend.

Where were you born?

In Guilford, Connecticut, on the Long Island shore.

So you did grow up on the ocean?

Four miles.

Were your parents into boating?

My grandfather was. He had a skiff, and he subscribed to *The Rudder*. [*The Rudder* [1891–1984] is considered by many to have been the greatest American yachting and boating magazine.] I guess I discovered boats looking at *The Rudder* in my grandfather's house when I was six or seven.

Can you remember the first time you saw the ocean?

Well, that was a strange thing because Long Island Sound is not the ocean. I can remember reading about the ocean at about sixteen, having never seen the actual ocean.

You and I must have different ideas of "ocean." I remember being in a storm in Long Island Sound and thinking,"This is all the ocean I ever want to see." Your idea seems to be a thousand miles offshore.

Well, 100 miles anyway.

When did it first occur to you that you might want to spend your life around boats?

I built a boat when I was twelve. A Blue Jay, a Sparkman and Stephens design.

Was it a success?

Yes, it was a success. I remember thinking, "This is pretty good, this boatbuilding."

Did you sail it? How did you do?

Mixed bag; In the end I never really won the Blue Jay Nationals. When I was sixteen, I borrowed a better Blue Jay and qualified for the Nationals. [Designed in 1947, the 13′6″ Blue Jay continues to be one of the most popular boats for training young racers.] The year I did the best with the Blue Jay, we were racing on the Connecticut River. There wasn't much wind, and I was a pretty good light-air sailor.

Also I sailed at Tabor [Academy]. I wanted to be on the *Tabor Boy* crew. [*Tabor Boy* is a 92-foot, gaff-rigged, two-masted schooner.]

What was your next boat?

I sort of graduated pretty quickly. The next boat was an Invicta yawl, which is a Bill Tripp boat. I sailed it in an Annapolis-Newport Race, which happens on the even years, alternating with the Newport-Bermuda Race.

I imagine you've also done the Bermuda Race?

Seven or eight times.

How were you making a living while you were sailing?

My parents had some money. I went to Tabor, then I went to the University of Vermont.

What did you major in?

Skiing [laughs]. Actually I started out in engineering, but I was baffled by calculus. I could never figure out why anyone would study calculus. Basically I flunked out of college.

So you have an innate sense of how things work, but you don't want to use formulas?

Actually I can't make sense of how anything works. I'm still trying to figure out how the computer works. I keep looking for the little man inside.

But you have been very successful at building boats. You must have a good sense of the strength of materials and the strength of connections.

A lot of that I've picked up from other people.

When did you first get the feeling that you were going to spend your life building boats?

When I was building the Blue Jay at twelve, I think I decided right then that I wanted to build boats.

When did you first get on a multihull?

I knew a guy who had a Hellcat. It had round hulls; it went pretty good in light air, but it was no "wow!" The next time I sailed a multihull, it was Phil Weld's *Trumpeter*, a 44-foot trimaran. *Trumpeter* was built in Britain for the Round-Britain Race, and Phil got a second.

Now you were into serious multihulls. How did that feel?

It felt like a piece of junk! [laughs].

Why? Did you feel, "I could build a better boat than this?"

Yeah. But the experience was pretty mind-blowing. I had been sailing monohulls pretty seriously. *Trumpeter* did eight or nine knots, while the monohulls did about five. So immediately I said, "Hey, these multihull guys are not bullshitting us. This is real."

Phil Weld asked me to do the Bermuda Race with him, and I immediately said yes.

How did you do?

We were the first boat to Bermuda. But I could see lots of things that could be better on that boat.

Well, you saw that multihulls were faster, but were there other ways in which they were better?

Didn't heel. You could walk around on them. The heeling thing didn't bother me, but for cruising …

And shallow draft, so they wouldn't go aground?

No! One of the first things we did with *Trumpeter* was run her aground!

Are there any disadvantages to multihulls?

Plenty. Marinas aren't set up for them. They are so beamy [wide], you have to pay for two slips instead of one. And most yards can't pull you [haul out].

After my senior year at Tabor, 1963, *Tabor Boy* went to Bermuda, and I went on her. We had a lot of wind and seas. I thought it was great fun, but a number of guys got seasick. She was slightly topheavy so we got a lot of motion. Some of the guys flew home.

Why are you in Maine rather than Connecticut or Rhode Island?

More open space. There is no open waterfront down there. And Merle Hallett offered me a job at Handy Boat building custom boats. The idea was that Merle would deal with the customers, and I'd build them. It worked—sort of. We built Merle a racing boat, *Scaramouche*. That was a 43-footer. We had a crew of six. Then we built a trimaran, *Moxie*, for Phil Weld. And we built the prototype for the Freedom 33, a Jay Paris design.

And we built a 56-foot trimaran for a French movie company making a film about Donald Crowhurst. [Crowhurst entered a round-the-world race, hoping the prize would save his foundering company. When it became clear he was losing, he formed a plan whereby he would loiter about the South Atlantic while his competitors raced each other around the dangerous Cape Horn and Cape of Good Hope. He would then turn and race ahead of them back to the finish line and claim the prize. Later, realizing his log books would be scrutinized by experts and his scheme uncovered, he committed suicide by jumping overboard. The winner, Robin Knox-Johnston, gave his cash prize to Crowhurst's widow and children.]

I was at Handy Boat about two and a half years, but Merle's restaurant, "The Galley," was also in the same building. It was just too close—the smell of epoxy resin and the fiberglass powder, and the Awlgrip fumes. It was probably also illegal.

So I came and started this place, Greene Marine.

I have noticed that multihulls, with their large center hulls and smaller outriggers on wings, look like gliding seagulls. Is that an aesthetic thing, or is it purely for speed?

You can fool around with the aesthetics and not lose much speed. The most important thing is the part of the hull in the water. I remember when I was first learning about multihulls, there was a Dick Newick trimaran called *Three Cheers* in Rhode Island, and it just looked like it was dancing on the water. I said to myself, "Boy, I'd go sailing on that thing!" I was off to Bermuda on some monohull. *Three Cheers* was tied to the dock, but it looked so alive!

You could race on the Great Lakes, you could just race in bays, but what is it that draws you to racing across oceans?

It's not hard. To sail a modern boat across the ocean is nothing.

How many times have you crossed the Atlantic?

I stopped counting at twenty when I got Parkinson's. That was twenty years go.

How long does it take to cross the Atlantic?

Twenty days for racing trimarans; thirty days for monohulls.

Some guy who crewed with you across the Atlantic said one should never let Walter provision the boat—that you once showed up with just two dozen Big Macs. Is that a true story?

That's a tue story, except they were hamburgers, and they were pretty good for the first three or four days.

Why just hamburgers?

I was in a rush. The race was about to start.

Another time, Bill Fulton told me he saw you headed for the dock with a stick of French bread sticking out of a grocery bag. When he asked where you were going, you said, "England." Is that also true?

Could be.

What is it about racing sailboats that you like so much?

I guess it's being able to see a boat sail well, properly. If I go on a boat and people aren't sailing it properly, it bothers me.

It doesn't matter so much whether you win the race, as long as the boat is sailed well?

Yeah, but even if it's just day sailing, if the sail isn't trimmed right, it bothers me no end. I'm not saying I'm a perfectionist, but I have a hard time just cruising.

Because it's like having a thoroughbred race horse and using it to pull a wagon?

Something like that.

So whenever you are on a sailboat, you are always looking for something that can be just a little better, whether it's the design, the equipment, or the trim of the sails?

I'm actually pretty competitive. I do want to get there first, but I've gotten more conservative as the years have passed.

You don't like to capsize or lose the rig anymore?

No, I don't want to break boats. Breaking a boat is hard on the owner financially and it's hard on my mind as a boatyard operator. When you have completed a boat so it's finally perfect in every detail, and then you see the same boat dismasted or the rudder busted off, it's gut-wrenching.

When you win a race, what is the nature of the thrill?

I'm not interested in going to the cocktail party afterwards. One second after we cross the finish line, I'm ready to go home. I'm not saying I'm a great sailor; I just want to know how things work and how to make them work better. And it's not just doing well. It can also be, "Why didn't we do better? Is it because the bottom was dirty, or the propeller wasn't faired [smoothed]?" I just want to know why.

Do you mind telling me the story of *Gonzo*?

Gonzo was a 53-foot trimaran we built in 1981 for Mike Birch, a Canadian guy, a racer. He's building a boat over in the shed right now. He was second in the OSTAR in 1976 and third in 1980.

What is the origin of that name?

Well, "gonzo" was what the hippies used to say in the 60s, the 70s. Like, "I'm gonzo." ["Goodbye, I'm out of here."]

We built her in 1981 for the Two-Star Race, a two-handed race from Plymouth, England, to Newport, Rhode Island. Mike and I raced her. We lost an outer hull. It broke off.

That would be a handicap!

[Laughs] *Tele 7 Jours*—"television 7 days a week" in French—was the name of the boat. It's the French equivalent of *TV Guide*. When we lost an ama [outer, smaller hull], we were second in the race. We were about 600 miles offshore, and we headed for Liverpool, Nova Scotia. We could only sail on one tack, so we'd sail on the good tack for maybe a day, then we'd heave to until the wind shifted, then we could sail again. Like anything, good seamanship requires patience.

Good seamanship means getting there safely?

Yeah, with your boat intact. Anyway, we sailed her to Nova Scotia, then we came back here and built a new bow.

The bow was damaged, too?

Yeah, the bow was gone, too.

What caused you to lose *both* an ama *and* the bow?

Basically, we built her too light; we were pushing the limit.

Tele 7 Jours had a sister boat, sponsored by an Italian clothing company, that took third, so we knew the boats were pretty fast. Both boats went back to France with new amas.

They raced in "LaRochelle-New Orleans," which was a race the French dreamed up. But then they found out you couldn't sail to New Orleans because it is 100 miles up the Mississippi!

Didn't the French found New Orleans? Shouldn't they have known where it was?

I guess their GPS was off.

Both *Star Point* and *Gonzo* raced in that race, but we didn't do very well—third and fourth out of twenty-five, I think. The next race was the "Rum Race."

Rhumb as in rhumb line?

No, as in the stuff you drink.

Bacardi?

No, the Rum Manufacturers of Guadalupe. French rum is a lot different than American rum. It's probably the same process, but it tastes like mouthwash [laughs].

After that Mike said, "I want a faster boat." He said he wanted a catamaran [two hulls, instead of the trimaran's three]. He got a sponsor and they built a catamaran in Europe. He went in the Rum Race, and I was back here with *Gonzo*. Mike still owned her, then he sold he boat with the stipulation that I could race it in the Rum Race. The guy he sold it to owned a bunch of supermarkets, and he said, "I'll sponsor you."

We were sailing *Gonzo* over to France for the start of the Rum Race. We left in October, probably not the best month, but the race was in November, and shipping the boat would have been too expensive.

To make a long story short, we left Maine, and about four days later we ran into a nor'easter. We were in the Gulf Stream, about 250 miles east of Nantucket. It was blowing out of the east-northeast.

Was it really rough?

Yeah, but I wasn't really worried. On the second day we decided to run, so we turned the boat downwind. Going upwind wasn't much fun.

With minimal sail?

No sail at all, just the bare pole [mast].

Making what speed?

Oh, six to twelve knots.

The next day we got a whole bunch of junk together and dragged it [a "drogue"] behind us to slow us down. Mostly empty sail bags, and the anchor to hold the whole mess down. That worked—sorta. We sailed all that night.

Did the drogue slow you down?

A little. It kept us down to twelve knots.

This was to prevent the boat from surfing down the big waves and burying your bow?

Yeah. And I would never do that [run downwind] again. Maybe in protected waters where the waves weren't so big.

Did your bow bury?

Not the bow, but the ama. Scary. We were hand steering. That wasn't difficult.

Is hand steering better than being on autopilot?

Yeah, you can see what's coming and react to it—take it at a better angle. Nye Williams said, "I think this boat is foolproof." He said, "Capsize proof." That was bad thing to say.

I think it was about 10 a.m.. I was steering, and the other guys were down in the cabin. We came down a wave that was a bit like a whirlpool. It was a big wave, and the boat capsized.

Did you understand how it happened?

No, there were three people on the boat. One guy said we went sidewards, another guy said we pitchpoled [end-over-end], and I thought we went over at a 45-degree angle.

I was steering and had a life jacket on, but no lifeline. I was thrown out of the boat, so I swam to the upside-down boat. I swam underneath the net [the "trampoline"—the netting between the hulls]. I wasn't knocked out; I was just surprised that all of a sudden I was immersed in salt water.

We had decided the night before we didn't want to be tethered to the boat, in case it capsized. And we had taken precautions. We took the EPIRB [Emergency Position Indicating Radio Beacon] out of its automatic deployment holder and put it in a locker secured with sheetrock screws. And we had a waterproof, handheld VHF radio. And we had a couple of handsaws. There was no escape hatch in the boat, just a 15-inch porthole. We opened that up and I said, "How are you guys?" And they said, "How are you, chief?"

They handed me a saw, and I cut a bigger hole in the hull.

Now, a monohull would sink because of the heavy lead keel. But Gonzo wouldn't sink, even with the hole you cut, because she was lighter than water?

Yeah, and the amas were watertight, so they were flotation.

We later learned that we had cut the hole in the wrong place. The waves came in and sloshed around. We got rid of a bunch of stuff, like the generator, to make the boat lighter.

Phil Weld, who had capsized the year before, told us one thing you wanted to make sure was your flashlights were tied down, not just put in a nice holder. When you capsize everything turns upside down. Up has become down and down is up. You can't count on gravity any more.

Did you have faith in your EPIRB?

Yeah, Nye Williams had been in another boat that capsized about a year before that. We had survival suits with mittens. We stayed warm. All that day we sort of made the best of what we could. There wasn't any question we would be saved—just how long it would take. The EPIRB was on. Nye, he put the EPIRB inside his survival suit with the aerial sticking out [laughs].

We kept a lookout for ships. If we saw one, we could call them on the handheld VHF, which is line-of-sight. So we were sitting there all that day, all that night, and at seven in the morning an airplane came. The airplane circled around. He was out of the Coast Guard Air Station in Elizabeth City, North Carolina. We talked to him on CH16, VHF, and we said we had capsized [laughs]—in case he didn't know what we were supposed to look like right side up [laughs again].

Crew of capsized trimaran, after cutting escape hatch in center hull, hangs on while awaiting rescue by U.S. Coast Guard cutter Vigorous (foreground). Tanker California Getty, which also came to the rescue, stands by.

"Gonzo," 300 miles offshore and upside down in an October nor'easter.
Popular Mechanics, *May, 1983.*

Was is still blowing?

Yeah, it was stormin' pretty good. The waves were forty feet.

The C-130 said, "There is a tanker about thirty miles away and a Coast Guard cutter about 100 miles." The tanker appeared about one in the afternoon. I talked to the skipper on the VHF.

How big was the tanker?

Big, probably 1,000 feet.

Was the tanker a help?

He was going to try to rescue us.

Pretty hard to maneuver a 1,000-foot ship in 40-foot waves and high winds?

The guy was pretty good. Maybe he wasn't 1,000 feet, but certainly 900 and change.

This gives new meaning to "Permission to come alongside?"

Yeah [laughs]. He tried to come alongside. He came upwind [headed into the wind] one time. We were right in front of him, and when we rose on a wave, his anchor punched right through our hull. When that happened we all bailed out. He was dead stopped. He was just like a big sea wall. Our rig [mast] came out of the boat and was banging around.

He tried shooting a line to us. There were a couple of guys on deck with this line shooter. It was a pretty elaborate thing. One guy was carrying it; another guy would aim it. They ran down along the deck as we drifted by; they'd aim it; we'd drift some more; they'd run some more and start to aim it, then run again. Anyway, they finally ran out of ship, and they just chucked the whole shooting match overboard. They must not have practiced much because they never did manage to shoot it.

I talked to the skipper and said, "I don't think there's any future in this." He agreed.

Then he said, "I'll stand by." We weren't in any great peril, and—again—seamanship is patience.

The aircraft came on the radio and said the Coast Guard cutter was now thirty miles away, so we said, "We don't have any other plans, so I guess we'll stick around."

The Coast Guard came, a 240-footer, the "Vigorous." Once, when she turned and was sideways to the sea, she rolled on her side about forty degrees, and one of her props came out of the water. But as long as they kept her headed into the sea she was all right.

We talked to the skipper on the radio, and he said, "I'm going to approach you upwind, and we're going to throw a monkey's fist [a massive knot at the end of a line to give it momentum] and a heaving line."

Then we pulled a horseshoe life ring over—the kind of thing they pick people out of the water with on a helicopter.

He pulled one guy on while he backed away. Then he returned and picked off the second. It took about twenty minutes. I went last, and then we were rescued. That's the end of the story.

Did you learn anything from this experience?

Yes. I said, "These trimarans are pretty dangerous." And I said, "I'm never going to sail on one again."

Have you stuck to that?

No.

WILLIS SPEAR
Fisherman
Cousins Island, Yarmouth
Age 56

Willis prepares his traps for another season.

The first thing you notice about Willis Spear is his hands. Like those of most fishermen, his hands are oversized, from years of handling cold, wet rope, fish nets, and lobster traps.

Next you are drawn to his face: weathered and creviced like barn boards from long exposure to sun, wind, salt spray, and harrowing North Atlantic storms.

Then he speaks. The voice is sonorous and measured, what you might expect from a Shakespearean actor. Each carefully measured word portends a significant thought.

We are sitting in the Spears' kitchen on a cold, gray March day. I think to myself, "This is not Martha Stewart's kitchen. This is a kitchen where a lot of biscuits and fish chowder have been made and consumed." Willis's wife sits next to him in silence.

My father worked for the Portland/Montreal Pipeline as an oil dispatcher, but he was a seaman. He graduated in the second class at Maine Maritime, and he had gone to sea in World War II as an engineer on Liberty ships. But he liked most to lobster on the side.

He built his own traps, sawed his own oak, did his own trap heads. I remember being seven and going down with him to a place we called The Point at Willard Beach. He was a little nervous because he'd built these traps himself without much of a pattern to follow.

They were square, and they looked like traps, but he was afraid some of the local lobstermen would have a few comments to make on his workmanship. So he went down really early in the morning and looked, and nobody was there. He came back and I helped him load half a dozen into the back of our '41 Ford.

Well, we went down, and now everybody was there. So when we took the traps out of the car .... I remember his trap door [the hinged opening used for baiting and removing the lobsters]. Most of the other fellows' lobster traps had four-lath doors. He had built his five laths wide. Sure enough, someone made the remark, "What are you trying to catch, elephants?" But that was the only snide remark I heard. His heads [the netting] came out okay.

I remember going out with him. He would row, and I'd just sit and watch.

Did you get seasick?

I wasn't seasick. The smell of the bait was a little....The first time, you know, it was red fish. It was strong. I remember the smell. You baited the trap with a string through the eye socket. He made his own bait needle for threading the string.

Willard Beach was a very, very old fishing village. Actually at one time it was the biggest seaport on the coast of Maine, in the 1600s. The other name for Willard Beach was Gurry Cove. The fishermen used to clean their fish right in the cove, so there was plenty of fish gurry [guts].

"The Point" at Willard Beach, South Portland

How did you get into lobstering yourself?

Some of the local color, the characters, a lot of them were originally from Long Island, Maine. There were Floyds, there were McVanes, there was Riches, there was Braileys, Woodburys, all Long Island names. So I kind of gravitated. I seemed to really like the water a lot. Liked the boats. It gave you that sense of independence, which is kind of a false thing. Once you get that taste in your blood, anyhow, it's hard to get rid of.

I had my first lobster license in 1965. It was the first year it went to ten dollars. It had been five. I was twelve or thirteen. My father didn't get me a pair of boots because he didn't want me down there. But my uncle felt sorry for me. He was in the fire department, and he got me a pair of fireman's boots.

After that, my father bought a double-ender. It had a torpedo stern. It was twenty-four feet long by six feet wide—narrow boat— twenty-four horsepower, flathead Universal 4-cylinder engine.

There was another boat like it in the cove that had belonged to the boxer Gene Tunney, who had summered in Maine. We saw our boat again in the late 70s on Mt. Desert. I knew it was my father's boat because it had a wet exhaust on the port quarter, and where the wet exhaust had come out it had cracked a couple of ribs, and the old man had sawn ribs to fit in there to sister the broken ones. Those ribs were still there, so I knew that was his boat.

Did you ever think of being anything but a fisherman?

I don't think I ever did. As a kid I just always liked boats and always was pulled to the water. I never did anything else. Melville said that people are drawn to the sea, to have a look around, who knows? You'd wake up in the mornin' to the sardine whistles at the house, and you could smell the tide changing. That stuff I can still smell, still hear. So that got into me deep. It was like oxygen. Couldn't live without it.

As a kid, I lobstered in my rowboat, and then I lobstered with those fellows from Long Island. One in particular was Donny Rich. I loved the guy; I loved the man. I was his sternman. I was the fellow that baited the trap, opened the doors of the trap, picked out the lobsters, banded the lobsters.

I enjoyed being with him a lot. He was a very even-tempered man, never swore, he was actually pious. I'd go with him in the winter and during school vacations. He always had a story to tell. He had a very good memory; still does. He told me of the islanders, of his family living on that island for 200 years. He had a big influence. Believe me, we suffered dearly in the winter with the storms. So I knew what it was like to fish in the wintertime, and lobstering. The messes we got into, after those big storms with those traps.

Did the storms damage the traps?

Terrible. Smashed up, broken off. One winter, I think it was the winter of '71 and '2, we did nothin' but just untangle snarls all winter long. Traps in thirty fathoms [a fathom is six feet] of water were all tangled up. The seas would start pulling the buoys together.

Storm damaged traps

They acted like a drogue, and dragged those traps. I can remember in March reaching down into the water with a knife, water right up to my ear, cutting traps off. He'd have his gaff hooked into a trap and I'd cut it off from the ball because we couldn't get them to the surface. Just get the traps, that's all you could hope for.

It was so cold, I couldn't wear enough clothes. You'd wear those rubber gloves. The only heat we had was from the exhaust pipes, put your hand on the exhaust. His circulation was so good his hands used to steam, and on a good winter's day he'd roll his sleeves up, with bare arms on a good winter's day.

I did that right up until I went to that vocational school over in South Portland—Southern Maine Vocational Technical Institute, it was called. I wasn't smart enough to go to Maine Maritime, so I went there because they offered a marine science program which taught young people small boat engineering, or small boat navigation. The first year they give you a little of both. The second year you specialize. They taught me the basics of small ship engine rooms.

A lot of kids got jobs as marine technicians. I got a job with Texas Instruments doing environmental work on the Hudson River. Con Edison, if it had built a nuclear power plant anywhere on the Hudson, they built it in the wrong place. They built it in a place where there happened to be a deep hole that they put their suction lines in to cool the nuclear reactors. The striped bass and the white perch would collect there because it was warm. They would suck them into the turbine, so they had to set a revolving screen in front of the intake pipes.

I remember the summer of '72 was when Con Ed was having brownouts, because they started to get a large number of striped bass on the screen. When the number approached 1,000, they would have to start cuttin' back on the amount of water they used.

Then I went to Halifax on the seismic ship the *J.E. Johnson*. I was a seismic sound source engineer. My job was to take care of the compressors. They built up a charge of compressed air, almost 3,000 psi, to these things they called air guns. They had what they called a tuned gun array where they made little pops with little guns the size of soup cans up to the big air guns, which would be bigger than a gallon bucket. The array would send off different frequencies 35,000 feet down into the earth. They had a machine that printed out the echoes that came off the bottom. They were looking for salt domes, where the pressures of the earth were pushing salt up through the earth's crust. It would make a dome where oil would collect.

Then they sent me to Barranquilla, Colombia. I was in Barranquilla, Santa Marta, and Cartagena. They were very tough towns back then because of the cocaine. Then we went down to Brazil, and I spent the rest of the time off the Amazon River looking for oil. Came home in June. Went lobstering through the summer.

How did the work in a seismic ship compare to lobstering? Was it like, "I really hate this. I gotta make money, or …."

It was an ok job, although it didn't have that sense of independence, that cursed Maine sense of independence. I had a boss who left me alone. But always in the back of my mind I thought I'd like to come home and go fishing. That sense of independence of having your own boat, watching the sunrise come up—that was the curse, that was always with you.

You're always out there at sunrise?

Yes, sunrise. I used to go with another old timer who always made sure the first trap came over the rail just as the sun came up.

Were you hauling the traps by hand back then?

We used a "niggerhead" —you're not supposed to say that any more—but that's what it was called. It was driven by the engine. You took a couple turns with the rope, put a little tension on it, and the turning drum does all the work.

I used to watch the old timer's arms. They'd go ninety miles an hour, and some of those guys would do it like they were playing the fiddle. They were just as in tune, just as coordinated. They could haul traps as fast as a hydraulic hauler could. But you still had to hold onto the rope and pull the trap in with one hand. It was almost like a ballet, watching a good guy doing it.

I remember one day in June '67, the shedders [soft-shelled lobsters] hadn't shown up yet. We were out on the Cod Ledges, about six or seven miles from here. It came up a hard breeze, sou'west. Everybody went home, but he got into the rhythm. And he got me into the rhythm of the waves. I mean, it was rough. We hauled the whole day long. It was no trouble at all once a man was in rhythm with nature. I never forgot that day because he was so in tune, with the way he maneuvered that boat through the waves. It was what we called a feather-white sou'west. It was actually fun when you're tuned in like that.

I went with another fellow, Jimmy Floyd in the spring. He had a Novi [a design built in Nova Scotia]. Jimmy knew where he was. Just compass and sonar machine. And looking at the land from seven miles out, he could tell where he was within fifty feet. And he said one day, "Do you see this place here?" I mean, we're a long way out, I'm looking at Half Way Rock and the shore is seven miles away. "This is the place that the Bailey Islanders called "Jim

Floyd Ground," not after me but after my father. My father fished so many traps here that the Bailey Islanders couldn't get a trap on it, so they called it Jimmy Floyd Ground."

He says, "Look how she goes through the water?" [There was southwest breeze in the afternoon]. She went good. But his trunk house windows were broken out from where the spray and the waves had come over. There's literally a fountain of water going down into the cabin, but she went good, she went right along. He was a good man, a good seaman.

What did you do after the seismic work?

I got off in '76 and came home and was lobstering in my punt with my wife—she and I weren't married then. She was in nursin' school.

Did you call her your sternman?

No, never did. We was kind of a package deal, you know. She was my sternman, but I didn't dare call her that.

She was a great person to have in the boat. She knew her stuff because she'd been on boats with her brothers. Its a good way to know your future wife. I'd highly recommend taking your prospective wife out lobstering in a punt in the summer, because if you can get along in a punt, you can get through most of life's travails. We managed to get through the lobstering without killing each other. It was a good trial. She may not agree with that. She just sits there peaceful and quiet, but she was good.

That fall a friend of mine and I, we bought an old Novi boat that had sunk. There was a lot of fish on the shore, a lot of gillnet fish. This was 1976, they were doing so well that there were actually some fellows who sunk boats, from loadin' them with so much codfish and pollock. The whales were around, the Russians were there fishing for herring, everybody was doing real good.

So we rigged the boat for gillnetting. We didn't know a thing about it. It was coming on winter. We took an older fellow with us, a fellow who had fished his whole life. He would go with us and show us how to go pollocking. We put out thirty-six nets.

The weather was bad, terrible bad. The winter fisheries are altogether different from the summer fisheries. The nets set a long time, some of the fish got rotten, and it was horrible.

But we did all right. Pollock was 20 cents, and we were getting like 4 to 8,000 pounds a day of pollock. Then the pollock left; we fished on cod till the spring. There was a resident family of cod around the shoals. There used to be so many fish, there could always be a resident family of cod, of pollock, of something along the shore. They weren't the school cod; they just stayed. They were different looking. The school cod were nice and clean and green and had snow white bellies because they were always moving. But the residents, they were kind of brown looking. They hung around the rocks. And they were wormy.

We started to catch a few haddock in March, around the 65 fathom edge, southeast of the Portland Light Ship, place they called Trinidad. We got down off a place called Cape Porpoise Peaks around the first of April, and honest to God, we hit it at the right time. There was haddock and codfish; they came together. We were getting between 3,000 and 8,000 a day. Haddock was a buck, and the cod was 50 cents. We were right on 'em, and we were the only boat for about two weeks. It was something I'll never forget, to see that school of fish and to be on 'em.

We fished up and down the whole coast, with the migrating schools. We'd stay out overnight. We slept with the 471 [Caterpillar diesel engine] in the cabin. Kept the boat in Port Clyde for a couple of months. We weren't married then, but she'd [his wife] come down and visit. We'd stay right down there.

I ran a steel dragger for a fellow the winter of '78–'79. The price of haddock was a buck then, flounders were a buck. I knew nothin' about dragging. I stove the net up a lot. They called it a "New Bedford 35." It was built out of rayon and nylon—stuff that they made tires out of. Once it got dirt in it, it got wicked heavy on the bottom, but it would catch flounders like a son of a gun. That net would tend bottom. We did real well.

I was able to procure a government low-interest-rate loan to build a boat. Things looked really good. Fuel was cheap; the price of fish was a buck. A man could do real well. We had two or three good years with that boat. We launched it in '79 but by '84 I could see things were changin'. The fish, they were further out and further out. They were going south. People were enjoying fairly good fishing in other parts of the coast, but where we lived, around Casco Bay and the area outside, it, you could see the tide was going out on the fisheries. By the late 80s it was kind of destitute.

Then the federal government said, "Because you only ground fished fourteen days last year, we'll give you fourteen days this year for ground fish," and I said, "Geez, guys, I fished fourteen days last year only because there wasn't any ground fish. There was shrimp, and Maine people have always done whatever it takes to survive. Why don't you look at it in the big picture? Why don't you look at what I've done continuously for thirty years?" I said, "Even though I built my whole life's business around continually ground fishing?" They said, "Tough luck." So I lost my ground fish days. I went from 130 days a year down to fourteen. Consequently the value of my boat went down. Then the value of shrimp started to drop. In 1984 it was $1.20; by 2004 it was thirty cents. Fuel had doubled or tripled. Lobsterin' was still good, but I needed a winter fisheries to carry me through the year.

Tell me about the day you decided not to do it any more?

I had 4,000 pounds of shrimp on the fish auction in Portland. It was beautiful shrimp. It was a Friday night auction. They called me up Saturday afternoon and said, "Hey, your shrimp didn't sell Friday night. We don't know what happened." I says, "Okay, we'll see what happens Sunday. But I got thinking about it and I said, "They won't be looking too good on Sunday." I went in Sunday morning and paid to have 2,000 pounds moved back onto my boat. I went out and dumped 1,000 pounds into Portland Harbor, and I took 1,000 pounds down to the islanders: 500 pounds to Long and 500 pounds to Chebeague. The Chebeaguers wrote me a letter, saying it had fed thirty-seven families on the island. The last 2,000 pounds went for nineteen cents a pound.

I had seen a *National Geographic* special on television about these Brazilian diamond miners working in just loincloths in a deep pit in the heat and humidity digging out diamonds. There would be an avalanche of dirt and thirty or forty of them would get buried. Everybody else would scurry over the tops of them to pick up the diamonds and didn't bother to dig out their compatriots.

Fishing was starting to look like that Brazilian pit mining. I said to heck with it. I had to try to elevate myself a little bit from throwing away my catch or begging people to buy it. So I got money from the government to be re-trained. I got my AB's [able-bodied seaman] ticket. I got a job on a McAllister tug pushing an oil barge up and down the coast.

My favorite part of the job was riding up in the bow of the barge with a walkie-talkie. My job was giving the captain distances as we came into a dock. They speak their own language. You have to talk in a succinct, clipped voice because you have to give distances and numbers very quickly because you're in a dynamic situation. If you're thirty feet up on top of a 400-foot barge that's eighty feet wide, and you're coming into a dock, and the dock is a dogleg in and out, and you're giving the distances, and they're changing every time you come up to another fender, you've got to let the guy know at the wheel of the tug, because he can't see.

Barge language is a special language. Words like "good barge" and "bad barge." Now that means a lot. If the bow of the barge is inside a fender, and you're telling the guy you're six feet to the bad, and it's fifty feet ahead, he knows exactly what you're talking about. If you say you've got ten feet of overlap on a fender, that means it's ten feet of good barge beyond the end of the fender. But if you tell him you've got sixty feet of overhang, that's not good.

It's like that old joke about driving. Your wife says, "Take a left," and you say, "I'm supposed to take a left, right?" And she says, "No, left, not right." You've got to have your system of communicatin' figured out.

How long do you think you'll continue doing tugboat work?

Right now McAllister hires me seasonal. But I'm able to come home and go lobstering, which is a real good deal. It's all right for an old guy. I'm no spring chicken. It's satisfactory work. I knew what I was getting into.

I'm nobody special; I just do what I have to do to survive. It's not an easy thing, and I accept that and just do it. Parts of my life have been a real struggle, but I'm still a pretty happy guy.

Did I choose this life on purpose? I don't know. I just kind of went that way. Like a salmon swimming upstream, I just found myself going there.

WILLIAM GRIBBIN
Retired Portland, Maine, Docking Master
Little John Island, Yarmouth
Age 74

Docking Master Gribbin at ease

Ship pilots are experienced seamen with local knowledge who assist ship captains in navigating the often-dangerous waters at the entrances to ports. Most of the world's major ports require that a ship employ a licensed pilot in order to enter.

The pilot is responsible for the navigation of the vessel from the time he assumes control from the master until the vessel is safely moored or docked, including steering and engine orders and the operations of the tugboats.

Until recently, Portland, Maine, was the largest tonnage seaport in New England, receiving 150,000,000 barrels of oil per year in tank vessels up to 900 feet in length.

We are sitting on Captain Gribbin's deck, perched on a ledge overlooking Casco Bay. The height, the immediacy of the water, and the port-side navigation light give me the feeling of being on the bridge of a large ship.

My father always had boats of assorted sizes. In 1947 he bought a place up to Sebago Lake, a big place, about thirty acres, 1,200 feet along the shore.

When I was seven he bought my brother a bicycle and me a boat. I had a little six-foot punt. I got a one horsepower motor for it. Before I could use that boat, I had to learn to swim, so I had to have swimming lessons. But before I could do that, I had to be four feet tall, so I could stand up in the shallow end of the pool. My father was very safety conscious, and it spilled over onto me.

Then he sold the lake place. He bought half a yacht with a friend of his—a raised-deck, Marblehead Cruiser, vintage '20s-something. His friend died, so in 1954 we came back to the salt water. We stayed mostly in the bay and cruised weekends as a family.

I was taking courses at the Power Squadron. Then I got a job with Casco Bay Lines, the ferry service here in Casco Bay, as a deckhand. I was on the Portland Boy's Club swimming team, and many of my teammates were working for Casco Bay Lines. Some of the kids misrepresented their ages to work there. This is in 1954. I was fourteen.

Old Walter Sweat was the manager. He'd come along and ask when your birthday was, almost every other day. So you had to be on your toes to fib a little bit about when your birthday was. That's really how it started, on Casco Bay Lines. I worked there for a couple of years.

I don't remember how it happened, but the fellow who was the brother of the man I worked for in the grocery store, before I worked at Casco Bay Lines, had gone to Maine Maritime Academy. He knew somebody who hooked me up and helped me get a job for one summer as an ordinary seaman on a tanker, when I was a junior in high school. So I went to New York. All these things enabled me to get my seaman's papers from the Coast Guard. I was an ordinary seaman, the lowest-echelon job on the ship. I was sixteen.

I flew to New York City a few days before my seventeenth birthday. Went to the Mobil Oil Company office on East 42nd Street, had a physical, and a couple of days later I was on a tanker.

The tanker ran coastwise between Beaumont, Texas, and New York. I made four runs that summer as an ordinary seaman, and I learned a lot. It was hard work. It was not the kind of work I'd been used to. These men were all experienced seamen, but they took me under their wing and they were good to me. The old bosun, Axel, a Norwegian, a little bit of a man, would work my head off. But he liked me and every evening before supper, we'd sit around and do knot tying and making fancy rope work and things like that. I learned a lot. Back in those days I could splice a small line with one hand. I was eager to learn, and it was fun. There was nothing else to do on a ship but read in those days. That was a test to see whether or not I wanted to go to sea for lifetime work.

I only got seasick once. I was painting the overhead of the midship house on this tanker, and I think we were in the Gulf of Mexico. The ship's name was *Socony Vacuum*. The crew had taught me to chew tobacco. The ship was moving, and I was breathing the paint fumes. The chief mate stood there watching me paint, and I had a mouthful of tobacco juice. I didn't feel as though I should spit in front of him, so I swallowed it. I was only seventeen; I shouldn't have been chewing tobacco in the first place. That was the only time I didn't feel quite right.

After that summer I worked for Casco Bay Lines again, then went down to Maine Maritime Academy as a freshmen in August of 1958. I graduated from Maine Maritime with a Bachelor's of Marine Science, which really didn't mean a lot unless you were in the marine industry. More important, I had a license as a Third Mate, Unlimited Tonnage, Any Ocean. It's a good license—a good way to start. You have to have 365 sea days, working days, in order to take the examination for the next higher license.

When I graduated there were six of us in the deck department that got job offers. Shipping was beginning to slow down. It was after World War II, and the merchant marine was shrinking, as it continues to do, and there weren't that many jobs available. There were bunches of maritime academies cranking out graduates.

Back in those days, in order to get one month's sea time, I had to spend three months ashore. It took three years to be able to sit for a Second Mate's license. Jobs were scarce, and you had to wait your turn. I joined the union—Masters, Mates, and Pilots, Local 88—in New York, right about where the World Trade Center was. It was a rotary hiring system. You'd come ashore, go to the union hall, take a number. I'd just keep going down to New York once a month for the union meetings in order to keep my number current so I could use it to bid on a job.

I did Third Mate on many ships. I worked on a couple of troop ships, then freighters, then freighters out across the Pacific, and over to India and different places. They were all adventures.

What are the duties of a Third Mate?

Well, the Master is in charge of the vessel; he's the head of everything. The Chief Mate supervises what's going on with the cargo on the ship, plus the maintenance of the ship. The Second Mate is primarily concerned with navigation. The Third Mate stands the watch. He may have some collateral duties like life boats.

It's all about growing into becoming a Master. It's an apprentice program—a wonderful way to do it.

The training at Maine Maritime Academy was enormously valuable. Still, there's nothing like just doing it. There were some times when I was dealing with people that got their license by way of coming up from the fo'c'sle, without going to school. I experienced some resentment along the way because of that.

How did you get to be a pilot?

Whenever I was home from sea I would go down and hang out around the Portland waterfront. The tugs were tied up down there. I started talking with one of the crew. He said, "Come aboard and have a cup of coffee." So I did and, "We're going out to do a job here in a little while," so I went along. That's how it all started. "This is it; this is good," I thought.

I was married and had children. I thought, "I think it's better to be at home." I'd be making seagoing wages, at home, and working a lot more. Back in those days, 1964ish, the crew were working six days on and one day off. They were available twenty-four hours a day.

So I worked for Brown Ship Chandlery waiting for a job to open up on the tugs. We were on the same pier, and I would have coffee with the tug crews every day. I put myself in a position that if anybody ever left there, I would be available. My message is that if you want something, you've got to have the right certificates and be available and willing and ready to jump at a moment's notice.

At some point, one of the pilots got ill. They needed a deck hand temporarily, so I quit my job. I had a family, so I was taking a risk. It just evolved from there. People started taking vacations. It was the beginning of the summer, and by the end of the year I was a full-time employee. I worked nine years as a Deck Hand, one year as a Mate steering the boat, then five years as Master of one of those tugs before I got to be a pilot.

What does a pilot do?

First of all, I was a docking pilot; I wasn't a sea pilot. The sea pilot goes out in the pilot boat and boards a ship at the sea buoy, out beyond any navigational hazards. I go out with the tugs, climb up from the tugs, introduce myself to the Master, relieve the sea pilot, and take the ship to its berth or to anchor.

Pilot boat (At right) approaching ship to deliver docking pilot

Why are pilots required?

Local knowledge. A foreign vessel with a draft over nine feet coming in to Portland Harbor is required to take on a pilot for assistance through the hazards: the tides, the currents, the bridges, the traffic in the harbor. When I go aboard the ship, I command the ship and the tugs.

There are tankers coming to Portland now with a draft of fifty feet. We're required to have a three foot under-keel clearance. Three feet under fifty feet—that's not much. We bring them in at high tide.

And these ships are up to 900 feet long, three city blocks. The beam is 160 or 165 feet. They're just enormous.

What is your relationship with the captain of the ship?

Good question. I'm an adviser, a mandatory adviser [chuckles]. I've only had a couple of difficult situations, when the captain just didn't want me there. Sometimes there's a lot of ego stuff going on with these captains, so I'd say, "Go ahead, Cap."

When you take one of those ships through Portland Harbor, how fast are you moving?

As slow as the individual ship can go while maintaining steerage, because when you're moving through the water, and you have not much water under you, you have what's called "squat and sink." That is, the ship sinks down. You could be a couple of feet deeper. When you have a clearance of three feet, and you squat two feet, that's something you have to be very careful of. In addition to that, a list [lean] of one degree over half the width of a 160-foot wide ship can add over a foot of draft.

Let's say that you were moving through the water at four knots and you needed to stop as quickly as possible. How long would that take?

If it were a total emergency, you had lost power, and the ship was taking a sheer towards the shore, or towards a ledge—with all tugs backing full, or doing whatever maneuver was best, and all anchors down, you'd probably stop in a quarter mile. You can't just stop the engine and start it up in reverse. This is not your car, pushing the clutch and throwing it in reverse. Occasionally it takes a full minute before the engine can start up in reverse. In a tight harbor, a quarter mile is huge!

Do you take Tums along with you?

I did develop a gastro problem over the years. Maybe because I drank a lot of coffee.

What's it like to take a ship like that through a narrow bridge?

When you're looking at that bridge from a mile away, it doesn't look like you'll fit. A lot of captains get very nervous. But you know the width of the ship, and you know the width of the opening. You have to have faith.

You only watch one side of the ship. You don't stand in the middle. You might need two feet on the starboard side, sometimes less than that: half the difference between the opening and the width of the ship.

If you're standing on the ship's bridge on the Portland side, you sight up that side of the ship. The bridge has a couple of lights that make a range. If they're open a little, one way or the other, then you are not in line with them. You are off to the port or starboard. When things are right, those two lights look like one light.

Did you ever approach a bridge and all of a sudden the bridge tender said, "Sorry, we can't get the bridge up?"

Lots of times. That's when we do the emergency crash stop at full astern. As soon as that happens, you get out of shape. By that I mean, as soon as you go astern, the stern will swing to port, due to the torque of the propeller. You're cockeyed, and all out of shape. When you're going ahead you can steer, but when you put the engine astern, you're no longer steering the ship because there's no pressure on the rudder.

What happens if you hit the fenders on the bridge?

I've got some pictures. The fenders used to be wood timbers; they're not now. Most times the fenders would just spring in and bounce back, sometimes they would break. Twelve-inch timbers breaking—that's an awful sound. It's a sound you never want to hear. These ships weigh up to 45,000 tons, 90,000,000 pounds—imagine.

One of the greatest compliments I ever had was on a warm Sunday afternoon. I was bringinging a tanker into the Mobil dock. The captain was Norwegian, and the ship was drifting in there just beautifully. The thing I like to do is just let the ship find her own path. Don't fight her and work too hard to do it. Find the easiest way.

This captain said to me, "You have the touch." And that was just the biggest compliment to me. There were other times I would get a, "job well done" from a captain when, in my mind, I hadn't done the best job. Then I knew he didn't know what he was talking about. But I always appreciated a compliment from somebody who knew the difference.

What percentage of recreational boaters do you think know the Collision Regulations, what a landlubber would call the "rules of the road?"

Depends on the time of year. I would say in the middle of the winter probably most of them have a rough idea. In the summer there's a lot of scariness. It just gets my goat when someone tries to cross ahead of me...they just don't realize.

They're assuming their engine is going to keep running, or if they're in a sailboat, the wind is going to continue. I remember I was going up the channel. I was shaped up with a pretty good sized ship for the bridge, and there was a little sailboat running along, right ahead of me. Even at dead slow, I was overtaking him. It was just a little sailboat, probably twenty or twenty-five feet. He was sailing along. I blew the danger signal [five rapid blasts of the ship's horn]. I stopped the ship's engine, and I'm drifting, and nothing is happening. All the tugs were blowing their horns, too, and I couldn't raise him on the radio. Finally I sent one of the tugs ahead ...the man was deaf! He couldn't hear! He was just blissfully sailing along, enjoying a sunny day on the water.

We were creeping up behind him with this immense ship. When the tug did come up alongside of him, that scared him. He got his engine going then!

There are traffic rules on the water just as there are on land. First, Rule Number 5 in the Collision Regulations states: "Every vessel must maintain a lookout by sight and hearing, as well as all available means, in order to be able to appraise the situation and risk of collision." Second, Rule Number 9 states, "Sailing vessels and vessels less than 20 meters [about 65 feet] are not to impede any vessel confined to the channel."

Do you remember a time you were really scared as a pilot?

There have been a few times that had my heart racing. One of the tugs caught on fire. It was blowin' hard, and we were just coming alongside the pier with a big ship at the pipeline. First thing in the morning, blowing out of the west probably forty.

900-foot tanker tied up at Portland Pipeline pier

I needed all of the tugs. We were right at the margins of getting the ship in as it was. Just as we were getting her in position, I saw the ship's stern start dropping away from the pier. I thought, "What is going on?" I'm calling down saying, "Can you give me any more?" Sometimes the engineer keeps a few revs up his sleeve. The tug on the bow looked back and saw smoke coming out of the after tug. They had a base explosion in the engine. The engineer got burned pretty badly trying to shut the engine down so that it wouldn't destroy the whole boat. We managed to get a line forward. I put the other tug back in the middle of her. In the meantime, the men on the pier got a line on the stern and got a line on the bow. By hook or by crook we kept her there. She would have drifted out and gone aground. I was really in a pickle, sad that one of our crew got hurt, pretty badly burned. It's dangerous business, tug boating. A lot of people get hurt. Some people get killed doing it.

In your business, you can't afford to make an error?

Can't afford to take a chance. Whenever I got in trouble, if I reviewed it afterwards, I recognized that I had taken a chance. I rubbed a bridge hard one night with a ship that was just a dog of a ship anyway, and I knew it was a bum of a ship. All ships are not created equal. There are different steering gears, different lines of sight, lots of variables. When I left the dock, I was shaking my head, saying, "I'm not sure I should be doing this." But I did. I whacked the bridge good; crushed the timbers on the way out.

I should have said, "Not now, Cap. We have to wait." We used to sail only on the flood tide, to gain the advantage of steerage. This particular ship was just a dog. She was so big. She was just a real dog.

Picture yourself down on the waterfront, and a tourist from Iowa comes up to you, taps you on the shoulder and says, "You know what, this is the first time I've ever seen the ocean." What would you say?

It's beautiful, isn't it? It's different every day. It's not like looking at the mountains from your back porch. The sea is different every day.

TOM CROTTY

Artist and Gallery Owner
Freeport
Age 74

Had I $100,000, I would buy two things: a 30-foot schooner and a Tom Crotty painting. Like Andrew Wyeth's paintings, Crotty's are more real than real, yet inspire awe at the primordial beauty of the Maine coast.

I don't know Crotty, but I know his Frost Gulley Gallery is on the old road between Freeport and Brunswick. I swing in on a whim.

The gallery is in a barn attached by ell to an old farmhouse. I enter the door of the ell. Behind a desk piled high with books on art and politics, a rough looking character is peering at photos of Maine scenes on a large computer monitor. I say, "I'm looking for Tom Crotty." The character looks up and says, "What for?" It is Crotty.

I describe the idea behind this book. He likes it. He says, "What the hell, why not?" and so we begin. The text here represents about ten percent of our four-hour conversation. Talking to Tom Crotty about anything except politics is like driving a car with a flat right-front tire. The conversation constantly veers to the right, and I struggle to bring it back to the subject of his art. Perhaps I will write another book, this time on the evils of socialism.

Tom Crotty is not only an artist. He is an intense man, fully and passionately engaged in life. I look forward to future conversations.

My father was a journalist. He worked for UP and for BUP [British United Press], so we bounced around in the Maritimes and New York. We lived in Canada for my first fourteen years.

I'm the quintessential dropout. I dropped out of everything. I dropped out of grammar school; I dropped out of high school; I dropped out of college. I came to Boston at fifteen, and what I had accumulated in terms of knowledge in less than eight years in Canadian schools equipped me to breeze through two and a half years at Boston Technical High School without cracking a book.

In the Canadian system you were responsible in the final exam for the material covered for the entire year, and the final exam counted for 60% of your grade. It was an introduction to real life; it was what you remembered long-term that counted. If your grade was below a certain number, you did not advance, period.

Did any of your teachers stand out?

Not particularly. It was just a good system all across the board. If you were slow, you weren't given any slack. I have a hard time reading. I've always had a hard time reading. I had a heck of a time with poetry. Shakespeare drove me nuts. French was a nightmare. But I did those courses, and I passed them. It showed me what I could do when I had to, when there was no excuse.

When did you first start drawing, and did anyone comment that your drawings were exceptional?

I can remember we were in Prince Edward Island. I was three or four. Of course all parents rave about their own child's drawing. So many youngsters are talented with what they can do with a pencil and a piece of paper. The irony is that if parents and teachers would treat them properly, we'd have a world full of artists.

Do you mean if we didn't discourage budding artists by saying, "You're just wasting your time."

Not only discourage, but destroy, rather than helping young people develop. Drawing is a natural human inclination. It's not a challenge to get a child to do something with a pencil and a piece of paper.

One of the greatest encouragements I received was in grade one of the parochial school in Montreal. I was driving the teachers nuts, and this priest took me aside one day. He said, "Look, Tom, we're going to have to do something about this. I'll cut you a deal. If I don't hear any complaints from your teachers, you can take the last period and go in this office here, and I'll give you all the paper and pencils you want."

Ah! This had so many positive components: One, I was getting special attention; Two, I was able to draw; and number three, he raved about my drawings. That is probably when my art took off. That is where I began thinking of drawing as the most important thing in the world. I would go to summer camp, and I would draw the other kids, and everyone would just go nuts over my drawings.

The lesson here being that parents should take seriously what their kids show interest in?

Absolutely. Let the child pursue an interest as far as they want. If it's something flimsy and not that important for the youngster, but is only a device by which he is gaining attention, then most of the time he will just become bored.

At what point do you think one can be a little more critical of the child's effort? Like, "That's good, but..."

I don't think you need to be critical at all. If you turn the child loose, and if at the same time you expose him or her to great art— take him or her to museums, have really good art in your home— the youngster is going to soon realize that this is not a narcissistic proposition. He is going to discover the rewards of doing something with his talent that communicates to other people.

Tell me about your more formal artistic training.

One of the best moves in my life was quitting art school. Massachusetts College of Art was practicing a version of modern education, the attitude that excellence was secondary. Rather than creating an environment where students could test their abilities and extend their reach, they were after nothing more than experimentation.

I believe the trick is to challenge the student all along. When you see young people copying things in museums, that is good. If there's a painting in a museum that you cannot duplicate, that should tell you something—like maybe you'd better try again, or maybe you should rethink your program. Maybe you shouldn't be an artist.

To copy a great painting well you have to learn the same skills as the original artist?

Almost, but it's a lot easier than creating the original because it doesn't require the imagination, the ability to conceive of the painting. It does require the abilities to draw and to control a paint brush, however. And paints don't do what you want them to do. Brushes don't do what you want them to do.

Then is it comparable to mastering a musical instrument?

I think it's a little more challenging in that when you do a certain thing to a musical instrument, it responds in a given way—always. A musical instrument is a machine, a mechanical thing. The basis for music is that you can reproduce a given sound infinitely, for ever and ever.

Painting is not as reproducible. One of the most obvious examples is that paints change as they dry. Lighter paints will darken, darker paints will lighten a bit, and the color will change. That's one of the interesting lessons learned from copying paintings. You paint one to look exactly the same. When you go back a week later you think, "Oh my god, what happened?" You have learned something important. Before you may have been a little cocky. Now you are not so cocky.

The biggest thing is that the materials of painting are not predictable. You will never find the same brush. You find a brush that you love, and a couple of months later the brush has had it. There is no way to keep brushes from wearing out. They lose their quality, their behavior, so you just have to keep buying brushes until you find another one that works.

Let's go back to the Massachusetts College of Art.

OK. I thought I was going to put myself through art school by lobstering. Shortly after my wife and I married, we found a winter rental down in Cohasset, south of Boston. A lady rented this big old Victorian house to summer theater people. We rented it in the off season. We had the top floor, and it looked out over the harbor.

I started hanging around Cohasset, and I got to know some of the old-timers, and they were building a few traps. I said to them, "You think the other fishermen would mind if I tried it?" They said, "The only way you'll know is to try it. You might get away with it, and you might not."

Was fishing as territorial there as in Maine?

Oh, even more so, because Cohasset is like a tiny piece of Maine along that sandy coast. As a result, the lobstermen came from all over to work that small rocky area. Plus, the locals in Cohasset were mostly Portuguese.

So I bought this 18-foot Novi skiff. I took the rear axle out of a beat-up old Crosley to use as a trailer to go to Rockland, Maine, to pick up the skiff. I was going to haul it with a Volkswagen Beetle. When I got to Rockland, these guys who were going to load the skiff said, "So how are you going to get this skiff down to Massachusetts?" "With this trailer and VW," I said. They cracked up.

How I got it home I'll never know. There were no brakes on the trailer and it was the dead of winter. The boat dwarfed my little Beetle. Later I put the Crosley engine in the skiff with the transmission that came with it. It wasn't very fast, but it worked.

Two old-timers let me build pots in their shop, and I started out with a few traps. The other fishermen tolerated me the first year because I was just fishing a dozen traps off the beach.

Then I bought a 41-foot Novi. I bought it for $750 in Kennebunkport. It was in great shape, but nobody wanted it because it was way too big. I could load 125 traps on it at a time. In fact, I got more money for the 18-footer than I paid for the 41-foot Novi.

Things still went along ok because the locals saw this scrawny little redheaded kid with this huge boat, and they just laughed. "Let him be," they said, "He's fun to watch."

But then in my third year at Mass Art, I was out there one day in late October—the most gorgeous day—and I thought to myself, "Crotty, you idiot. You're going to go back in, drive through all that traffic to get to Mass College of Art, for what? For what?" That's when I said, "Screw it; the hell with it." I just couldn't get past this amazing experience on the water.

I continued lobstering for one more year, but then I decided this wasn't what I wanted to do the rest of my life. I was twenty-seven and needed more money because I had a wife and children. So I took a job at Rust Craft Greeting Cards. They had a process. I was in the design department. I learned more in six months at Rust Craft than in two-plus years of art school. This was the real world. You had to produce; you had to perform. There were twenty designers, and the quality of the art was the important thing. It was still an era when people were trying to be the best they could. I did that almost two years, and then I moved to Maine.

Why did you move to Maine?

Because I'd always wanted to. We had sailed up to Maine in '52 or '53 in a converted 26-foot Coast Guard surf boat. My mentor, Joe Lee, loaned me the rig he had in his English sailing lifeboat: three telescoping aluminum masts with sleeved sails. We put leeboards on the surf boat, and seven of us sailed it up to Casco Bay.

What did you think of the Rockbound Coast of Maine?

Oh my god! There was nothing like it in the world I knew. The irony was that my first wife grew up in Bridgton, Maine. I met her in Boston, and not long after we married I told her I wanted to move to Maine. She said, "Oh, my god, I've spent my whole life getting out of that place!" But I finally convinced her. I had this idea of running an art gallery, because one of the first things I discovered after just a year of living in Maine was there weren't any galleries.

You found this lovely spot, Frost Gully in Freeport?

Yes, we were lucky. We started the gallery. When we first started, it was the cat's meow. People back then so looked forward to coming to Freeport, especially to the openings. The openings were some of the biggest parties around.

The *Maine Times* loved the gallery. Peter Cox [Publisher of the *Maine Times*] was a discriminating guy. He knew what was art and what wasn't. So he was very kind to me and to the gallery.

Then I moved the gallery to a much larger space in Portland. That was a mistake. It took me a long time to realize that the people of Maine are not interested in an urban experience. Even for the people who live in Portland, the big attraction is to get out of Portland. And the few Portland people who are interested in art are more interested in the art world outside Portland.

It took me twenty-seven years of banging my head against the wall in Portland to fully understand this. For ten years I had the most beautiful gallery this side of New York City. Gorgeous space: multilevel, with 2,500 square feet. Not only beautiful in its own right, but in the stable of artists I had there. Outstanding. And nobody paid any attention, so we moved back here to Frost Gulley.

So what do you think of the current art scene in Maine?

I'm probably on thin ice here, but everything in life is a combination of frustration and reward. The people who run the Maine Commission on the Arts, or the Portland Museum, or the Bowdoin Museum, or the Farnsworth—these people are not risking anything. They are on salary, so they don't have to worry about their performance vis-a-vis how they are rewarded. They tend to be unqualified to do their jobs at an elevated, inspired level. The opportunity for the visual arts in Maine is staggering, mind-boggling. We could have an art scene here that would be like nothing else on the planet.

Isn't there a lot of money coming into Maine for art museums?

Yes, but it's going into the hands of people who are more interested in what I call anti-art, nihilism, dada, just nutty stuff, and with a wink and a nod to what is considered the great art, for example Winslow Homer and the old war horses. These movers and shakers of the art world can't ignore the giants of Maine art, so they give them lip service and keep them in the picture, not because they are crazy about their work, but because if they didn't, they'd be laughed out of town.

Didn't Andrew Wyeth face that same problem, going against the current art scene with his traditional realism?

Wyeth had the greatest gig that the art world has ever seen! Think about it: to be the quintessential traditionalist, and to be able to convert that into the role of a revolutionary! Because the establishment was all about everything he was not about.

Was he a great artist?

He was phenomenal, a veritable genius. And the guy was prolific!

I had a date to see him one day in October and, as I drove in, he was in the driveway. We'd had this unusual 6-8 inches of snow on the 9th or 10th of October. I had done a painting I called *Fall Snow*, but on that same day he'd done TWO paintings by three o'clock in the afternoon! Mine had taken a couple of weeks, working from a photograph. He'd done two in one day!

Did Wyeth's example give you permission to stay traditional?

Yes. One of the important milestones in my art education was seeing an exquisite little exhibition of his small works at the Fogg. These were drawings and watercolors and dry brushes, and it just .... wow! I mean, this is legitimate stuff! I can do this, and it can be great. There is no limit to where I can go with realism.

The main quality you need in life is humility. You need to be able to be in the presence of something greater than yourself, and enjoy it. Andrew Wyeth did that for me.

I think of my life as a simple manifestation of how in awe I am at being alive and at having the opportunities that entails. To be a human being, to be alive, and to have all these possibilities. How can anybody be any less than thoroughly excited about that?

Any activity you become involved in, you can do at any level. What I find interesting is the way people place limitations on how far they are willing to go. I don't think you should place any limitation on it at all. If it's interesting enough to you, then I think you take it as far as you can. In forty-odd years in the art world I've seen a lot of people who have very limited goals. Whether they are artists, collectors, or people involved in the management of the art world, they reach a certain point and they simply shut down.

Is that because they lack passion for their subject? Because I think when you are passionate about something, there are no limits.

I think you've put your finger on it. It is a question of passion. But how have we, as a society, lost the excitement about being alive? You don't need much beyond being alive. You know, the whole Eastern thing about contemplation and just thinking about our existence.

It's fascinating to look at the Renaissance—how it worked and why it worked. What's missing today is the passion for excellence the Renaissance artists felt. Look at the religious paintings that were the heart and soul of the Renaissance. Think about those artists having to deal with both physical limitations and a Pope dictating. "You are going to illustrate a moment from the Old Testament or the New Testament."

Those guys said, "Hey, big deal!" They painted mind-boggling paintings. They just saw it as a challenge, and what is so remarkable is that, with those limitations, they went way beyond what was asked.

Another example is the American artist, Frederick Church. Here we are in the middle of the 19th century and this guy painted all the way from the Arctic to the South American Andes! I can't imagine what it was like just trying to get to those places in that era. He and so many other painters in the mid-nineteenth century produced these incredible landscapes in these hard-to-get-to places. But nobody is touching that stuff today.

Behind me is one of your paintings of the coast of Maine. When I look at it, I feel I have been there; I have experienced those rocks in that light: the light of a cold, dry December day, with the contrast between dark stone and pure white snow. You have nailed winter on the Maine coast. That painting is as inspiring to me as one of Frederick Church's.

I'm a piker compared to Church. I'm not demeaning myself, just acknowledging how great he was. I give a painting my best shot, but I'm not the final judge of how good my work is.

I remember walking into the Dallas Museum. I walked into a room, and the only painting on the wall was this huge Frederick Church painting of icebergs in the Arctic.

Was it like actually being there?

Oh more! Because what you are really looking at is the ability of a human being to make this thing, this painting. Nature is amazing, but it's almost as amazing to have a human being create this thing. It's not making a copy of nature. It's having reverence for the subject. It is a truly sublime experience to look at this painting and to be able to feel what this artist felt.

What I think I just heard you say was that the artist felt something, that being in the presence of nature created a feeling in him that he was able to put onto canvas and inspire that same feeling in the viewer. That is art.

That is art.

Your passion for life reminds me of Thoreau, who said, "I did not wish to live what was not life, living is so dear; nor did I wish to practice resignation, unless it was quite necessary. I wanted to live deep and suck out all the marrow of life ..."

My feeling about life is that it is such a rare gift. Combining that with the natural world we live in is the basis for my art. Of course you could line up 100,000 people and they could all say that life is important, and nature is important, and the environment is important. Then the question is what do you do with that? How aware are you of it? And how much do you value it? And how much humility are you capable of? Are you really capable of being just in awe? I think what you can do with that is in direct proportion to how much you can be awed.

Conversely, if you are arrogant and insensitive, the result is what a lot of our artists are doing today, which is this very narcissistic thing of suggesting that, "I am the epitome, the zenith, of

Frederick Edwin Church, "Fog off Mount Desert"

Tom Crotty, "View with Jaquish Island"

the visual arts." It has evolved into just, "Look at me." Clint Eastwood, in the book, *Wisdom*, put it well, "Don't take yourself too seriously; take what you are doing very seriously."

You can either live looking for life's sublime experiences, or you can be arrogant and self-centered to the point where you don't care about what is around you.

People sometimes criticize representational art as being no better than photographs. Are they correct?

I often work from photographs. One artist I know is so narcissistic he can't benefit from the wonderful world he lives in. He'll come in here, look at my work, and say, "I just can't see myself sitting around copying photographs all day."

I think to myself, "You poor, stupid son-of-a-bitch, you are depriving yourself of possibly a great experience. Don't knock it." What is the difference between that optical device you hold in your hands and your eyeball, which is wired to your brain? You can supplement the information gathered by your eye with that from the camera.

The camera enables you to see better?

Exactly. It enables you to capture the moment, to take that information home after the scene has changed.

You have to be brain-dead not to feel the difference between a photograph and a painting of a subject done well. The painting allows you to feel the artist, to see the scene through the eyes of the artist. One of the problems in the contemporary art world is that most of the people selecting paintings for exhibitions and writing reviews are looking at appearances. "Does this *appear* to be contemporary, and interesting and new? Or does it *appear* to be conventional and traditional?"

What if you were able to do something in a representational style better than it had ever been done before?

It wouldn't matter. They wouldn't be able to discern that. Because getting to that level of understanding requires passion, which they sadly lack.

RICHARD PULSIFER
Boatbuilder
Mere Point, Brunswick
Age 68

R. S. Pulsifer

It's a drizzly cold day, and we are sitting on sawhorses in the middle of Richard Pulsifer's boatbuilding shop. In the corner is a nondescript woodstove to which Richard has just added three large chunks of oak. The walls and floor are covered with hand tools, power tools, paint cans, drawings, odd fasteners, scraps of marine hardware, and wood shavings, giving the impression that a powerful explosion had occurred. Rising from the chaos, however, set on blocks as if on a throne, sits a watercraft that makes you long for the ocean. The object d'art is a Pulsifer Hampton, a recreation of the open lobsterboat universally favored by Maine fishermen in the early 1900s.

Building with wood must be healthier than building with fiberglass because you don't look a day over 50.

Wood is a wonderful medium because it's natural and because of the people from whom I get it. The loggers and the sawyers are all very special people. I enjoy visiting and culling through piles of logs and timber with them.

So there is more to it than just purchasing wood at a lumber-yard and fastening it together into a design?

Creating a wooden boat is an integrated process starting with a standing tree and ending with the finished vessel. I can show you the stumps right here [His shop is surrounded by roughly twenty acres of trees] of trees that are in this boat. We use trees that have died due to the Brown Tail Moth, or the trees from the Bowdoin Pines that needed to come down for a variety of reasons. These trees have been called to a higher purpose than stockade fencing or paper pulp.

I've read that the old shipwrights used to search the woods for natural tree forms that would lend themselves to particular uses, such as the bends where the trunk joins the roots.

Very true. We are sitting next the to the boat's stem, a curved timber which rises from the forward end of the keel. The grain in that stem has a natural bend; the tree grew that way.

I take it that the wood is stronger left in its natural shape than were it steamed and bent or sawed into a curve.

Correct. Fortunately I can, through searching, talking with loggers and giving them templates, get this piece. If the log is big enough, I can get two stems from it. If I were to cut a curved piece from a straight log on the bandsaw, I would be cutting through the wood fibers at an angle—what is called cross-grain—which would weaken the piece. Also, wood left in its natural state is more stable with moisture changes.

Next to someone calling and saying, "I want to buy one of your boats," the most exciting call I get is a logger saying, "I'm on a lot, and there is some nice oak or pine. Come take a look." They know what I'm looking for. It also helps if the logger has a saw mill and I can be there to make decisions as the log is sawn.

Since these boats are made entirely from wood, except for the fasteners and the propulsion system, I imagine that the keel and stem are the equivalent of the foundation and sills of a house. If either is off, then the entire boat or building is off.

I think of the keel as the backbone of the boat. It needs to be, when seasoned, reasonably straight. If there is too much curve, or sweep so-called, or poor wood in them, you never should have put them in the pile of keel wood. Keels come from big logs, twenty-two feet long, nice straight trunks. You can't cut a straight piece of wood out of a curved trunk and have it stay straight.

In the large vessels, back in the day, they'd box the heartwood for the big timbers, so the center of the tree would be right down the middle. These are smaller pieces, so as you set up the boat you can horse them over or punch them down. But what I try to do is cut any of the sweep in the seasoned piece out with an electric plane before we bring it down to final dimension.

Are there books that show you all these tricks?

These are tricks you learn by screwing up. On a recent boat I forgot to take this curve [sweeps the air vertically with his hand] out of the stem timber before I planed it, so I had to cock the stem over to minimize the visibility of the curve. It's invisible to the untrained eye, but frustrating to me when I put the 4-foot level against the stem to get it plumb. That's the sort of thing I still have to remind myself of even after 100 boats.

I'm now the old-timer. Not to be prideful, but some wonderful boatbuilders were very gracious and generous in suggesting and helping back when I started. They're all gone, so I'm now the repository of this priceless knowledge.

Are you mindful of the duty to pass this knowledge on?

In many ways the myriad Bowdoin [Bowdoin College just up the road] students who come to help me are getting little pieces of it.

I suspect the value of what you are teaching lies not in the specific details but in a way of thinking.

You have nailed the process exactly. It's the doing it, the "Why do you do it this way instead of another way?

Richard and a Bowdoin College "apprentice" at work

As you build a boat you are mindful that it is a process, and that every step is critical to some later step and to the end result?

Coming back to your foundation analogy, getting the foundation plumb, square and level makes every later step so much easier. Further on, if at any point in the framing you allow a half-inch error to creep in, that half inch will be magnified to several inches by the time you reach the peak of the roof.

The temptation is to assume that all boards are the same width. In fact, due to milling tolerances and seasonal moisture changes in the wood, they are not, so you end up with a trapezoid instead of a rectangle. We process all our wood. We get clear, green pine boards, plane them after they have air-dried, and strip them [cut into narrow strips, the boat's planking].

After 105 boats, you are still learning?

Every day.

Does that keep you going, making a new discovery every day?

There are those mountaintop moments, no question about it. An example is the cedar strips in the decks. You want to get the cedar into the shop, even though it is air-dried, at least two weeks before using it. Recently I didn't, and the wood dried just a couple percent more, and hairline seams opened up in the deck. I will not omit that step again very soon.

So building a wooden boat is not at all like assembling an automobile in a factory. The boat is an organic thing. Every boat is different because the wood grain in every piece is different. You must feel like you are creating rather than assembling.

Tight cedar deck seams and Monel™ fasteners

Definitely. Although the hull material is of high quality, northern white pine, you can't just pull a piece of pine out of the working pile and assume it is going to work. You have to give it a bit of a spring test because sometimes the piece is a little shaky. You have to give it a stress test to see if it can bend and twist. Better to have it break before you fasten it down and then have to pull the fasteners.

What do you mean by "shaky?"

"Shake" is where the annual growth rings have separated, perhaps due to a hurricane or to an ice storm, or even in crashing to the ground when cut down. The tree hasn't broken, but it has been weakened; it has lost some of its integrity.

Some of these really tall, centuries-old trees have seen storms we have long forgotten. They can contain surprises. It's often the 22-foot clear pine or oak pieces that look perfect to the eye. But a long piece with defects can provide two perfect shorter pieces.

I wonder what generation of Maine boatbuilder you are.

Of course the Native Americans were making dugout and birchbark canoes long before the Europeans arrived, but building with wood timbers goes back to the *Virginia* at Popham Colony [in present-day Phippsburg, not far from Pulsifer's shop]. *Virginia of Sagadahoc* was built by the Popham Colonists over the winter of 1607-08. It measured about fifty feet in length and carried the surviving colonists back to England.

So, 1608 to 2009, about 400 years. Assuming a generation every twenty-five years, you are the fifteenth or sixteenth generation Maine boatbuilder! Will there be a seventeenth generation?

Sure! There are many younger people and older career-transition people attending Maine boatbuilding schools, both traditional wooden boatbuilding and composite. There won't be as much going into the woods to find the perfect stem as there will be developing strong new materials. The best material for the purpose. That's why most lobster-boats today are fiberglass, and many of them are truly beautiful.

Is wooden boatbuilding in Maine in good shape?

I would say that the wooden boatbuilding business, in this economic climate, is actually better off than the fiberglass business. There is little demand for fiberglass workboats right now because both the economy and the fisheries are off, whereas the demand for wooden boats has always been small, and there is a lot of "brand loyalty" among people who love wooden boats.

A fifteenth-generation Maine boatbuilder at work

I think wooden boats have a quality that is hard to define. You could put me blindfolded in a wooden boat, and I would know it was made of wood.

Doug Whynott nailed that in his book, "A Unit of Water, A Unit of Time." He wrote, "There is 'soul' in wooden vessels." There is a great debate about when that goes in: when you first start fondling a piece of wood, or when the last piece is done and the hatch is closed, but it's a gradual instilling of something "other."

John Cole described that same thing when he wrote about wood in "From the Ground Up." He said, "With every change in temperature, with every ray of sunshine, drop of rain, breath of salt fog, or splash of ocean spray, wood responds. It swells, shrinks, curls, changes color; it reacts as if the soul of the tree still locked within has never departed."

I agree, it is very much alive. And because of the air in it, it's buoyant, it's quite soundproof, it doesn't "drum" and shudder with engine vibration.

And it's thicker.

Yes, a scary thing I remember is going aboard somebody's fiberglass lobsterboat, going up forward, and you could see—not like through glass—but you could see where the light changed, the line between the water and the air. It was an eerie feeling to realize that my feet were actually below the surface.

But with all that, fiberglass is a very good material. The craftsmen in that field—I think of someone like Glen Holland—turn out awesome boats: looks, the way they ride.

But I think there is another, equally significant, difference between fiberglass and wood. It's the same sort of difference as between electric baseboard heat and a fireplace. For however long human beings have been on earth, we have lived with fire and with wood. I think this familiarity and this comfort with fire and natural wood are in our genes.

As we worry about petroleum resources, we should take pause at embracing too much synthetic material because it contains hidden costs. These synthetic materials work too well. We are going to see phone poles and wharf pilings made of composites because they last indefinitely. Unfortunately, what we use today is decided purely by economics. Some day we will realize the additional element of social cost.

We may, right now, be at the inflection point of that realization. Say! I didn't think of it before, but your boats are "green!"

Organic and green.

Let's go back in time. Where were you born?

Born in Children's Hospital in New York City. Dad worked in town. We lived out near Glen Cove on Long Island. From a very early age, from the age of being toilet trained, we were able to come to Yarmouth Island in Harpswell for the summer. That was a magical experience for me because I was on the water, in the water, all summer. Boats such as the ones I build were the standard lobsterboat: small, open, low-powered, homemade, or at least made by a local fisherman/boatbuilder. This was before lobsterboats got big and powerful and fast. Lobstering was all done close to shore. The lobsterman rarely travelled more than a couple of miles from his own wharf. Some lobstermen even rowed. The gear was hauled by hand in relatively shallow water.

If you were little and lucky enough to ride in one of these boats, you could just hang over the side and there was the water. You could drag a boat hook, or if you were daring, your hand. Everything was wood: the bottom, the sides, the gunnel, the oars. The engine was running right there beside you, "chug-a-chug-a-chug." It was very organic.

And there was the lobster bait, rotted fish skeletons, adding to the aroma.

And a mixture of gasoline, and motor oil, and clamflat mud. It was just...perfect. It filled all of my young senses with what it meant to be a waterman.

I was never comfortable going with someone with a fast boat: showing off, waterskiing, rushing from here to there and in circles.

No speedboats in your family?

My family had a little 2-horsepower Johnson on a Penn Yan cartop that we would use to get back and forth from the island to the mainland. With a boat like that, seamanship becomes very important. You are inches from the water, you need to trim ship by where you sit, and you just putter along. Easy does it.

Did you go out with local lobstermen?

When I could wrangle an invitation. Got picked up at the wharf early in the morning, about 5 in the morning, as soon you could see.

I remember going out with my grandfather at that hour, and it was always flat as a mirror.

Just beautifully still. You'd be out there, laying to, watching the fellow haul his trap up, hand over hand. You'd watch this wooden trap come up out of the deep, out of the gloom, then up on the gunwale, open it up and see what's in it. And you'd see the other boats off in the distance, toiling and spinning, doing the same thing. That fascinated me.

Like a dance, the boats pirouetting in unison.

It is a dance, particularly when two or three boats are all working the same spot. Those fellows could handle boats. Amazing to watch them come into the dock and spin around.

And the way they could work the ledges. Right up within feet of the ledges, even between the ledges, with the swells throwing the boat back and forth, seemingly unaware of the danger, yet never touching bottom.

That's in the genes of the Hamptons, too, because of the way the hull is shaped underwater. The rudder and keel arrangement allows the boat to track straight, yet spin in its own length.

One of my joys is to get owners to think like the fishermen in running their boats. Instead of reverse, forward, wheel-the-wrong-way, crash and bang, put her in neutral, let her do what she naturally wants to do, put her into reverse at the right time, and just stop. With the fishermen, it's a gentle process, whereas the big plastic recreational boats have too much free surface, too much windage, and no ability to just glide. It's painful to watch: thrusting forward and reverse, bow thrusters going, skippers screaming at crew. It's ugly.

Can you recall the point in time when you thought, "I want to build boats for a living?"

Yes, I was eight. My mother and I built a little square-ended punt: very crude, flat sides, square end. I wanted something small that I could manage.

Pogo's punt?

Pogo's punt, yes. That's where the image came from. It hasn't seen the water for ages, but I still have it. We called it *Jupiter* after a character in a children's book.

That was both exciting and frustrating. Frustrating because we were cutting the boards with hand saws. Even so, as E.B. White said of Joel's first little boat, "It's the boat that launched a thousand ships." Maybe an exaggeration, but that is where it all started.

I had various summer jobs with fishermen: helping on the dock, building traps, getting dories ready, painting, doing minor repairs. I sometimes watched fishermen, boats pulled up on the bank, lengthening them, just cutting them back and splicing on.

As a child I saw the building process, step-by-step. It was a magnet. I would just go there and watch. Maybe hand them something, hoping to become part of the job.

These old lobstermen were natural teachers. They loved having children around. You weren't a threat; you weren't stealing ideas; you were just inspired.

I remember my grandfather and his brother—both lobstermen. They'd be down on the float getting ready, loading the tubs of lobster bait and the whatever, and they'd occasionally take a moment and say, "Do you know how to tie a bowline?" Then they'd show you. One lesson a day, or maybe a week, and you'd be there every day waiting for that prize, that little piece of special knowledge. If only public schools could be that enticing.
So why did you choose to build your boats in Maine?

Maine is a place where you can wear your individuality without being thought of as a crackpot. You walk into Morin's Auto Parts to get batteries or oil or something, and the counter doesn't fall silent. There's also the legacy, the tradition, of doing things off the land. Maine is not the best place to go back to the land in terms of agriculture, but is for boatbuilding. Maine is a great place to do things on the water because we have a lot of it, a lot of shore, 3,600 miles. Think of it.

And there are plenty of boatyards and marinas for those who don't live right on the water. Last summer I encouraged a new owner to put his boat at Great Island Marina—very protected from wind and wave, fuel right there, helpful people. Last June the wife and two daughters would go down: get the boat ready, fire it up, let go the lines, and go out to the "No Wake" buoy, turn around, land the boat, then do it all over again. Just idle and get the feel of the boat—like a child mastering their first bicycle. The next thing you know they stick her nose out beyond Yarmouth Island, into the open bay, and England, here we come!

How long are you going to continue building these boats?

As long as I can. There's no end in sight.

The concept of retirement is nowhere on your radar?

Not at all. This is what life is all about. The expending of this energy. If not building boats, I would have to go to a gym and exercise like a rat on a treadmill. This type of boatbuilding is manageable solo. There is simply no reason to stop.

The Hampton will go on. I'm not the last generation of Hampton builders. I've had a lot of help over the past ten years from John Lentz, but less now because he has built up a fulltime business refinishing the older boats. But if someday I get only halfway to the house, he could take over where I left off. And the boats we have produced, if cared for, will last 100 years.

No, there are no plans to shut down. The thing that would throw a wrench into continuing this would be no interest, no orders. But that hasn't happened yet.

Well, I know of at least one future customer. I have coveted the Hampton ever since I saw one of your first ones, forty years ago. I'm only seventy, so I still have plenty of time. Just keep building them!

Look at the phoebes (points to a nest on a beam over our heads)! They built a nest on that beam last year. I didn't think they'd be back, but apparently they like my company. Maybe it's the music on NPR. Maybe it's the warmth from the woodstove I keep going on rainy days. I leave the big doors open all summer so they can come and go as they wish.

MID COAST
Brunswick to Searsport

CHARLIE JOHNSON
Offshore Fisherman
South Harpswell
Age 68

Charlie Johnson's beloved swordfishing boat, Seneca

I meet Charlie and Gail Johnson at 8 p.m. in the kitchen of their South Harpswell home. Charlie has spent the day rebuilding the ice-making machine in their 78-foot longline swordfishing vessel, Seneca. Gail has just returned from running her neighborhood general store. Both are exhausted but congenial.

He is rugged and weatherbeaten, as one would expect from thirty-six years of fishing on the Grand Banks. His answers are short, to the point, and delivered in a resonant voice.

She, as her seafaring husband would say, is "ship shape" and speaks in measured sentences with a dulcet voice.

It soon becomes apparent that the two have developed a symbiotic relationship: he the hunter-gatherer; she the keeper of the family finances and the fire.

There are more Johnsons in the Harpswell phone book than any other name. I counted thirty-eight in a town of 4,000.

[Charlie] There's a few.

Before I came over I looked up the famous statue of the Maine Lobsterman down at Lands End, Bailey Island. I found the bronze statue was of Elroy Johnson of Bailey Island and was commissioned by the State of Maine for the 1938 Worlds Fair. Besides the one on Bailey Island, there is one in Portland's Old Port and one at the foot of Maine Avenue in Washington, D.C.

Statue of Elroy Johnson, "The Maine Lobsterman"

Elroy? God, I remember him. He was lobsterin' when I was. He was a great guy. Used to go up to the hearings in Augusta until he couldn't hear any more. He was the only one that ever made any sense. He was the greatest guy on the water, too. His boat was like a log in the water. Didn't roll. Just rose and fell in the waves.

[Gail] There's a diary upstairs by Charlie's grandfather, Fred, that kinda shows what the Johnsons are like:

"July 17. Not much news today, but delivered of a fine baby boy and thirteen eggs."

Was your grandfather a fisherman?

Like most down here, he did about everything. He went lobsterin' some, he went clammin, built skiffs.

My grandfather, over in East Harpswell, cut and sold ice to Grand Banks fishing boats, built his own house, built boats and floats, lobstered, raised cows, horses, pigs, chickens, just about everything.

That's the way it was on the islands. When they went to town, they went by boat. If they wanted to go by horse, they had to take the horses across to the mainland on a scow. Fred used to row his dory to Portland and back. If it started blowing too hard, he'd stop and load the dory up with rocks off the shore to make her more stable.

Where were you born, Gail?

I was a war baby, born in California just before my father shipped out in the war. He had a summer camp here in Harpswell, and after he was done with the GI Bill, we moved here. I was six. Charlie says I'm a "highlander" [a person from inland]. One day he looked at me quizzically and said, "You talk funny! And you're teachin' our kids to talk funny." [we all laugh]

So how did you meet?

I worked summers at Dain Allen's wharf and seafood stand, and Charlie brought his lobsters in to the wharf. I was fifteen, he was nineteen. I wanted to go to college, Charlie wanted to get married. I didn't know what to do, so I split the difference. I went to a two-year college in Massachusetts.

[Charlie] She dumped me when she went off to college.

[Gail] He still remembers that. Charlie, I was away!

[Charlie] Not THAT far away!

I interviewed Dain the other day, and he told me he remembers you, Charlie, getting off the school bus, running down to the shore, throwing your books in the bushes, and hauling your traps. How old were you when you started doing that?

Twelve or thirteen, I guess.

Did you know then you were going fishing instead of to college?

Fishing was a good business. I always had all kinds of money. I started out making my own traps, sawing my own laths. I made square traps. I didn't have enough money to buy a steam box.

Lawrence Wilson, who lived down at the bottom of the gully at Bunganuc Creek, he was an old dude. Always had an old suit jacket on. Great guy. Used to go musselin' in that suit, quahog diggin', whatever to make a buck. He had a crab pickin' house.

He showed me how to knit trap heads. Used to buy oak boards up to Marriner Lumber and strip 'em out. Rounded the ends and stuck 'em in the sills.

Were you the first fisherman in this area to go swordfishing?

Harpswell, yes, but there was a few boats down to Portland. Bob Griffin and I decided to go out for swordfish in '74. He was supposed to be out there fishing with me, but I didn't even know where he went. He never showed up.

Jeff Johnson had a side trawler. He was supposed to come out, too. We were going to load our fish onto him, but he never showed up, neither.

I only had a 42-foot Bruno and Stillman lobsterboat, but Jeff had a much larger boat. I could only hold 10,000 pounds. It just wasn't worth it to steam all that far, so I decided I had to get a bigger boat. We went down and bought a 72-footer. Nice boat.

Where were you based with the 72-footer?

I had her down here on a mooring. We went out to Georges Bank, then to the far side of the Grand Banks, the Flemish Cap. We used to land them in Portland and truck them to Boston. This was before they had the Portland Fish Exchange.

How long does it take to get to the Flemish Cap?

Four, five days at eight knots.

Just chugging along?

That's about all I do. It won't go no faster, really. You'd burn an awful lot of diesel to go any faster. The more power you put on her, the more the bow wave increases. You just end up pushing a big pile of water. You could get ten-five out of her, but you'd burn twice as much fuel.

How many crew did you take?

We went out four of us one trip, but a couple of guys quit. They got discouraged when the shaft busted. Can't blame them for that. We had to get towed back, and they figured it would be a long time before we got goin' again. I was outa that mess in ten days.

I think we hit something, but where the shaft broke it had discoloration, so I think it was probably weak. It was forty years old. There was this big bang, and suddenly we were just drifting. One of the crew dove under the boat and said, "There's no propeller, Cap!" There was just this stub of a shaft sticking out. Luckily, she broke outside the hull, so we didn't take on any water.

So five days, or about 1,000 miles, to the Flemish Cap?

We're over there most of the time now because we can't fish inside the 200-mile limit because of the Canadian mess.

Linda Greenlaw found that out, didn't she? [Linda was arrested and fined $38,000 for drifting inside the Canadian 200-mile limit while filming a television documentary.]

Oh yeah. I was in there one time. I was trying to set up the west side. It was in November, and I was settin', and it was coming on a gale of wind. I wasn't going to set all the gear, and while I was deciding whether to set it all, I was kinda drifting closer to the line. Finally I said, "Throw it overboard." So we shot it overboard, and then I got up to near the line, and I turned off to the west and paralleled the line.

The current has been running off southwest every day, so my gear always went southwest, but when that wind came, it went the other way. I was outside the line, but my gear drifted inside the line.

I reported myself. I thought they'd let me take it in. I tried calling around five in the morning, but I couldn't get anybody. It was just getting worse and worse. The weather was coming on.

Did you haul the gear back in?

No, I couldn't do a thing. I got ahold of the Coast Guard finally, and that was about eight o'clock. By then my gear's in there in good shape. A plane flies overhead and says, "You're inside the line." I said, "I know I'm inside the line. I'm following my gear, not haulin'. When it comes back outside the line I'll haul it in. I'll wait until the Coast Guard comes, because they'll want to watch me haul the gear and make me throw the fish back."

Did your gear ever float back outside the line?

No, we just hauled it and cut the fish free.

Then the Canadians wanted to board me. I said, "You guys comin' aboard tonight, or what? No problem for us. Might be a problem for you." They decided they'd wait and see me in port.

They still was givin' me a hard time. The Coast Guard was right behind me with that big ship, right behind me with a spotlight on my block [the pulley where the line comes aboard]. We was messed up.

When you are going down sea [with the waves], you can't stop the boat when it's blowin' fifty knots, so you've got to keep coming around. The line goes under the boat, and you've got to go around in a circle and come back on the gear. It's usually easy, but with that ship right behind me....

Soloman's down there in the stern, and he's yellin', "Watch it! He's right behind you!" I said, "That's his problem. I'm comin' around." I asked the guy when we got to port, "How'd you like them turns? There was nothing I could do. I was goin' downwind."

Tell me about the swordfish. Does the sword have any purpose?

They use it to get their prey. You'll see a swordfish bill, and it's hard as a rock and all beat up. They use it to root around on the bottom. I know they go down 500 fathom [3,000 feet]. That's where the red-fish are lots of times, and they eat them.

But I've seen a Mako eat a swordfish when it's on a hook. Go right underneath the swordfish, a 200-pounder, and take him right up in the air, six feet out of the water. When that Mako got done, I had a chunk left about this big around.

What you do is called "longlining." How long is the line?

It could be twenty miles, or it could be fifty. Depends on how much gear you want to put in the water. It's one continuous 700-pound-test monofilament line. There's no steel at all. When we get done attaching gear, we just cut it off, put a knot and a buoy on the end. We put on ninety leaders and hooks per section, and each section is three or four miles long.

What is the spacing of the hooks?

We're going eight knots, and we're putting on a hook every fourteen seconds, so the hooks are spaced every 150 feet or so. We put a buoy, like a lobster buoy, every three or four hooks. The leaders are eighteen feet long, so the hooks are down eighteen feet.

The line is just drifting, held up by the buoys?

Yeah, the boat runs along; the line just drifts in place. When we retrieve fish, we're just lifting the line up to the rail.

What do you use for bait?

Mackerel and squid. Mostly mackerel, a pound or a little less. And we reuse them if the swordfish doesn't eat it. Sometimes we reuse the same mackerel three days.

How big are the swordfish you catch?

The average size last trip was 207 lb, cleaned. **[Gail]** Once they get over 200 pounds, you get less money because of portion control issues. Chefs like a certain size steak.

When do you call the boat full and come back in?

When I can't squeeze any more in it. [laughs] About 60,000 pounds if I fill the tanks that's on deck, too. It could take eight or ten sets. That would be eight or ten days fishin'. Then it takes five days to get out and five days to get back, so its a total of about three weeks. Sometimes we're out there a month foolin' around.

Where do you land your fish?

We've got this Brazilian crew, so we can't come to the U.S. with the fish. They work hard. They're gettin' old, though. That's a problem. I can still get my job done, but I wonder about them sometimes. Sometimes I think they party a little too much. Those boys have a good time, no matter where they are.

You don't have any crew from the U.S.?

Oh, I have people who want to go. I kinda keep a couple of spots open for those guys if they want to go.

[Gail] But here's another thing. We pay our Brazilian crew the same wages as the U.S. crew, but it costs an order of magnitude less to insure them. We don't have to give them insurance, but we don't want to lose the boat. Besides, if somebody gets hurt, and they have troubles, how can you afford to pay them what they need to live?

Because medical care in Brazil costs less?

Because Brazilians are less litigious. They don't have American ambulance-chasing lawyers. It's wicked! I see those Joe Bornstein lawyer ads on TV, and I....

[Gail] The hard part is they sometimes do get hurt, and they do sometimes get run roughshod over. Then there are other times when... Well, there's a man in Portland Harbor who told his insurance company, "You fight this claim; don't settle." But the boat owner knew, both by reputation and by talking to the guy, that he had feigned a back injury. He wanted disability for the rest of his life. The boat owner hired somebody to follow him, and they caught him doing things he couldn't with the injury he claimed.

We've been sued, but never successfully. One guy, way back in 1976, he decided at the last minute that he didn't want to go on a trip. The lines were off, the boat was rounding Spring Point on the way out of he harbor, and the guy said he wanted to get off the boat. He'd changed his mind. When it appeared that Charlie wasn't going to turn around, the guy got so mad he ran down, got the vacuum cleaner, and threw it overboard. "There now, take me home!" he said. That should have told us something about the guy.

We figured he'd get over it, but he sued for false imprisonment. Then he wanted to jump onto another boat out on the Banks and hitch a ride home, but the other captain wouldn't take him.

There was another guy that got clunked in the head by a really freak accident. We won that case, too, but we could have lost it if the guy hadn't lied. The suer said he hadn't been able to work because of all the pain and anguish. He really did get clunked in the head, but too many witnesses came forward and said, "Hey, you were working here and working there!" Case dismissed. It's too bad. He may have had something of a case, but he lied.

In the old days a handshake was good as a contract. Now even a signed waiver means nothing once a lawyer gets involved.

[Charlie] No good comes of hooking up with lawyers.

You started swordfishing in 1974, so you've been swordfishing for thirty-six years. You must have been in bad storms during that time. Did you ever think you were going to lose your boat?

Nope. I know my boat. I know what she'll do. I suppose you could get a freak one that would do somethin'.

[Gail] Our son has gone with Charlie a few times, and he tells about a time when the water just went out from under the boat.

[Charlie] What hurts you is when a breaking wave hits you from the side. The wave is just a vertical wall and throws this 200,000-pound boat sideways, wham!

[Gail] I'm never scared on the boat unless I can tell he's scared. When we [Gail acts as mate transporting the boat between fishing trips] steam down to Brazil, it's nineteen days down and thirteen back [due to the powerful Gulf Stream]. Sometimes I have these strange dreams like I'm jumping up in the air trying to catch a balloon. I wake up, and I'm going airborne off the bunk.

Have you ever been caught in a hurricane, like *The Perfect Storm*?

More than once. We just shut the boat off and let her lay to [broadside to the waves]. We don't try to keep her headed into the waves. If a wave comes across the bow it can take out the pilothouse windows. Once the pilothouse floods, you've lost your controls; you've lost your electronics, your communications; you are done.

I'm struck by the fact that pleasure sailors, yachtsmen, socalled, when they get in trouble, they'll switch on the EPIRB, call the Coast Guard, and abandon ship. Then a month later their boat will be spotted still afloat. Fishermen, on the other hand, won't leave the ship until it is actually under water.

Young Phil Ruhle got lost tryin' to save his boat, *Sea Breeze*, last year. Old Phil had the *Audrey Lynn*. He was out there swordfishing with us. He was pretty old when he give up.

How was young Phil lost?

He was in the pilot house, the way the story goes, and the two crew got out on deck. He was in there tryin' to right the boat. His outriggers were up. Somehow the outrigger on one side got caught and sucked her down. She was layin' down and wouldn't come up because of the outrigger and the 100,000 pounds of squid aboard. He got caught when she went down.

He went down once on his father's boat, *Audrey Lynn*, too. He was standing on the pilot house when the stack was goin' underwater. He just don't give up easy. You've got to know when to give up.

Your boat, *Seneca*, is so stable she won't roll over?

[Gail] We had a stability test before Charlie took her to Brazil. I asked the surveyor to do it, and he had this hesitation, "What kind of a boat is it?" I described the boat, and he said, "What kind of fishing is she rigged for?" I said, "Swordfishing." "OK, I'll do it." I said, "What's the difference?" He said, "I don't do draggers any more. They've got too much weight on deck. The owners don't like what I tell them, and they don't pay me."

[Charlie] Like the *Katahdin*. They added a lot of heavy plate in certain places. They had great big net rails on it, two of them, and the guy used a lot of ground cables. They'd have 100 fathom [600 feet] on two of the reels.

I was on that boat one day when they were going out to test the engine. It come out around the corner by Spring Point Light. The first thing I noticed was the tool boxes fall in the bilge. She was layin' over hard in the turn. I said to myself, "Boy, this thing don't feel right."

They took her up to the Grand Banks, draggin' for yellow-tails [yellowtail flounder], and the crew give up. She put the windows of the pilot house in the water, and it was stayin' there for a while. No one would go on her again. It's a bad sign when a boat goes over and hangs up.

Do you remember Sir Francis Chichester? He sailed single-handed around Cape Horn. He said it got so rough, he just strapped himself in his bunk. One time he woke up and saw a can of tomato soup standing on the overhead, and he realized that his boat was upside down! [All laugh]

You know, judging the heights of waves is funny business. People overestimate them, especially pleasure-boaters. How can you judge the height of a wave?

Roy Knight said he saw waves that were as big as a barn.

They get that big all right! Oh, there's some pretty cruel-looking waves sometimes.

I'm sure you saw the movie, *The Perfect Storm*? Didn't you think that last scene when the boat was climbing up the 100-foot wave was overdone?

[Gail] That was a joke! I got a large charge out of George Clooney hangin' onto that boom that kept going down into the water. He never got washed off, and the burning torch never went out. That wouldn't of happened.

[Charlie] What I noticed was all the leaders lined up and hanging over the rail. Guess where they'd be. On the wheel [propeller].

Yeah, Looper, there, he used to run the *Andrea Gail* and some of the other boats. He was in on that film, and I seen him down in Gloucester one time—he don't go fishin' now—I says, "Boy, you didn't do a very good job tellin' them what swordfishin' was all about." "No," he said, "They had their own ideas how they wanted to do this stuff."

So, Gail, while Charlie's at sea, what do you do?

[Charlie] Nothin'! [both laugh] All she does is run the store.

[Gail] Last year fishing was horrible, and I began to get a little concerned. The general store down here went out of business, and we bought it. So now *Seneca* is Charlie's number one wife, and the store is my number one husband, so I'm stuck on shore. When it gets a little more solid and I can hire a manager, can afford a manager, I'll get to be mate again.

DAIN ALLEN
Allen's Seafood
South Harpswell
Age 79

Allen's Seafood, South Harpswell, Maine

It's January, 7 a.m., and the wind is blowing the crests off the waves in Middle Bay. I park next to the only vehicle in sight, a pickup truck missing its tailgate. You can tell it belongs to a fisherman because its bed is completely rusted through from hauling salty nets and traps.

At the land end of the wharf sits the ubiquitous "fish house." Usually containing a fisherman's equipment, tools, and foul-weather gear, this one has been converted to an office, as evidenced by a hand-lettered sign on a scrap of plywood.

I push open the door and am thrown back by the heat from a propane space heater. The radiant heater, glowing like a blast furnace, is large enough to heat a Walmart.

Behind a metal desk, possibly WWII surplus and likely recycled from the town dump, sits the apparent proprietor. The desk top supports three things: a disordered pile of paperwork, a goldfish bowl full of red-and-white striped hard candies, and Dain Allen's feet in rubber boots.

How would you describe Allen's Seafood?

It's what you call a "wharf." I buy lobsters, bait, whatever, and across the road there my wife runs a takeout shack. Crab rolls, lobster rolls, fried clams, fries, fish sandwiches, and what all. And then you got the freezer back up there where I freeze bait to sell to the boats.

How many boats sell lobsters to you?

I think there's eleven boats that produce enough to.... There's also a lot of little, bitty boats that's got to get rid of their lobsters, but hey.... I'm not countin' them. I think if you counted them, we'd be up around twenty one.

   Right adjoining the freezer up there, I got a processing plant that the State of Maine, in one of their brainstorms, came up with. They say you got to have a full processing plant before you can have a wet storage license for your clams. Separate building, concrete floor, stainless steel this, stainless steel that. I don't use it. I got to keep it right up to snuff, you know, so when the inspector comes I can show it all to him. And he does, he's doin' his job, but there isn't a clam in there. It's so I can hold the other license to buy clams. I had to spend over $100,000 into that buildin' just so I can continue on doin' what I been doin' for forty years.

I talked to a fisherman's wife who has been picking crabmeat in her kitchen all her life. It's the only way her family can make ends meet. The state came along all of a sudden and said, "You've got to build this separate building, concrete floor, with stainless sinks, or we'll take away your crab-picking license.

Ayah. Goddamn state. Did she do it?

No, and she's still picking. She just took her sign down.

Good for her.

So, where did you come from, Dain?

Right here. Where'd you think I come from, Mars? House up on the corner is where I grew up. From the age of five all I wanted to do was come to the water. I didn't give a damn about anything else.

Henry Barnes and dad built me a skiff. I think I was six or seven. I took that skiff and rowed from here to Birch Island and back alongside of my father, just like a duck and a duckling. He was goin' over clammin'. I took my own skiff, and he took the dory. The dory used to be quite a lot of our transportation. We wouldn't bother startin' the powerboat.

The dory was easy to row?

It was with him on the oars. Christ, two sets of oars. A big set for him, a small set for me. He'd sit in there, and you could hear them wooden oars walk right out, so much pressure on them. And me, I'd be back there flailin' them little oars like a son-of-a-bitch. Sixteen-foot dory. We went clammin' a lot in it. I don't know what you didn't do with that dory.

When there's no weight in them they're tippy as a bastard, but once you git some weight in them, down in the bottom, they're real stable. But they rowed real good. My father always told about him and his father, they rowed to Portland [a distance of ten miles] to get their groceries. It was quicker than taking the horse up to Brunswick.

Before I had that skiff, though, I had an old skiff that the stern was gone outa. I picked that up adrift. Albert Allen, my cousin, and I, we'd set in the bow of that skiff and paddle it.

I was five when I had my first traps. Father said I could have a trap in the cove as soon as I could swim. It didn't take me long to learn to swim.

Did you catch anything in that first trap?

Oh Christ almighty! I'd catch a lobster every now and then. But they was old traps that was discarded. Christ, the lobster could crawl out easier than he could crawl in. But I'd haul that trap half a dozen times a day. Sooner or later I'd catch that lobster when he was in the trap. I think it was a good way to grow up.

You grew up during WWII. Do you remember much about that?

WWII—I can remember that all pretty good—dad went to Bath Iron Works, and he stayed down there for, oh, maybe a year. That was the most he could take workin' indoors. He come out and they said, "Expect to get drafted." He said, "I can't help it. This is killin' me." He come home, and he went fishin', and he never did get his draft papers. They deferred him because he was producing food.

And I can remember up by Phil Pierce's garage, which is gone now, they had a tower there, and the women around town went up and manned the tower. You had pictures of all these airplanes, and you identified every plane that went by. Over to Haskell Island there was a guy they thought was a spy. They went down, a group of them, and shot him. They shot and killed him, and he's buried over there on the island.

Who shot him, the FBI?

No, just a group of vigilantes. It turned out he was just some young yahoo actin' peculiar, stalking one of the guys' young daughters. Didn't make no difference. They shot him.

You think the government interferes too much in fishing?

Damn fools always get in the way for no reason. The one biggest instance that I ever got involved in was I was fishin' on smelts. Now when I was a young man I sweep seined them at night. I always thought, wouldn't it be nice to be able to do this in daytime. So I bought a little boat and rigged it out for draggin'. I knew them fish were down there, and they had to be a way to catch 'em. I frigged around out there. It was a couple of summers before I figured out how to make that work. All of a sudden I went from catchin' a handful of fish to all the fish I wanted. I worked at that fishery for, lets see, twenty years that way, workin' on them smelts. No question about it, I made a lot of money.

The law said I could fish through the whole year, but I said, "No, I'm gong to wait until the fifteenth of September, when the water cools off a little bit. Then I can fish, get them ashore, iced and shipped, and get a better product into the market. And I did that. It worked, it worked good. I could go out, catch my fish, bring them in, pack em in ice, put them on the truck, and they'd be in Fulton Market, New York City, in the mornin'.

Then the state said we couldn't fish small mesh nets due to the shrimp. Dumb bastards don't know smelts and shrimp don't intermingle at all. Smelts are all up in the Bay. The shrimp are all outside.

I went up to Augusta, and I said, "I'd like to have a license to work on them smelts." "You can't do that." "Well, I've worked on the smelt fishery for quite a few years and all that." "No, there isn't enough fish out there to make an industry." "Well," I said, "I'd like to see your study." "We haven't done one."

Now doesn't that show how ignorant they are up there in Augusta? They think the smelts from here go all the way down and around Small Point and up the Kennebec River so that they can be caught through the ice! The goddamned fish are right here year round. I could go out today and catch a mess of them.

Dain advancing an opinion on government fishing regulation

[A younger man enters with two dogs.] This here's my son, Albert.

Albert, you gonna join us?

I'm going to set and have some coffee.

I have to go to the head. Where is it?

Why don't you ask my dog, here? He always finds a place. Just don't face upwind. It's blowin' pretty good [laughs].

[I return] Do you know Lewis Stuart? He's some kind of a distant relative of mine.

Let me tell you a funny story about Lewis Stuart. One day I was headed down to Pono's [Pono's Trap and Marine Supply] to get some traps. I was gonna order 50 traps. Well, I got to shootin' the breeze with him, and I ordered 200 traps. Now mind ya, I took off from the house in the mornin' with $200 in my pocket. That was it.

On the way down by I see a pickup truck that I liked the looks of, so I stopped and I bought that.

Then I went down to Lewis Stuart's shop, and I went in. I said, "I understand you're going to put the *Voop* [a fast lobsterboat Lewis built for the sole purpose of racing] up for auction." "Ayah. They're comin' down to list it tomorrow." I said, "If you ain't listed it, you could sell it." "Ayah. Make me an offer." "Well, let's go look at it." We hauled the coverin' off it enough to git a good look at it. Here's this boat with no engine, no rub rails on her, no deckin', no wash rails, just a bare hull. She was put together and designed for one purpose: to race. But I could see a boat in her.

I says, "Well Lewis, what do you want?" He said, "Make me an offer. I ain't puttin' a price on her." I sez, "Well Lewis, don't take offense, but I know what she's worth to me, I'll give you $5,000." Lewis braced back and hooked his thumbs in his suspenders like that [pretends to hook his thumbs in imaginary suspenders] and he says, "With the trailer or without?" I said, "I'd kinda like to have somethin' to haul her around in." He says, "I guess you bought yourself a boat." I'd just spent $20,000 of the $200 I started out with! [We all laugh].

My father had a niece named Gracie Allen. Are you related?

Gracie Allen is my cousin.

Dain rejects any claim of kinship with the author.

Well then, you and I are related!

Not with some of your ideas. If that's what you think, then I'm not related to Gracie Allen. [We both laugh a long time].

The life of a fisherman must be quite different from someone who gets up and goes to an office nine to five, five days a week.

When we was shrimpin' offshore, you know, you had to get out there by the time daylight came. And then you'd get home after dark. When we was tub trawlin' you went, took your gear, baited, set your gear, turned right around, hauled it in. It took twenty-four hours to go out and come back in.

Did it worry you to come in the dark?

Dhow! [Maine for emphatic "No!"] If you start thinkin' about things like that, you best not be in fishing. Really, you know, having brains enough to get out of trouble once you got into it, is the big issue. Is it any more dangerous than drivin' down the friggin' highway? Considering the number of boats fishing today, I don't think so.

When I started fishing, if you drawed a circle between Ash Cove, Chebeague, and Freeport, there was only thirteen boats. Now there's hundreds! Christ, just right in Ash Cove there's a hundred.

Why are there so many more boats now?

Because the bay [Casco Bay] is producin' that much! We've done somethin' right. The government didn't do it. The fishermen did it.

You are saying the lobstermen, without direction from bureaucrats in Augusta, developed a system that is sustainable, and as soon as the government gets involved, they screw it up.

I'm not sayin' we don't need any regulation. I was born to fish, and I admit that if there was just one smelt left in the bay, I'd figure a way to catch it. But them fellows up in Augusta don't use the brains God gave 'em!

Take the clammin' industry. They got so many miles of this coast closed on the *potential* there might be some pollution! Not actual pollution that they've measured, but the *possibility* there might be some pollution. And red tide closures: they close the clam flats if it rains more than two inches. Now the rain might or might not actually result in a red tide, but they don't care. They just automatically close the flats. They're sittin' up there on their fat asses collecting their paychecks regardless, and they're closing the flats without any thought to the clammers' income just because it rained.

Has anyone ever died from eating a clam with red tide?

Not that I've heard of, and I'm seventy-nine. I guess a few have got the runs, but no one has died. Christ, you can get sick by goin' to the movies! No, it's way out of control.

Is there a solution?

The solution is when somebody gits so worked up, they go up there and thumps one of those bastards... I mean, just haul off and thump 'em good. I don't think there is ever going to be any realization up there as to what they're doin' to the fishermen.

You can't talk reason to them?

You can talk to them all you want, but you don't get nowhere. It just goes in one ear and out the other, or maybe it don't even go in at all. They are there simply to be important, collect a paycheck, have two or three secretaries to generate all that paperwork. You go in there sometimes, and those secretaries don't have one thing to do. Granted, at the time of year when licenses are renewed, they're busy, but the rest of the time …

We had a fella on the wharf got a verbal warning for a problem. The warden took it back up to Augusta. A week, week and a half later or so, the warden come back down with a summons. Says his superiors wouldn't let him give a verbal warnin'.

Now there's somethin' wrong with that picture. You know, that man should be trained to the point of he makes that decision at that time, but his superiors undercut him. If he was gonna write him up, he should a wrote him up right then. That warden should have quit right there when his superiors undercut him.

Are wardens generally pretty good guys?

Ummmm [sucking on a hard candy] they like to be important, most of them. I won't say good guys or bad guys. The one we got here now, the one I was just speakin' of, he's the nicest kind of a fella, but he kisses ass in Augusta to keep his job.

So he's a nice fella who doesn't command much respect.

I ain't got the respect for him I used to. We got another one here, he's the fire chief now. He's a little bitty fellow. He's got that short-man syndrome. Who was that little French general? A little man with flashing lights on his truck and a big badge. Oh, Christ, didn't I used to wind him up some awful!

When he was the fire chief, or when he was the warden?

When he was the shellfish warden. He come down one year and sez, "The vent [the escape hole for undersize lobsters] is gonna have to be such-and-such." Brought a piece of paper with it all drawn out. Put it up on the wall for the boys to see. Come spring, back down he comes, "No, they changed their minds up in Augusta. This is not the way it is going to be. Tell the boys I didn't know."

I said, "You put that paper up there; you tell them."

Meanwhile, the boys had changed over the vents on all their traps, a hell of a lot of work. I didn't say a word. So when it come time, the wardens come down, two of 'em, to look over traps, to tell us what was right and what was wrong. They went through this one's and that one's. I had 400 traps settin' right there. They pawed around this one and that one. One warden says, "This one will pass." The other warden says, "No it won't." After a bit they said, "There, we've got that taken care of." I said, "No, you don't. There's 400 traps, and you're gonna do every one of them."

Oh man, wasn't they mad! When they went up over the hill, they was screamin' at each other. I mean screamin'. I'd a thought they was gonna kill each other.

Have you ever come close to sinking?

[Laughs] A few times. We was comin' in from Great Ledge [ten miles south of Cape Newagen] and we were runnin' her hard. She was right smolderin' hot. Coming up between the Whaleboats here [Whaleboat and Little Whaleboat islands, to the west of Harpswell Neck], she went off with a "boom." I lifted the engine cover and everything was just a ball of fire down there. She'd blown a hydraulic line. I dropped that cover right back down and reached up and got the fire extinguisher. The next time I lifted the cover, I lifted it just a crack, and everything down there was goin' "woof, woof, woof." I stuck the extinguisher nozzle in and pulled the trigger, and, bullshit luck, I put it out, and we come on in.

It seems like all the fishermen on the coast of Maine know each other. It's like a community without town lines.

Ayah, most of 'em. Speakin' of fishermen, you should talk to Charlie Johnson [see page 111]. That man has had more water run out of the ass of his pants than the rest of us have sailed over. The man goes fishing! By Jesus, when Charlie gits done, they're gonna haul him out of his boat and bury him.

Charlie grew up right here on Birch Island. The school bus dropped him off down to Mere Point [the nearest land to Birch Island]. He'd get off that bus, throw his books into the bushes, run for that boat—small boat with an outboard on it—and head out to haul his traps, go over and get his bait, sell his lobsters, whatever. I mean he was obsessed with fishing way back then.

I guess he married right. His wife is right in there helping, not complaining about the fishing life.

She'd be a very good one for you to talk to. She works hard right alongside Charlie. Grew up right here in town. Of course she also runs the general store down here now. Somethin' to do while Charlie's at sea.

Charlie went from a small boat to a bigger boat, then to another bigger boat, lobstered here quite a few years. Then he got into the swordfishing. He had a 42-footer first. Didn't take him long to outgrow that. He just wanted to go further. Needed more boat to do it. Then he had that one built down to Washburn and Doughty's. That was quite a vessel. Nice boat. I think that was the one he had up 'til this one, but he might of had one in between.

That boat he's got now, that ain't a very big boat for what he does, the weather he'll stay in. He just stays, no matter what. When the weather gets too much, he don't go home. He just lays down right there and takes it. Waits it out.

Do you know Jennie Bichrest?

Course I do! Her mother-in-law was my sister—still is!

Know what they call her over to Sebasco? The "Bait Bitch."

That's what they call her all up and down the coast.

It must be because she's strong-willed and runs a tight ship with her bait business. It certainly isn't because of her looks. She is a good-looking woman.

Yes, she is. Jenny as a young girl was quite plump, but she lost that, and now her body is groomed good.

[Chuckles to himself] One day she was over here deliverin' a load of lobster bait. She had that dump truck with the little chute in the back full of herring. She was up in the herring, and the body was tilted up pretty good. All of a sudden she lost her footin', and down she come. There's tons of herring behind her, all rushin' for the openin'. The boys ran up from the dock and had to reach up in there and grab her by her legs and ass until they slid her out the chute, hehe. Can't fault the boys. What else you gonna do in a situation like that? But it sure was an excitin' day at the wharf.

I heard you were the first to drag for mussels. My father told me the only people who'd eat a mussel were the French.

I spent twenty-eight winters draggin' mussels. I just gave up Maine Mussel License #1. I'm not goin' mussel'n again.

Back there in the sixties, my brother and Dick Merryman were pitchin' mussels [standing in shallow water and picking the mussels up with a pitch fork]. I was scallopin' in the wintertime. Come up through one day, they was in there, and I swung in to see them in Peter's Cove. There wasn't tide enough for them to pitch the mussels, so I said, "Wait a minute, and I'll get you some mussels." That was the first mussels that was ever dragged up this way that I know of. Christ, I had their skiff full in just a couple of minutes.

I figured it would be profitable to drag for mussels. Then a couple of other fellows rigged their boats. All of a sudden there's four of us goin', and the state said, "Hey, here is something else we can regulate!" So from then on we've had to have a license to do it.

[A pug jumps into his lap.] Does she go out on the boat?

Ayah, but you know, pugs can't swim. They got no neck or snout, so if they fall in, they can't keep their vent holes above water! They swim like friggin' submarines. This one here I've had to net three times!

[He starts stroking the dog. They are obviously very attached.] Now, I been married four times. You know, if this dog could cook and keep house, and her face was just a bit prettier, I'd marry her!

ROY KNIGHT
Lobsterman
South Harpswell
Age 54

*Harpswell Neck Fire Chief, Frank True, and Roy "Santa" Knight
collecting for the Harpswell Santa Fund*

*We sit at a round oak table in his kitchen. Through a large bay window
I can see all the way up and down Harpswell Sound. Directly across is
the famous cribstone bridge connecting Orrs and Bailey islands.*

*His twenty-year old daughter sits on the floor, lotus-style, tapping on a
laptop computer. Wife, Debra, sits at the table with us, also peering at a
laptop. I can tell that both are following our conversation, however.*

*Roy is a big man with a big, open face. Not tall, but solid: size XL
or XXL. I remember thinking. "If I were on a boat in a storm, this is a
man I'd want with me."*

My mother and father were born in this town; my grandparents were born in this town; my great-grandparents were born in this town.

Grandmother was a Randall. Grandfather was a Barnes. My mother told me many times that her family, way back, actually settled the north part of town. They were here before the Revolutionary War. We're also related to the Alexanders. My grandfather told me, "When it comes time to marry, go outside Harpswell or you'll be marryin' a cousin."

I got Debra, here, up in Brunswick [the next town, eight miles up the road].

Your grandfather probably had a little farther in mind.

I don't know. Back in the days of the horse and buggy, going to Brunswick was like going to Boston today.

My mother's mother is actually from Newfoundland. My mother's grandfather was a ship captain, as was his brother. I've got a pile of grandfather's old charts. They were both lost on separate vessels the same month.

My father was in the Merchant Marines during WWII. When he came home, times were tough, so he did clammin', sea mossin', musselin', whatever he could make a buck on. Then he went to work at the Bath Iron Works and lobstered at the same time. I used to go lobstering in the summer with my father as a kid.

When I was twelve, he built me a skiff and taught me how to build traps and knit the heads—the whole nine yards. The first year I had forty traps. Actually my parents tried hard to discourage me from going lobstering. They wanted me to go to school and look for a better life.

Why didn't you take your parents' advice and go to school?

I wasn't very good at the books. I liked the social part of school better than the books. I had a good time in school, though. I played sports. When I graduated from grammar school down here, there was two girls and four boys. Then I went up to Brunswick High School. More students, a cafeteria, it was a whole different scene. I loved it; I had a blast!

We were used to hard physical work down here, so when it came time to play football, we were a lot tougher than the Brunswick guys. I got along with the Brunswick guys ok. I sort of fit in wherever I am. I try.

But I was the only Harpswell guy that graduated high school. I said to them, "Why are you dropping out? School is fun. That's where the girls are, you know?"

Did they drop out to go fishing?

Not necessarily. They just didn't think they needed an education. My father didn't have a chance to go to high school, so when we were growin' up we were told, "Your father goes to work. That's his job. Your job is to go to school, and you ARE going to graduate." There was never a chance to even discuss quitting school. Other kids didn't have that.

I wanted to get on a big lobsterboat, so when I was fifteen, I got a job with a guy who went big time. I was his helper in the summer. I'd work for him on weekends during the school year. He went tub trawling, and I baited tub trawls; I built traps; I painted buoys; I did whatever I could to keep my fingers in it.

When I graduated from high school I went on the boat full time. But I had busted up my knees playing football, so I had to get off the boat and have a couple operations.

While I was having my knees done I was living at home. A couple of my Brunswick friends were going to SMVTI [Southern Maine Vocational Technical Institute], so I went there, too. I studied heating, air conditioning, and refrigeration. I wanted to get into refrigeration because of the coolers on the boat.

While I was in school, the guy I used to work for, Charlie Johnson, converted over to swordfishing. A couple of my friends were on the boat with him. I'm sitting one day in class, and I'm looking out over Portland Harbor, and here comes Charlie's swordfish boat back in. I go, "Damn!" So at lunch time I jump in my car. I went over and, "Hey, you know … blah, blah, blah."

Well, they'd had a slammer of a trip. I mean a slammer. Big bucks. And that's all I could think about.

Charlie says, "I had a guy quit, and I got an opening, and we're leaving again in a couple days."

So I'm like, "Damn. I want to go." So I said to him, "I'm goin'." Course he knows my mother. Charlie goes, "Yeah, what's your mother gonna say?"

I remember going home, and we were eatin' supper, and I said, "I'm goin' swordfishing."

Not what my mother wanted to hear. She's always had that fear of going out on the ocean because of her grandfather and uncle being lost at sea. My father had been in the Merchant Marine, and he knew what I was looking for, so he was like, "Whatever."

I remember my father tellin' about seas big as a barn, but I thought I'd already seen some heavy weather lobsterin' with Charlie Johnson. We loaded the boat up, and away we went. I was like, "All right!" And we steamed right up there to the tail of the Grand Banks.

Just like in *The Perfect Storm*?

I fished with the guys in that book. I fished out of Gloucester and spent a lot of time in that bar. They got the bar pretty good.

We steamed almost five days, and it's beautiful weather, late October. I'm saying to myself, "This is a piece of cake!"

We started setting out the gear. We set out 30 miles of wire containing 1,500 hooks, each with a good-sized mackerel as bait. The wire was just drifting, held up with buoys every so often with lighted buoys at each end.

So we set out all that night, flat as the top of this table. I'm the greenhorn, so I get the first watch that night. I took my two-hour watch, piece of cake, woke the next guy up, and turned into my bunk. We all slept up forward in the peak [bow].

I'll bet that was an active place in a storm.

I've been thrown out of a few bunks. Anyhow, mine was the peak bunk, and Jeez, durin' the night things started movin' around. Then I began hearing this sound, like a faucet trickling. I'm like, "Jeez, what is that?"

Time to haul back [retrieve the line and fish]. I get up. I remember looking around and the oilskins and shirts were movin' back and forth on their hooks. I'm thinkin', "Whoa!" Climbed up the ladder into the dog house and stepped out on deck, and I'm, "Jeezuss. What the hell happened here?" I'm like, "Now I know what my father was talkin' about. They ARE higher than a barn." Jesus, we took a beatin'! This was the tail end of October, and we were in a friggin' hurricane!

How big was the boat?

Almost eighty feet, wood. That's another funny thing. Back then there were no survival suits [Waterproof foam suits that fishermen climb into when they have to abandon ship. They typically allow survival in freezing water up to 24 hours.], no life raft, no EPIRB [Emergency Position Indicating Radio Beacon—an automatic transmitter that signals the position of a sinking vessel to a satellite]. There was just this old dory on top of the wheelhouse, and I remember thinking, "I ought to go up and check out this dory, just in case...." I got up there, lifted the top, and looked into the dory. I'm lookin' around and—Jesus—I can look right out through the side of the dory! Holy!!!! There was no drinkin' water, there were no emergency rations, no flashlight, nothing!

Anyhow it blew, and Jesus, didn't it blow! We got the gear back in, and we started to set out again that night, and it was screamin'. I remember letting go of the poly balls [the floats], and Jeez, they'd clip the poly ball on, and I'd let go, and the thing would just take off in the wind like a soccer ball. The skipper said, "It's blowin' too hard. We got to get this gear back." So we worked hours just to get a fraction of the gear back. We got the gear aboard and battened down the hatches, and started jogging into the wind. We jogged for seven days straight.

I'm telling you the truth. Seven days straight, and we were going backwards. Then the wind turned around, and blew the opposite way. We steamed into it three days that way. When the wind dropped, we set out again, and we blew some hydraulic lines. We worked to fix them up, but we couldn't, so we had to come home. We had only one set's worth of fish on the boat. I'd been gone three weeks. I remember comin' home to Harpswell.

What was your share?

Well now, I'm going to tell you. I got home and went to my parents house. "Roy's home! How much money did you make?"

On the books I OWED the boat $800. Charlie never made us pay, but the trip was a loss. The crew split the income and the expenses: the ice, the fuel, the food.... You can imagine my mother. "You idiot! You OWE $800 after three weeks work?" Anyhow, I'm like, "Oh my God, now what am I gonna' do?" Of course the skipper lives just up the road here, and I know some of the guys on the boat. "What are you gonna do?" "I ain't goin' again." "I ain't goin'."

I said, "I'm goin' again." My mother said, "You are out of your mind." I went, and we went right back up there. We were gone a month. When I came home I bought a Pontiac GTO, cash.

Did you continue swordfishing after that?

Are you kidding?. One of the guys I had been on deck with got a job in Gloucester as the skipper of a swordfishing boat. He said to me, "Want to go?" I said, "Is the Pope Catholic?"

We did the circuit. We went out of New Bedford, Gloucester, Sandwich. Come spring we fished Georges Bank, summertime we went to the Grand Banks. Thanksgiving we'd come home, pack the boat up, and head south. We followed the swordfish. We made trips down off the Carolinas. We'd go into Miami, then we'd go to Key West, then up into the Gulf of Mexico, Panama City. Then we'd go down into the Yucatan, down off Nicaragua.

I was twenty-one. We tied up at Key West a lot. We tied up at Mallory Square where all the venders and entertainers come at sunset. You can imagine what a bunch of young fellows with lots of cash would do in Key West.

We had a barbecue set up right on deck. We'd barbecue swordfish, and this and that. We had trash barrels full of beer. We made friends with some scuba divers with spear guns. They'd go down around the piers and come up with grouper and snapper—real good eatin'.

I grew up in Harpswell, and I'd only seen one black person all the time I was growin' up. I didn't have an opinion, whereas some of these other fellas who were from Boston and New York, they had a whole different view of people of another color.

I'm "ignorant," so I'd take some of the smaller swordfish down around the corner where all the shrimp boats with black crews were tied up. I'd say, "Hey, I want to trade swordfish for them big shrimp you guys have."

At first they'd looked at me like, "This guy is out of his friggin' mind!" I'm the only white guy down there. First they'd make fun of me, but I'd make fun of them right back. Then, all of a sudden, "Hey, you all right; you cool!" So I'd go aboard their boat, and we'd party up and tell lies, and whatever. I got along great with them. I'd see them later on and they'd say "Hey, man, come on down!" And the guys on my boat would say, "You can't do that!" I sure wish I could find some of those guys now. It would be kinda fun to party with them again.

I came home at the end of May and ran another guy's lobster boat. That ended the first of December, then I was out of work. What am I gonna do? So I took a job down at Bath Iron Works.

You hadn't put aside enough money to coast through the winter?

Money wasn't the issue. I was living at home, and at home there is no such thing as coasting. The way I grew up, you worked. Being unemployed was an unknown concept.

I lasted about six weeks down to BIW.

After swordfishing, working at BIW didn't compare?

I had a hard time at the yard. They'd give me a job to do, and I'd do it pretty quick. My lead man would come and say, "What do you think you're doin'?" I said, "I'm all done. What do you want me to do now?" I guess down there they allot so many hours for certain jobs, and I'm doin' the job in less time.

The way I was brought up, and the way it is on boats, if I get my stuff done, I'm supposed to jump over and help you. No, no, no—not at the Iron Works! I'd start sweepin' the floor, and I'd catch hell. "That's not your job to sweep the floor. That's Department 27." I said to myself, "This place sucks. This don't work for me." So I got done.

Then four or five of us lobstermen got together. We'd lobster our own boats all summer. Come Thanksgiving, we'd all get together and find a boat and go draggin' for the winter. Mostly we stayed in the Gulf of Maine, but a couple times we went up to the Grand Banks, draggin' in the wintertime.

I'll bet it was rough up there.

Rough! Rough? Holy Christ, we took a beating!

Now you'll think I'm crazy, but we had a system. When the weather got real bad the fleet would come in. When the fleet came in, they sold their fish, and the prices would go to hell. Our system was when the fleet came in, we went out. When we did come in, we had the only fish, and we made some serious money.

That's when Debra and I got hooked up. I had bought a house, and she lived in it while I went offshore. Here is a funny story. My mother is scared to death of my going offshore in the wintertime. My brother-in-law, he's watching the TV news. If you'll remember, back in the '80s, a lot of older wood boats were being lost, and it was that dramatic kind of news they liked putting on the TV.

We got in a mess. We were sinking. We built these shelves to stand on in the hold, and these shelves were plywood with foam in the middle. When the boat filled with water, the shelves floated up, and all these little white beads of foam clogged the bilge pumps. So the pumps weren't working, and we had no idea where the water was coming from. It's winter; it's the middle of the night; and we are goin' down.

Did you have an EPIRB?

There was no such thing back then. But we had the radio, and we called for help. Come daylight, we were in a hell of a mess. We called for the other boats in the area, and we called the Coast Guard, "We're goin' down," we said.

We passed 5-gallon buckets up to bail. It got crazy. I marked the level of the water, and we'd bail like crazy, and I'd look again, and the line was under water.

The Coast Guard came, and the helicopters came, and they dropped pumps to us, but the pumps didn't work. Finally they sent a damage control team with duffle bags full of rope and mauls and caulk and all this equipment over in a boat from a cutter. The last guy to come aboard lost his footin' and went down between the two boats. Me and another guy caught him and pulled him up just as their boat and our boat were about to slam together. If we hadn't pulled him up, he'd a been crushed right there between the boats. That's how wild it was. Anyhow, they slowed the leaks, and we made it back to port.

Debra, here, never knew we were in trouble. My brother-in-law heard on the news that the *Sisu* was in trouble, sinkin'. He calls my mother, so she's beside herself, but nobody called Debra. When we get back I call her from the boat, "I'm ok! We made it!" Debra says, "That's nice. Was it a good trip?"

I heard you originated the lobsterboat races.

In Harpswell, yes. They'd raced Down east, but it wasn't organized like it is now. Back then it was one guy challenging another, "My boat's faster than yours." "Oh yeah? Prove it!"

Twenty-three years ago Andy Johnson had a lobsterboat, and he was crazy about racing it. He kinda talked me into it. That winter we both swapped out the engines in our boats with turbocharged Volvos. But I wasn't doin' it for the speed. I had a 453 GM in the boat before, and I needed to swap engines anyway.

Long Island, here in Casco Bay, had lobsterboat races on the 4th of July. Andy and I packed up and went down to enter the races. When we got there they said we couldn't race because we weren't from Long Island. We suspected it was because they knew Andy had the fastest boat.

Andy got pretty hot. He's pumpin' on me for startin' our own races. So I said, ok, but we're going to do it a little different. We're gonna invite everybody. You could be from Mars, as long as you've got a lobsterboat and you want to race. Now we have boats come all the way from Massachusetts. We have a good time.

We started printing T-shirts, and then hats, then sweatshirts. Then companies started donating prizes. It really grew.

Then someone said, "Why don't we make it bigger and have a fireman's muster, and a fisherman's jamboree? We hired sheriff's deputies, and we got the wardens, and we closed off the town road. Down at the town wharf we had crate races, we had a blind man's rowing race, we had a trap-hauling race, we had a ten-man tug of war, and we had the codfish relay. Oh, my Jesus, wasn't that fun! What a howl! I did it with my father. It was a LOT of work, but it was worth it.

But then my father died. Kinda took the wind out of my sails [Roy tears up, and we all sit silently].

How long ago did your father die?

Twelve years now. [Roy gets a glass of water and looks out at the bay.]

Well, tell me about the Harpswell Santa Fund.

That's a tough one. It does it to me every time [tears up again]. One of the guys went overboard. Got tangled up in the ropes, and drowned. He had a wife and three kids.

He was settin' traps, and his foot got caught in a loop in the rope, and the string of traps just pulled him over the rail and down. His stern man was just a kid, and he ended up in the water too, trying to save the guy. Long story short, we were the guys ended up bringin' him in. [voice breaks and he has to pause again].

Deb and I were talkin' one day, and Christmas was comin' around. Oh my God, here's that woman with those three little kids. So we said let's help them out with Christmas. So we went out and got some gifts. Went to Lewiston and bought a Santa suit. We didn't tell anybody. Just the two of us knew about it.

Seein' those little kids' faces was somethin'. We came home and we said, "Now that we're all dressed up, we've got to do something else." So we went and saw some of the older people in town. Nobody knew who we were. Afterward we hid the suit away and shut our mouths. All over town, "Who was that, who was that?"

Next year come around, we looked around and found a couple other families havin' a hard time. And we went to the school and said, "Do you know of anybody who needs some help? But the deal is, you can't tell anybody who's doin' it."

We visited the old folks, too. I went up to this woman's house, who'd known me since I was born, and I knocked on the door. She opens the door and she goes, "Roy, what are you doin'?" I about fall over. I say, "How the hell did you know it was me?" By your eyes," she says.

I put a couple soda machines down at the wharf, and the money we made off the soda and the cans helped fund us. After a while people began to figure it out, so we kinda come out of the closet. Individuals would send us $50 or $100. Jeez, the next thing you know, its startin' to grow and grow.

Beverly's Hallmark Cards in the Topsham Fair Mall does what they call "the giving tree" and we get 95% of our toys through them. People will pull a tag off the tree that says, "Girl, Age 5" and go buy a gift and leave it there. The store will call and say, "Come pick up a box of toys." A lot of women knit hats and mittens and scarfs for us. We get blankets.

Have you ever thought of going non-profit?

We checked into it, but for a non-profit, you have to prove your income. We take their word for it. They say they need help, we believe them. There is a lot of pride in Harpswell.

I've had kids come to me that we've done Santa for, and they know, and now they want to help, which is kinda nice, you know what I mean?

We go see the older people, too. This year we had some boat race mugs left over, so I went to town and bought some of those funky beers, wisecrack labels, foolish stuff, you know what I mean? There's people we go see, they haul those bottles out like you would your Christmas wreath and use them for decoration. "It's Christmas time. Santa Claus brought us these bottles, we'd better get them out." It floors me how much it means to these old people.

We've got a guy we've been doin'—he's, what, ninety-seven now?—he's up at Thornton Oaks Assisted Living. Debra works at LL Beans, and they had ornaments on sale, so we picked up twenty, and we went in. They wasn't supposed to be many people there, but there was a pile of old people. I don't care if you gave them toilet paper, it was the idea that Santa Claus comes in and you go to each one of them, you talk the foolish talk, "Have you been a good girl?" Like the old man, I said, "Chick, I've been lookin' for you." "Oh," he says, and he's ninety-seven years old, tickled to death, the hell with supper, Santa Claus is here, "Oh, I've moved a lot lately." I said, "What are you, on the run from the law or somethin'?" Of course everybody is, "Haw, haw, haw." It is a howl.

This year the American Legion called us at the last minute, "Would you consider coming up to Togus [Veteran's Hospital]?" There was this blind guy. I thought he was asleep. I thought I should leave him alone, but someone said, "Don't forget this guy."

"Santa" Roy at the Togus Veteran's Hospital.

So I go over, and he's sittin' in a wheelchair with his eyes shut. I leaned over and, "Hey, guy, hey," and he says, "Who is it, who is it?" I say, "Open your eyes and take a look. "No, tell me, who is it?" I say, "No, I'm tellin' ya, you got to open your eyes and take a look." He's sittin' there, he opens his eyes, and I say, "See who I am?" He says, "I'm tellin you, guy, I'm blind!" I felt like about this big! [pinches his fingers together]. "Oh my God, I'm sorry, man! I'm Santa Claus." "That's ok," he says, "I haven't seen Santa Claus for years."

And I had some candy canes. I said, "Well I'm gonna put a candy cane in your hand." "Open it up, open it up," he says. I open it up and he says, "Put it in my mouth, put it in my mouth!" I put it in his mouth, and he goes crunch, crunch, crunch. "Jesus, don't that taste good! That reminds me of when I was a kid."

The nurses came down and got me. There was this guy wouldn't leave his room. I went in there and he said, "Don't you look like a GD fool!" I says, "What do you mean?" He says, "Who the hell are you?" I says, "Who the hell do I look like, the Easter Bunny?" And he laughed; that's all it took.

DODGE MORGAN
Record-Holding Single-Handed Circumnavigator
Snow Island, Harpswell
Age 77

Dodge at his home, Snow Island in Casco Bay, and Eagle,
his beloved 91-year-old 30-foot schooner

Where were you born?

I was born in Malden Massachusetts, a blue-collar town just outside of Boston. My father was a pharmacist; my grandfather was also a pharmacist—owned a pharmacy there in Malden.

Were they disappointed you didn't go into pharmacy?

My father died when I was two, of an illness related to being gassed in WWI. I don't remember him.

Twelve years later my mother married a lovely guy whose signature characteristic was being helpless. He was quite different from the other males in my family, who rejected the idea of being helpless. Even if they didn't know what the fuck they were doing, they were going to do it.

That was my father's side. On my mother's side, the Dodges, my grandparents were located in Harwich, on Cape Cod. Grandfather Dodge was a very important presence in my life—an obscene, obnoxious, son-of-a-bitch of a person.

Is that where you learned your waterfront language?

I think so. Learning it was one thing; being compelled to use it is what I learned from him. His son had a boatyard in Harwich called Allen Harbor Marine, where he worked just when he wanted to. As male members of the family, we were required to work there. There was a rule that, "This is a business; it's not a recreation." So we were not allowed to use boats or to enjoy them. We were there to repair them and serve the owners.

How old were you when you started working at the boatyard?

I was fifteen. Working with Grandfather Dodge was a challenge, seeing kids my age playing with boats while I simply worked on them. The yard sold Johnson Seahorse outboards and Lyman boats.

The Lymans were lapstraked, fastened with copper rivets. Working with my grandfather, my job inside the boat was to peen off [round over the ends] the rivets as my grandfather drilled and drove new rivets in from the outside, a process of refastening the boat. If I was not on a new rivet he was driving, I got a blast of anger from him so I was quite pleased when he drilled into my ass or the sole of my shoe. I took some of my earnings from the yard and rode my bike up to Bass River and rented a Beetle Cat [gaff-rigged sailboat about 9 feet long] from a wonderful guy named Ted Frothingham, who was a signal character in town and ran a yard devoted to sailing.

I remember him telling me, "Here boy, this will teach you patience." And one of those little catboats would do that.

I would sail out into Nantucket Sound. I found a particular thrill from sailing out of sight of land.

Was the thrill due to being scared, like when a rollercoaster plummets?

No, it was like, "Who knows what lies over that horizon, and wouldn't it be interesting to find out?"

When did it first occur to you to sail around the world?

Sailing around the world was simply one more step in my love of sailing towards another horizon, going out of sight of civilization. Just me and the boat. Out there you own all of the victories and defeats, and only you know about the mistakes you make.

Before I was old enough to work at the yard I learned a tough lesson from my grandad. I was digging cesspools and mowing lawns, and I used the money to buy a mail-order sextant. He had agreed to teach me how to use it.

Did you use an artificial horizon?

I'll tell you in a minute if you'll just have a little patience.

The instrument arrived in the mail, and I told my grandfather. We went out on his boat before dawn, and we hove to. I remember him saying, "You need both the horizon and the heavenly body at the same time, so you use the sextant just at dawn and dusk." He picked the thing up, and quickly went through a process, then handed it to me and said, "Here, you do it."

I said, "I don't have the vaguest idea what you just did."

He said, "OK, give that thing to me," and he went through the process again and handed it to me. I still had no idea what he had just done and told him so. He says, "Boy, you are really stupid!" And he took the sextant and threw it overboard.

So you didn't learn celestial navigation.

No, but I learned something else—that if you are going to be taken care of, you'd better do it yourself.

I got through high school, then went to the University of New Hampshire and got kicked out.

You flunked out?

No, I fired a cannon off in the Dean of Women's bedroom —one of those 10-gauge shotgun cannons.

Were you under the influence of anything at the time?

The influence of stupidity, no substances.

You hadn't connected the dots to see that this would probably get you kicked out of school?

She was an old maid, and you could certainly tell why. Two of us engineered this prank, thinking it was hilarious. But as soon as I pulled the lanyard on that cannon, after I'd put up the ladder and pried open her window, I knew I'd done something astoundingly stupid. The sound was deafening.When I turned around my accomplice was gone. So I'm running across the campus with an extension ladder and a 15-pound cannon when I was accosted by the campus police. Thus ended that phase of my education.

I didn't dare tell my mother what I had done, so I went running down to the Air Force recruiting office and joined up so I could tell her that I had quit school to serve my country.

Did your mother ever find out?

Years later someone told her, but she refused to believe it. She adored us...and we adored her.

The Air Force is where I grew up. I flew early jet fighters, the F-86, the F-94, the F-89. I was just 21. The training involved a lot of hazing, a lot of pressure, a lot of competition. Only half of the guys starting the program finished.

Got out of the Air Force, went back to college, got married, and earned a degree in journalism from Boston University, magna cum laude.

When I couldn't find a job in the lower forty-eight, I went to Alaska, did get a job at the *Anchorage Daily News* as sports editor. After one year, I left the paper to form my own advertising and lobbying operation, primarily representing oil companies that had an interest in the state's oil reserves but didn't yet have their own lobbying staffs there.

Were you a good lobbyist?

Good enough, more from my determination than my skills. My basic plan was to earn enough money to buy a boat and sail the world. Which I did. Bought this schooner [points to a photo of *Coaster*], thirty-six feet, four inches on deck. She was a double-hernia rig—not what you would call the ideal single-handed vessel. Built by Goudy and Stevens in East Boothbay, Maine, in 1931. I sailed her from Maine down through the Lesser Antilles, Greater Antilles, Central America, Panama to Hawaii, Hawaii to Tahiti and the Society Islands, then to Alaska. I never slept ashore in two and a half years, maybe passed out there a few times, but never slept.

Why did you stop sailing?

I was broke, and I had to see if I could rejoin civilization. It wasn't so much being broke because I was broke all that time. Money is of no use when you are at sea.

I became a writer. But when I figured out what I got paid for what I wrote, it was pennies an hour. No way I was going to earn a living that way. So I got a real job. From some real research, I found a Massachusetts company in an early stage of growth and learned its operating details. I gave them no choice other than to hire me. I invented my job title and wrote my own job description.

What did the company make?

They made ball valves and butterfly valves, but I didn't care what they made. I cared about the people involved. The CEO, named Bob McCray, gave me my business education in three years of work.

I had no establishment business credentials but was an avid student, and there is nothing a teacher enjoys more than an avid student. McCray and I bonded. The company started an electronics division which, it turned out, was a disaster. Because I wasn't on an established career ladder, he gave me this operation to run.

The product was a speech scrambler for two-way radio and telephone communications. I was actually able to build some sales, but not soon enough. McCray's board of directors—some very well-known New England business names—advised him to sell this loser division and I got that job. The only person I found to buy it wanted me with it, and I wasn't at all interested in working for someone else. So I said, "I'll buy it myself."

The price was right: $20,000, but I had to borrow the money and set up in a Littleton, Massachusetts, garage. My first year I had $127,000 in sales and managed to break even because the inventory I got in the buy gave me a very high gross margin. Slowly, I built deep and meaningful relationships with a group of manufacturers reps. In spite of the low sales level, the reps and I bonded. Somehow it was understood that some day my company would be important to them even as I mailed out commission checks each month and at least half of them read "Zero dollars and zero cents."

I got an outstanding design engineer, a graduate of the wartime MIT Radiation Lab, who was highly experienced in microwave technology. Dick Mosher was going broke trying to sell his design of the world's first and only hand-held marine radar, the Whistler. I could sell Whistlers and he could deliver a whole new family of products for me to sell. Our winner was a line of radar speed detectors, also named "Whistler."

No military applications?

We sold a few hundred receivers to the Naval Weapons Center in China Lake, a standard receiver that operated well in enemy weapon detection for fighter aircraft. The Navy sent us this huge military specifications manual. I sent the manual back with the note, "We don't have the capability or the time to read this son of a bitch, and the only Mil-Spec thing we'll do is stencil 'NO STEP' on the receiver case." We got the order anyway. By that time we were selling nearly a million Whistler radar detectors a year.

Now you are talking a huge market, potentially everyone who likes to speed and hates being caught.

Yeah, we were onto something. But in the early design stage I didn't have the money to tool the product for mass production. I went to the rep force with an offer to pay double commissions on sales for three years if they gave me $1,500 for each percent of the national market in their territory. I collected 49,000 bucks from them. I paid them back more than $860,00. This is now one of three case studies used at Harvard Business School and Babson College.

We had an extremely successful company now and it came to be time to sell her for my promise to myself for a boat that would sail me solo around the world non-stop. The company sold to Dyna-tech Corporation in Burlington, Massachusetts.

You were sitting on a pile of money, and you wouldn't have to work unless you threw it away, which a lot of people have done.

Like on the *Maine Times*.

Yes. Why did you buy the "*Maine Times*?"

Because I had been a journalist, and this was a premier Maine newspaper. So what if it had never made money? So what if founder John Cole, the spirit, and Peter Cox, the discipline and the money, could not get along?

As I recall those two were like oil and water.

But such a nice mix of oil and water. Peter finally gave up on John when John said, right on national TV, "The facts don't matter in a story."

Well, Farley Mowatt said essentially the same thing. He was asked in an NPR interview whether everything in his books was true, and he laughed and said, "Of course not. Facts get in the way of the truth."

John then left the *Maine Times* and started *The World Paper* in Boston, a bad career move.

Yeah, that was a big mistake.

Peter told me that when *The World Paper* folded and John came back, he spotted Peter working in the *Maine Times* garden. John leaned over the fence and said, "Well, Peter, I'm back. I finally met a bigger asshole than you!"

Yeah, John was a piece of work.

So you had a degree in journalism, you loved to write, and you had just had great success running a company. You thought you could shape the *Maine Times* up and make it profitable?

It was going to die, and I thought I could extend its life for a while. It had been a Maine treasure, but by then its time had passed. It was the only alternative weekly in the United States that stuck with issues and had a statewide paid circulation. But by then, the issues that put the *Maine Times* on the map, the environment and the Vietnam War, had been assumed by the national press. By then the *Maine Times* was preaching to the choir. It was a marvelous one-shot paper.

You didn't waste your entire nest egg on that venture?

No, not all, but a whacking amount. I don't consider it a total waste.

Let's talk about your record-setting voyage on *American Promise*.

I had promised myself, back on the old schooner, "Someday I am going to make a significant sail in a boat designed for the purpose." I always referred to the boat as *Promise*. One of Ted Hood's [designer and builder of the boat] people thought the name too soft for its mission and we learned that no American had ever gone around the world alone without stopping. So that is how she became *American Promise*.

What were the special design characteristics?

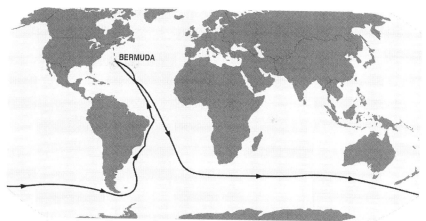

American Promise's *record-setting track around the world*

It was designed for a 56-year-old single-hander to get around the world without stopping. In the back of the book, *The Voyage of American Promise*, is a fifteen-page section on the specifications.

Give me a highlight.

I said I would trade a half knot of speed for an hour of sleep. The speed tradeoff was my way of saying my durability is going to be tested, so anything you can do to extend my energy I want you to do. And the only key equipment that isn't going to be redundant is me. Put two of everything in there.

After *Promise* completed her voyage, the French established a non-stop race, single-handed race. They held almost all of the round-the-world records, and they wanted this one, too [the non-stop]. Philippe Jeantot did a solo circumnavigation of 159 days, but it included four stops. They were pissed off when I turned in 150 days.

I read that you were taking psychiatric tests along the way.

Right. Manny [Dodge's wife] wasn't really all for this. She said, "You ought to include some socially acceptable goal here." She wanted to make it a medical project—she was into doctors and medical things—and I said, "No." But I'd agree to be a white rat for a psychological stress and solitude test. So she proposed this to Boston College, and they bought into it.

Jesus, they tested me, not to help me cope, but to learn how the solitude and stress might affect me. I was asked to take tests every day during the voyage. They were personality profiles and puzzles. The whole experience taught me that the soft science of psychology measures our mental state based totally on how we relate. I found the tests amusing. The personality profiles posed questions like, "Would you rather be an actor or an engineer? And this one really cracked me up: "Are you the life of the party?" WTF! I am the only party here.

Did you find yourself talking to yourself?

I talked to myself all the time, and I would answer in a different voice so I could keep straight who was talking at the time. Some of my conversations with myself are recorded because there were movie cameras installed, some of which automatically fired up for a half-minute every four hours.

Have you ever figured out why you wanted to make this trip?

It was a logical waypoint in my life's journey. I didn't wake up Monday morning and say, "Gee, I'd like to sail alone around the world." The "why" is a very common question, and I have trouble answering it. "Because it is difficult and different?" "Because it is there," the Edmund Hillary answer to climbing Mt. Everest? I have no real explanation.

Did Manny know of this waypoint when you married her?

Yes, but I doubt that she took it seriously, because when it came time to do it, she said, "Wait a minute! I thought that was just a nice Friday night conversation, not a real plan."

Were you ever scared?

No, I knew the risks, and I was ready to accept what came. Death was possible. You live with it. A hell of lot of guys have gone around. Less than half who start finish. In the last non-stop race thirty sailors entered and eleven finished, and there is usually a death for every fifteen racers.

American Promise, *Dodge Morgan at the helm, crossing the finish line at Bermuda after its record-setting non-stop 150-day circumnavigation.*

You grew up in Massachusetts, and you did your early sailing in Cape Cod...

How did Maine come in? I sailed to Maine and lost my heart here. This is the most attractive and compelling coastline on God's earth.

Is it the combination of beauty and challenge?

The challenge of the rocks and the fog are part of the joy. It's always a thrill to overcome a challenge. If you're never challenged, then fuck it, there's no thrill.

Do you still race?

I don't race. Ocean racing, I am sure, is a thrill to many, but I think it's tainted with male arrogance. Pouring money into a sailboat to compete at eight knots of speed is on the face of it, dumb. If there's a racing fleet somewhere, I am going someplace else.

I know what you mean about the male thing, the "Mine is bigger or faster than yours." One summer I worked at Yankee Marina in Yarmouth. There were races between the big boats, the 40- to 50-foot boats with deep fin keels, every Thursday night. The owner of the boatyard used to salivate in anticipation of boats limping in Friday mornings with their keel hanging from the bolts because a few juiced racers tried to win by cutting across the ledges.

I know how to compete, but I don't use the water as the medium. I feel sorry for the guys who think sailing is a matter of budget and brute-force competition.

There are three reasons people sail. One is to get somewhere. MB [Mary Beth, his companion] thinks I'm wrong, but I think there is no less efficient mode of transportation than sailing, so sailing to get somewhere is dumb.

The second reason is to compete, and I do think that is arrogant. Let the kids race dinghies, but grow up after that.

The third reason is to do it simply for its own sake. That is why I sail.

I remember taking my boat down the Intracoastal Waterway to Florida. I was chugging along at maximum speed, 6 knots. I looked over at the highway running parallel, and a car passed me at 60 mph. Then I looked up and saw a plane, probably from New York to Florida, going 600 mph. Suddenly I felt stupid, so I know what you mean about reason number one.

You must have a spiritual connection to the water, because when you are not on your schooner, you are in this house on an island. Why would you live on an island unless you want to be a hermit? But I suspect you enjoy having company, such as the lovely Mary Beth.

I enjoy visitations as well as hermitage.

Is Snow Island essentially a big anchored boat to you?

You could say that, except she never drags her anchor.

Dodge sailing his beloved Eagle, *"simply for its own sake."*

DAWN BICHREST
Block and Tackle Restaurant
Cundys Harbor, Harpswell
Age 77

Where else can you get a good corned hake?

Few outside of Harpswell have heard of the Block and Tackle Restaurant in Cundys Harbor because it doesn't advertise. It doesn't have to.

Besides the food, which is Down east cooking at its best (Where else can you find corned hake?), an appealing feature is the wait staff. At every visit there seems to be a new crop of delightful, fresh-faced young ladies, all of whom refer to the proprietor as "Grammie."

At the restaurant I am directed to an old clapboard house behind a white picket fence down the road a piece. I would know the house by a hand-painted sign, "Grammie's House," over the side door.

Grammie admits me to her kitchen but informs me she has changed her mind about our interview. "My husband, Frankie, would kill me! He says I blab too much, never mind doin' it in print."

"Grammie" Dawn offers me a consolation coffee or tea. We sit at her sunlit kitchen table. I mention fond memories of summers spent in Cundys Harbor with my lobsterman grandfather, Clarence Goddard. She doesn't recall Clarence. I tell her my mother was a classmate of Sid Watson, the now-deceased fourth-generation owner of the local general store. Grammie is beginning to warm up.

I remember hearing that Lewis Stuart, a local contractor, had provided the former motel building that became the Block and Tackle Restaurant. Thus informed, I deliver my last and best pitch: that Lewis Stuart's wife, Virginia Goddard, is my first cousin, once removed.

Frankie, watching a baseball game in the next room and listening to our conversation, groans.

Were you born in Cundys Harbor?

No, I was born in Harpswell Center. [Cundys Harbor and Harpswell Center are both fishing villages in the same Town of Harpswell. The distance by road between the two is so great, however, that the residents think of them as separate towns.]

What did your father do for work?

Fisherman. My mother was a schoolteacher.

What grade did she teach?

All of 'em. It was a one-room school. But my husband was born right here in Cundys Harbor, so he's a true native.

Did you ever go out with your father in his boat?

Oh, yes! We were always busy doing things, because any time you're around the water you are busy—and happy. But my parents were divorced, so I was kind of back and forth. It was a very mixed-up marriage, but a good life.

It didn't seem to affect you too badly because you've been married...?"

Fifty-two years, I think.

Psychologists make a big thing about the negative effect of divorce on children.

Sure, but life is what you make it. Sometimes a divorce helps because it makes you more determined to keep your family together. You work a little harder than a person who doesn't know what divorce is all about. And when you don't have money you work harder, because love is all you can give them.

More important than taking your kids to Disney World?

Oh, by far.

Do you think kids today have too much?

Yep, mine are spoiled—not my kids, but my grandchildren.

Kids today are so plugged in to television, the internet, iPhones, they don't get a chance to use their imaginations. Their heads are so full of external noise, there's no room for thoughts.

Not my children, but my grandchildren are more into that modern way of livin'. I don't think it helps them in any way.

You might think that here in Cundys Harbor, they would be isolated from that, but it's electronic. You can't keep it out.

No, no, and I wish you could. Kids today are missin' out because the way we lived is—we'd grab the kids, and we didn't have much money, so we had a camp up country. We'd head up there, and that was our big outing. We are lucky in Maine that we have the ocean, the woods, and the mountains, all within just a couple of hours. Our camp isn't much, just an old farmhouse. There's no running water and no plumbing, or any of that stuff. No electricity.

But isn't that a positive?

It is to me because I've gotten away, and I've taught the kids another way of life. Because we have no electricity, we can't have a TV, a telephone, or a computer. People have to talk. We tell stories. If we had all that other stuff, they wouldn't do that.

Do you suppose that's why the people of the Maine coast and of the North Woods are such great story tellers?

Ayah, it's a long way to a movie theater. They learn how to tell a story. Some of them do add a little to the stories, but I think the best stories are "added to."

I once asked an old fellow up in Houlton whether he'd ever been to Boston. "Nope," he said. "You ever been to Portland?" "Nope." "Well, would you like to go to Portland?" He said, "I hope to never go south of Island Falls." [Houlton, population 4,500, is the county seat of Maine's largest county. Island Falls, population 754, is twenty-seven miles down the road toward Portland.]

That's right! [laughs]. I have to go to Florida for a week every fall just because my husband, Frankie, plays baseball. He won't go without me, but if he would, I'd stay to home. [Dawn's husband, Frankie, is a remarkably fit 72-year-old fisherman. Every fall he travels to Florida to play for a Rhode Island team in the Roy Hobbs Over-47 Baseball World Series. In addition to playing any position, he is the team's designated runner.]

What keeps Frankie in such good shape?

Lobsterin', keepin' busy. He never sits. [During our two-hour interview, Frankie reminded me of a hummingbird. He was in and out of the house half a dozen times, always carrying something. At one point he threw a dozen traps into his pickup truck and sped off.]

What do you think of Florida?

I can't find any good reason why anybody would leave Maine, as beautiful as it is, even in winter. I think winter is as pretty as it is in the summer.

We're never tied down by snow for more than a couple hours before they come through with the plow. You get up in the mornin' and by 6 o'clock, the road is plowed and sanded.

I went down to visit my mother when she had a place in Florida. In the mornin' the buses would pick up one or two kids for school. Everybody else is so old, they're still sleepin' when the buses are pickin' up the kids. And those gated communities: "Children not allowed." That's not for me.

How did you meet Frankie?

My brother fixed me up. The first date, I hated him. Another girl came up to me and said, "I was going to go out with him, but I couldn't, so he got you." I didn't want to be second choice, so I treated him like dirt that day.

The second date was the same. My brother twisted my arm and made me go on a double date again. That's how it started.

Why did you keep going out with him?

I wanted to find out what made him tick. He was different from the other boys. He liked goin' smeltin' in the brooks and some of the stuff that I liked doing. And he liked dancing; he was a good dancer, and I liked dancin'. That was more interesting to me than the other boys who just wanted to go to the movies or some stupid thing like that.

Have you figured out yet what makes him tick?

Nope, I'm still working on it.

How many children do you have?

Five boys. I wanted a girl, but we didn't have much, and I figured if we didn't stop it at five, those kids would never have anything. They're all forty-five and older now.

They all still here in Cundys Harbor?

Yup. All fishermen. All self-employed with their own boats. They've done all right for themselves. Some of them go about a bit, but they come right back to the Harbor.

What is it about Cundys Harbor that makes people want to stay? There are a lot of families who have been here for five, six, even seven generations. Can you think of anything you'd change about it?

No, I can't, but I don't like some of the things that are trying to change. Like people comin' in from outside and sayin', "We're going to put these rules in." It changes it for the natives.

People from New York, New Jersey …?

I'm not going to say where from. They come and see this and say, "I want to live in this place." Then they move in and start changin' things and ruinin' what they moved here for in the first place.

That happened in Portland, too. Someone built a condo development on one of the wharfs, and rich people from away bought them up, thinking they could sit on their balcony and take in all the fishing boats in the harbor and on the next wharf. Then another developer built condos on the neighboring wharf. Suddenly these people were drinking their cappuccinos and eating their croissants, and staring, not at fishing boats, but at people just like themselves, and they said, "Wait a minute! Where did all the fishing boats go?"

Yeah, they don't think about what they're doin' to the community. It's all about them. We're lucky to be built up enough in the middle of town so they can't come in. No more land is available. But you'll still see people that will come in and buy a house for $200,000—and I've seen this happen down here—tear it down, and put another house up for a million dollars! It's just crazy. [laughs] It's crazy!

More money than brains?

That's it. Why not have a friend instead? I'd take one good friend over a million dollars any day. They are the one that's going to be there at the end. It isn't going to be that money, and it isn't going to be that expensive house. You're still going to be put in the ground just like everybody else.

I had a man tell me once, "I dried some leaves and put them in my pocket, so I could rustle them and feel like I had a pocket full of money." [laughs uproariously] And he was just as happy as a clam.

I'll tell you one thing—money will never buy you a genuine friend. Oh, it might get some types to hang around, but they won't be the real thing, the real friend. There is no amount of money that will buy you anything of real value, absolutely nothing. Everything I value is right here.

What was it like raising five boys in Cundys Harbor?

I'm a strict mother. I'm the first to admit that my boys knew what it was like to be paddled.

Didn't they used to make and sell paddles up to the State Prison in Thomaston?

Ayah, I've had some of those. It makes their bottoms pink; it smarts; but its gone in a short time. I never whacked them with a whip or something really harmful, but they respected me, and I think they turned out good.

Did you spank them for swearing?

They never did. That was something that was understood. They were fishermen, and they could talk any way they wanted to aboard the boat, but when you are in the house you don't.

There was one kid that visited—one of their friends—and he slipped and said something he shouldn't have, and I kicked him out. He went over in the corner on the floor, and he cried, and he cried. I got mad. I said he had to be gone for a week.

My kids went over to him, and he said, "She'll never let me back in the house." They said, "Yes, she will. Mama gets over things, but you are never to do that again." And he never did.

Another kid I baby sat. He was just a monster with everybody else, but he was good with me. He was scared of two people: one of the wrestlers you see on TV, and me. I never laid a hand on him, but he had heard my reputation.

Was there any problem down here with drugs or alcohol?

Oh, there was in the Harbor, but my boys never got into them. Probably because they thought I'd kill them!

Why did you start the restaurant?

Because my kids started getting married, and I didn't want to be a pain in the butt, havin' nothing else to do but meddle in their affairs. It would keep me out of the way of my daughters-in-law. Keep me out of trouble. And I'd always wanted a restaurant.

We didn't have much money, so I went digging clams; I shucked scallops to pay for my restaurant. And Lewis Stuart hauled it in there. It was part of a motel he had bought. I paid $700 for the building, and Lewis hauled it in there for nothing.

"Grammie" Dawn fixin' a batch of good corned hake

Why did Lewis Stuart do it for nothing?

Because he really cares about the town. He thought the town should have a restaurant where people could get together. If he likes you, there is nothin' he wouldn't do for you, but boooy if he don't! [laughs]

When I go to your restaurant, I notice all these girls, pretty girls, and they all call you "Grammie."

Well, most of them are my grandchildren, and the rest of them have been around me long enough to be my grandchildren. The restaurant is definitely a family deal.

Do you teach them how to smile and be so friendly?

No, they're just happy girls.

Of course a pretty, happy waitress makes a happy customer, and that leads to bigger tips....

That's right [laughs]. They do good on tips. Sometimes they make more money than I do!

Now you have to tell me where you get your haddock. Fried haddock is about my favorite food, and I have never tasted anything like yours.

To be honest, it's Icelandic flash-frozen.

No! Frozen haddock from Iceland?

Yup. I would never tell a lie to anyone for anything. I have tried the fresh haddock off the boats, and it just doesn't do as well. The water is colder up there, and they freeze it the minute they catch it, so it's actually fresher than if it come into the harbor on ice on a boat that's been out there a couple of days.

I remember a story by Jack Aley in the *Maine Times* back twenty years. They wanted to see what New York restaurants meant by "fresh haddock" on their menus, so they sent Jack out on a boat. He put a tag on one of the fish, then he followed it: a couple of days longer out at sea, then into the dock, shipped by truck down to Fulton Fish Market, bought by a wholesaler, sold to a retailer, and finally bought by a fancy, upscale restaurant. Jack hung around the kitchen until the haddock was cooked and served. When the people were half way into the meal, Jack went up to the table and said, "How's that fresh haddock?" "Oh," they said, "there is nothing in the world like fresh haddock just off the boat." Jack didn't tell them the fish was a week old!

Fresh haddock you cannot keep together. If that haddock don't fall apart when you cook it, then that isn't fresh haddock. Never mind the smell; that doesn't tell you. It's the fallin' apart.

How do you make your haddock chowder?

The same way my grandmother and her mother made it. Sauté the onions in salt pork scrap until they get translucent, but not brown. Boil the potatoes in that, just barely covered in water. When the potatoes are about done, throw the haddock on top of the potatoes, turn the burner off, and put a cover on it. If you continue boiling, the fish falls all apart so you can't even tell it's in there, and everybody bitches that there's no haddock in the chowder.

When we serve it, we warm the chowder up in a big fry pan with a big chunk of haddock on top. By the time the chowder is warmed up, that big piece of fish is cooked just perfect. Then we add the milk, and the chunk of haddock sits on top where you can see it.

Do you use cream or milk?

One can of evaporated milk to one quart of whole milk.

Any butter?

Nope, just the salt pork.

Salt and pepper?

The salt comes out of the salt pork. I let the customer do the pepper.

Any other spices, like rosemary?

Oh, no! No, no, no. God forbid! You don't want to ruin it.

I have to tell you a funny story about my Aunt Marjorie, who grew up here in Cundys Harbor. Toward the end of her life—she lived to 90—she was in intensive care up at Midcoast Hospital. I had medical power of attorney, and they called me in. There were a couple of doctors, a psychiatrist, a couple of nurses and me, all sitting around her bed. They said, "We can't get her to eat or even drink water."

Marjorie was lying there looking like she might go at any minute. The psychiatrist said, "Marjorie, listen to me carefully. You haven't eaten or drunk water for five days. If you don't, you will die. Do you want to die?" Dead silence. You could hear a pin drop. The psychiatrist looked at me and shrugged his shoulders as if to say, "What now?"

Of course I've never been able to keep my mouth shut, and I knew that haddock chowder was her favorite food, so I said, "Marjorie, how about a bowl of haddock chowder?" Marjorie rose up, as if from the dead, and said, "That would be good!" I came down and got a bowl of your chowder and brought it to the hospital. She had it that night, and they discharged her a couple of days later.

Now you have all these granddaughters working up at your restaurant. Any of them going to go to college?

All of 'em. But I've got four or five granddaughters that go lobsterin', too. Two of them have their own boat.

How old were they when they started?

Twelve or fourteen. The cook, Emily, and one of the waitresses go haulin' together. The two days they're not running the restaurant they haul their traps.

I don't know how Emily gets time to do all the things she does. Right now she's goin' to college, she cooks five days a week for me in the summer, she lobsters, she takes care of a little girl in the "Big Sister" program, she's taken a welding course, she's got her captain's license, she took flyin' lessons, but I don't think she finished that yet.

She'd be interestin'—but I doubt she'd talk to you.

Dawn was right—Emily wouldn't.

CARROLL "BUD" DARLING
Unschooled Mechanical Genius
Cundys Harbor, Harpswell
Age 82

Bud and his 60-foot portable sawmill

Everywhere I went, from Portland to Rockland, someone always asked, "Have you talked to Bud Darling?" Story piled on incredible story until I wondered about the reality. I became afraid the stories would prove exaggerated, that the mythical man would prove to be an ordinary human being.

I spent five minutes searching for his unmarked driveway, a landmark "just down the road a piece" which the locals insisted I "couldn't miss." What turned out to be the drive could have been the set for a war movie. Strewn with boulders and washouts the size of my little car's wheels, it explained why the most popular vehicle in Maine is the Ford F-150 4-wheel-drive pickup.

Fear was replaced by wonderment, however, as soon as I pulled into the yard. Bud Darling stood next to a sixty-foot-long steel trestle bridge on wheels that supported an automobile engine and gigantic circular saw blade on a railroad track.

"Some fella needed a 40-foot log sawed up. He couldn't find a mill in Maine that could do it, so I built him one," said Bud.

My ancestors come over from Germany in 1780- or 1790- somethin'. There was two brothers, and Germany wouldn't let them leave, so they went to Norway.

They was young. This is what I got from my grandmother. She had pictures of the graves of our great, great, great, great people there in Germany. I don't know what become of the books and all her writin'. Some of it was good, some was bad, and some was terrible.

Are you saying your ancestors were doing bad things?

Ayah, but anyway, they went to Norway, and the two brothers met two sisters, twins as I remember it. And these two brothers married the two sisters, Norwegian girls. They had this fishin' boat, and they loaded that thing up with everything they could get on to it, and they headed for this country.

They landed up here in the New Meadows River on Birch Island. Birch Island has the oldest house in Harpswell on it. It was built in seventeen somethin', and it's still there today. My family, for years and years and years, owned that. Uncle Arthur lived there for years. Arthur's been dead for years, but he was my grandfather's cousin.

Anyway, when they landed they got in with this man that owned Coles Island. He said, "If you'll clear that island, which was all heavy, heavy timber, I'll give you half of it."

That sounds like a lot of work.

I guess probably! You stop and think what you had for tools.

Did they sell the timber?

No, they built with it, and they burned it to keep warm. But they had to have the land cleared for gardens and for sheep and cows. Mostly everybody had sheep and goats 'cause they browsed and kept the bush down. Goats and sheep was what would keep it down.

Everywhere you look in the records of the Town of Harpswell you come to "sheep pasture," "Sheep Pasture Pond," "Sheep Island," "sheep" everything.

Cundys Harbor has always been a unique place, a very unique place. Why if they took that bridge down [the recently built Ewings

Narrow bridge, connecting East Harpswell and South Harpswell]
and moved the Town Office over here, why people over here
would be thrilled to death.

They's two different mindsets. Over there to South Harpswell,
all they want is tourists. Well, over here, we don't want no tourists,
just the Cundys Harbor community, which is all fishermen.

Would it be difficult for someone from away to move in here?

Yes, it would. I had this land all divided up into lots. I wouldn't
sell a lot to anyone from out of town. We've got these outa staters
and this selectman, and they've messed the town up so bad, we'll
never get it back.

They never shoulda' built the bridge. That destroyed the town,
that did. They was always talk of Harpswell, but that over there is
Harpswell Neck. This over here, Great Island, is East Harpswell.
They shoulda' been two separate towns. When they built that
bridge we lost our school over here. It was the most beautiful
school there ever was. I didn't get to go to it much, and I didn't get
along with it, but it was beautiful. It was a community thing.

Well, let's get back to you. When and where were you born?

I was born in 1929, right there in that room in the corner, me and
my brother.

And your father was a fisherman?

Oh, ayah. Born and brought up doin' it.

And did he keep animals?

Ayah, we all had farms. Everybody did everything.

**I see an awful lot of machinery out there [in the yard and in
several nearby buildings]. Were you the town mechanic?**

I was mechanical, I guess. I done construction work. I done marine
construction, mostly, when I weren't fishing. I built wharfs, and I did
quite a bit of dredging and pilings. I done blasting and drilling. I was
the only one in it full time around the Harpswell Islands.

You said you didn't get to go to school much?

Well, that's a long story. We never got along too good with the teacher. She hated my family, and she took it out on me.

I guess I musta been rebellious 'cause she used to beat me somethin' awful, until finally, through a hint from my grandfather, like t'fix my mother, he said, "Buddy, there comes a time in life when you're going to have to stand on your own two feet. Now you can keep on goin', and you can take it, but there comes a time when you've got to make up your mind enough's enough."

That teacher, she bled my nose; she hit me over my head; she stove up the desk; she tore the clothes off'n me. I never passed a grade.

Well, one day she done a job on me. She come up behind me, and I was readin' a book I wasn't supposed to be readin'. I had a big geography book, and I had a history book down inside it. I dunno what grade I was in, but I was readin' way up in tenth grade books. I'd finished what she told me to do.

She come up behind me, hit me over the head, and drove my face down into that oak desk [chuckles], bloodied my nose and my eye. Well! I come up outa there—and she was a big woman, about this big around and about that tall—she was a miserable thing, a miserable thing, and her husband was one of the sweetest guys that ever existed. Well anyhow, I nailed her, and she went over backward, and I never stopped. And nobody interfered. All them big boys just stood around. Oh man, it was a terrible mess. Shut the school down.

They shut the school down because of you?

Yes, they did. It was a big deal. It was big because she claimed she was pregnant, and I killed the baby. I was just a kid, so I run up to my grandfather's. He washed me up, cleaned me up. Course it wasn't a minute before they got aholt of my mother to come down. My mother chewed out my grandfather. She said, "You see what you done?" He says, "Sounds to me like the boy done some good." Grandfather was a calm man, a very calm man, but he had his limits. Very uneducated, but smart.

You can be smart, but uneducated, and you can be educated but not smart.

Ayah, that's the way the most of 'em are today, overeducated.

My friend, John Totman, over in Phippsburg found out how much education I had [MIT PhD], and he said, "You know, you've had so much education, you're foolish. They've bred all the common sense right out of you."

Well, that's just exactly what happens. They want that common sense outa you. They want everything book learnin'. This whole country is goin' that route.

So that was the end of your school career?

Not quite. One day we was repairin' gear over on the island, puttin' off our fall gear. I knew dad had somethin' on his mind. He was quiet, and he wasn't sayin' much. He said, "Bud, I got somethin' I want to talk to you about." I said to myself, "Oh, no, here it comes!" He says, "I've found a school I'd like to have you go to. You ain't got to go. That's up to you."

I said, "Dad, I'm too old to go to school." "No, you ain't!" he says. "You think of all them men that's gone to school while you was in school down here." See, in the winter the older fellers who never got their education, they'd come into the school to learn to read and write. They'd sit in the back row, right in with the children, and they was learnin' to read.

I knew that it was on dad's mind so heavy that I had to do it for his sake. Mom and dad, they did everything they could for all of us boys.

Well, I went up, and I met the teachers, and they knew the whole history before I ever got there. I weren't stupid, and I put two and two together, and I could see that this had been goin' on for some time.

This teacher, Mrs. Leach, she says, "Do you read?" I says, "Ayah." And she says, "Let me get a book. Here, read this." So I read it, and she says, "Now wait a minute, I thought you didn't have no education." She went and got a book of somethin' way up, way advanced. I read that, and she says, "Where did you learn to read?" I said, "The boys on the boat. When we weren't fishin', they'd make me read. They said, 'If you don't know what a word means, you stop and ask us. We don't know nothin' either, but one of us will come up with somethin'.'"

Then she started askin' me about our country, and I told her about the whole country, the beginnin' of our country. She says, " You know about the Constitution?" I said, "Yes," and I named a bunch of the men that signed it. She said, "I can't even get that out of my students."

We talked a little bit about geography, then she said, "What about this writing thing?" I said, "I can't write." "Why can't you write if you can read?" "Well," I said, "I don't know how to spell the words." She said, "Write a bunch of words that you know how to write." I did. I wrote a bunch of words I knew how to write. She says, "Spell Mississippi." So I said, "That's easy: M I S S crooked letter crooked letter I." She said, "There's somethin' that ain't gettin' through here. Do you know how to sound your words to spell?" I said, "Why no, I never was taught anything about spellin', never anything at all." She said, "That's what you're missin'. You don't know phonics." It ended up I agreed to stay. I liked her right. She was a sweetheart, right from the word go.

Well, they was these three girls, one to either side, Edith Snow and Edith Decker, and another girl in front. She says, "Class, we have a new student, and I want to explain a little about him." She told them that I hadn't been to school much, and what schoolin' I'd had weren't good. She says, "I want you to help Buddy when he needs it and kinda guide him."

Goodness sakes, it was like a circus! It was more fun. I learnt more in them few months than I'd learned all my life.

Oh, what a difference a good teacher can make!

Did you ever lobster?

Yes, I lobstered. Oh yes, that's what me and my dad used to do. As a kid, me and my brother went together. I dunno how old we were, but my mother and grandmother used to stand on the shore and watch us haulin' traps, because once we got out there we'd go down on the islands and explore. We'd camp right in the skiff. We used to throw a canvas over it and stay overnight in that thing. Kids today, they don't know how to do it. They don't know how to do anything. If they ain't gone to school to learn to lace their shoes, they don't never lace them up; they strap them up.

All these guys what comes out of college, they won't touch a lawn mower any more. They got to ride around on it. If the thing quits in the middle of the lawn, that's where it sits until somebody comes repairs it. They can't lift the hood to see if it's out of gas. This repairman I know, he says, "I go to this place every week to fill the gas tank and check the oil." He says, "The man's got no clue. He called me up one night, 'You got to come right down. I've got an hour to go, and my motor quit.' I said, 'Well, have you checked the gas?' He said, 'How do I do that?'" So he goes down. The spark plug wire's fell off!

Something similar happened to me. I knew this recent college graduate who had a nice gas grill, and I noticed he never used it. I said, "How come you never use your grill?" He said, "It's broken." Well, it looked pretty new to me, so I figured it could be something simple to fix. I said, "Maybe I can fix it. How much would you sell it for?" He said, "Ten bucks." You can guess what was wrong with it. The propane tank was empty! I didn't have the heart to tell him.

I'll tell you another one. I was at the hardware behind this guy who was complainin' about his propane grill. He said, "It has this little button you're supposed to push, and it's supposed to light the fire. I've pushed that thing a thousand times and nothin' happens." The clerk said they'd send a man down to take a look. A couple days later I see this fellow again, lookin' at propane grills. I said to him, "I thought you just bought one of these things." He said, "I did, but the igniter wire fell off so it wouldn't light. I figure if I buy another one, the wire won't fall off for at least a year." [laughs]

How did you get into blasting?

I had to do it. One day we was quahoggin' and we had to drain a flat [mudflat]. I went and got some dynamite, five sticks. I knew Mr. Black [Black's Hardware in Brunswick] real well. I said, "I need some dynamite. I want to drain a place that we're quahoggin'." He said, "Bud, be careful, won't you?" I said, "Oh yeah, no problem."

Well, we drained it all right. Made a fortune, me and Wes Alexander. He got drowned down here a few years back. Yup, we drained 'er, and I think I made somewheres around $1,200 out of it. We drained her down good. Today you can't even get dynamite. I got to be careful tellin' you what I got and what I don't got around here!

And now the stupid town has passed a law that dynamite noise might bother somebody. One time Taylor [a cottage owner from away] over here tried gettin' a law passed that the lobster fishermen couldn't haul their traps down by his shore before noon!

Was he from away?

He was, least ways in his head. That was one miserable son of a bitch.

Tell me about the submarine I hear you built.

I'd done deep-sea diving with a suit and helmet for years. Me and my brother started in by putting buckets over our heads and pumping air into the bucket. I never could swim a stroke. Course I had to move from one spot to another underwater. I don't know if you call how I did that "swimmin'." With the suit on, I could swim. Take the suit off, and I'd sink. Why I'd sink even with a life preserver on!

I understand that most lobstermen can't swim.

That's right. Water's too cold. But as kids, why we'd all go skinny-dippin', girls and all. I'd run and jump off the wharf, but that was as far as I could go. Back in those days, that was how we got a bath. We didn't have indoor plumbing, so jumping off the wharf was a fun way to get a little cleaner.

Anyways, I was doing deep-sea diving, and I had some real deep work to do, so I said, "I'm going to build a submarine." It was

Carroll O. Darling of Cundy's Harbor and his son, Orville with Darling's home-made submarine, the Sea Puppy. (Don Hinckley photo)

Carroll Darling's submar...

Newspaper clipping of Bud Darling and the Sea Puppy

powered by a motor, batteries, and a long cord that went up to a generator. She carried her own air supply. I had my own mixture. I had a mixing valve. It was all stuff I made up. We had these packs that absorbed the carbon dioxide.

Where did you learn how to do all of that?

It's just common sense.

[His wife, proud as punch, shows me a newspaper clipping with a photograph of the sub, the *Sea Puppy*. Bud stands erect and proud with his hand on the sub.]

That's a good-looking submarine. How deep would it go?

Somewhere around 1,400 feet. I made two and sold 'em both. I see in the paper that one of them found a treasure ship down south. The fellow who found it and the state are fighting over who owns the treasure.

So your sub is still being used, fifty years after you built it? I think it should be in the Smithsonian. Wouldn't you like to be in the Smithsonian?

Nope. I'd like it to stay right here.

[His wife pushes another photo in front of me. This time it is of a gigantic windmill]

You built a windmill, too? How long ago?

About twenty-five years. She was 125 kW, See that shaft? [a 10-inch steel pipe] That goes eighty feet down into a drilled well casing. She's usually jacked up out of the casing about sixty feet. When I want to shut her down, I just lower the shaft down into the well. She rotated horizontal. The blades were like canvas sails. When a blade was goin' downwind, it was flat to the wind. When it turned and went upwind, it feathered into the wind so there'd be no resistance.

[Now his wife pushes a fat scrap book toward me. She says, "This will give you some insight into his life. This here is to haul boats." She points to a photo of a hydraulic boat trailer. similar to the ones used today. Next she points to a photo of a steam engine with a gigantic flywheel. "This is his generator."]

Why were you generating electricity?

Why do you think? To sell it to Central Maine Power! But that lasted just a very short time because I took sick, very sick. I thought I was gonna be done for, so I took and scrapped everything out. I thought I was finished.

[His wife says, "The teacher up at Potter Academy told me the kids used to make fun of him. Called him a dumbbell. 'No,' she said, 'Bud's got more knowledge than any of you booklearners'"]

You've sure had a lot of fun! [His wife giggles like a little girl]

I still do!

Do you have any ideas you still want to try? [now his wife lets out a loud guffaw]

[Bud goes back to the scrapbook] Here's the gyrocopter I built.

No kidding! Did you fly it?

Course I flew it! Flew it a lot. It was my plane, my helicopter.

Bud holds the trophy he won for his homemade gyrocopter.

Why did you built it?

[Now Bud gives me a look as if to say, "What are you, stupid?] So's I could fly it!

You had to read something about how to build a plane!

No, not really. I'd read some stories about this and that, and I said, "I can do better than that. That ain't nothin'."

I'd always played with kites when I was a kid. Unbeknownst to my father and mother, I built this kite. Well, the miserable thing, we got it up but we couldn't get it down.

It was big. I guess it was big! It was blowin' a pretty good breeze when we put it up. It ended up over Holbrook's Wharf [a distance of at least a quarter mile]. We had it hooked onto grandfather's cod line.

Well, we got the thing up, and there was two of us hangin' on to it. We finally had to tie it off to a tree. The next mornin' we went back, and she was gone. The cod line was draped across the trees. We hauled in the line, and it was busted halfway. The kite must have ended up across the river or out to sea.

She was eight feet tall. It wasn't bad at first. The wind down low was not so much, but then she climbed into the Jet Stream, I guess, and she took off! She was somethin' else!

[Bud hands me another scrapbook.] These are my boats. Here's salvaging boats. Here we're raisin' her up. We put tanks down, tie them to the sunken vessel, pump air in the tank, and up they come.

Here's my lighter [a barge without an engine]. That boom's a hundred and somethin' feet tall. She'd pick up 150 ton. She was never made to pick up more than ten ton. I went to New York to buy a barge and crane, and they was eight of these for sale. Pennsylvania Railroad, they used to use lighters to load ships that couldn't get in to the docks. So I bought one. It didn't have an engine.

I come home and I built an outboard motor for it. I had a big six-cylinder diesel engine with a big gear box. The shaft was fourteen feet, and the wheel [propeller] was fifty-six inches.

We took it down to Bayonne, New Jersey. We lived right on the barge. These men—oh, I almost said their names!—they said, "We hear you're pretty handy at raising vessels. We've got a boat sunk right over here. You told somebody that this rig would lift 100 ton." I said, "Yes, she will." They said, "There's no way this barge and crane will lift 100 ton. Her limit is 10 ton."

I says, "I wish I had some money. I'd like to bet with you." He said, "Would you like to have that salvage job?" I looked at it, and I said, "Ayah, I'll raise her, just as soon's I get this outboard goin'."

The name of the sunk boat was the *Victor*. She was a steam lighter, and she was big. She'd blowed up. Somebody blowed her up. Gang wars, you know.

So, we got the outboard goin'. Well, they couldn't believe it. We took that barge outa there, yanked her outa that canal, took her out around. They just couldn't believe it.

Well, the same guy come back three or four days later, and he says, "We've got a job for you." They wanted me to take all of them vessels that had been up in there in Liberty Park for years, sunk on the shore, and cut them up for salvage. There was a wicked bunch of them, and they wanted me to take charge of the whole thing.

They're probably still talking about you down there.

I'm sure they are. They was an awful good bunch of boys. Mafia. Nobody come near. If anybody come down snooping on them piers, that's the last you saw of them. They said, "You'll never have to worry." I says, "But I'm in your territory." "Well, you're an invited guest. You..." Oh, I almost said that name again! They said, "You're worried about the Mafia? You ain't never got ta worry. We're gonna send the Chairman down."

This guy shows up, a nice-dressed man. He says, "Bud Darling?" I says, "Yeah, right here." He said, "May I have a word with you?" He says, "I'm so-and-so." I said, "Yeah, well, nice meetin' you, but I'm scared to death!" He says, "You don't have nothin' to be scared of. We know who you are, we know all about you, and we know you're a good man."

He said, "You ain't never going to have a problem, and if you EVER need anything, I don't care what it is. You need money? It will be in cash, and it's yours. No paperwork.

Now, you are welcome here, and you can have any job you want. You can bid on any job and it's yours. Just tell us you are going to bid on a job, and we'll take care of the rest. One more thing. The police will be around once in a while. They'll be taking care of you."

You remember that Swedish liner got run down in the fog?

The *Andrea Doria*? I read that it had a safe with $1,000,000.

That's right. Well, this man drove up alongside the tug. He said he'd been sent by the Mafia. He said, "You've been invited to attend a meeting." I said, "Oh, what have I done wrong?" "No, no, you're the honored guest. They just want to talk to you."

So I got ready, and you'd never believe this building. We park the car. The car goes and disappears down into a pit. We're standin' there within four feet of the building, and there ain't no windows and no door! I says, "Where do we go?" He says, "Right here. Just stand here for a minute." Suddenly I hear a little noise, and I turned around and looked. Here's a door! And there weren't a thing there before, not a thing!

We steps in, and two guys, one on each side, are standin' there. "Hello, Mr. Darling," one of them says. "Come with me." We got on a little elevator. The elevator would go up four feet and stop, waited a minute, then it went up another four feet and stopped, waited a minute, went up some more.

Finally it opens up into this room. Here's this long table with twelve men on each side. The man at the head of the table says, "Mr. Darling, it's good to see you. This is the board meeting, and these are the members. We're talking about something that's kind of interesting to us. We're always looking for a project." [Bud halts—a long pause—and he gives me a funny look.] Look, I think I'm into this too far. I don't want to get into trouble.

I don't want to get into trouble, either.

It's not just you and me. You'd better turn that thing [points at my recorder] off.

OK.

JIM HENNESSEY
Winter Point Oysters
Winter Point, West Bath
Age 57

James [Jim] Hennessey is one of nine children in the ninth generation to occupy Winter Point in Mill Cove near the head of the New Meadows River estuary. The family homestead had long been a dairy farm, but when dairy farming became unsustainable, Jim found a way to keep the homestead together: farming oysters in the cove.

Summers, I used to live on a boat moored just off the oyster farm dock. Every evening an old green van and a pickup truck would appear side-by-side at the head of the pier. In the van was a man with a snow-white beard: Jim. In the truck a man with a black beard: Jim's son, Johnny.

No doubt occasional words and thoughts were exchanged, but mostly they just sat there, each in his own truck, watching the setting sun paint the sky and the water of the cove.

I once asked Jim why he sat there. "Because I'm in awe," he said. "This is as close to God as I can get, I figure."

What is the earliest memory you have of the ocean?

Like do I remember the first time I ate carrots? Memories are always made from profound or outstanding things or events. The first time I opened my eyes, the water was just there, so I don't have a first memory of it.

If I think of the first time I remember being around the water, it was the first day I swam. That was memorable because it meant freedom. Before that your mother had to be with you. You couldn't go down to the shore alone. You don't remember learning to walk, but when you learn to swim, that's something you have to accomplish.

I learned the dog paddle. I think everyone knows the dog paddle; it's an animal instinct. We went in shallow water and just dog paddled. There were nine of us kids. My cousins were around, too. In the summertime that was what you did. Wait for the tide to come in and go swimming in the cove.

How do you describe your occupation?

I guess you'd say I was a shellfish harvester. I dig clams, as well. I also run a gillnet and run a few lobster traps, which is very common for somebody on the water. Most of us don't do just one thing. Take for instance Jerry's brother [Jerry Wallace, one of Jim's friends], one of the best fishermen in Phippsburg, which means he's one of the best in the state. He taught half the people around here how to catch tuna.

Jerry's old man sailed on the fishing schooners. He died a couple of years ago of a heart attack. Like me, he wouldn't bother to go to the doctor if he had a pain. He wanted no part of it.

"Gooch," I think they called him. There's all kind of funny names given to people on the water. Another one that struck me: a guy named "Tinker" Moore, for Tinker Mackerel, which is a small mackerel. I think he was 6'4", so I don't know why they called him "Tinker." Maybe when he was little the old man called him that.

Then there is "Dirt" Murphy. This is the name he goes by. I imagine when he was a little kid he got dirty a lot, so his mother called him "Dirt."

Jim gill-netting for lobster bait

But back to my work. I guess I'd have to say that work is my life. I say I grow oysters, but half my life is fixin' roads, plowing snow and shoveling docks, you know what I mean? There's so much involved with working on the water.

I'm getting the picture that "work" will be your life until you simply can't do it any longer, until you can't get out of bed in the morning.

But that won't be the end of my life. If I can't move, I'll be working at something with my hands or just my head. You don't get involved on the water unless you intend to work, and that's why a lot of people don't do it. It's work. It's not easy work.

I know I'll never retire. I don't even think about that. When you wake up, you've got to do something. That's why I don't talk about my life as an occupation. It's just whatever I do when I get up.

How did you get into oyster farming?

When my brothers and I were digging clams, we'd talk about farming them. We lived on a farm, so why not farm clams? When I was ten, eleven years old, we were out there talking, digging clams, just for something to do. Then we found out we could make money at it, $6 a bushel at the time. I also had a job doing maintenance on some local summer cottages. My mother encouraged me to have a steady job, but I just wanted to dig clams.

But you did venture out into the world for a while, didn't you?

I took a look at it. I spent ten or fifteen years down in Baltimore.

And what did Baltimore look like to you?

Looked like civilization.

Was that good or bad?

It was what it was, still is I guess.

What did you do in Baltimore?

I worked as a tilesetter. Used to drive the Beltway down to D.C. a lot, but I always wanted to get back to the water. I'd seen enough of the Beltway. I said I'm going back to Maine while I'm still young enough and well enough, and get goin', start somethin'.

I guess I had breathed too much salt air growin' up. It caused me to have a sense of being independent, of being free, but also being part of this earth, this remarkable creation.

Speaking of creation, here we are, on Winter Point, and what we see around us are all God's creatures: cormorants, herons, seals, crows, sea gulls...

There's always somethin' going on here. Life is goin' on, whether you are watching it or not. That has a way of affecting you. It gives you a perspective—at least if you're not brain-dead.

In the city I was aware of the traffic, the stop signs, the red and green lights, the sound of sirens, the clothes people were wearing, the things they were carrying.

Here, I am immersed in nature. I realize where I fit. Humans did-n't create nature. Man is just one small part of nature. Not better than, just part of. I'm feeling this twenty-four hours a day. I don't consciously think about it, but I am, at every moment, aware of the direction and strength of the wind, the direction the clouds are moving in, the angle of the sun on my face, the state of the tide.

And, like the squirrels, you are probably concerned about the coming winter: how your oysters will fare, if your firewood will last. But you are not worried-worried, not losing sleep, because your family have survived winters here for ten generations.

Survival is a constant concern for all creatures. One of the reasons we started farming oysters was to pay the taxes on this land. Our roots are deep in this land. If we lost it, where would we go? Plus, I always thought that if you had land, it should pay for itself. I suppose that's the Yankee in me. If something doesn't have a use, why have it? My ancestors cleared the land, built barns, built ships, cut lumber, mowed the hay.

And you build your own wharf and floats and equipment. You maintain your own boats and motors, maintain—hell, build— your own roads.

That's the way it was and still is. When I was young, not having any money, if I wanted something I had to do it myself. Farmers had to be carpenters, gardeners, mechanics, welders, veterinarians. We didn't think anything of it. It was just the way things were.

I have a friend who is a groundfisher working on the draggers. I tell him I can tell he works on a dragger, not because he smells like fish, but because he's always covered in grease. He spends more time being a mechanic than fishing!

You know, mine was the first generation prohibited from digging the flats that we owned. Times have changed; the family has been here since the country, before the country. But who the hell no-ticed? Who the hell cares? Only the people affected directly.

I didn't want to become a lobsterman. I didn't want to work on somebody else's boat. I decided I wanted to oyster.

Does oyster farming require a permit?

A hell of a permit. They had this ungodly bureaucratic, fifteen-page application form. You had to pay for a biological study on your property. Getting a lease is a huge thing. Fortunately I had the time to do it and the determination to do it.

At the time I got our lease, you could get a three-year permit, because it takes three years to figure out if your site is any good. There are very few really good oysterin' sites. You have to have that very particular hard bottom, but it also has to be silty enough and have the right nutrients for the oysters to grow. People look hard for these sites. People fly over in the air, drive all over looking.

Getting a permit is incredibly involved. In addition to environmental studies and an environmental impact statement, the Army Corps of Engineers has to come and look at your site.

Would you like to send a message to the government?

I sure would. I am someone who loves freedom. and I gain that sense on the water. When you stand as a young child on the edge of the water, when you look out at the wind, there's a sense of life out there, that you're alive.

There's a lot of options. That's one thing I like about being on the water. You can be on it, or not. You can go in a boat, or not. It's a whole other world.

There's something about being in nature that conveys a sense of rightness and freedom. I have trouble with bureaucrats, because they are people who either don't sense that feeling that you get growing up on the coast of Maine, or they don't appreciate it. If they did, they'd regulate a whole lot differently.

Some regulation is necessary, but it needs to be sensible. The government can hurt a lot of people. They can put them out of business. They can change a historic and successful way of life and family. They can destroy whole communities instead of protecting them.

I think it's because they're so far away from the creation.

Aside from, and in spite of, government interference, how does one raise and harvest oysters?

We get our seed from Mook [an oyster hatchery in Walpole, Maine]. A million seed. They're like grains of salt, smaller than that.

You want to start no later than the first of June. There's a one-week window. You can get them a little earlier, but they don't grow any better. If they're not in the water and ready to go on June 1, you're going to have a setback in how they develop.

They have a sense of feed; it calibrates their metabolism. A lot of animals have that. It mechanically locks them into a certain rhythm of pumping and feeding. If they're not pumping at the rate that was set at a certain time in their development, they feel hungry.

How does water temperature figure in?

Somewhere around the first of June the water temperature gets up and creates the algae bloom. If you put them in the 15th of June, your oysters are going to be slow growing. Trial and error. That's how you learn. We've gotten seed in the middle of June and been set back six months in the harvest.

When I started ten years ago, every one used to put them out on float trays on window screen so that they wouldn't sift out. You take them out of the hatchery when they'll sit on a window screen and not fall through. I went out and bought some gnat screen so we could get even smaller oysters and try to grow them earlier, but we had no better results.

The big improvement back a few years was the upweller. That's what most people do now. An upweller basically forces water up through a cylinder, hence upwelling.

We have to rinse the seed off every day. The bigger they get, the more care they are. Four or five cups will hold a million seed when we get it, and it fills 120 racks by the time we deploy them to the upwellers.

By the time they reach a half-inch size, the volume is two or three 55-gallon drums. Then we put them in plastic mesh bags held in racks. Some peoples' leases are in forty feet of water, so they have to float the bags on the surface, but I was able to get permission from the town to have some intertidal waters. Most towns won't give you the flats because that's where the clams are, too.

Are the oysters exposed to air at low tide?

Yes, they'll come right out. You can put an oyster up on the shore for two or three days. They're hardy creatures. A clam would die in a day or two. You wouldn't want to eat a clam after the first day. It's also good to have oysters exposed to the sun because it cuts down on the fouling.

If we floated the racks, we'd have a lot of trouble with seaweed. Seaweed attracts mussels, so you'd have mussels all over your oysters. Give mussels something to cleave to, and it's not long before you're just infested with mussels.

One of the things we're looking at is going directly from the upweller to the bottom. We could do that because our bottom is hard. If it was soft mud, they'd suffocate. The clam has his siphon, the long neck that sticks up out of the mud. The oyster doesn't have that, so he can't be buried in the mud.

Oysters will attach themselves to anything hard. Porcelain fixtures, have you heard about that? They found that they cling to porcelain good, so some places they're bustin' up old toilets to make oyster ground.

What size are they when you take them out of the racks and put them on the bottom?

By the end of the year we hope to get them an inch and a half. Anything less than an inch won't make it through the winter. We used to plant in the fall, but the last couple of years we've been holding them over the winter in the racks. We move them into deeper water so they won't come out and freeze in the cold air.

How long does it take an oysters to reach commercial size?

With good seed, it will take eighteen months to reach three inches. If you get bad seed, it could take three or four years. Some sites will take that long anyway, but where we are, we have a pretty fast-growing, nutrient-rich water. You want fresh water running into the salt water to create brackish water, which grows the algae the oysters eat.

And when you get up into brackish water, you don't have the predators—the crabs and lobsters and stuff. Oysters sit on the bottom, so anything walking by looks at them as lunch, especially when they're small and thin shelled.

How often do you harvest the oysters?

Three or four times a week. The most laborious thing about this business is counting and inspecting. Every oyster we sold last year had to pass inspection. Size, shape—we don't ship the real ugly ones. They go back on the bottom to try to straighten themselves out.

Some people want a 3-inch, some people want a 4-inch. We've had 6- or 7-inchers. They're sorted by size. The ones that are too small go back to grow some more.

How do you account for the increased popularity of the oyster?

Cable TV. People watch the cooking shows. When I first went into Harbor Fish in Portland, he had one oyster supplier. He said, "No, I already have an oyster grower." Now he has twelve different oysters in there.

I've been down to Harbor Fish. That seems to be the preeminent fish market north of Boston. I noticed they sell oysters from a dozen different sources. But the Winter Points are always the most expensive. Why is that?

They're not expensive enough considerin' what it takes to grow them!

But what sets Winter Points apart?

The combination of water and the marine clay, the mudflats, in the cove. It's just the right combination of the elements we have been given here.

Is it generally true that cold-water fish taste better?

I believe so. Johnny [Jim's partner and son] reads a lot about fish. He tells me the taste of a fish is a function of the fat content. Like all animals, cold water oysters put on fat to get through the winter.

Well I know it's cold here because I've come down in the winter and seen you and Johnny cutting through the ice with chain saws to get at the oysters!

We do what we do to get by.

How long does the cove stay frozen over on average?

Only a couple of months, usually January through March.

Do you wear immersion suits in case you fall in?

Nope, we're just careful.

I knew an old carpenter who still had all of his fingers. Usually, by the age of eighty, they've lost a finger to the table saw. So I asked him why he hadn't lost a couple to his table saw. He said, "Cause I'm scared to death of the damn thing!" [we both laugh].

So, are oysters your favorite food?

Truth be told, if I want to eat a shellfish, I'll get a clam. I steam 'em; fryin's too much trouble. And I'd rather have a clam than clam chowder. Chowder's ok, but you dilute the clam flavor by adding potato. I won't eat a potato mixed in with clams—just heavy cream, half and half or somethin'.

Oyster stew is good. That's when you really like an oyster, when it's in a stew, because it's no 'tater in there, just cream. I'll tell you, another way you'd like is that casserole Joyce [Jim's sister-in-law] makes. That is a delicious thing.

I can see why oysters are a rage among chefs because, to the discerning palate, they have an incredible flavor. It would take an artist to describe. The chefs know it when they eat one of our oysters. In wines, they talk about bouquet and all this stuff, but it's the exact same thing with an oyster. It's where it grows. The taste of an oyster is basically controlled by the type of fresh water and what they feed on, just like corn-fed beef is different from grass-fed. So when you go down to a fancy restaurant in Boston or New York, they're very proud of the particular oyster they serve. Most places offer a variety, just like a wine list.

When you get a good one, you'll know it. You can taste how fresh that oyster is, so one of the things we do is expedient delivery. We take them directly from the water, get them right to the wholesalers. When someone gets our oyster, they'd have to go out and get it themselves if they wanted it any fresher.

Now to change the subject, I've been told you are a deeply religious man. If you don't mind telling me, how would you describe your religiosity?

I wouldn't. I'm not religious. I don't like organized religion. The idea may be all right, but once you form an organization to promote the idea, the idea gets corrupted in the name of promoting the organization.

Well, would you describe yourself as a moral person?

I don't think there's any such thing as a moral person.

Then do you have a conscience?

Oh, I've got one of them.

Let me recast this. Are you a spiritual person? Do you, for instance, feel like you are but a small part of a much larger thing going on?

I believe true spirituality is an individual thing. Nobody can tell you how to be spiritual. If it's not your own thing, then it's not real. Then it's just you acting out a part someone else wrote.

A lot of people read book after book about the spiritual life. They go to conferences and travel far to listen to gurus, but they never seem to get it enough to live it.

See, I grew up independent. I was given the freedom to think my own thoughts, to make my own decisions. Who is to say if someone else is spiritual, or if they are spiritual enough, or if they've got the right sort of spirit?

I don't talk about it; I don't try to instruct other people. If people care enough, they'll find they're own version.

When you sit down here in your truck every day from about 4 p.m. until sunset, what are you doing?

Reflectin'. Considerin' things.

What sorts of things?

Things like what am I doing? What the hell am I doin' here? And then I reflect on which motor needs to be fixed. It's a combination of the big picture and the little pictures.

Being alone allows you to think clearly?

Well, I wouldn't go so far as to call it "clearly." But I'm Irish, and that means I think a lot, maybe too much. In my opinion most people are too busy doin' what they're doin' to ever stop and think. They don't know, and they don't care, and they don't care to know.

It's a great mystery to me how people can live their lives without ever stopping and asking, "What the hell is going on here?"

If you don't know why you're here, then…. Let me put it this way. If you don't have a foundation, then how do you expect to build a house? If you don't know where you're comin' from, you certainly don't know where you're goin' to.

That salt air has affected my thinking, I guess.

WILLIAM "BILL" HAGGETT

Former President, Bath Iron Works
Birch Point, West Bath
Age 76

Bill Haggett runs a tight ship at the Bath Iron Works

I lived in the Bath area for nearly twenty years. During that time Bill Haggett's name was synonymous with Bath and the Bath Iron Works, but I had yet to meet the man.

He agreed to meet with me at his home, which is perched on a ledge overlooking the New Meadows River. I am already there when he arrives from work. He parks, exits, and walks toward me. An image flashes across the screen of my mind: Ted Williams, the legendary Red Sox hitter, ambling in from left field. Loose-limbed, athletic, and handsome as a movie star.

He shakes my hand. His hand is large and deployed with a just-right, self-assured grip.

He leads me into the kitchen and introduces me to his wife, Sally, and an enthusiastic Golden Retriever. Sally is crafting pastries for a political meet-and-greet they will host that evening.

I'm thinking, "This man could run for governor, possibly president."

I grew up in Bath, attended Bath schools, and graduated from Colby College. After college I served in the Air Force for three years and got a lot of responsibility at a young age, which was a good experience.

After the Air Force, I sold steel throughout Maine for a company in Massachusetts. That was also good training. I had been selling to BIW, and they'd gotten to know me a little. They offered me a job at $2.61 an hour, and that sounded good. The shipyard had been an interest of mine since I was born. Both of my grandfathers worked in the yard as mechanics, and my father worked there for forty-two years in the sheetmetal department. I also had an uncle who was a purchasing agent and another one who was foreman of the pipe-covering department.

It sounds as though you had a pretty good overall view of went on at the yard.

Growing up, I wasn't tuned in to what was happening at BIW except that they were building a lot of WWII destroyers, and people like Pete Newell, one of the founders of the company in the 1920s, was a hero of mine. I'd been conditioned by everything that I heard in my family and growing up in Bath to believe that the Newells were really special people.

We hero-worshiped people like Ted Williams at that time, but also Pete Newell was a great name in Bath. I thought that he and a few of his associates had really saved the community in the '20s. The yard was in trouble when he came in, but because of his ability to raise money and his managerial skills, the company survived and went on to do tremendous things in the Second World War.

Anyway, I joined the company thinking of the future and opportunities that might exist there for me. My expectations were not very high. I remember graduating from Colby, hoping I lived long enough to earn $10,000 a year.

Sure, at that rate a person could retire.

Yeah, I'd be in fat city! I enjoyed the purchasing department at BIW but was also involved in the community. I ran with a slate of five people for the Bath City Council, and we were all elected. Because we were a slate, one of us had to serve as chairman. At the first meeting I ever attended I was voted in as Chairman of the City Council.

Why do you suppose they elected you, the youngest member, as chairman?

Probably because nobody else wanted the job! They knew it was going to be a challenging year because we were dealing with urban renewal, and people were polarized on both sides of the issue. The arguments swirled around whether or not this was a federal program, and was urban renewal the right thing to do, or was it a socialistic kind of thing? Because I was chairing the city council, and that issue was very much in the press, I got a lot of attention which I probably never would have gotten otherwise. I was also coaching a very good American Legion baseball team in Bath. We won the State Championship and almost won the New England Championship, so I got some visibility for that.

And you weren't even trying!

Yes! At the company I was being promoted and moved into a job as assistant purchasing agent, and then became assistant contract manager, director of public relations, and eventually vice president of marketing. Those changes occurred over a period of eight or ten years. I was fortunate: the timing was right, the circumstances were right. Someone upstairs probably thought I was doing ok.

At the same time I was involved in other things in the community. During my years on the city council I also served for a couple of years on the school board. Over the years I was involved in the Chamber of Commerce, and ran United Way campaigns.

That's a LOT of work! What motivated you?

First, I love to work. Second, I love this community. I didn't stand out academically in high school, probably due to lack of effort because my priorities were in sports, but I grew up loving the community of Bath.

My family had limited resources. I think in hindsight we were probably poor, but I never felt poor at all. I managed to do the kinds of things I wanted to do, but my expectations weren't very high. Saturday we typically went down to the YMCA and hung out, played pool and basketball and ping-pong. We were down there with our friends, and we developed great friendships. Those friendships have continued to this day. By the time I graduated from Colby and began to progress at BIW, I felt as though I owed the Bath community. They had provided this safe nest, a nice education, a chance to play sports—the things that were important to me.

So you feel you were parented by the community as much as by your parents?

I've always felt that way. I still do to this day. Those kinds of feelings conditioned a lot of what I did in my later life.

Let's get back to the Bath Iron Works.

From vice-president of marketing I moved on to vice-president of operations, and then president and chairman of the board, and CEO. My college major of history, government, and economics wasn't ideal for running a shipyard, but I spent a lot of time with the operating people—the chief engineer and the production managers—and acquired enough shipbuilding knowledge by osmosis to feel comfortable.

I also spent a lot of time on ships and in the production shops, and I got to know the people in the business as well as possible in a company of that size [we grew to 12,000 employees]. By the late 1980s/early 1990s, BIW was booming. We built twenty-five Navy frigates, cruisers, and destroyers, but we also built freighters, tankers, container ships, and roll-on/roll-off ships.

The shipbuilding business was very competitive. There were more shipyards back then: Ingalls in Mississippi, Newport News in Virginia, General Dynamics in Massachusetts, Avondale in Louisiana, and Todd Shipyards on the West Coast. We were always in a competition, yet we won the majority of competitive contracts.

I have heard over and over that Bath-built ships are the best.

Oh yes, the ships BIW builds ARE the best, the best in the world, and the cost of building ships at BIW was lower than anywhere else. It's a tribute to both the workers and the management of BIW. The leaders and supervisors and the mechanics in the company embrace the notion that they want to be the best. That doesn't happen in a lot of other places. I've visited and observed what happens in other shipyards and wondered how in the world they ever built a ship!

Pride is a large part of BIW's success.

Is that a function of the quality of the Maine worker?

I think that is part of it, and perhaps an important part. But BIW has a great tradition and heritage. BIW is the oldest shipbuilding company left in this country. As was true in my case, there are generations of family members involved in the business, coupled with a continuing influx of capable people from the outside. That combination has motivated the work force to want to continue to excel, to maintain its reputation.

When building a warship you need to focus on the fact that the ship must be capable of engaging the enemy and prevailing in a hostile situation. You're always aware of the fact that there will be 200 to 300 young people on that ship. No matter what happens at sea, the ship has to bring them home safely. You can't emphasize too much building quality into a vessel whose performance means life or death to its crew.

I think because Maine has so much coast, and so many people own boats, BIW workers are more aware of the demands placed on vessels at sea.

I never thought of that connection. I'm living on a boat now, and being out there in bad conditions always reminds me of how important the quality of construction is.

Absolutely! Think about being in the North Atlantic in a frigate or destroyer in a twenty-foot sea. You're up and down and taking water over the bow. Well, at times seas get to be forty feet or more, and the wind blows eighty knots!

One of the things we did when we were building the frigates, which looked a bit top-heavy, was take them out into the North Atlantic and expose them to the worst icing conditions we could find. We made a conscious effort to demonstrate that the ship could remain stable and functional with a huge ice buildup. Weather can build up inches of ice on the superstructure of a ship, and it gets very top heavy. We proved the frigates could survive under the worst conditions.

I have built houses from plans. Those plans contains hundreds of details of how it all has to fit together. I cannot imagine the millions of details in the plans for a modern warship. It boggles my mind.

It is amazing. Ships today are built in large modules. The ship goes together like a series of building blocks, one block at a time, each block weighing a thousand tons or more. That's 2,000,000 pounds! Every module is pre-fitted with ventilation, piping, electrical cabling, and connections. All interface connections have to match the connecting module within a small fraction of an inch. Gigantic cranes move modules into place. The fit has to be perfect, close enough so you can bridge the gap with a weld. It is a very complex business, and BIW does it very well and is a leader in the use of that construction technology on combatant ships.

Why are the ships built in modules?

So that you can build them on flat ground indoors, in a controlled environment. Maine winters are severe, and working outside on steel staging covered with ice and snow is tough work. Just cleaning off the snow and ice before you can begin to work is time-consuming, not to mention dangerous.

Think of just going to the bathroom. Inside it's a two-minute walk to the bathroom. Outdoors you'd have to climb down off the staging, walk 500 yards, take off your heavy coveralls, and then reverse the process.

Building inside, everything is better, easier, and more cost-effective. Every generation of management at BIW has found a way to build larger modules and a way to outfit them more extensively. Today they are installing machinery and equipment, shafting and components which are very sensitive to alignment that we never would have attempted to install twenty years ago.

After the modules have been welded together, the ship is very close to being complete and ready for launching?

Yes, and the earlier you install the outfitting, the lower the cost. Once the hull is enclosed, just moving machinery around inside is difficult and time-consuming. Without pre-outfitting, shipbuilders would have to cut large access holes in the hull, remove stiffeners, slide the machinery in, then reweld the stiffeners and replace the piece of hull cut out for access.

How's this for a housebuilding analogy? You have framed the bathroom walls, attached and finished the drywall, installed the cabinets and fixtures, hung and trimmed the door, and then you notice you forgot the tub.

That's a very good analogy!

I left BIW in my late fifties and thought, "I'm out of the ship-building business forever." But then I got a call.

Jim Irving asked if I would be willing to manage his Irving Shipbuilding operations in Canada. They were having some difficulties, which wasn't surprising because Canada had been out of the Navy shipbuilding business for about thirty years. I agreed, and Sally and I moved to Canada and bought a home in Saint John. We both had a great five-year experience in Canada, and the shipyard eventually produced some excellent work. Today, those ships are the backbone of the Canadian Navy. There's a lot in common between the people of New Brunswick and Maine. Building good ships is just one example.

I think Maine people are more similar to their neighbors in the Maritimes than they are to people in Massachusetts.

I agree with what you say about Massachusetts. The program ended up successfully for both the Canadian Navy and Irving Shipbuilding, so I felt good about those five years spent in Canada.

In 1998 we moved back to Bath and got involved building a new YMCA. I spent a year and a half raising the funds, doing most of the solicitations myself. Half of the people in Bath have been approached by me requesting money. Thanks to a lot of friends, there was a tremendous amount of support for that program.

In the middle of that, the Libra Foundation [funded by the late Elizabeth Noyce, ex-wife of the founder of Intel, and devoted to helping startup Maine businesses] approached me and asked if I'd be willing to help manage a potato company in Mars Hill, Maine. I said, "I've just come back from Canada, and I'm sixty-five. I will do it with the understanding that I can continue to live in Bath and commute. I'll go up there two or three times a month for a couple of days." Fortunately, the man who founded the company had been a potato farmer and understood the industry. The business just had problems with sales. The founders had built and opened a beautiful factory, but after a few months the business was almost bankrupt because it didn't have enough customers.

What was the potato product?

Refrigerated potatoes. They are about eighty-five percent cooked: mashed potatoes to half a dozen different recipes, other potatoes that are sliced, diced, shredded, or cut into wedges, everything but french fries. We used Aroostook County potatoes and within a couple of years were selling them all over the United States. Our big customers were chains like Ruby Tuesday's and Bob Evans.

Our potato products cut a chef's prep time to five minutes. You could go into a Ruby Tuesday's restaurant and order a potato dish, and it would be served in five minutes. In 2005, the owners sold the potato business, and the investors, including many Aroostook potato farmers, got their investments back plus interest and dividends.

As soon as the Libra Foundation sold its share of the potato business they turned their attention to the Wolf Neck Farm natural beef business and again asked me if I would be willing to serve as chairman of the board and CEO. By then, I was seventy-one and hardly an expert in cattle or beef. But if you know anything about management, you can adapt to new challenges.

Wolf Neck grew rapidly. We acquired a facility in Fort Fairfield that had been used for composting potatos but had a couple hundred acres of land with it, so we created a cattle feed lot and put cattle in there.

Is the beef organic?

It's natural, meaning the cattle receive no antibiotics, no growth hormones, and eat a vegetarian diet—the way our grandfathers raised beef. We're focused on treating the animals as well as we possibly can and producing natural beef that tastes good.

By 2011 we had 2,700 cattle in the feedlot and were buying 300,000 bushels of barley every year from local farmers. That's 5,000 acres of barley. The facility produces 300 tons of cow manure and bedding material a week, which we truck eight miles to the old Loring Air Force Base where it's spread into half-mile windrows and becomes composted cow manure. Then we sell the finished compost. Our largest customer is a Maine company that bags compost under the name Coast of Maine. They mix our compost with seaweed, clam shells, mussel shells, and all kinds of things.

One of the things we're trying to do is convince farmers in Aroostook County to use this compost on their fields, not only to reduce their fertilizer costs, but to build back the organic matter in the soil.

When you wake up in the morning, do you look forward to getting to work?

Oh, Jesus, yes! I wake up two or three times every night thinking about the job and the issues I'm dealing with. The only reason I'm working is because I WANT to work. I try to avoid pulling a lot of money out of the businesses for myself and often pay the people who work with me more than I pay myself. My primary objective is to make the businesses succeed. Obviously I measure our success in financial terms, but also the company's impact on the state of Maine, particularly as it relates to employing people, either directly or indirectly. Recently, we reacquired the potato business and merged a cheese making component into that company. Now Pineland Food produces meat, potatoes and cheese.

Maine has such a rugged climate, you have to be a pretty together person just to survive. I think many Mainers take pride in toughing it out instead of abandoning ship and running down to Florida. I saw a sign on a lawn the other day that said, "WINTER—BRING IT ON!"

Sally and I don't go to Florida. We wouldn't be happy living there. I suppose I could live here and not work, but sitting home so many days in winter would be difficult. Being stuck inside, reading a book or watching TV, isn't my cup of tea.

Speaking of winter, I had an interesting experience at BIW. It was the middle of February, and I had gone home sick. John Sullivan, who was then president of BIW, had issued a directive, "No use of company property for personal reasons. Anyone who violates this rule is subject to termination." The work force was paying attention.

About 5:30 in the afternoon BIW got a call from the Coast Guard, asking if it would send the company tugboat across the river where there were smelt shanties on the ice because a lady had called saying she thought she saw a light on the ice.

It was a terrible night. The wind was blowing such a gale you couldn't walk to the location of the light. The captain of our tug said, "I'm sorry, we've been told we can't use the tug for anything but company business."

The night superintendent called me and said, "Mr. Haggett, would you approve taking the tug up the river to check out this light?" I said, "Oh, God, I can't overrule the directive, but I'll come down and go with you. If anyone gets in trouble, Mr. Sullivan will have to fire me."

I got dressed, went down, and got into the tugboat. We crossed the Kennebec, and Jesus, was it a terrible night! The little tugboat went across the river, under the bridge, and plowed through a half mile of solid ice. The captain said he thought he saw a light, so we kept pushing. Sure enough, there was a light, and it was coming out of a little aluminum dory. We pushed up to the point where the bow of our tug was against the boat. Lying in the bottom of the boat was a man holding a little pocket flashlight over the side, praying someone would see it.

The crew got off the tug and lifted the guy up. He was frozen solid. Have you ever seen anybody who is frozen solid? He was alive, but he was like a piece of wood. We couldn't bend his legs; we couldn't bend his arms. Fortunately he couldn't bend his fingers, or he would have dropped the flashlight.

There were four of us on the tug, and we brought the guy up to the small pilothouse. I had a heavy coat on, so I took him inside my coat and wrapped my arms around him.

The man had been checking out smelt shanties. He was apparently planning on putting fishing equipment in the dory, but he got disoriented, went in the wrong direction, and broke through the ice.

Fortunately, he managed to pull himself back out of the freezing water. He knew he was on thin ice because he'd already gone through once, so he climbed into the little boat and laid down.

He had this little pocket flashlight, and the lady on shore saw it and figured that something was wrong.

The tug captain backed out of the ice and recrossed the river to the shipyard. We called ahead, and an ambulance met us at the dock.

The person we had picked up was Freddy Pecci, a tree climbing expert in Bath. He was the guy who would go up and limb trees. God, was he skinny! By the time we got back to the shipyard, he'd got his teeth going, but they were chattering so fast he couldn't get a word out. You got a feeling that night what it's like to work on the water in Maine in winter!

They took Freddy to the hospital but released him a day later, none the worse for wear. The next Thursday night Freddy went to the Yankee Clipper [a notorious local bar] and was sitting at the bar. He got into an argument with the man sitting next to him who pulled out a jackknife and stabbed Freddy in the back. The bartender called an ambulance, and Freddy was back in the hospital.

The Bath paper ran a story the next day with the headline, "It's Been a Tough Week for Freddy Pecci." One of the all-time great headlines in Maine journalism! [we both laugh]

I'm sorry, but I just can't get away from the Bath Iron Works. It was such a large part of your life. Can you tell me any more about the pride of the BIW workers?

Well, one interesting aspect of what happens to workers who have been with BIW a long time, is their ability to identify the ships they have helped build. They see a concept start as nothing but a design and end up as a finished ship years later. They launch and deliver a ship, and then, for the next thirty or forty years, they follow its life.

Once you work on a ship you never forget its name, and because most BIW ships have been warships, they are always doing important things in distant places under interesting circumstances. BIW employees take great pride in following the accomplishments of Bath Built ships.

It's not like working on an automobile where you have no idea where it ends up?

Right! A ship in the Persian Gulf was chasing pirates. They were assigned snipers who set up on the stern of the ship—kind of a gruesome story—and the snipers shot the pirates. That was a Bath-built ship!

The *Samuel B. Roberts*, a BIW frigate, hit a mine in the Persian Gulf, blew a hole in the bottom of the ship thirty-three feet long and thirteen feet wide. Blew the engines and the reduction gears up. Fire shot 200 feet into the air. The stern of the ship cracked and dropped down so water was coming over the stern. The crew fought the fire for hours, and eventually the fire died out.

The commanding officer called me from the port where his ship had been towed. He said, "Bill, we owe our lives to the welders of Bath Iron Works." He said, "That ship should have broken in half and gone down. Do you know what it's like to be in the waters of the Persian Gulf? The Persian Gulf is full of snakes and sharks. It would have been a disaster."

There wasn't a single loss of life on that ship. Whether you were a BIW painter, welder, or CEO, building one of those ships is like birthing a child. The child goes out into the world and does things that reflect on you. It's a very special feeling when they perform well.

I have been involved in seventy-five BIW launchings and can't recite the names in sequence, but I know the histories of these ships. Each one reflects directly on the workers, Bath Iron Works, and Maine, and the vast majority have brought great credit to their builders, past and present.

JAMES "JIMMA" TOTMAN
Pine Tree Service Center
Phippsburg
Age 64

Jimma Totman, Chief of the Phippsburg Volunteer Fire Department

Coastal Maine villages consist of more than just fishermen and boat-builders. For a period of six years I lived in the Town of Phippsburg, which contains no fewer than five small fishing villages. If the social fabric of the town could be compared to a network, there would be two nodes: The Center Store and Pine Tree Service Center. The latter is presided over by "Jimma" Totman.

For some reason Jimma wants to meet me at the Phippsburg Volunteer Fire Department after locking up the Pine Tree Service Center.

Jimma is waiting just inside the door when I arrive. As he steps out to greet me I can see why we are meeting here. Jimma is the Chief. Festooned in the Chief's uniform and badges, Jimma resembles General George Patten of World War II fame.

Jimma, I've met three of your brothers. How many children did your mother have?

Seven in all; I'm the youngest.

And are they all in Maine?

All except one. Adele moved across the line to New Hampshire. My oldest sister moved to New York for a while, but she came back.

I have heard that your family goes way back, that one of your brothers has an original deed from the King of England.

Brother, John. Seventeen sixty-nine. Has it framed up on his wall. But my brother Tommy is the real historical one.

I also noticed driving through the town center that there is a Totman Library.

That was a great, great uncle of my father's. I guess he bought the building and made it into a library.

And your mother?

She was the librarian forty-seven years. She was born in the Spite House.

What and where is the Spite House?

Well, it used to be down at the Center, but now it's up to Rockport.

How the hell did it get up to Rockport? That's fifty miles!

By barge. Down the Kennebec, then up the coast to Rockport.

[I looked up the Spite House on Wikipedia. It said, "In 1806, Thomas McCobb, heir to his father's Phippsburg, Maine, land and shipbuilding business, returned home from sea to discover that his stepbrother, Mark, had inherited the family 'Mansion in the Wilderness'. Upset about his loss, McCobb built a home directly across from the McCobb mansion to spite his stepbrother. The National Park Service's Historic American Buildings Survey photographed and documented the 1925 move of the McCobb Spite House by barge from Phippsburg to Deadmans Point in Rockport, Maine.]

The Spite House

When you were growing up, was there a big emphasis on people doing public service?

Oh, yes. When I was really young I can remember what was called the PTA. It was a lot of volunteer men and women. They helped with all kinds of kids' programs.

Was that the Parent-Teacher Association?

It was a school thing, but they didn't meet in the school. They met in an old wooden building that used to set right next to the water [Kennebec River] here, by Center Pond. I can remember going there for the fluoride treatments for your teeth. They used to do that for all the kids in town.

That was pretty advanced thinking for this part of Maine. I remember moving to Woolwich, right across the river, about forty years ago, and it seemed that few people over thirty had any teeth of their own. I asked why that was, and I was told because no one ever went to a dentist until it was too late, and then they had them all pulled out.

Ayah, I remember a whole bunch of us walking down from school to the PTA once a week for four weeks. They put this clamp in so you couldn't close your mouth, then they swabbed this fluoride on and told you not to swallow. That was a big thing.

Another thing they had while I was growin' up was a little, small fire department. It was an old wooden building up here by the Center Store, and they had an old panel truck they had a pump in. That's all they had.

Did it carry any water?

No, no water. Just a pump it took four people to lug. They'd lug it to a well, or a pond.

Did they ever put out a fire?

They saved a lot of foundations [laughs].

And chimneys?

Ayah, them, too [still laughing].

My father was Fire Chief for quite a while. While I was growin' up Bill Blaisdell and Hammy McCourt and Maurice Blair, they got together and bought this old truck and built a tank on it. They did the plumbing. They put a 200-gallon pump on it, and a 500-gallon tank, and a ladder rack. It was an old telephone company truck. Yup, they painted it bright red. Had that quite a while.

They had that old truck right up to '58. That's when they built this place. Three bays. One bay was longer than the others. They used to store the winter highway salt in here, too, along with the telephone truck. The salt come in bags at that time.

Later we picked up a couple of old oil trucks to carry water in. We had one that would carry 700, maybe 800 gallons. Of course we had to plumb them, too. Then in '65 we bought a brand-new fire truck.

That must have taken a lot of baked bean suppers!

Ayah, I think the truck was around $22,000.

Then we had three old Dodge Army trucks that we got surplus

from the government for a dollar, or somethin' like that. The guys just built tanks on them. Them things would go anywhere. You couldn't stop 'em.

A lot of fellows around here handy with plumbing?

Very handy. A lot of them worked at the Iron Works [the Bath Irons Works, a major builder of naval ships].

Do you suppose any of the plumbing materials came from the Iron Works?

Oh, it come from everywhere: the Iron Works, Sebasco Lodge [a local summer resort where three of the Totman brothers worked for years].

Were BIW and the lodge aware of their generous donations?

Well, the fellows who donated the stuff certainly were. Anyway, around '59 or '60 they started an ambulance service in town. The three volunteers used their own station wagons. They borrowed a stretcher from the Bath Hospital. They started it because one of their mothers had to go to the hospital, and the nearest ambulance was in Bath.

This is a big town, so it would take a long time for an ambulance to get down the peninsula from Bath. How many miles of road are there in town?

There is about thirty-three miles of road, so they started that service and ran it for a long time.

The next vehicle we got was a hearse. We run that for a while, but the fire station wasn't big enough to hold it with all the trucks and salt. That's when my brothers and I had started the fillin' station [Pine Tree Service Center, still owned and operated by Jimma]. So we used to keep the hearse in there overnight to keep it warm.

Hearses are generally black, so did you paint the old hearse red or white?

No, we just put some red lights up on top.

Where did you all get the training to work on an ambulance?

The first ambulance licenses we got at a class at Morse High, a bunch of us. It was done through the hospital. We had doctors as teachers. Now you have to have the EMT [Emergency Medical Technician] license. Some of the paramedics we've got now are real good.

When did you start volunteering for the fire department?

I started with the fire service by following my father around when I was ten. All the guys was on it at one time.

The guys?

My brothers John, Owen, and Tommy, and the Doughty boys, and the Harringtons, the Bowkers. That's about all there was right here in the center of town.

Of course Sebasco Lodge had their own fire truck, too, and they'd show up and help out. If it was bad enough, Bath would come down, too. But now we're in a mutual-aid system with the whole county. There's ten towns in the county, so we could all get called out.

Since I've been in the fire service [fifty-four years, since age ten] we've traveled quite a bit around.

I see from the patch on your shirt that you are the Fire Chief.

Yup, I took over from Robert Beals in '92.

I heard about you being named "Citizen of the Year."

2001, I got the "Mainsail Award" from Morse High School.

What was that for?

For volunteerin' I guess. I try to do a lot with the kids and working with people.

Phippsburg is a big town. I looked it up, and it is forty-four square miles in area. Is the Pine Tree Service Center the only service center in Phippsburg?

The only one I know of. We started it in '67 or '68. Started with my brothers, John and Owen, and Albert Gray. I did all the work days, and they all worked nights. I did the mechanic work. How we really got into the service station was I worked a while at a filling station in Brunswick, and right across the street was this Esso station. Well, they was busy just all the time. Then I worked at the lodge for a summer with my brothers, and I kept tellin' the boys, "We ought to build a garage and go Esso." So Albert owned the land, and we built the buildin', and we signed a contract with Exxon. We were with them for over twenty years.

The four of you owned it equally?

Ayah, and we were all in there together about seven years. Then my cousin, Clint Richardson, decided to buy them out and go into the heating oil business, too. So we bought them out, and Clint lived up where I am now. He had a big piece of land there, and we built a new garage and put in big bulk oil tanks.

Back then a service station wasn't just a convenience store where you pumped your own gas. They really did offer auto service, like fan belts, tires, hoses, and minor repairs.

Ayah, there aren't many of those around any more. The other day I had a fella come in, from New York City, I believe. I come out to pump the gas, and he couldn't believe it. Said he'd never seen anything like it.

Someone told me that the people in town will actually go out of their way to buy their gas at your station and pay ten cents more a gallon, just to make sure you don't go out of business.

[Jimma chuckles and looks embarrassed.]

I actually heard a fellow said that if Jimma's station folded, he'd have to leave town.

I don't know about that [still chuckling, but not denying].

Yup, we do quite a few of the vehicles in town.

I remember a few weeks after I had moved in I sent my wife down to get her brakes fixed. When you were writing in your

appointment book she said, "I'm Judy Wing." You said, "I know who you are." It seems there isn't much you don't know about what goes on in this town.

Ayah, we have a lot of ears.

You might compare Pine Tree Service Station to the Internet: all information flows through your station.

Well, it actually starts at five with the mornin' coffee crew at the Center Store. The information flow can get pretty heavy there.

What time do you start work at the station?

Well, after the Center Store we have more coffee at the station. We generally get to actual workin' at about eight or nine.

Do you think your sense of giving to the community was instilled by your father and mother?

Yes, oh yes.

Are there other families like the Totmans in town?

Yes, the Doughty family and the Harrington family and the Bowkers, they give a lot to the town. And there's the Blaisdells; they gave a lot for years.

Why do people think they should give back to the town?

I think it all started because people didn't have a lot, so everyone tried to help each other.

I remember being in a group of liveaboard sailors in a remote harbor in the Bahamas. There were 300-400 boats there for the winter, but there were absolutely no hardware stores, no marine supply stores, no boat-repair businesses. Every morning at 8 a.m. everyone would turn their marine radio to channel 82. Some volunteer would act as a moderator. I'm sure it was illegal, but he'd say, "Does anyone out there need anything this morning?" A boat would come on, "This is *Fairwinds II*. We have a dog aboard who cut his paw on a shell and his leg is all swelled up. Does anyone have any antibiotics?" Another boat

would say, "*Blue Waters* needs an O-ring, ¼ inch by 1-1/4 inches." Then a few minutes later, here would come a dinghy with the antibiotics or the O-ring. The person might get some homemade muffins in exchange, or they might get nothing but a thank you.

I always thought that was similar to the way it was in small towns in Maine.

Yup, that's the way it was. Now its a little harder to get volunteers. One thing is people have to work so much now. Families aren't what they used to be. They have both the husband and the wife workin'. Some have two jobs. And the kids! Parents spend hours chasin' the kids around.

Are there any young people coming along to volunteer?

There's a few, but they're gettin' harder to find.

Are they from the same old families?

Some are. My son's on the fire department. my daughter's on the ambulance, my other daughter has been tax collector–treasurer.

How many Totmans have been selectman?

My father was and my brother, Tommy. My son run four years ago; lost by one vote. Pretty good for just a couple years out of high school. Number of people tried to get him to ask for a recount, but he said, "No, the other fella's ok; I'll get another chance."

My father always said that if a fellow came to see him personally, he'd vote for him. It'd show the fellow wasn't lazy.

I usually see your wife down at the service center.

Ayah, she does the books. She's also on the Fire Department Ladies Auxiliary. They do all the fund raisers. They have the Christmas Fair. They have another fair in July, one in November. They have different sales and stuff.

How much do they raise in an average year?

Oh, they do real good. They raise close to $10,000 a year.

Didn't I get stopped in front of the fire station one summer by someone asking for a donation?

Oh yeah, we have a toll booth on the main road. We only do it once a year, the day of our Field Day. It's always the last Sunday of July or the first Sunday in August, when the tourists are comin' or goin' to the state park or to the lodge.

People from New York might think you were a bunch of terrorists, except you always seem to have the prettiest young girls in town as the toll takers.

Oh, we have it set up so its completely voluntary. You don't have to stop, but a lot do just to flirt with the girls.

Are a lot of people moving in here from away?

We've had a few from Massachusetts and New Jersey. They move here and stay for a year or two, but then they sell out and move.

Why don't they stay?

A lot of it is there's not much goin' on. All they have to do is spend one winter and lose their power. In the ice storm a few years back we lost the power for a week. This last winter we lost it again for three or four days. They're just not used to this type of livin'. Too slow I guess.

You know how it is around here. You call up a fella to do a job, and he says, "Yeah, ok, we'll get you Monday." Course he don't tell you which Monday. You don't want to rush into things.

I know that if I wanted my car fixed in Portland, they'd take me in right then. Of course they'd take my wallet, too. But here it might take two or three weeks to schedule a look at your brakes.

Oh, now, you know. First thing in the mornin' we don't do much. After coffee at the Center Store, we come down here and open up. Then we have to discuss town affairs. Then of course the contractors are all there. Someone will come in and say, "When are you going to get to my job?" "Oh, we'll get to it; don't get all nervous now."

I remember needing Harry Doughty to dig a foundation hole. After three weeks of waiting, I asked your brother, John, what to do. He said, "Well, you have to call Harry before 5 a.m. when he leaves the house." What I didn't know was that Harry wasn't headed out at 5 a.m. to a job; he was headed to the Center Store to catch up on the news. Anyway, I commenced to calling him every morning at 4:45. He'd always pick up the phone, and the answer would always be the same, "Well, I've got you right top of the list. I'm doin' the best I can, but its been awful wet."

Eventually Harry showed up, and he did a great job. And the bill was more than fair. I never questioned his integrity.

Another example is your nephew, John Totman, Jr. I wanted this new house, and I spent all winter drawing up detailed plans for it. I had seen the one he built for himself, so I took my plans over to him. I said, "I'm quite impressed by what you've done here. Would you be willing to look at what I've drawn up?" He sat down and unrolled the plans. Within a minute he said, "You don't have enough headroom in this stairway, and the landing at the bottom is too short." I was impressed. I said, "Are you building for others?" "Yes," he said. "Well, would you mind looking at these plans and telling me how many man-hours it would take?" "Just a minute," he said and started writing down numbers. After about five minutes he said, "2,200 hours." "How sure are you of that?" I asked. "Sure," he said. "Sure enough to do the job for a fixed price?" "Yup."

He built the house in 2,180 hours and deducted the 20 hours from his fixed price. After I wrote the last check I said, "John, you could have gotten twice what you charged." "Might be," he said, "but I charge what I think it's worth."

Yup, he learned that from his father.

When we built the service center, his father, John, helped us. We was putting the roof on. We had just started putting the rafters up, and John said, "You know, this is a big area up here. Why don't we put on a dormer and make an apartment?" No plans or nothin'. After about the third rafter he said, "We'll cut her right here, and put the dormer in here." Worked out fine.

Phippsburg is surrounded by ocean, but you are miles from the water. Do you feel connected to the ocean in any way?

Oh yes, I deal with the fishermen. Biggest part of my customers are fishermen—probably forty percent. Occasionally we do some boat davits, or some fellow will come in and say, "Can you straighten out my propeller shaft?" But mostly we do their trucks.

A lot of rust from the salt water?

Yeah, we see a lot of that. Actually, when they're that rusty, you can't even weld to them. But we do a lot of patching up—brake lines and stuff. But of course now a lot of them are making so much money, they just buy new pickups.

They say they are suffering from the cost of fuel and bait, because of the low prices they get at the dock.

Oh yeah, yeah, I listen to that every morning, and then here they come with a brand new truck. If a fisherman don't complain, you know he must not be feeling well.

Remember when the draggers were doing poorly, and the government was buying back the boats? The government had this program where, if some one could prove he was a fisherman just by showing two past years tax returns, it would buy his boat and pay for two years of retraining. Do you remember what happened? Not a single fisherman showed up, because they couldn't produce the tax returns!

Not too many could. You might say their taxes were a little shaky. Still, they're good people.

WILL BARNET
Artist
Sebasco Estates, Phippsburg
Age 100

"Vigil." part of the series: "Women of the Sea" by Will Barnett

Will Barnet, an iconic American artist, painted summers on the coast of Maine for nearly sixty years. His works are found in the collections of every major art museum in the United States.

When I heard he would be residing and painting at his daughter, Ona's, Rock Gardens Inn in Sebasco Estates in the summer of 2010, I called to ask for an interview.

His enthusiastic response: "I have tried to write how I feel about art for fifty years, but after writing a few lines I always pick up a brush and start painting again. Perhaps you can write down what I have to say!"

Will lost the use of his legs two years ago in a fall. When I arrived at his cottage, he was seated in an office chair with wheels, busily sketching at an easel. I held the screen door while his wife, Elena, helped Will propel the office chair onto the porch. We sat looking out at the sea.

Years ago we spent summers in Italy, and I used to drive on the Amalfi Drive, the one you see in the Hollywood movies. Then one summer we decided we'd rent a house in Maine. We rented this house in a beautiful spot just up the coast from New Harbor. It overlooked the ocean and out toward Monhegan Island.

Well, I was captivated by it because, as I stood on the porch and looked down the coastline—we were high up—I said, "My God, this looks just like Amalfi Drive!"

I love the ocean, I think, because I was born on the ocean. I was born in Beverly, Massachusetts, in 1911. My father built a house just three blocks from the ocean. I used to row from Beverly over to Gloucester with a friend. So I grew up more or less an ocean person.

Can you put into words the appeal the ocean holds for you?

In the first place, from where we lived on the top of the hill, the ocean had a wonderful color. It was dark, almost black, and under the surface were all these rocks and ancient species you could pick up and hold in your hand. It was like being in prehistoric time.

And I like the way the light strikes the ocean, the variety of light as it reflects from the surface, and then as it penetrates. But the thing I like best of all about the ocean is the feeling of space. Space is important. It allows you to dream.

Did you fantasize about what was over the rim of the ocean?

Where I lived in Beverly there was a big lighthouse. I used to sit on the rocks below the lighthouse, and across the bay was Marblehead. I wanted to go to Paris and become an artist, so I dreamt that Marblehead was Paris.

Do you have a first memory of the sea, perhaps some event when your mother or father took you to the beach?

I don't remember anything of that nature. The sea was just something that had always been there.

I asked a fisherman that same question, and he said, "The sea was there when I arrived into the world. It was just always there in my awareness."

He's right. That's the way it was with me, too. It was there when I was born.

Well, how old were you when you starting thinking, "I want to be an artist?"

I decided I wanted to be an artist when I was ten years old. Seriously! I used to buy watercolor sets from Mr. Foster on Cabot Street in Beverly. Mr. Foster was six-foot five, a very tall guy who ran a store where he sold art supplies along with a lot of other things.

Did he treat you as a serious artist at the age of ten?

He had to take me seriously! One thing about me was that I was a tall kid. By the time I was twelve I was almost six feet. I looked more or less like an adult. Back then, three or four generations ago, people weren't that tall. Today I would have been six-foot ten!

What sort of work did your father do?

He worked for United Shoe Machinery.

Like so many New Englanders back then.

That's right. He made an income. He kept the family alive. He worked day and night. He also felt that he didn't want his children to work in factories. I used to laugh when he mentioned that. I said, "Are you kidding? You'll never see me in a factory!" I told him, "If I'm not going to be an artist, then I'll be a gardener. I am **not** going to be inside. Forget it!"

Did you have brothers and sisters?

I had one brother, about fourteen years older. All my siblings were much older, so I was essentially an only child.

Do you think, "Hey, maybe I was a mistake?"

Yeah, my mother had me when she was forty-five. I guess I must have been a surprise, a BIG surprise!"

But an auspicious birth for you! You made it into the world.

Yeah, I made it, just in the nick of time!

What about your schooling?

I went to a wonderful school in Beverly. It was like a little red schoolhouse. It was actually bigger than that, quite a nice big building, but the education was like that in a little red schoolhouse. Very New England: wonderful teachers, kind women, but very few men teachers.

Strict, but very nice, too. And if you were cute and nice the women liked you even more! I had a nice relationship with my teacher.

I fell in love with my third grade teacher, Miss True.

That's possible. That is possible. It's very natural. I remember Mrs. Cressy, my first-grade teacher. How many years ago was that? Ninety years ago! She was lovely. Another very good-looking teacher was Mrs. Montgomery, in seventh grade, a beautiful woman.

And I began to have trouble with the girls. They used to chase me! I was a good-looking guy.

I don't feel sorry for you. [Will beams and laughs, obviously relishing the memories of being pursued by girls.]

So I had a pretty good start in life. It wasn't easy, though, because the mills caused in an influx of Canadians from Halifax. They were rough, very backward, and I used to have a lot of problems with them, a lot of fist fights. There were a lot of bullies.

Were you good at fighting?

Not particularly skilled, but I had long arms. I never got beaten up because I could hold them at arm's length. Most of the time it was a draw.

When and where did your art education begin?

At the Beverly Public Library. They had wonderful books on art, and I studied them. I used to borrow all their books. When the librarians saw I was so involved in the history of art, they gave me the key to the top floor, which had all the great volumes and portfolios of reproductions and things.

Libraries are one of the great institutions in the United States. The Beverly Library was a godsend to me. It was a glorious library to go into, like a museum.

Did you have art courses in high school?

No, we didn't have art of any kind in the school system.

Did you attend an art school later?

Yes, after dropping out of high school, I went to the Boston Museum School. I spent two years with Phillip Hale, a wonderful man of the old school. He had studied in Paris and taught at the Academy in France. With him I studied drawing—mainly cast drawing [drawing plaster casts of sculpture] and life drawing. He was a good man.

In those days the teacher was way up there, "Sir." You didn't call him by his first name. But I was already having my own ideas, so I didn't worry about whether I was as good as my teacher. I wanted to study what he had studied, and then do whatever I wanted outside of the school. We had a very good relationship for two years.

After two years I said, "Boston is too damned small. I want to go to New York." I was nineteen, and it was the beginning of the Great Depression. I remember 1929 when everything went down, like a bolt of lightning hitting the ground, BANG. Mr. Hoover was the president. The other president I remember really well was Mr. Coolidge, who used to take a nap every afternoon. He was a farmer, and he wasn't much of a president.

They say he may have been our least intellectual president.

He sure was! And Hoover wasn't far behind. I hit New York with ten bucks in my pocket when the bread lines were around the block, people waiting in line for food.

Wasn't there some good art created during the Depression?

Yes, there were some good artists, but art wasn't very popular at that time. But it didn't make any difference to me. I was going to be an artist anyway. I remember my supervisor in high school, Mr. Gaylord—isn't that a nice name, Gaylord? He asked me what I wanted to be. I said I wanted to be an artist. He looked me straight in the eye and said, "Barnet, are you crazy?"

Artists didn't make any money back then. No one did art for the money. Artists in those days came from wealthy families. No one ever talks about that, but I was very aware of it because I was so poor.

I had a good relationship with a fellow artist whose parents had old New England money. With that old money, they could paint any time they wanted and not worry. But some of them did have talent.

But I was on my own with no money, so I came to New York. I was lucky because the real estate market had collapsed, and you could rent a room for a dollar a night.

Where did you get a dollar a day? Were you selling your art?

Oh no, I used to do different things. I painted signs, a sign painter. For a while I was a part-time librarian because I liked books a lot. I always wanted to do prints, graphic stuff, and one of my great heroes during that time was Daumier, a famous French artist. So I began to work on lithograph stones.

I also won a scholarship to the New York Art Students League, a four-year scholarship. That was given me by a well-known artist. I didn't even know him. He just saw my portfolio and wanted to help me.

I began my studies at the Art Students League in the graphics department, where I learned how to print stones, lithographs. I became a professional printer. I made my living in the '30s as a printer, printing fine art for other artists.

Later on I was a supervisor for a short time at the WPA [Works Progress Administration]. They wanted me because I was technically very good. I eked out a living between my salary of eight bucks a week, plus a few bucks from the government. I ate at the Automat. My regular meal was Boston Baked Beans.

That was smart because baked beans give you everything you need: protein, fiber, carbohydrates.

Right. I was doing heavy work, lifting stones, and there was no
meat. So I lived on baked beans, beans and bread. The Automat
was a wonderful institution.

How old were you at that time?

I was twenty years old. I had left high school in my senior year. I
knew what I wanted to do with my life, and high school was holding me back. I was anxious to get on with my dreams.

As it turned out, dropping out of high school didn't hurt me a
bit because years later I became a professor without even a high
school degree! I was exhibiting, I was becoming pretty well known
as an artist, so when I applied to the university, they put me in,
not as a student, but as a professor! [laughs] They don't do that
anymore. Today you have to have degrees by the tons. I have
taught at universities all over the country. [Among others, Will has
taught at Cooper Union, Yale University, Cornell University, and
the Pennsylvania Academy of Fine Arts.]

Pretty soon I came to be recognized in graphics, and I showed
in galleries that were very good. But art was not popular as an investment. Today art is an investment. Collecting is still only for
the wealthy.

Back then there was no money for art, for music, for any form
of art. Artists made only enough to exist. Things today are very
different. Young people today go into art thinking they are going
to make money. They are like Mr. Gaylord. They are crazy!

My father's generation worked like slaves. My father didn't want
me to be an artist. He wanted me to be a lawyer or a doctor, because
they made money. He almost disowned me because I didn't listen to
him. But years later he appreciated me. Just before he died, but up
until then, boy, oh boy....

After graphic art, was there another period?

Then I became a painter. There was a distinction between graphic
art and painting. Graphics people did etchings, woodcuts and
things like that. I went into oil painting because there is a preju-
dice in the art world. If you do graphic, they identify you as a

graphic artist, limited in technique. So I played down my graphics and pushed my oil painting. After I became well known as a painter, I could do my graphics and still be considered an artist.

But to you, graphics has always been equal to painting?

Oh yes!

What about computer-generated art? Is that looked down on because the computer is involved?

Well, it's mechanical. I don't want to criticize it, but when you have the human touch on the canvas, and your mind is interpreting the reality, not a machine, there is a difference. I'm not in a position to get involved in that argument any more because I have argued enough already.

What about photography?

I have always looked upon photography as something very different from painting. When I first came to New York I tried out photography just to see what it was like. I had a dark room and everything. At the end of a year of doing photographs I found that I didn't have a feeling for it. Photography bored me, so I went back to painting.

Photography limits you because you can't alter what the camera sees. And the result is very flat, too. In painting you can get a sense of physical presence. The paint and the canvas have life, like real skin. The brush strokes add to the feeling. It's very different. But that's just the way I feel.

I read somewhere that your art balances the universal and the personal. A lot of your paintings have to do with your personal life.

That's right, my family, but also the universal. The scenes in my "Women of the Sea" series are not personal. They're personal only in how I feel about them, but they're really about history, the role of women, like the woman standing on the widow's rock looking out to sea.

Like Winslow Homer's "Watching From the Cliffs?"

Yes, in that vein.

Your paintings actually remind me of Winslow Homer!

In many ways, when I work in Maine, I am like Homer, no question about it. Yes, very Winslow Homer, yet different.

Your paintings are stripped of all unnecessary detail.

Yes, they are more abstract.

I saw a painting of your daughter, Ona. I know Ona, and I immediately recognized it as her, but at the same time, she could be any woman.

That's right, universal! I'm glad you caught that! The personal: Ona and the universal: young woman.

I've done a lot of portraiture, but my portraits are different. They are not photographic, yet you know it's the person. I capture the person. I can be realistic if I want to be, but I choose not to be. You don't have to show every detail to capture a person.

Are you the only popular artist working in this graphic style?

Yes, my work is very individual.

That's good for you, isn't it?

Well, it's good and bad at the same time because you are like a lone wolf. You are not disagreeing with, but you are diverging from, the mass of artists. You leave yourself wide open to criticism.

When you sit down to start a painting, do you ever have the feeling, "This could be my best ever?"

No. When I start I am always excited, I feel it is going to be an interesting piece, I hope it MIGHT be my best thing, but I don't start with the feeling it will be.

I spend a lot of time on my work. It's not knocked out. I'm like a man building a castle. I have a foundation, and I build it up slowly in small sketches. It becomes bigger and bigger and bigger. My first idea is sometimes that size [holds his hands to indicate about six inches square], and then they become larger and larger, and pretty soon they are big canvases.

So you do a number of versions.

Yes, I don't go, like van Gogh, and lay down the final canvas. It has to do with the way I am as a person. If you were van Gogh you would start right on the final canvas. I have nothing against that, but it's not what I do.

So you don't envision the final work before you even begin?

Right. First I do a little sketch. Only then do I begin to see what it's like. Then I consider whether it's going to be a big painting or a smaller painting.

But the part we haven't discussed is my teaching. When I began in my twenties, I was the youngest teacher at the league, and I taught there until I was in my eighties.

You must have really enjoyed teaching to do it for fifty years!

I loved it.

What was so gratifying about teaching?

To communicate with younger people and discuss your ideas. You don't tell them they have to be just like you, but you show them the principles of good art, what makes a good painting. You see, painting is a language. It's not just something to look at. It has a language, and its language is visual.

When I look at a painting, should I look for a message?

That's right, so I taught them the language of painting.

Did you consider teaching to be your duty, something you wanted to give back?

First it was just for income. Later on it was just a love of being in contact with younger people. For instance, after the second World War we had the GI Bill. That GI Bill was one of the great bills of democracy. The GIs used to come to study with me. They were grocery clerks before the war, and during the war they changed their minds and wanted to be artists.

Did any of your students gain fame?

Some of them made more money that I ever did! I don't mind that at all. I like it.

Back to your "Women of the Sea" series. Is the coast of Maine necessary to these paintings?

Yes, it is. There is something about the Maine coast. The series could only have been done in Maine. Understand how the series began. My wife, Elena, was standing on the porch one evening, and she was looking out to the sea. She made this wonderful silhouette against the sea. It suddenly struck me that she was all women who have scanned the sea, over the ages, for the return of their loved ones. Elena has been the model for all of the women in the series.

Elena brought me to Maine. She loves the sea and the light in Maine, so, in a sense, she introduced me to the very elements. I was born into the world of Maine through my wife.

NICHOLAS SEWALL
Hermit Island Corporation
Hermit Island, Phippsburg
Age 74

Nicholas Sewall, steward of a Yankee tradition

Between 1820 and the early 1900s, the Sewall Shipyard on the Kennebec River in Bath, Maine, built approximately 100 square-rigged sailing vessels of wood and of steel. In fact it has been said by maritime historians that the Sewall Shipyard defined Maine shipbuilding.

Nick's father, Sumner Sewall served as the governor of Maine from 1941 to 1945. Arthur Sewall, Nick's great-grandfather, was William Jennings Bryan's running mate for president in 1896.

We are sitting in the office of the family mansion, surrounded by ship models, large paintings of Sewall square-riggers under full sail, and an imposing floor-to-ceiling bookcase of leatherbound nautical volumes. Take away the rotary phone and the single green-shaded desk lamp, and we could be sitting in Arthur Sewall's office in the 1800s.

The first memory I have of the sea is listening, while taking a nap in the afternoon, to the steam-powered fog horn on Seguin Island. It was the most strange yet enticing noise that a young boy could probably ever experience. That was 1940; I was four or five.

We spent the whole summer at the family cottage at Small Point, and as I grew up, we sailed boats in Sprague River. We had a beautiful 12-foot lapstrake lugger-rigged sailboat that we moored in the Sprague River, right below the cottage. A beautiful little river at high tide; you couldn't get into trouble unless you went out the river on the outgoing tide and went crashing through the breakers ... which my brother and sister did, and actually sailed that little lugger lapstrake all the way to Seguin [six miles off the mouth of the Kennebec River, a treacherous area of the Maine coast]. Unfortunately my father found out. There was quite a commotion that day at dinnertime.

You come from quite a nautical family. Can you tell me a little about the history of the family?

Our immediate family—father and mother, and even grandfather and grandmother—weren't nautical in the sense that they spent much time on the water. Grandfather's job was really selling the remnants of his father's shipyard, which was located right here on the Kennebec River.

It was a wonderful shipyard. It was actually the shipyard that built the first steel sailing ship in America, the Scottish-designed four-masted bark, *Dirigo*, that's right there [points to a model in the corner].

They of course started with wood. That [points again] was a cargo ship, the *William D. Sewall*. Then there's the *Edward Sewall* in the hallway. I'll show you the very first ship, built in 1820, just around the corner, the *Diana*.

Shipbuilding was very good to the family, but it all went to pieces when the Panama Canal was built [the canal opened in 1914] because steamers would have to take so damned much fuel to get around the Horn [It is 14,000 miles from New York to San Francisco by Cape Horn vs. 6,000 miles via the canal.] They couldn't really carry cargo as cheaply as a sailing ship. Although the sailing ship might take two months or more to make the trip, at least when it arrived it was stuffed full of cargo.

Anyway, the steamer came, and that was the end of the sailing ship. Then the First World War came, and tonnage went up, and I think there were still some Sewall sailing ships, and they kept them during the war. In fact, the first cargo ship sunk in the First World War was the *William P. Frye*, which was a sailing ship. It was bringing grain to England.

After the war, the Sewalls stopped building ships. They leased the yard to the Texas Company, which at that time started to rivet together tankers to carry oil. The Texas Yard burned, and right now we have just forest and woodlands and river where used to be a very busy yard.

Everyone was building a ship. At one time there were twenty shipyards in Bath. But the canal ended the building of ships.

The sailing of ships, as I said before, commenced in the Sprague River in the forties. It bloomed into the family buying a Small Point Class sailboat, which we raced as a family.

My father also had a very nice Gomes-built Hampton, and my brother, father, and I would go out and troll for tuna around Casco Bay. That went on for a few years, then all the kids had to go into the service, or went to college. The Hampton was covered up and stored at Hermit Island.

The last boat we had was the passenger vessel *Yankee,* which we got at Montauk Island in 1964. It was built in '46 on Staten Island by a company named Peterson, that actually specialized in building tugboats. She's built like a tugboat, and hopefully will last as long as a tugboat. Sixty-two years later, she is still sailing out of Hermit Island on scenic cruises and fishing trips.

I ran the *Yankee* out of Hermit Island for a couple of years. I can't really call that work. It was the nicest occupation I could think of. But things got busy at the island. The campground grew, pressures grew, problems grew, and I finally left running the *Yankee* and became very involved in running Hermit Island Campground.

Nick and his treasured Yankee

How did Hermit Island Campground start?

It started after dad's political days. He wanted to get involved in Maine business somehow. He got hooked up with the Brown Brothers in Boothbay, who were at that time packing sardines, buying lobsters, running a smack out to Monhegan. Chet Brown, one of the younger brothers, persuaded father to build a lobster holding pound. These are tidal pounds, dammed to the half tide level, and above half tide wooden slats that allow the water to go in and out to exchange the water. A nice circulating pound. He thought that was a wonderful idea. He said, "I've just bought this piece of land at Small Point called Hermit Island," and lo and behold, there was a nice cove at the northern end. In fact the cove was used in the 1700s for tidal power to run an up-and-down sawmill, which we uncovered when Mace Carter built the dam. Incidentally, Mace Carter was a wonderful New Englander.

Mace had the barge and the crane and the forge on board, and he would make his own hardware, drive his own piles, and he probably drove every piling from Boothbay to Portland. A real

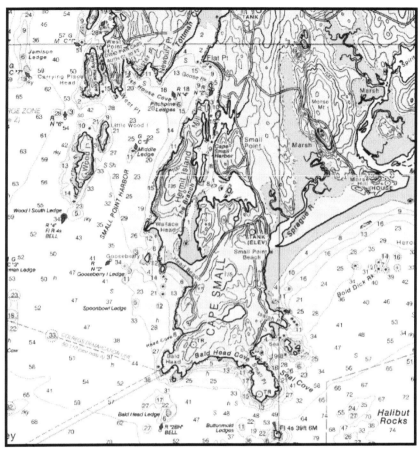

Hermit Island Campground [in center]

New Englander who would put on his diving gear—not the modern rubber diving gear but hard hat and air hose—and jump off the edge of the barge. He'd make sure everything was good on the bottom. Hardworking, good man.

Mace built the pound in '48, the Brown Brothers would lease it from father, and they would put 30,000–40,000 lobsters in, and father would get ten cents a pound. That was a very, very good business, and I've carried it on, although it's a different game than it was a few years ago.

Basically, we ended up with a beautiful piece of land, Hermit Island. It's called Hermit because when Dad grew up at Small Point, one of the things the kids would do would be to steal a skiff and row over across, and spy on the hermit. According to history, it was Morse's Neck at one point, and was Macintyre's Neck at one point. It was just the Neck at one point. So it's Hermit Island now, and goodness knows what the next name will be.

It's about a mile and a quarter long and a half mile wide. It expands at low tide. I can tell you a story about that, too, as far as being taxed. I think we're taxed at low tide.

That's how we got into the camping business. We had to generate more income to keep the island. That is sort of the story today, isn't it, with land? We thought of cottages, we thought of motels, we thought of every possible thing, but one afternoon father got my brother, Dave, and me, and we hopped in our '52 Pontiac and went to Sebago State Park. We wanted to see what was going on there. We spent the afternoon riding around, came back that evening, and said, hey, that's the least damage to the land.

We started with 14 sites, and it was very successful. We now have 275 campsites on 275 acres. We've kept two thirds of the island wild, with nature trails and so on. Still at the northern end we have some commercial fishery business, and we have a shop that we lease out to a boatbuilder. It's balanced quite well.

However, the future is really clouded by the inheritance tax. My brother died a few years ago. We experienced how good the death tax is. Good at killing businesses. The problem is that the town has zoning only to 250 feet back from the shore. In the middle of the island you can do anything you want. What happens is that death comes, your estate is appraised, and the land is appraised. Having no zoning in the middle of the island, it's zoned at the highest use. The highest use for oceanfront property is for wealthy people to come from out of state and build these million-dollar cottages.

So it's going to be very interesting to see what happens when it has to turn over again. I suspect that it will probably have to go to some sort of conservation agency.

Is that double taxation?

It's multiple taxation! But it's been a good life. It's interesting that our government designs the economy in an indirect way. They don't do it right up front; they come in the back door. The government, in effect, said to Dave and me—well me, because Dave was now dead—you guys were suckers, spending your life in the camping business. You should have been selling that unique, beautiful island to the "highest purpose" out-of-state millionaires instead of offering an ocean camping experience to less affluent folks.

That annoys me very much [now quite agitated], the idea that government was telling us what we should have done. It's bad enough that they tell us what we should do, but to, after the fact, say oh, you guys were suckers. Basically that's what they said.

Why didn't you sell it as lots and pocket ten million dollars?

Basically, a certain affection for the land, and a certain lack of importance to the second million, third million, fourth million in life. Every year we met 2,500 campers. In the winter we'd deal with fishermen and so on. I thought it was a very rich life.

I have heard that Hermit Island campers don't recognize you as the owner because you are in disguise as the garbage collector.

That's right. But I haven't gone as far as pasting on the mustache and glasses. It's a small business. In a small business, if the garbage man gets sick, there's still garbage, so what do you do?

You earlier referred to your affection for the land. Does that affection have anything to do with the fact that the island is surrounded by the ocean?

Definitely. It is a very special place, and I feel that we have to take care of it. As long as I'm involved, I want to protect it and I want to see it forested, and I want to see it not beat up, I want to see people enjoy it. And I want to make a living from it.

Now that you're at the end of your career, is there anything that you would rather have done for a living?

I wanted very much to go to Maine Maritime Academy. I wanted to really try being a mariner. I wanted to be that close to the sea. I couldn't, I didn't, because of pressures. Family pressures. Society pressures. Being born into in a social group where people don't go to Maine Maritime—they go to Harvard, or Bowdoin, or they go to Colby. The expectations were such that the Maritime wasn't one of my options.

I can't say I feel sorry for myself. The opportunity is gone. Forget about it. That's my feeling. Even when I was in graduate school in New York, I used to go down, wander down to the piers at 44th Street and listen and look at the old Pennsylvania Railroad steam tugs. They used to go back and forth pulling railroad cars. It was a yearning.

The *Yankee* is your last connection to the sea?

That's right. No, I have one more—the skiff in the lobster pound. The *Yankee* was sort of my way of keeping a connection with the sea. It was a way of combining Hermit Island with respect and love for the sea.

In your 74 years, have you observed the ocean changing or is it ever constant?

It's changing by the number of people using it, both from the standpoint of watercraft and the use of beaches, recreation. I think the ocean has gotten warmer. In fact, I know it's gotten warmer. I remember cutting ice in the pound, which sometimes would get as much as twelve to sixteen inches thick, with a chainsaw, and poling it out through the gates on the outgoing tide. We haven't had ice for six or seven years.

One of our pound keepers, with a straight face, remembers his grandfather taking a pung [a one-horse sleigh] and going over the ice from Small Point all the way to Portland. I think if we ruin the sea it's going to be from increase in global temperatures. It isn't from pollution. We're doing pretty well on pollution.

The ocean is actually cleaner now than it was fifty years ago. I remember in the early days Small Point cottage owners going out in the middle of the channel and sinking their garbage. They'd put it in a paper grocery bag along with a heavy stone or brick. Of course the bag got soft, the brick went through the bottom, and the garbage popped right back up. But they had disposed of their garbage.

Is there anything else you'd like to say?

Yes. Just a little bit of romanticism which you can cut out, but our involvement in shipping, in building ships, affected me about three years ago when we had a charter for the *Yankee*. We picked up a group of environmental reporters at Bath. It was one of those perfect summer days. We took them up the Kennebec to Richmond. I wasn't in the pilothouse; I was aft. We went right by the old Sewall shipyard, and I noticed up on the *Yankee's* masthead the Sewall flag flying in the breeze, blue with white [he chokes up]. It just struck me as being strange. That Sewall blue-and-white flag, still flying. It was on a very small wooden vessel, but going by the old yard was emotional for me. Looking at that blue flag.

HERBIE LOVEITT
Lobsterman
Five Islands, Georgetown
Age 94

Herbie Loveitt: from the film, "Where's Herbie?"

I had seen a trailer on YouTube for a fifteen-minute documentary titled "Where's Herbie?" It featured a buoyant 91-year-old Maine lobsterman, still hauling seventy-five lobster traps. The movie title derived from his wife's poignant query prior to his daily visit to her Alzheimers ward.

It was now three years later, and I had heard his wife had passed on. I wondered whether Herbie had lost his enthusiasm for life. I called his home and a voice boomed, "Here's Herbie!" Assured that he was still afloat, I asked if he might give me an hour or two for an interview. "An hour or two? Got plenty of them; you can have all you want!"

Five Islands, Georgetown

Herbie, when were you born?

I was born on September the 18th in 1915. Now I can't remember the exact hour because I was pretty young then. I was born at home on Georgetown Island.

Were your parents farmers or fishermen?

No, my father was a city slicker. He was born in Portland [Maine's largest city, 1910 population 58,571].

What did he do for work?

Horses, workhorses. Everything went along fine because there was plenty of work for horses. They was just exactly the same as a tractor or 18-wheeler today. But then along come gasoline motors, and the bottom fell out of horses.

There was a lot of barter system in them days. Someone would have a bushel of potatoes, and your neighbor would have a bushel of peas, so you'd get together. Now the fishermen, they didn't have any land. Didn't want any. They just wanted to get close to the water.

I had relatives that were born sailors. There was a couple of them with Captain licenses.

When you were small did you go out in boats?

Did you say, "Go out in boats?" My father didn't care about boats at all, and I couldn't get my hands on one when I was four, five, six years old.

You were on Georgetown Island, but inland?

Two and a half miles from the water. Might's well of been up country. Could have been in Aroostook County [Maine's largest inland county, in fact the largest U.S. county east of the Mississippi] just as well.

Were you expected to work when you were a child?

Expected to?! [incredulous]. We wasn't expected to do anything. We done it because we was told to. As soon as we could do anything, we done it. There was lots of things we did that we weren't too happy about, but we didn't question them.

What were some of the things you had to do?

I had the animals to feed and water, and this was before daylight. In the winter it was dark, and we had to get up and water them horses and feed them horses, and after that we could have breakfast. Then we'd get up from breakfast and get on our feet and walk two miles to school.

When you came home from school did you have more work?

Oh, the same thing. Had to feed and water them. All of that livestock had to be fed and watered.

Did you have chickens?

Chickens? Yes, we had chickens. Why, if we didn't have chickens, we wouldn't have any hens; if we hadn't any hens, we wouldn't have any eggs!

Did you have a cow?

A cow? Of course we had a cow. If you hadn't a cow, you wouldn't have no milk or cream or butter or cheese.

Did you heat with wood?

Wood? Yes, all wood. My grandfather, probably at one time, owned half of Georgetown. It was all trees. As soon as we could lift a saw and an ax, we had to cut wood. We had a woodshed, probably fifteen by twenty feet, attached to the house right next to the kitchen. That woodshed had to be full before the first snow. That woodshed probably held ten cord [a cord of wood measures four by four by eight feet and is equivalent to about 250 gallons of heating oil].

We cut it all by saw. It was nothin' to walk up to a tree, two to three feet in diameter, one on each end of a cross-cut saw. Why you can't find a tree today on Georgetown Island that's more than eight to ten inches in diameter.

What did you have for breakfast?

Hah! Anything that didn't bite you back. I'd say the typical breakfast was eggs, fresh eggs from under a hen. They was still warm—just come out of the hen.

The yokes stood right up?

Oh yes, they stood right up, three-quarter of an inch.

Did you ever lift a hen up to get the egg?

Yes, and the hens frowned on it. At a certain stage, when the hen got close to settin', you could tell by lookin' the hen in her eye, and you'd say, "OK hen, I'll go on to the next one." When they're settin' they don't want to talk to you.

What happened after a hen stopped laying?

Why, they went into the vinegar or salt to preserve them.

No refrigerator?

Refrigerator? What's that? Later on we had an icebox. You'd put a big block of ice into this insulated box. Before that we had a well, probably thirty feet deep. That was our refrigerator. Put the butter into a container and lower it into this well. It was probably forty-five degrees all year round, 368 days.

Was the well close to the house?

Close to the house? How about eighty yards, in three feet of snow, with fourteen horses and twenty-eight hens and a cow to water twice a day.

How many trips would you have to make?

That's what I asked my father. I said, "I know if I went to the water bucket I'd take about a glass of water. How much do I give that cow?" He said, "When she stops drinking, you stop haulin' water." Well, I know for certain that cow could drink 325 gallons of water! You wouldn't believe how much water that cow could hold. I was only six years old. I couldn't lift a whole bucket, so I carried two half buckets. When I got to the cow I poured them together. That cow would stick her nose down into that bucket and [makes a sucking sound], that bucket was empty—just like that! So back to the well! Now this in three feet of snow!

How long did you go to school?

Well, the law said you had to make eight grades. You had to start when you was seven, and you had to make eight grades.

It was 1930 or '31 when I graduated from grammar school.

That was during the Depression.

Depression! We was in the depression five depressions before that one!

What did you do after you graduated from school?

Now it's possibly in '32 or '33, in the summer, an old buddy of mine and I walked up to Bath, seven or eight miles, and we went to a carnival. There was a lot of carnivals back then. We was up there, lookin' for—oh, well, anything exciting, you know.

Like a girl?

A girl? What's that? No, we was up there, just snoopin', trying to get in trouble, and somebody walked out from the "Terraplane" and they said, "You workin'?" We said, "No, we aren't workin'."

He said, "You want a job?" We said, "Course we want a job. You gonna pay for it?" He said, "Sure, we'll pay you." We said, "Then of course we want a job."

Well, it was about ten, eleven o'clock at night, and they started taking this ride down. They'd take a part off and set it down, and they'd say, "This has got to go on the truck to go down to the train station."

Everything went along just fine. We got the whole thing torn down, and down to the train, and into a boxcar. Then he said, "OK, I'll pay you." I don't know what it was, but it wasn't a dollar. Nobody back then had a dollar. Then he said, "You want a job?" I said, "What do you mean?" He said, "You want to go with us? You want to work for me?" I said, "Well, I wished I knew. I dunno." I never thought about leaving Bath. I said, "I dunno.... Yep, I'll take it."

Did you have to ask your parents?

Oh yes, my parents had to know everything that happened, everything that was going to happen, because you was taught that right away when you came into the world.

You were fifteen. Were you a strong kid?

Oh yes, I could pick the world up while you put a rock under it. I was physically perfect, nearly. Anyway, we went to Gardiner. I got paid. Everything went along good.

Were there girls working at the carnival?

Ooooh... that was part of the excitement! And they was pretty girls. Can you imagine one of them pretty girls walkin' up to you and sayin', "Would you like to pay my rent for the week?"

I said, "No ma'm." I didn't have any idea what she was talkin' about, but I was pretty sure it was too excitin' for me!" I didn't have much schoolin' but I had a fair amount of common sense, which when you come down to it is all you need. I think what you should have is ninety percent common sense and ten percent education.

How far did that carnival go?

Just in Maine, all the country fairs. Did that for five years. Worked at home winters; worked the carnival summers.

What were the carnival people like?

You know, carnival people are misrepresented. There is better people in a carnival right today than there is down there in Washington, D.C.

In the spring of 1937 my brother got ahold of me and said, "You want a job at the Bath Iron Works?" I had been working in the carnival and things were getting monotonous and whatever, so I said, "Yes I do."

They was building more ways [ship's ways, where a ship is built and launched] because they knew they was going to have trouble, what with the goin's on in Europe. So they put in three more ways. I ended up working for the Iron Works as a shipfitter.

In 1940 the government passed a law that any man of a certain age would get one year of compulsory military training. We didn't know it, but the government could see it coming, and they was getting ready.

I got drafted the spring of 1941. I went to Fort Devens, Massachusetts. Away we went; that was the end of living, I tell you. The military is a caste system and I hated the whole thing. I didn't like anybody telling me what to do. The first thing they tell you is, "You're in the Army now; you belong to the Army; you can stop thinking right now 'cause we will do your thinking for you."

I'd been thinking ever since I was knee-high to a duck, you know? I didn't like that worth a damn. But I see'd the handwriting on the wall.

Course I'm a gabby old soul. I talk to everybody. I like everybody. I don't care whether they're big or small, tall or short, black or white or red or yellow. And everybody likes me, so I'm talking to these fellows who had been in there for eight or nine years. I said, "What's the best thing to get into here?" "Well," they said, "what are you looking to get away from?" I said, "People telling me what to do so GD much." "Motor Transportation," they said.

"There ain't no money in it, and you won't be a First Sergeant tomorrow. What are you looking for down the road?" "To get out of this GD thing," I said. "Motor Transport," they said. "No night watches and a mess hall ticket twenty-four hours a day."

So they put me to driving a fire truck. We was laying there, twelve hours on, twelve hours off, just the same as a fireman today. Then some guy comes in and says, "Anyone here ride a motorcycle?" Now another thing the old veteran had told me was, "Don't volunteer, ever, for nothin'." So I kept still. Another guy volunteers, and they take him out. Forty-five minutes later he comes back, and he says, "They do have a motorcycle, and they want somebody to ride it, but I couldn't get the thing started."

Now I'd had an old 1928 Harley Davidson. I knew how to start a motorcycle. I went with the fellow down to the field where they had twenty-five or thirty motorcycles. "Jump on and ride that thing around the ball field here," the fellow said. I found the magneto ignition; cut the switch up on it, and [makes a whirring sound] started up. Rode around the field, and the fellow said, "You're riding motorcycles now." I rode that son of a bitch right up 'til it started snowing. "Dispatch riding" was what they called it. Best job I ever had!

But then they replaced the motorcycles with jeeps. So then I was back to motor transport, driving anything with a motor that needed to go somewhere.

It was December, 1941, and my year of compulsory training was just about up. I was looking forward to getting out of this place. In fact, I vowed I'd never ever set foot in Massachusetts again. Anyway, we got up one morning and looked at the bulletin board, and it said, "No more discharges." They had bombed Pearl Harbor, and I was in the Army then. I didn't get discharged until 1945.

Went to the South Pacific. That was a nasty business. Every coconut tree had a Jap and a rifle in it. I know just how a deer feels in hunting season. Just waiting for "bang."

I got along; I did my job. But then my skin started going to hell. Jungle rot. Some of those soldiers got fat. It improved their whole being 100 percent, but mine went the other way. This area here [points to a spot on his leg] was just meat, no skin at all.

Finally a doctor said, "I've done everything I can. The hell with this. I'm sending you home." "Oh, Jesus," I said, "don't do that, doc." [laughs]. That was 1943. I came home on a hospital ship, but them bastards still wouldn't let me out.

I got back to Letterman General Hospital in San Francisco. They had some wing-dingin' dermatologists there. The doc said, "Where you from?" I said, "Maine." "Oh, that's good, that's good," he said. "I can guarantee you'll be all right when you get back to Maine."

They sent me back to Fort Devens, and I got better.

Did they discharge you then?

Hell no! They had a point system. Enough points and you were supposed to get out. I had points forty numbers long: two years in the jungle with Japs shootin' at me, jungle rot with my skin falling off, and they still wouldn't let me out!

They said, "We're going to give you a train ride." I said, "Good, its about time you did something nice for me." Well, they sent me to Lake Placid, New York, for two weeks R&R."

At least that's a cold place.

Cold place? I guess it was cold. Cold as welldigger's ass!"

So, where did you meet your wife?

In Bath. We'd co-inhabited for two years before I got drafted.

Did your parents know?

Oh, yes, and her parents, too. We didn't leave any question marks around.

That was very modern thinking for 1940.

Oh yes, but I think it ought to be the law. Works better that way. You should have to co-habit for six months before you go marry because in six months you'll know whether it is going to work with that woman.

Marrying a woman you don't completely know is responsible for 102 percent of the problems today. You don't know who you are marrying.

Hell, you don't even know yourself!

Very true, very true. Gorry, I wish I'd thought of that. [Hands me a photo of a young couple.]

She looks sweet.

Yes sir, sweet she was; that she was.

Do you remember how you met?

I can remember it just as good as it was yesterday. Late one afternoon I was down on Front Street. I had my old Chevrolet car. She and a friend were walking down the street, and I was parked alongside the street there, and they come up and stopped for no apparent reason I could see. I just tucked my head out the door and said, "Hellooo!" That has worked quite well for me in the past.

Well, they kept on walkin'. Some time later in the afternoon, here comes Virginia—that was her name—and she was alone. She stopped, and we yacked, yacked, yacked, probably two or three hours. I said, "Want to go to lunch?" She said, "Well, I dunno, well yes, I guess prob'ly." So we went somewhere and had lunch.

I dunno where that was, but I do know that later on that afternoon we ended up in Brunswick because I said, "I've got to have a beer." I used to drink quite a lot of beer. She didn't make no comment about it, so we went to a little place in Brunswick. I ordered two beers. The lady brought them over, set them on the table. I drank mine before the waitress had set it down, but Virginia's beer just sat there. I ordered another, and that disappeared, but her's was still sittin' there. Well I drank about five, which was about normal for me, and her's still set there. So I said, "Ain't you going to drink your beer?"

"Yech," she said. "I don't like that stuff!"

This was 1939, and I haven't had a drink since!

She was more important to you than beer?

Yes, she was.

Were you aware of a feeling that...?"

Yes, that this was the woman, this was the woman. I knew the first time I see her.

How long were you married?

Sixty-three and one-half years.

Did you ever stray?

Nope. Never crossed my mind; never had a fight. Oh, we had to sometimes compromise, but nothing ever came between us.

Any children?

No, no children. I blame that on medical science. In the thirties and forties, they didn't even know where a child come from, medically speaking. You know what's happened with medical science between 1940 and now?

Yes, now they know how to make a baby out of nothing!

That's right. You go down to the doctor's office, and you say, "Let's see, I think I'll take three." "Well," they'd say, "they come in sixes, but you'd better hurry home because you'll have 'em before you get there!"

Well, when did you start lobstering?

1963.

You were forty-eight then. Did another lobsterman show you how to do it?

I worked with some of the best fishermen around as an apprentice, as a sternman.

So the older lobstermen taught you the tricks.

Yes, and they teach you the hard way. When I first started, I'd set out five traps, and them bastards would cut off six. They don't want more competition. I went to grade school with ninety percent of them fishermen on Georgetown Island, and they still give me a hard time. It's greed; like anything else, there's a lot of greed involved. The way they look at it, every lobster you catch is one they won't.

In the old days some of the more ambitious lobstermen had two or three thousand traps!

That's right. Now they have a limit on the number of traps.

Is it 400 now?

It was, but I'm not sure. The state makes a new law every twenty-four hours, so its hard to keep track.

You've been lobstering forty-six years. Did you ever take a break?

I retired in 1983, at sixty-eight years of age. Sold my boat and traps. Borrowed a travel trailer and went to Florida. Went to Key West.

Down with Ernest Hemingway?

Who's that? Name sounds familiar, but I don't know the fellow.

Well, did you like Key West?

Not too much. Too many people and too many bars. Beers was five bucks, and you'd have to drive twenty miles before you found a parking spot.

What did you do when you returned?

Went back lobstering. I was bored. There was nothin' to do, and I can't stand that.

Watching television wasn't enough?

Watching television will kill you. You have to have something to get your ass out of the recliner. That's why I go lobsterin'.

I see you have an exercise bicycle in the corner.

What's that? Oh, that thing! Somebody give me that thing, but it has only one wheel! No, that's what I use to bend up my wire traps. Bend them over the seat. I made five traps last winter. Saved probably fifty bucks.

REV. ROBERT E. "BOBBY" IVES

Carpenter's Boatshop
Pemaquid
Age 63

Bobby Ives in the Carpenter's Boatshop

We parked under a huge oak in the center of what appeared to be a working farm. Behind us, a pile of logs awaited milling. Ahead, a flock of chickens policed the unfenced yard of a weathered farmhouse. Across the road stood an imposing Amish-style barn, no doubt The Boatshop.

Seemingly from nowhere, a slender, unpretentious man appeared. From my science background, I knew about fields, both electric and magnetic. We were in a field, but of what I did not know. Talking to my wife later I found she had experienced a similar feeling: that we were in the presence of goodness, if not godliness.

Mom was a Quaker and Dad a Congregational minister. One was a little louder than the other, one a little more soft spoken, but they were close in spirit. My mother was the stronger influence, though, so outwardly I'm Congregationalist, but inwardly I'm a Quaker.

So would your funeral service be Quaker, or Congregational?

[Laughs] It would be an ecumenical service, blending and celebrating all traditions. I'm a pacifist, a person who believes in equality, dignity, and reverence for life. I am not a card-carrying Christian but a blend of many traditions. The tradition at the Boat Shop is one that encourages deep spirituality, but it doesn't matter whether you are Jewish, or Methodist, or Quaker, or even of no religious tradition at all. The common thread is simply thinking of life as sacred. Relationships are sacred, life is sacred, and how you live your life is the most important.

Tell me more about your family.

My dad was a Congregational minister from Portland. His mother, my grandmother, was a minister, one of the first women to be ordained in the State of Maine. She was raised a Unitarian, but ordained as a Congregationalist. My Grandmother's father, Charles Freeman Libby, was the mayor of Portland, so my roots are in deep Portland and Maine.

When it came time for college, Bowdoin was about the only school that would take me, principally because I was the fifth generation at Bowdoin starting in 1838. I deeply loved Bowdoin.

After graduation in 1969, Bowdoin asked me to join the admissions office. I was a pacifist, and during that time the war in Vietnam was raging. So I applied for status as a conscientious objector.

Did your Quaker background give you a basis for CO status?

Yes, I did get a CO, but then I had to find an acceptable alternative service position. The classic CO jobs were working in hospitals or as a medic, so when Bowdoin asked me to work at the admissions office, I told them that my draft board would probably not accept it. To my amazement, since the job in the admissions office was focusing on the recruitment of African-American and Native-American students, the draft board did accept the position.

So I worked in the Bowdoin Admissions office for a year as a CO, but then proceeded to hand in my draft card to protest the war in Vietnam. Even though I was a CO I still felt like I was a part of the American system which was waging war in a foreign land.

For doing this my draft board decided to punish me. They took it as an insult to them and to the United States, and so they changed my classification from CO to 1-A, which meant that they were going to put me in the Army.

I was required to take the Army physical, but many suggested I should take the case to court, which I did. I won it fairly easily because six months previously, the Supreme Court had ruled that a draft board could not use the draft system as a means of punishing a registrant. In other words they could put you in jail, but they couldn't draft you into the Army as a punishment. So at this point I was free to do what I wanted.

When I finished at Bowdoin I decided to attend the University of Edinburgh graduate school of theology. The only problem I faced, however, was that I needed to get permission to leave the country from, of all places, my Draft Board. So once again I appeared before the Board and asked them if they would give me permission to go to Scotland to attend University of Edinburgh.

They said, "Oh, American graduate schools aren't good enough for you?" [laughs uproariously]. I said to them that I thought it would be helpful to leave the country for awhile to gain a perspective on what was happening in America. They said "No." I replied that I would be going anyway, and gave them my address in Edinburgh where I would be staying if they wanted to contact me. They said, "If you leave this country, you will never come back again." I said, "I love this country; I deeply appreciate what goes on; but I despise what our government is doing in Vietnam. If you feel that I'm not worthy of coming back, that's your decision, not mine." They said, "If you leave, you will never come back again."

That's the way we ended it. I left, and they were right. I could not re-enter the United States. I was a man without a country. I had been admitted to Edinburgh, so at least I could stay there until I finished my graduate degree in theology. I had originally thought I would go for just one year and then come back to Yale Theological Seminary, but when they said I couldn't come back, I decided to remain in Scotland.

To this day I do not know why, but about two years after my leaving, I received something called a 1H classification. I think it was a quiet way of granting amnesty to people who had not just run away.

I probably wouldn't have availed myself of it, except I had just met a lovely lady in Edinburgh who came from, of all places, Wiscasset, Maine! We were the only theology students from Maine at Edinburgh University.

You must have thought, "Someone is putting us together!"

Edinburgh is a very formal place, and they always start the academic year with a lecture, usually given by its most esteemed professor. The opening lecture that year was where I met Ruth. Interestingly enough the subject of the lecture was "divine providence." [We both laugh]

We were both from Maine, and we had done nearly identical things. I had worked in a program at Bowdoin called "Upward Bound," and Ruth had always wanted to teach on an island off the coast of Maine in a one-room schoolhouse. That's what we ended up doing.

In physics there is a phenomenon called "sympathetic vibration." Put two strings, tuned to the same note, in a room. When you pluck one string, the other string begins to vibrate. Was it like that?

Absolutely. We were knit together. We were meant to be together. It was just a remarkable relationship. [At this, Bobby chokes up, and we pause. Ruth died three years ago, and it is obvious just how remarkable their partnership must have been.]

We came back to Maine. Actually we had planned to go to Nova Scotia—"New Scotland"—but Ruth was friends with the Rev. Stanley B. Haskell, the minister on the Seacoast Mission boat,

Sunbeam. He told Ruth that the people of Monhegan Island were looking for a school teacher and a preacher. One of the families with young children said, "In the old days we had a preacher/teacher. If you ever find one of those, send him out." Stan said to Ruth, "Before you go to Nova Scotia, at least take a look at Monhegan."

So we said, "We'll give it a try. Perhaps it will be a stepping stone on the way to Nova Scotia." So we interviewed together for the teacher job, and they liked us. Technically they hired Ruth, but we both did the teaching for the one salary. We ate a lot of beans, but they provided a house.

Then the islanders heard that I had a divinity degree, so they asked, "Would you ever preach for us?" I said, "I'll give it a try." I never really wanted to be a formal parish minister. It wasn't my cup of tea. Having said that, I did enjoy it. I enjoyed the connecting with the people especially.

Monhegan was such a powerfully emotional experience. I would visit individuals and talk with them about simple things for maybe an hour. Then, as soon as I said, "It's time that I left," out would come the most remarkable stories I've ever heard. They were about adultery, about theft, about deeply secretive events in their lives that they simply needed to share with another person before they died.

I was overwhelmed. I became a trusted figure. I was a psychiatrist, a psychologist, a minister, a confidant, a bridge-builder, a person who tries to work toward reconciliation.

Originally when I thought about the formality and pomposity of the preaching, I had no interest in becoming ordained. But earning people's deepest trust, building bridges, working toward reconciliation, and helping individuals live more meaningful lives, that was the ministry I really loved.

And is that why you are here?

That is why I am here.

Did you ever become ordained?

Yes, they asked if I could be their minister. The Monhegan church is nondenominational. It's not Episcopal; it's not Quaker; it's a community church, and so I did become the minister of the community.

You could have been a Buddhist for all they cared!

Exactly. [laughs]

Yes, Ruth and I were the teachers and ministers on Monhegan for two years. Then, although we loved it out there, we thought it was important for the kids of Monhegan to have a variety of teachers. So we decided to leave. The two previous summers we had served as the summer ministers on an island called Louds or Muscongus island which we came to love as well.

In fact we wanted to buy a farm on Louds Island and so we inquired if there was any land for sale? Many said, "Yes, there are people who would sell land, and even a house. So we wrote to Edward Loud Poland, a direct descendant of the first settler. I wrote, "Mr. Poland, people say you might be interested in selling land." He wrote right back and said, "Sure, I'll be glad to sell you whatever you want." We said, "We don't want much, maybe ten acres, and how much would you charge us?" He said, "You can have ten acres for whatever you can afford to pay."

But then he wrote and said, "Nope, I'm not going to sell to you, but I'll tell you what. You can live in my island house for a full year, and then if you still want to, you can buy the land for whatever you can afford." He just wanted us to be sure that island life was what we wanted.

Louds no longer had a year-round population, since the last full-time islander moved off in 1964. Eddie Poland had grown up on Louds, and he wanted it to be a year-round island again.

Where did Mr. Poland live at that time?

Washington, D.C. He worked in the nautical chart division of the national cartography office [laughs]. In fact it was Eddie Poland who surreptitiously changed all of the government charts to read Louds Island instead of Muscongus Island. Any chart printed before 1962 reads Muscongus Island. Now they all read Loud's Island.

So you moved to Louds Island?

Yes, but we had actually written to two people: Eddie Poland and Hilda Libby. Hilda had come to the U.S. from Edinburgh, Scotland, and married a fisherman from New Harbor. She had bought and fixed up an old farm on Louds right next to the church. People said, "If you're interested in buying land or a house, write to Hilda Libby because she may be selling." After corresponding with Eddie Poland all fall, suddenly in the spring a letter came from Hilda Libby, who hadn't responded before. She wrote, "You had written me back in the fall, and I'm awfully sorry that I never responded. You see, my life was in shambles. I was going through a very sad divorce, and my whole life was turned upside down. I've decided that now I will return to my native Scotland, and I would be honored to sell you my farm. I will give it to you for what I paid for it.

But how were you going to make a living as the only year-round residents of Louds Island?

Good question. We lobstered; we clammed; we raked sea moss. When we first went to Loud's there was a retired Norwegian boatbuilder. He had come across from Norway when he was twenty-four years old. He had built boats up until WWII when wooden boats phased out. Then he became a carpenter, but his love was traditional wooden boats. His name was Edvard Salor. He had fixed up an old fish house on Louds, and he and his wife lived on the island from May until September. But he was always working on wooden boats. Every summer person had Edvard fix their dory or skiff. As soon as I met Edvard, he became a father figure to me.

With my love of wooden boats and my love of traditional things, we just hit it off. So he helped us get going.

We had a dory, and we used it for lobster fishing and getting back and forth from the mainland. But getting back and forth when it was 10 below zero, with ice in the bottom of the boat, was something else. So one morning as I was cranking on the outboard, trying to get it to go I said to Ruth, "This is crazy! If we had a good rowboat, rowing would be so much easier." "I'm going to build a good rowboat."

That's when my boatbuilding really started. Edvard showed me about lofting [laying out a boat's lines full-size], all the techniques, the basic way of building a boat from his traditional perspective. He started me off on a 14-foot peapod.

There was no electricity on Louds. Everything was hand done. Even if we'd had power, he wouldn't have used it anyway. It was all handsaws, planes, and chisels. Edvard and I framed up our boat and started the planking. I finished the planking, and then I made another peapod, then a dory. In fact The Carpenter's Boat Shop, our eventual ministry, and school really started on Louds Island because of Edvard, and all that he taught me.

What was Ruth doing?

Everything we did, we did together. We built the peapod together, we fished together, we cut wood together. The total population of Louds Island from October till May was two. Just Ruth and I. So you had to get along with your neighbor.

Why did you leave Louds?

The spring of our second year on Louds Island, we became friends with the minister in Round Pond and New Harbor, Dr. John Wesley McKelvey. He had cancer, and I became very close to him. I used to come off the island one full day every month to help him out by doing jobs for him.

I did that for six months, and then one day he said, "No work this time; I just want to have a meal with you and Ruth together." So we rowed over, and John said, "You know, I'm going to die pretty soon, but I'd be deeply grateful if you would take over the churches in New Harbor and Round Pond for me." I didn't want to go back into the formal ministry, but how could I refuse? It was John's last request, and so I honored it.

I served the churches for two and a half years, and in doing so I became a part of the New Harbor and Round Pond communities. It was such an honor. I disliked the formality of the church, but the experience was the same as on Monhegan. Entering the houses of the local people, being at one with them was such a meaningful experience.

We served the New Harbor and Round Pond Churches for two and one-half years until the Bishop asked us to step down since we were not Methodist ministers.

Ruth and I then decided that this was the place to do what we had started on Louds Island. This was the place to begin the Carpenter's Boat Shop ministry and school. But we had nothing. We had no furniture, no tools, nothing, and yet within literally two weeks the fishing families of Round Pond and New Harbor had supplied most of our needs through a "pounding party" they gave to us.

A pounding party?

Yes, it's an old Maine tradition. When you move into a new house, the community tries to make it into a "home" for you. They give you a pound of everything: butter, sugar, flour, but the people of Round Pond and New Harbor also gave us a pound of table saw, and band saw, and drill press, and nearly all the carpentry tools we needed. They even gave us a pound of money. We were just so grateful for all that they did.

Did they know your plans for this place?

On our last Sunday at the churches, I simply described what this new ministry and community was going to be. It was to be a home for individuals in transition who needed to regain their footing. It was going to be a boat shop to sustain our daily living. And it was to be a community where all would work for the common good of others.

Is there something healing about boatbuilding?

Absolutely. There's an old saying which goes, "People build boats, but boats can build people." When you build a boat you have to do it with great care because peoples' lives depend upon your craftsmanship. And as you build carefully you become more caring as a person. I've seen this happen over and over again. In fact many of our boats have saved the lives of a number of people.

In 1986, for example, the Coast Guardsmen out on Manana Island received a call at 2 a.m. that the Monhegan Light was out. It was blowing 30 to 40 knots, and it was about 10 degrees. The Coast Guard called Manana and said, "Get over to Monhegan and relight the light." So they took their peapod down the ways on Manana, and as they were going down, the painter fouled and the boat flipped over and threw the men into the harbor. This was February, and the sea water was 39 degrees.

The men were swept across to Smuttynose Island where they were literally freezing to death. They called the Coast Guard in Boothbay Harbor with their VHF radio, shouting, "We are dying. We need help immediately." The CG responded, "We can't get to you, but we'll try to raise the fishermen on Monhegan." They called Sherm Stanley, and Sherm said, "I'll try to get them."

Sherm went down to the shore with a couple of other fishermen, but they couldn't get their boats off the shore. Their skiffs were too small, and the wind and waves pushed them back on shore. Then they saw a 20-foot dory the boat shop had built. They were finally able to launch it, and rowed over to Smuttynose, where they rescued the two men. That dory was the only boat that was able to save them.

As our apprentices are building the boats, I tell them, "This is what your boat might be called upon to do, so you must build it as well as you possibly can."

"You are important, and what you do is important?"

Exactly. While they are building their boats, they are also building themselves and their personal lives.

In addition to boatbuilding, do you offer any group therapy?

Yes, it's called living a balanced life. The apprentices don't just build boats. They garden, they take care of the chickens, they do chores, they take turns cooking the meals for all twenty people. When they leave here they know how to prepare and cook healthy breakfasts, lunches, and suppers. It's a one-year course in the basics of life: eating around a table, sharing and learning to be thoughtful, and how to cooperate with other people.

The Carpenter's Boatshop

Toward the end of the year, each apprentice goes to an island and stays there alone for three days. It's not a Hurricane Island experience where you have to forage for food, but a time for reflection, and for thinking about what you want to do and what you truly want to be in life. Amazing things happen when you are totally alone on an island.

Do you practice any sort of formal religion here?

We do begin every meal with a silent or sung grace. And every meal concludes with a reading that hopefully might bring a sense of interest and inspiration. But no, we do not practice any one formal religion.

The Carpenter's Boatshop is simply based on the Benedictine tradition, which goes back to about the 6th century. The Benedictine tradition is based on seven important elements: working, worship, prayer, study, recreation, hospitality, and service. It's a balanced life. William Sloane Coffin, Jr., the chaplain of Yale once said, "The aim of life is not to prove yourself. The real aim of life is to honestly reveal yourself. Our hope is that apprentices are able to achieve this.

I'll bet there have been plenty of stories about you in the press.

Unfortunately, and occasionally it was a large mistake. For example the television program "The Today Show" was doing a piece on Jamie Wyeth out on Monhegan, and the producer had landed at the Portland Airport to do it. We had one of our dinghies on display there. The producer looked at the boat and saw the Scottish prayer that we place in every boat. Then, when she was interviewing Jamie out on Monhegan, she saw the same prayer in his boat. She said, "Where did you get that boat?" He said from the Carpenter's Boat Shop."

So she called, and asked if she could come over? Ruth said, "No, we have sixty-five kids here doing special projects, repairing homes in the community, and we are just too busy." So they said, "Well, we're coming whether you like it or not." She said, "No, we can't have it." They said, "Please, just for a short little time." Ruth said, "If you can keep it to one hour you can come, but only one hour."

They came over and shot the video. The problem was that on the day the program aired on "The Today Show" within two hours after the program we had received three hundred calls. People from all over the country wanted to come to the Carpenter's Boat Shop.

We are not a college competing for students. We are just a small community which tries to help its members to live without fear, to love without reserve, and to willingly work for the common good of all.

The dories your apprentices build seem symbolic of what the Carpenter's Boat Shop is about. Could you recite that Scottish poem they carve into the transom of each boat?

Gladly.

> *'Round our skiff be God's aboutness*
> *Ere she try the depth of the sea.*
> *Seashell frail for all her stoutness,*
> *Unless Thou her Helmsman be.*

ALVAH MOODY
Moody's Diner
Waldoboro
Age 83

Alvah and wife pose in Moody's bake shop

Moody's Diner in Waldoboro is my favorite diner in the world. At Moody's I am time-warped back to my grandmother's kitchen of sixty years ago. I never look at the menu because it hasn't changed significantly in those sixty years.

I am looking forward to meeting the oldest working Moody, born the year the diner opened. Goosebumps rise on my arms as I am ushered through the swinging doors into the kitchen. We file past the "line" where the plates are filled, past Alvah's beaming wife operating the dishwasher, past two flour-covered girls making the pies and biscuits, and through the door to Alvah's office.

Alvah swivels his chair to face me. His smile lights the room. He has stories to tell.

Alvah, someone told me you were born the year Moody's opened.

Ayah, 1927. My father started the diner up there on the hill in a house he bought. Route 1 [U.S. Route 1, stretching from Fort Kent, Maine, to Key West, Florida] used to go up over the hill, and he bought the house next door to ours. He built three cabins to rent, and he put a little dining room in the front of the house and hired a couple of local women to cook.

That was smart because the local cooking is good. What did your father do before he started the diner?

Mainly Christmas trees. Labor Day he'd leave home and go up north to Greenville, Monson, Harmony. He'd buy trees off'n these farmers, Christmas trees. Their pastures were all grown up with balsam firs in 'em.

Did they plant the trees, like in a tree farm?

Nope, they was just wild trees grew up. They grew up wild, but they was good shaped trees.

And where did he sell the trees?

Boston. He used to cut fourteen freightcar load of trees. There would be 600 bundles of trees in each freight car, and there would run anywhere from four to six trees to eight to ten to the bundle.

Fourteen cars times 600 bundles times, lets say, seven trees. That would be 58,800 trees! Did he cut them by hand?

Ayah. He had a little axe. He had a man that followed him around. He'd whack 'em off, trim 'em, and throw 'em on the ground. The man behind him would cut the stump down. He might just take the top off if that made a good tree. Then the other guy would cut the stump down, trim it out, and leave it flat on the ground.

I've gone out and cut my own tree a couple of times, and that is hard work. How big was he?

Oh, prob'ly five-two or three, but you wouldn't want to tangle with him. He could run, too. Oh, he'd run like a deer.

Was he a strict father?

We weren't allowed off'n the hill. Not until we'd go to work down here or go to school. The rest of the time we stayed on the hill. If we wanted to play with friends, they had to come up there and play with us. That was his rule. "Forty acres here," he'd say. "If that ain't enough, you'd better stay in bed."

Were you afraid of him?

No, we respected him. And mother was a great woman, a great woman. She run the camps for him. Did all the reservations and let 'em, all that stuff.

We used to have a little Cocker Span'l dog, and dad would come in the kitchen, and he'd grab my mother and spin her around, dancin'. That dog would come out from underneath the stove and grab my dad's pant leg and growl. He didn't want nobody touchin' Momma. [laughs]

How tall was your momma?

Oh, she was average height, prob'ly five-, prob'ly four, five, six, right around there. She was taller than my dad.

How many kids were there?

Nine in all. There was Dewey, Nellie, myself—I was third.

Did all of the kids work at the diner?

Yup, every one of them. Some of 'em didn't much like it, but they worked there.

How old were you when you started working at the diner?

Let's see, I was prob'ly in the seventh grade. I'd a been ten or eleven.

There was a great aunt, Nell, that used to run the diner for my dad. She did all the bookkeeping, then went down there and did the cookin' in the day time. She stayed at the house with us.

In the mornin' I'd come down here with her, quarter to seven. In the winter I'd go in the pond [a small pond adjacent to the present Moody's Diner] and chop some ice out and bring it in and put it in the rootbeer machine and the Coke machine. Then I'd bring in the coal for the stove that heated out front. Then in the kitchen they had a woodstove, and I'd bring in wood from the woodshed.

After that, sometimes I'd get a ride down to the village with people that would come in there and eat. Then I'd got to walk down to the school, and I'd come back at 3:30 and do the same thing all over again. I'd help Nell clean up the diner, do the dishes, get all that stuff done. She'd cash out, then we'd walk up to the house around 6 o'clock.

Did your father cut the firewood, too?

Oh yes, he used to cut wood and sell it, about forty, fifty cord a year, with the farm crew. He always had a crew of four, five working on the farm. We had twenty-four, twenty-five cows up there, too.

Did any of the kids go on to do something else?

Oh yes, after they went off to college, most did, yes. I've got a brother worked for GM Diesel, another brother was a surveyor, you know, surveyin'.

Why did you stay on for the rest of your life?

Well, dad couldn't do it. Somebody had to do it. But my sister, Nancy, used to do the hirin' of the help. She has that gift shop over there [Moody's Diner gift shop, behind the diner, sells touristy things like tee-shirts and postcards.] She wrote the cookbook, "What's Cooking at Moody's?"

I bought one of those books, and the first thing I did was look to see how you made your fish chowder and your blueberry pie. Those are my two favorite things. I followed the recipes exactly, but somehow they didn't come out quite as good as yours.

I'll tell you something else I really like. The last time I was here I ordered blueberry pie. The waitress said, "You like the juice?" I said, "Oh, yes, I love the juice. That's the best part." She took a big spoon and ladled about three tablespoons of pie juice over the crust, just like my grandmother used to do sixty years ago.

The author's favorite: blueberry pie with a dollop of extra juice

Ayah, ayah!

You don't get juice in pie anymore. You buy a pie in the store, and it's all full of corn starch.

Too much thickenin', ayah, ayah. They thicken it right up solid so they can ship it.

In fact, when no one is looking, I lick the plate.

Ha, ha, ha. Ayah, me too!

Where did Moody's recipes come from, your mom?

No, no, some of them, but most come from the women that worked for us. They'd bring in a favorite recipe, and we'd try it. Like the Indian puddin'. There was a lady that worked here, she used to make Indian puddin' and she brought it in. She made it in a double boiler, and it took all mornin' to make it. Don Mortison, the other cook, and I, we just cut that double boiler foolishness out. We never told her.

When was the last time you added something to the menu?

Well, fish and chips. When they first started that I was cuttin' up fish. My dad come in. He looks at me, and he says, "What are you doin'?" "Cuttin' up fish," I says. "What are you cuttin' it up in them bitty little pieces for?" he says, "They don't want them little pieces." [Alvah laughs]. I said, "Well, it's called fish and chips." Course he'd never heard of it. "Ayah, well ok," he says, and he walked out.

He'd come in, and I'd be cuttin' up the haddock, and the other cooks would say, "Alvah, your dad's comin'." So I'd put it away real quick. It upset him somethin' wicked to see that good haddock cut into those little strips.

You must use tons of wild Maine blueberries. Do you buy them Down East in season and then freeze them?

We used to buy them local and freeze them. Now we buy them flash frozen from Down East, but we don't have storage enough for a whole year's supply.

How many pies do you go through in a day?

Pretty near sixty altogether.

Sixty pies a day? Times 365 days, that's 22,000 pies a year! How many girls does it take to make all those pies by hand?

Two of 'em. They come in 2:30, 3 o'clock in the mornin'. They start right in on the muffins and the doughnuts. Then they go to the pies and the biscuits afterwards.

What would you say is your most popular dish?

Well, that would be the special. Each day we have a special, and it's the same special every week. If you come in on Monday and the special is Yankee Pot Roast, why you know that if you come in Monday a year from now, you can have Yankee Pot Roast.

The same with the desserts?

Right. That way people know when to come and git 'em.

Well, that's both good and bad. My wife loves Indian pudding. If she comes here, and it turns out not to be Indian pudding day, she's mighty upset.

Then she'd better come on Thursdays! [laughs]

Another thing that gets her going is lard. She's one of these modern, health-conscious women, you know? I said to her, "The only way to make a good donut is to fry it in lard."

Right. No lard, no donut.

So she says, "You're wrong. No one cooks in lard anymore, no one." So we're sitting here at the counter, and I said to the waitress, "Are these donuts cooked in lard?" The waitress looked kind of embarrassed, and she said, "I'll go ask the cook." She came back, and she said, "The cook said, 'course they are!'"

Ayah! [Alvah breaks up laughing]

If it ain't broke, don't fix it, that's what I say. When I come to Moody's, I know exactly what I'm getting on my plate, and I know exactly how it will taste. The recipes never change!

Right. Yup, we always use the same ones.

I was just noticing, driving up here, that the last time I saw a McDonalds was back in Bath, and the next one up Route 1 is in Rockland. That's a fifty mile fast-food dead zone!

Ayah, right. Yuh. [laughs] Actually I think now they've snuck one in over to Damariscotta.

Alvah, I have to tell you a story. I was here about a quarter to noon one day, and I sat down at the end of the counter, right at the corner. I had a bowl of chowder, and everything was going along pretty well. About five minutes before twelve the waitress comes up and says, "I'm sorry, but you're gonna have to move over." I said, "Why do I have to move?" She said, "Cause Mr. Spoffard is comin'."

Parker Spoffard?

Parker Spoffard, yes! She said, "That stool there is Mr. Spoffard's, and the one next to it is his wife's." So I obliged and moved over two stools. Sure enough, right at the stroke of noon, in comes an elderly couple, both white-haired, he wearing a houndstooth jacket and bow tie. They come right down the counter and sit on the two empty stools.

Now, how long has that been going on?

I dunno, but a long time. Could be forty years.

The original counter, where the locals meet

Do you have other customers like the Spoffards?

There's a John Picher comes in here. His father and mother come here years ago. John come here when he was a little kid.

And how many years ago was that?

Well, he's retired now, so I guess fifty or so. He still comes in. Lives up the road in a trailer. Never got married. I pick on one of the girls that works in the kitchen about him, 'cause he always comes in wearin' shorts, and he has these spindly little legs, and I says, "Carolyn, here comes John, Don't look out. I don't want you gettin' all excited." [breaks up laughing] She gits wicked mad at me.

Your waitresses are something special, too. Is it possible that half of the women in Waldoboro have worked at Moody's at one time or another?

Yup. Lot of kids earned their money here to go to college. They get good tips. My dad used to tell the girls, "That smile is worth a million dollars." Old dad used to get after them when they wouldn't smile.

My first wife, when I was getting $40 a week cookin' out back, she'd make $100 a week waitin' on tables. She was a little blonde, real cute, pleasant. Finnish girl, a full-blood Finn. She worked here forty years, until she passed away. She's been gone twenty years now.

I met your current wife running the dishwasher when I came though the kitchen. She's cute as a button! How did you meet?

Well, her son is married to my sister's girl. She was down here living with her son. He was going to fix her up a room in his house, but he didn't git it done, so my sister, who was livin' in my house up around the corner, she took her in there. They got her a job down here, and that's where I met her.

What were your thoughts when you first met her?

Oh, I guess I liked the looks of her, ayah. Really pleasant. Really smart, too.

Isn't it great when you meet a woman who has matured into what she's going to be. No more guessing.

Right. It's pretty good. Ayah.

Did you ever think of something you'd rather do than work at Moody's?

Never crossed my mind. I built my house, and I built a house for my son, one for my daughter, and then I built seven cottages on the lake, and I still own three of them—the one I live in and two I rent. I sold the other four.

My first wife, she was in the hospital to Portland three months, and I didn't have a very big health insurance. It cost me three hundred and somethin' thousand. I had to sell four of my cottages.

All of my children worked here. My oldest boy worked here. Then he got clammin', diggin' clams, here and Vinalhaven. He'd go t' Vinalhaven and make a thousand dollars. He took two clam forks; he cut one in two and welded the other to either side, so his clam fork was about that wide [spreads his hands about twenty-four inches]. Oh, he is right rugged. He'd pull that fork with one hand, an' with the other hand just pickin' the clams.

When he was goin' to high school he said to me, "I want to build a house for myself." He was goin' with this girl, and they were goin' to get married. He said, "Grandpa give me some land up in Nobleboro." A lady up there lived in a house, and she got sick and had to go in a nursin' home, and my dad, brought up there with her, she came to him and she said, "If you pay for my nursin' home, I'll deed my farm over to you." So he did, and then he give some of that land to my children. Mark's got a lot there; Charlene's got a lot there.

But anyway, my son says to me, " I want to build a house." I said, "You got any money?" He says, "Ayah." I says, "How much you got?" He says, "Forty thousand." I said, "Well, I guess you can build one if you want to."

$40,000 while he was still in high school? Do you think working hard is just in the Moody genes?

Must be. My other son's a worker, too. I sent him to the university, environmental engineer. Come back, went divin' for sea urchins with his brother, and he saw all that money he was makin', so he goes Down East and gets certified with a diver's license. He comes back, buys an old wooden boat, goes down there divin' for sea urchins. He made enough money and had a $100,000 fiberglass boat built.

Now what's he doing?

Lobsterin'. Got a brand new house, cars, trucks. He and his brother both lobster outa New Harbor.

It seems to me that the young people around here are different from young people elsewhere, where they just sit around playing video games. Are you worried that attitude might come here?

Ummm, prob'ly work here eventually. But it takes a long time for anything to work itself here.

Is there anything you wish you had done different in life?

Hmm, I don't think so. I get a lot of satisfaction out of what I did, even when I was workin' late, double shifts. I still do.

When I came through the kitchen, your wife was running the dishwashing machine.

Ayah! They need help, she'll wash dishes. She don't care.

So that's the attitude around here? Anybody will do anything, whatever's needed?

Ayah, anything what's needed.

MOODY'S DAILY SPECIALS

Sunday

Roast Turkey with Stuffing	8.99
Roast Pork with Stuffing	8.99

Monday

Yankee Pot Roast	9.49
Macaroni & Cheese with hotdog & vegetable	6.99

Tuesday

Meatloaf	7.89
Homemade Lasagna & tossed salad	7.99

Wednesday

American Chop Suey & vegetable	5.29
Homemade Turkey Pot Pie	7.89

Thursday

New England Boiled Dinner	9.49
Shepherd's Pie & vegetable	6.29

Friday

Baked Stuffed Haddock	10.49
Boiled Haddock w/ egg sauce	10.49

Saturday

Smothered Beef & Onions	8.99
Baked Beans, Brown Bread, hotdog & vegetable	6.69

Daily Dessert Specials

Sunday	Apple Crisp
Monday	Apple Crisp
Tuesday	Grapenut Custard
Wednesday	Tapioca Pudding
Thursday	Indian Pudding
Friday	Grapenut Pudding & Bread Pudding
Saturday	Gingerbread

ROBERT SKOGLUND
AKA THE HUMBLE FARMER
St. George
Age 74

It's hard to miss the humble Farmer

Loving classic jazz, intelligent conversation, and Down East humor, I had been an avid listener to Maine Public Broadcasting's weekly radio show "The humble Farmer" for twenty-eight years.

It would be difficult to miss humble's homestead on Route 131 in St. George, Maine. First, the farmhouse is not the classic white of most of the homes in coastal Maine, but a bright American-cheese yellow. Second, on the lawn in front is a Model-T truck bearing his moniker in foot-high letters.

Humble, his pants held up by a pair of wide red suspenders, bounded toward me like a Labrador retriever. He insisted I tour his rhubarb patch, pile of roadside giveaway zucchinis, and gigantic array of solar panels. After asking how he might convert the Model-T to solar power, he led me through the kitchen door.

Bathed in the aroma of fresh-baked wild Maine blueberry cake, stood humble's pretty wife, "Marsha, the Almost Perfect Woman," as humble calls her. I'm thinking, "Where's the imperfection, humble?"

I didn't want to leave either Marsha or the blueberry cake, but humble dragged me into the living room, where he sat me in an office chair under lights in front of a tripod-mounted video camera. It appeared our interview was going to be conducted both ways.

It's a terrible thing to be seventy-four and suddenly discover that you have attention deficit disorder. Before they put this label on me, I was doing pretty good! If you want to make a lot of money, invent a disorder and a pill to fix it.

Remember the old days when people died of old age? Nobody dies of old age anymore, not even people who are 101. Nowadays there's always some technical reason why you die, as if dying were an unfortunate accident.

Humble, I'm putting down for the record here that I am talking to Robert Skoglund, The humble Farmer, in St. George, Maine.

Ayah, I was born up the road. You could see the house if there weren't no trees. My great, great, great-grandfather was one of the insurgents fighting with George Washington. Great, great, great-grandfather got shot the same week they hung Nathan Hale. They were both twenty-one years old.

He belonged to the same church in Boston as Henry Knox. Henry Knox, you know, was Washington's Secretary of War. Knox might have been instrumental in bringing great, great, great-grandfather here to St. George.

So you were born in St. George?

Weren't you listenin'? I told you, in that house right up there. And the woman that delivered me was the sister-in-law to my grandfather. She lived down there [points in opposite direction]. That Model T out front I bought from her son back in '51 for ten bucks.

When I go on a stage, sometimes I say, "I still live seven houses from where I was born and brought up. How many of you still live in the same town you was born?

You know...

You ain't listenin' to the story! This is a story I'm telling you! I say, "How many of you still live in the same town you was born?" Three or four put up their hands, and I say, "Oh, there's three or four of us here without no ambition."

In the interviews for this book I am beginning to see a pattern. These are families reaching back eight or nine generations. They don't seem to be able to get off the peninsulas! One fisherman told me that when he came of age his grandfather said, "You've got to go out of town to get a wife. Otherwise you'll end up marrying a cousin." So he went four miles up the peninsula to get his bride. Is life here so good that nobody ever wants to strike out for greener pastures?

Most of Moses Robinson's descendants moved away. If they hadn't St. George would look like downtown Hong Kong. It's just those of us with no ambition that are still here.

When I called yesterday you said, "Are you the Charlie Wing that amounted to somethin'?"

Ayah, I thought I'd heard of a Charlie Wing that went out in the world and done good, but I guess that must have been another fellah!

You're not the first person with that opinion. When my grandmother died at ninety-five, I had taught at Bowdoin College and written half a dozen books. Just before she died she looked at me critically and said, "Buddy, when are you going to get a job?"

Ayah! There was a fella out on Vinalhaven that did some bush cuttin' for Thomas Watson, the President of IBM. Watson could see that he was clever, so he fixed it up so the fella could go to Harvard. He went to Harvard for four years, did very well, and came back to Vinalhaven to cut bushes. He's still doin' very well.

So what is the purpose of an education?

So you can be happy! They're testing people now—this "No child left behind" thing. We have to test every child, and the teachers are responsible if the child can't learn. They're gradin' the students; they're gradin' the teachers; everybody's gettin' graded. Meanwhile, what I think of as education is goin' out the window.

How do you test for kindness, generosity, thoughtfulness, giving of yourself? You won't know if you've succeeded in educating a child until you have lived next to that person for twenty years.

Someone might graduate top of his class and be a son of a bitch.
He might be someone who'll shoot your dog.

What was your early education?

I was lucky enough to attend the one-room school here in St.
George. I did take one year off. My father was working in Sample's
Shipyard down to Boothbay Harbor, so I did a year in Boothbay.
Because I was the only one in my class in St. George, I did two
years in one in Boothbay. Big mistake. Made me a social retard.
You are not ready to go to high school when you are twelve.

The kids back then were very poor. But we didn't know we
were poor.

**I went to a one-room schoolhouse too. Up in West Gardiner,
and my mother was the teacher! She knew some of the kids
were poor because they would bring mayonnaise sandwiches:
two slices of white bread with just mayonnaise between. She
made me a bologna sandwich every day, and every day I had to
trade my sandwich with one of the poorer kids. I got some
pretty plain sandwiches. Sometimes the filling would be just a
slice of raw potato or cucumber.**

There's nothin' wrong with a cucumber sandwich! Remember
Oscar Wilde: "I'm sorry, there aren't any cucumbers to be had,
even for ready money." Remember that, from the "Importance of
Being Earnest?" You don't remember that? Well, you were educated as a scientist. No wonder.

You know what a scientist is? That's someone who thinks if he
can put a number on something, then he understands it. I'm reading a book right now that would be close to your heart, "Philosophy and Physics."

**Yes, that is a favorite topic of physicists. Einstein was quite a
philosopher.**

The fella I admired was that Werner Heisenberg with his "Un-
certainty Principle." Now there was an honest fellow! Another
smart guy was Schroedinger. Remember Schroedinger's cat para-

dox? This cat is in a box, and either the gas explodes and kills the cat, or it doesn't. There is no way of knowing which is goin' on until you open the box. So the cat is both alive and dead at the same time.

Now you ask how does that apply to life? Well, here is humble's wife experiment. Marsha went away for a week. She left instructions that the bed be made every morning. [I begin to laugh. I can see where he's headed]. See, you understand. The bed is both made and unmade until she gets home and opens the door.

So you see there is a profit in studying scientific principles. It can make you happier. That is what a true education is all about.

I remember wearing my fathers's made-over pants to high school. The pockets were worn through, so my mother just sewed them shut. You ever seen a pair of man's pants with no pockets?

I remember putting cardboard in the soles of my shoes, but then I realized that if I put a piece of tin can in there, it wouldn't wear out so fast. We didn't realize we were poor. Poor is a relative thing. We were poor, but there were even poorer families, so we didn't feel poor.

When I got out of high school I thought you had to be rich to go to college. I went into the Coast Guard Reserve. I drove a boat, and I learned to navigate. But I couldn't get out of there soon enough.

When I got out of the Coast Guard, I wanted to learn the clarinet. My sister was a good trombone player. She went to New York City on the Ted Mack show, national TV. She got into the Eastman School of Music.

So I went down there and my eyes got opened up. I said, "This is a good place. I'm twenty-one, but I can start with the five-year-old kids and learn to play the clarinet." I didn't realize that learnin' an instrument is like learnin' a language. If you don't have the aptitude, there is no way you can learn to play anything. Think about it. You'd never learn to talk if you waited until twenty-one to start. You'd become a wolf man or a wolf girl, barking. The Pope says, "If I can have them until they're five, I'll have them for life."

I tried playing the clarinet. They said, "You will never play good enough to get into Eastman, but they do have state teachers colleges where you can learn to be a music teacher." "Music teacher?" I said. "That sounds good." So I applied to the music college in Potsdam, New York.

Did you learn an instrument?

I learned the bass well enough so that, seven years later I had the house band at the University of Rochester, and all the best guys from the Eastman School were playing in my band! And these are all famous guys now.

And you learned a great deal about jazz, judging from your radio show. I love the selections you play on your show.

That's because I never played anything I didn't understand. You understand the mathematics of music? Let me play this for you... [Humble jumps up and sits down at a piano in the next room.] Listen to the math in this Woody Herman piece, "The Four Brothers." [He plays the tune accompanied by scat singing.] The mathematics of that are fascinating!

But I flunked out of Potsdam after two years. I never could learn to play musically. I could play the bass because it was just one string at a time, and it was all math, dum, dum, de dum dum.

So I was back home in St. George. One day I was drivin' my Model T around Tenants Harbor. These three girls come off a yacht in the harbor, and I picked them up. Model-Ts are good for that. When the yacht left, one of the girls stayed. She was a Vassar graduate who had translated German and French documents in Munich. We lived together in Portland while I went to Gorham Teacher's College.

The dean heard I was living with a girl. I was twenty-nine, she was twenty-five, she'd lived in Europe, I'd done my service time, and I was living with this girl in an apartment in Portland. Well, you could not do that in 1965. They were going to throw me out of college.

The dean said, "Skoglund, where do you live?" I said, "Post Office Box 35, Gorham." Well, he made me rent an apartment in Gorham, and we got married that summer.

Then I wanted to get a master's degree and applied at the University of Connecticut. Couldn't get in. We went down to Connecticut and taught. One of my students was Eben Ostby. I had my students pretend they were on television. We had a big cardboard box with a hole cut out for the screen. He got in the box, tied up a package with string and paper, looked out and said, "That wraps it up for tonight." That was Eben. He went on to make the movie, *Toy Story*.

Another one of my students went to Thomaston State Prison. Now, do I get teacher of the year award for having a student that I guided toward success in the movie industry, or do I get thrown out of teaching for having a student in jail? How can you grade a teacher based on the success of his or her students? You can't tell what they're going to do.

Then my wife and I both applied to the University of Maine. She applied for a masters in history; I went for a masters in English. I never got my degree. I never wrote the paper. Now I know why. With ADHD you may do wonderful work, but you never finish what you start.

So I learned to take the words of others and twist them around to suit my own needs. That's what I do. That's why I'm recording you right now.

You are apparently adept at this yourself. You have turned it into profit so you can ride around in a boat! [Unwisely, I had bragged to humble that I was living on a boat.]

Humble, you've seen through me! These stories I'm collecting are not mine. I'm just collecting stories from characters like you for the entertainment of others and the benefit of myself!

I know! I got you figured, but that's all right. So then a teacher down in Friendship had a nervous breakdown from some kids who were so bad, a couple of them later ended up in jail. Well, I had learned behavior modification in a psycholinguistics class at Rochester, so I went down to Friendship with four years of graduate study and restored order. For my master's degree I wrote a thesis on the correlation between acoustic and articulatory parameters.

Say that again.

I was attempting to ascertain if there was a one-to-one correlation between acoustic and articulatory parameters.

Of course you were!

I said that to a fisherman down to Port Clyde, and he looked at me and said, "God, ain't that good!"

[Marsha enters with a tray of tea and warm blueberry cake.] Humble says, "He wants to interview you." Marsha retorts, "I'm from away, and I'm going away!"

In the meantime my first wife, being an editor of *Downeast* magazine, assigned herself to write an article about Ossie Beal, the President of the Maine Lobsterman's Association. Ossie Beal was a Type A. He'd go to lobstermen's meetings until 2 a.m., get up at 4 a.m., and haul 800 traps.

She went down to Beals and wrote an article for *Downeast* magazine: "Ossie Beal, Maine's Most Active Lobsterman." When she didn't return, even I figured out what she meant by "active."

Now my wife is gone, and my mother is dead, so I buy a tractor, a new Mercedes, and a truck. I'm thirty-seven. I'm driving this tractor, mowing bushes, cleaning up the land. What else can you do when you have four years of graduate school in linguistics?

There was a weekly newspaper called the *Maine Times*. Every week I would send in a personal ad. "Antique dealer seeks attractive young woman interested in one night stand."

"Maine trapper seeks attractive lady taxidermist eager to mount four skins."

"Ornithologist seeks attractive young woman willing to sacrifice everything for a few cheep thrills."

A couple of guys at Maine Public Radio were cutting out these personals and pasting them on the wall. One day my neighbor next door comes over and tells me Maine Public Radio is playing a song by a communist folk singer from El Salvador. He's singing, "Kill the landlords and sow their bodies on the field. Their blood will make good fertilizer."

I call up Maine Public Radio, and with great feigned indignation I say, "Why are you playing this communist folksinger from El Salvador who is singing, "Kill the landlords and sow their bodies on the field." I have Spanish-speaking tenants who are listening to this!

They said, "We don't know Spanish. We just get the program from Boston. But do you want to do a jazz show?" I said, "How do you know I know about jazz?" They said, "You sent in five dollars one time to hear Harry Carney [Duke Ellington's baritone saxophone player]."

So I went up to the station, and did a pilot, and I was on the air for twenty-eight years. Never paid me for 28 years. I did it as a volunteer.

Putting together the weekly "humble Farmer Show"

I know you are still on the air around the country, but you are no longer on Maine Public Radio. What happened?

In 2003 I went on the air, said I didn't care for war, read a description of a man, and ended by saying he wrote a book called *Mein Kampf.* A few Maine people in influential places found my "war rant" offensive because they thought George W. Bush had written *Mein Kampf* and that I was, therefore, talking about him. You can still read "The War Rant" on line and decide for yourself. But some people realized that if you could describe the man who wrote *Mein Kampf* and have people think you were talking about the President of the United States, this country was in serious trouble. This kind of humorous commentary might give Maine people something to think about, which is obviously not the purpose of a Maine Public Radio. Although I was kicked off the radio, my friends immediately bought me a video camera and asked me to make the same show for cable television. So the same old-fashioned music and humorous social commentary show is now distributed by PegMedia in Rockport, Maine, and presently goes into a million homes in several states.

And now, if we can get back to the 1970s, I was drivin' my tractor and cutting bushes. Sam Pennington, who owned the *Maine Antique Digest*, asked me to write a weekly column satirizing feminists. I guess it was pretty good because it generated a tremendous amount of hate in the feminist community. They had me on one page and Abby Zimmet, who wrote for the *Portland Press Herald*, on the opposite page.

I finally decided there were better things to do in life than making feminists mad. So here I am, I'm making this radio program, and I'm writing for papers. I discovered you've got to go see people, look them in the eye. So I drove my pickup truck all over the country. I went to every newspaper in Arkansas and said, "I'm The humble Farmer. I hope you'll run my column."

I went to see Art Buchwald. I said, "Will you do a promo for my show?" He said, "Sure. What do you want me to say?" I said you say thus and so. So on the radio he says, "Hi, Art Buchwald here. If you read anything in my column that's funny or about Maine, I stole it from The humble Farmer."

I said, "Could you say that again with a little more conviction?" So he booms out, "HI, ART BUCHWALD HERE. IF YOU..."

I did mailings to 5,000 newspaper editors across the country. I'd send little funny stories and say, "Please test run my column." And I would invite them all, all 5,000, to my home for a free lobster dinner. We had a picnic the second Sunday in August.

How big did that picnic get?

A thousand people would show up. It was a beautiful thing. Top entertainment in New England would come: bluegrass bands, folk bands, rock bands, jugglers, mimes, humorists. It was all free, and these friends would come and do $10,000 worth of entertainment for free.

Oakhurst Dairy would send cases and cases of lemonade. Coca-Cola would send up a truckload of Coke. Paper manufacturers sent cases of toilet paper for my privy. Everybody wanted to be there and be seen there.

Everybody got 20 minutes and they were off. Bam, bam, bam. It took 50 people to run the event. Angus King [former governor of Maine and now Senator] would speak.

I remember Angus stood on the stage, and he said, "Well, I can see that the Democrats believe in recyclin'" The Democrats were running former Governor Brennan again, this time against Angus. I said, "None of that, now." We had a good time, a real good time.

When did that end?

Ninety-four. My wife hated it. $1,500 was a small price to pay to reach 2,000,000 people on 50,000-watt radio stations across the country, and I was getting $750 for every talk now. Even with ADHD I was able to do this thing. But Marsha said, "You will stop having that picnic." I said, "You don't have to be here. Go away, go away for a week." She said, "We can't afford those lobsters." I said, "We can't afford not to." I was getting five, six speeches a week. She hates dealing with the public. She'd rather scrub toilets.

When I met Marsha I had been a single man for twenty years. After my wife left I came here and slept on the floor. I wrote for papers, I wrote on the walls, newspapers all over. I was writing for fifty papers, and the papers were being sent to me. They weren't in the computer. We didn't have computers then, so I'd kept all the newspapers.

Humble and his wife, "Marsha, the Almost Perfect Woman"

Piles and piles of newspapers? You read about people like that. When they die the ambulance people can't even get into the house for all the papers.

Yes, but one night I went to this Camden singles club, the "Black Fly Club." I met Marsha, and that's all she wrote. She can't stand disorder. She has done everything in this house. Painting...she will paint, she will stand and scrape the paint off old woodwork with a spoon for eight hours. For two weeks she had a little white cloth, with no solvent, and worked on this old floor. She can do that, but she can't sit here and call someone and say, "Hi, I'm calling for Robert Skoglund, an after dinner speaker. He'd like to be considered for entertainment next time you have a meeting. To whom should we be sending out promotional material?" She is fantastic on the phone, but she just can't stand doing it. I don't mind, but killin' that picnic was a big mistake. That was our marketing tool. It was runnin' smooth as a clock. The entertainers were calling me to see when and if they could appear.

This may seem a stupid question, but how do you think the coast of Maine is different from other places?

It's miserable and cold on the coast of Maine. I've written stories about how there's no stress on the coast of Maine. I've written satirical pieces about a farmer trying to get his tractor out of the barn. He's trying to get the door open, and he gets his ax, and his wife is late to teach school. Ice has frozen the door shut, and he's chopping at the ice. He breaks the ax and chips off a piece of the doorstep, and he can't get his tractor going because it's a diesel, and it's 40 years old, and it don't have a cab, and the wind is whipping and howling, and his wife steps out and gets snow in her boots because she ain't had time to lace them up.

That's when someone calls you up and says, "Oh, it must be wonderful to live there on the coast of Maine where there's no stress."

That's so true! Look, you've got hundreds of stories like that on your website. Do you mind if I reprint my favorite one?

If you think it will get people to look at *www.thehumblefarmer.com*, my website, go ahead.

THE HUMBLE FARMER'S
SPAGHETTI FOR THE SINGLE MAINE PERSON

1 box of spaghetti
2 quarts of water
1 bottle of Ragu, Meatless Spaghetti Sauce
1 green box of Kraft grated Parmesan cheese

Bring two quarts of water to a boil in one of those blue double boiler colander things [the top one has holes in it]. Put in only as much spaghetti as you want to eat right then.

Do not break spaghetti. Stand over it and swirl it with your fork. Be careful so the spaghetti don't poke out in the little holes.

As the bottom part of the spaghetti gets soft, the rest will sag like a frozen rag into the boiling water. Reduce heat so it don't boil over.

Set timer for twelve minutes and read Maine Times *personals.*
Shut off heat, lug boiler over to the sink, lift out top part and slowly
dump spaghetti on plate that came from Sicily and bears the inscrip-
tion: "Ristorante Borgia."

Open bottle of Ragu Meatless Spaghetti Sauce and pour just the right
amount of cold sauce onto the hot spaghetti. By the time you shake on
some Kraft grated cheese the whole thing is room temperature, and you
can get the whole business into you in about two minutes standing right
there at the kitchen counter by the sink.

Do not move feet. Lean to the left and rinse off plate, fork, and
spoon under the faucet. Double boiler does not require washing.

Leave plate, fork, and spoon on the counter because you will use
them in another three hours.

TIM HOLMES
Tenants Harbor, St. George
Age 67

Gold Jaguar XKE
[The fellow in the driver's seat is NOT Tim]

"Meet me at the lobster-buoy tree down the dirt road a half mile," Tim said. When I get there, I see a man standing next to a tree with a dozen brightly-colored buoys hanging from its trunk. He is tall and loose-limbed, like an old baseball player, Lou Gehrig or Joe Dimaggio.

Like a small boy showing me a prize frog, Tim wants me to see his vintage Jaguar. He opens the garage door with a flourish, "Ta-da!" The finish is gold, and the car is mint. "Sit in it! Feel the leather!" He commands. He opens the hood. "Look!" he says. "Triple carbs, 4.2 liters!"

I'm afraid he's going to insist we take it for a spin, but he says, "I know you want to see what she'll do, but I take her out just once a year."

Finally he leads me across the road to the house. It is rough-sided and appears to be owner-built, but it sits on a point with a 270-degree view of Tenants Harbor.

Tim points to a couch that takes advantage of that commanding view and heads to the kitchen to make a pot of coffee.

We moved to Maine when my father took a job with Cushman Baking Company. I was six.

I remember the Cushman man! They used to come around all the coastal towns in black and white station wagons. They'd have bread, but also cakes, cream puffs, molasses doughnuts, filled cookies, even potato chips and B&M beans. I used to wait for the toot of his horn. I'd run out with grandmother's order and a five-dollar bill. As a reward I always got a raspberry-filled cookie.

My grandmother's favorite was the molasses donuts. They're hard to find today. Grandma would slice them in half, put them under the broiler to brown, then spread them with raspberry jam. They were to die for, hot and greasy like they'd just been lifted from the hot lard, and then slathered with that tart, sweet jam.

Oh, Jesus, yes! That's the way to have 'em, when the grease is runnin' right out of them. It was a Maine tradition. It's a terrible thing that you can't get doughnuts and pie crusts cooked in lard any more.

Did you ever help with your father's deliveries?

Every night after school. When I was seven or eight, my father would pick me up after school, and I'd go on the truck with him, sometimes until nine or ten at night. Dad was a route manager. He ran a route, but he oversaw a dozen other routes, too.

When I was seven he taught me how to make change. I had a little pouch, like a carpenter's nail apron, and I could make change as fast as anyone. He showed me the tricks. When I got into school, mathematics was no big deal because, from making change, I could add and subtract and multiply in my head.

I also had a way with people. I could just go up to people and talk with them, people I didn't even know. Dad would load up a basket with things he knew they would like and send me to the door. I was this itty-bitty kid carrying a heavy basket, and people would take things out of the basket just to lighten this little kid's load.

I learned a lot from working with Dad. One thing was to not eat donuts out of the boxes between stops. People got real upset when they had paid for six donuts and found only five in the box! And I got to know people. We had poor customers, and we had rich customers, and I got to find out that they're not all that different.

I remember one lady asked me, "Whose boy are you?" I said, "I'm my father's boy." I don't know if she thought I was being a wiseass, but I thought that was what she wanted to know.

That showed you already had the Maine sense of humor. Did you have any trouble with dogs along the route?

Sometimes. My father had a little baseball bat. One time we went to this house where my father knew there was a bad dog, so he took the bat with him. I took the house across the street. Unfortunately the dog happened to be visiting across the street.

What did you do?

I did what my father taught me, to walk right past like the dog wasn't even there. Don't ever lock eyes with them.

Remember the joke about the salesman and the dog that didn't bite? A salesman pulls up in front of a general store. Two old fellows are sitting on the porch, and there's a dog lying on the ground. The salesman says, "Does your dog bite?" One of the old fellows says, "No, my dog don't bite." The salesman gets out of the car, and the dog immediately jumps up and muckles on to his leg. The salesman jumps back into his car and yells, "Jesus! I thought you said your dog didn't bite!" The old fellow says, "My dog don't, but that one there does."

That story probably originated in Maine, but I also saw it in a Peter Sellers movie, *The Pink Panther*. Peter enters a hotel through a revolving door, and as he comes in, a fellow asks, "Sir, may I take your coat?" Peter says, "That would be nice," and hands him the coat. The fellow puts on the coat, walks out the revolving door, and is never seen again. [At this point Tim laughs so hard and long I have to fetch him a glass of water.] And THEN [still laughing] he goes up to the counter and asks, "Does your dog bite?" And it just continues like that, one slapstick joke after another. Priceless!

What did you do after high school?

I went to Maine Maritime Academy. I graduated there in 1965. It wasn't a very good time to graduate because the draft was on, and I got sucked right into the Vietnam War, right into the Military Sea Lift Command. They leased these old American Export Line freighters to transport bombs and missiles and weapons of mass destruction to Vietnam. They had what we called "the long gray line," old Victory ships from WWII. It was our job to go out to California and reactivate these ships. Once we got them going we took them to Oakland and loaded up with bombs, and missiles and napalm, all that good stuff. We supplied the Special Forces.

I befriended a lot of Special Forces guys. I had the honor of working with some pretty fine guys in the Rangers and the Navy Seals, and the Green Berets. Some of those guys didn't come home. A lot of them are still over there. They never found them. The military wouldn't even say where they had been. We were in a lot of places we weren't supposed to be: Cambodia, Laos.

Once in Cambodia I was watching TV, and someone asked President Johnson if there were any U.S. servicemen in Cambodia. He said, "No." He was correct, because we were civilians, stockpiling stuff in places where the Army was planning to go.

For a time I was working for the NSA [National Security Agency]. I thought "NSA" stood for "National Shipping Agency." I was paid by something called "NSA," and we never knew what we were doing or where the hell we were going!

I use to go up to the bridge and chew the captain out. I'd say, "Where the hell are we headed?" He'd say, "I'll be damned if I know!" And I said, "You're the captain, for God's sake! You don't even know where the hell we're going?" He said, "No, they keep changing our orders. Nobody knows where we're going." He'd get these coded messages, "Change heading to... ," then half an hour later, "Change heading to... ." Finally they'd shoot us into some little hole somewhere.

Everywhere we went we had escorts: PT boats, mine-sweepers, destroyers. You might as well have painted "Hey, look, we're carrying bombs" on the side of the ship. Going up the Saigon River was not a lot of fun! They knew we were carrying something important. It got so bad in Da Nang and Cam Ranh Bay we couldn't even stay overnight. What a pain in the ass! Every night at sunset we had to go out and steam around in circles. The Viet Cong had frogmen who would attach mines. We lost a couple of ships that way.

Did you save up your pay during the war years?

I saved a lot because there was nowhere or no way to spend it. That's how I got this piece of land [a deep-water point with a million=dollar view of Long Cove in Tenants Harbor]. By the time I got home I had enough money to pay off my school debts and put a down payment on this piece of land.

How did you meet your wife?

I was working down at Hall's Market in Tenants Harbor. I had worked there off and on since I was eleven. I used to flirt with my future wife's sister, who was married. I worked the meat counter, and she used to stop in. She was real cute. She was German and had met her husband when he was stationed over there.

One day I said, "Are there any more like you where you came from?" She said, "I have a younger sister. In fact she's coming here Labor Day." I said, "Are you going to introduce me to her?" To make a long story short, her sister came up, and she introduced me to her.

Now the first thing I had bought when I got out of the service was this land. Then I had bought the Jaguar XKE. I had a pickup, too, because I found an XKE couldn't carry much lumber. I was building my house at the time, and I said, "Shit, this thing is useless in building a house."

I said to myself, "I'm not going to take this girl out in no XKE because I won't know whether it's me or the Jaguar she wants." So I picked her up in my pickup. I brought her down to this house which was unfinished. I had just a couch that pulled out into a bed, and the only plumbing I had was a toilet in a bathroom with no door. The couch looked right at the toilet because there was no door.

She was sitting on the couch. Before we got to go anywhere I said, "Look, I've got to wash up a little bit. I'll be right with you." I had mixed her a nice drink to hold her over. Unfortunately I put too much whiskey in it, and it almost killed her. I wasn't trying to get her drunk or anything. I was just nervous.

She sat right there with her drink, and I said, "I'll be right with you." I was afraid my feet were smellin' bad, so I went into the bathroom, took off my shoes, and washed my feet in the toilet. I dried my feet, and then I took the lid off the tank, and I started washing my face and under my arms—a sponge bath, you know?

She's sitting there staring at me. She says, "Are you washing your face in that toilet tank?" I said, "Of course I am. I wouldn't wash my face the same place I washed my feet!"

When I came out she was ready for another drink because I think she thought she was hooked up with a fruitcake, and she didn't know how else she was going to get through the evening. I'm sure she thought I was some kind of nut, but we got married a year later.

How did you support yourselves?

I worked at Hall's Market, now the Tenants Harbor Market. There are so many stories about Hall's Market I don't even know where to begin.

How about one involving people from away?

OK, here's one. In supermarket delis they'd always have you take a number. We were never that busy in Hall's Market, but I said, "These summer people will probably get a kick out of us having numbers." I used to make homemade coleslaw, and the containers had these big plastic lids. I put a nail in the pole by the meat counter, and I put numbers on these big lids.

When you'd come to the meat counter you'd take a number. Well, people were taking the lids home because they thought they were funny—a souvenir of Maine, I guess. Pretty soon it got down to where there was only one number, #23. So I hung #23 on the pole under the sign that says, "Take a Number."

Hall's Market, Tenant's Harbor

One day I was working away, and I was busting my ass. I was trying to make sandwiches, and I kept getting interrupted. I was making these Italian sandwiches and putting them in the deli display case, and [Tim's voice drops to a conspirantal whisper] this guy from Massachusetts come in.

Massachusetts people are some of the worst?

The absolute worst. We had a name for them: "Massholes." Maybe you don't want to print that, but anyway, here he comes, and the first thing he says, which really got me, was, "Are those fresh?" Jesus Christ, I'm standing there putting them together! I don't know what come over me. I said, to myself, "What is the matter with these people anyway?" I said, "No, sir, they are not. They are tomorrow's." He said, "I'd like to have one." I said, "You can't." He said, "Why not?" I said, "I just told you they're for tomorrow. Today's are all gone."

Well, a couple of more people drifted over, listening to this conversation, and I kept going with it. This guy wasn't going to get the best of me! So he said again, "Well, regardless, I'd really like to have one." And I said, "I just told you today's are all gone." "Well, couldn't you make an exception?" I said, "How can I make an exception if these sandwiches are all for tomorrow?" He said, "Is there any way I can get a sandwich?" I said, "Yes, take a number." He takes #23 off the pole, and the minute he did it everybody started to laugh. He's here looking at #23, and I call out, "Number 24." He's looking around. So then I went to #25. Finally he put the number back on the pole and went off. Never saw him again. I said to myself, "Well there, I finally got one of them bastards." I lost the sale, but it did me a world of good. It got me through the rest of the day.

Did a lot of tourists come into the store?

Oh yes, quite a few. There was guys came in with big cigars goin' and smokin' up the store. They'd say, "I gotta have this, and I gotta have that, and I'm in a hurry." Well of course then I went extra slow.

I had another thing. My wife finally made me take it down. Up in front of the store we had a long counter with a big cash register. I had the idea of putting a second cash register at the other end of the counter for people with just a few things, so I made this great big sign over my little cash register, "SPEEDY CHECKOUT—ONE ITEM OR LESS."

A guy comes up with a pack of cigarettes and a Coke. I said [Tim's voice drops again to a whisper], "You're in the wrong lane." He says, "I only got two items." I said, "Yeah, I know." I pointed up at the sign that says "One Item or Less." I said, "You've got two." "Jesus," he said, "there's ten people in line with shopping carts full of stuff!" I said, "I'm sorry. One item or less." Jesus, didn't we have some fun!

Another guy come up and said, "I've got nothin'." I said, "Then you're in the right lane!" He said, "I just want to know how the hell to get to Port Clyde." I said, "You can't get there from here. You've got to go back and start over." He said, "What do you mean?" I said, "Have you crossed the bridge yet?" He said, "What bridge? I didn't cross no bridge. I came down Route 131." I said, "So you didn't cross the bridge! Well, Christ, you gotta go back. If you haven't crossed the bridge, you ain't here yet, and we can't even talk to you!" He says, "Jesus!" turns around, gets in his car, and goes back up the road. On the way out the door my wife heard him say, "These people are crazy. They ain't right in the head!"

But we did have other people that came here every summer. I got to know those people. Some of them were all right. They were from away, but they were a different caliber. They grew up here summers, so they knew the rules.

Your store stories remind me of one down in Harpswell. They had a general store, and it was a great place for the older fishermen to congregate. Besides conversation, the main attraction was just watching people from away. Well, they took a nickel, which today would be worth a buck, and they soldered it to a roofing nail and drove it into the wooden floor. The old fishermen would sit there all day long, like they were fishing, and wait for a tourist to come in and try to pick that nickel up. I'm sure the store lost a few customers, but as you said, it was worth it.

We had this guy who hung around the store, Eugene. Eugene was a tad on the slow side, but he was a very good human being, and he liked to help me out in the store. We all called him, "Tookie." Tookie Morris was his name, and he was a character. You never knew what he was going to say, but he had manners and was very polite.

He couldn't see too good, and he was a little dyslexic, too. He was in eighth grade three years, and they just wrote him off. There was no special education back then. If he'd a had special ed and a set of glasses, I think he could of gotten though high school.

Anyway, Tookie was the greeter at Hall's Market, like they have up to Walmart. He and I really hit it off. He used to get there early and help me put the papers together, and he swept the floor and cleaned up at the end of the day. I paid him in things to eat. He never ate regular meals, but I let him eat anything in the store.

He was the only guy I ever knew could eat a cream horn—you know, those pastry horns filled with whipped up Crisco and sugar—and drink a glass of grape juice at the same time. I said, "How the hell can you do that?" He'd laugh.

On Sundays we'd have 150 papers we had to stuff with the advertising and the comics. People would be beating on the door. We're on our hands and knees putting these papers together. We'd get all done, and there would be 30 *Boston Globe* inserts left over. I'd say, "Tookie, what did you do with the *Globes*?" He says, "I put them over here with the Portland papers." "Jesus, Tookie," I said, "You filled all the Portland papers with the Boston inserts!" Meanwhile all these people are standing outside pounding on the door and yelling, "I just want a paper. Let me in!"

We fixed most of them. I can only imagine what some people thought when they saw the Portland paper was filled with Boston advertising.

This brings me to one more story about Tookie. We practiced this routine all summer long. I told Tookie, "We're going to wait until Columbus Day, when the crowd thins out. I said, "When someone from Massachusetts comes and asks for directions, this is what we're going to do. When I point to you, you say your line."

Columbus Day come. That's when the leaf peepers start appearin'. This big Lincoln Continental slithers up the road and slows down. Tookie is out on the porch and spots the plate. He comes running in and yells, "Mathachuthetts!"

Tookie and I go out on the porch. Understand now that Tookie wore his baseball cap off to one side, and he had this wandering eye. I could make one of my eyes wander, too. I took my hat and I tipped it the opposite way.

The Lincoln pulls to a stop in front of the store. The window comes down, and the driver yells across his wife, "How do you get to Martinsville?" Tookie looks at me and then at him, and he says, "My brother here takes me." The guy looks at his wife, Tookie laughs, "huh-uh-uh!," and the guy says to his wife, "These people aren't right!" The window goes up, and the car lays rubber.

That made my whole summer. Tookie and I had been practicing that all summer, and we pulled it off perfect. That's one guy will never forget the Tenants Harbor General Store.

Did Tookie have family?

The whole town was his family. Everybody in town loved him. He mowed lawns around town, and nobody ever complained about the strips he missed because of his poor eyesight.

People always picked Tookie up when he was walking. One day two women from away pulled over to look out over the water. Tookie, walking by, opened the door and jumped into the back seat. The two women are terrified. They don't know who the hell he is. Tookie thought they had stopped to pick him up [breaks up laughing].

Tookie was a great asset to the community, a genuine friend to everybody. Everybody in town attended Tookie's funeral.

Do you have any memories of the Wyeths?

Oh yeah. Jamie used to hang out in the summer and do things with the rest of us.

The Wyeth homestead is in Cushing. Eight Bells, where Andy did a lot of painting, is at the end of Horse Point, five miles down the road. Betsy, Andy's widow, owns and stays on Allen Island. They have a big sheep thing going on out there. Jamie has a place on Southern Island and a house on Barter Street right here in Tenants Harbor. I see Jamie quite a bit. We grew up together, not real close friends, but in the same gang. He was a regular kid.

I've got some Jamie Wyeths here. That's one [Tim walks me around the living room, pointing at Wyeth prints and paintings], and that's one. That's the Thomaston church—that's Andy's. And this is Walter Anderson, Andy's boyhood friend. And this here is Jamie's "Buoy Tree" [brightly colored lobster buoys hanging from the branches of a tree, like a Christmas tree]. That's like my buoy tree. I had mine before he painted that. I got that picture for my wife, and he doctored it up on the bottom with what they call a "remarque."

I went over to Jamie's house to see if I could get a copy for my wife for her birthday. He knew Gaby from the store, so he did that little thing on the bottom, a little personal note from the artist. You notice the buoy there? He put our name on it. He gave it to her for her birthday.

I also have a book Andy gave me. One day Andy came into the store, and he was really down in the dumps. Toward the end he was depressed a lot because all his friends were dying. He was real upset about Walter Anderson dying. [Walter Anderson, known locally as "Uncle Walt," was the subject of many of Andrew Wyeth's most famous paintings].

Is it true that Andy went into the hospital and painted Walt while Walt was still in his deathbed?

That is true. Anyway, he came into the store one day really down. I could tell he was upset. He had this Stutz Bearcat automobile, a beautiful gold machine. You knew some celebrity was driving that. Anyway, he couldn't get the goddamned gas cap off. He had arthritis somethin' terrible. So I went out and got the gas cap off.

He said, "Damned arthritis! I don't know how the hell I'm going to be able to paint." I said, "Well you gotta take care of those hands. Don't be foolin' around with no gas caps." So I pumped the gas for him. And I filled a one-gallon can, too. He said, "I've got to take this gallon back to the fellow who loaned it to me to get down here." I said, "That would be nice since he come out and helped you." And he said, "Well, you're helping me too. You're pumping the gas." I said, "Well, that's the least I can do. You're some kind of friggin' celebrity, and I don't want you hurting your hands at my store. You take care of them hands. He said, "Thank you very much. I'll be back. I've got something I want to give you."

I never thought no more about it. I went up to New Hampshire to see my folks one weekend, and I called my wife. She says, "Jeez, Andy Wyeth was in here, and he's given you this book. You ought to see it! It's got a nice inscription inside that says it's for you!" It was the book of paintings by the three Wyeths: N.C., Andy, and Jamie.

Later Jamie was over at the house and Gaby showed it to him. He said, "Let me have that. I'll add something, too, but you'll have a hard time getting N.C. to write anything!"

Here's another Andy story. Every Friday Andy wanted two dozen white chicken eggs. I said, "What the hell is it with the white eggs?" He said, "Can you get white eggs?" I said, "No, I can only get brown ones around here. The only time we get white ones is at Easter so the kids can color them. Nobody eats those." I said, "You into paintin' Easter eggs now, Andy?" "Naow!" he said. "I'm not into painting Easter eggs. I use white eggs to make tempera for painting! White eggs make better tempera than brown eggs. I want two dozen every week, standing order, maybe even three dozen." "Well," I said, "I'll try to get them." He said, "If I paint anything good with these eggs, I'll bring it in to show you."

A couple months later he comes in. He says, "You got any *New York Times*?" I says, "Yeah, I got five or six," He says, "I'll take them all." I said, "You want ALL of them? What the hell you want all of them for? If you read one, they're all the same." He said, "I'll take them all." So he took them all. As he was puttin' them under his arm, I see on the front page this big headline about Andy and this romance he was havin' with Helga.

Helga was into the store a lot. She was actually Andy's nurse and assistant. Supposedly. She was a good friend and a helper to him, and Betsy was always out on the island. Andy liked to paint at Eight Bells, and that's where Helga lived. I don't know that there was anything goin' on between them, but he painted a lot of her, and a lot of them with not too many clothes on. But that was what Andy did, and he did it with real class.

Helga is still around. I saw her last week. She kinda looked after Andy and was his assistant. Andy's sister, Carolyn, also lived at Eight Bells, and I used to deliver groceries down there. Andy was always there, but you didn't bother him because he was down in the shed, painting. You didn't want to bother him. He had a sign over the door that said, "If this isn't the second coming of Christ, don't even knock!"

Helga sure looked like an interesting subject to paint.

She was German, rugged. She struck up a friendship with my wife, Gaby, who was also German. She loved to come into the store and talk German with Gaby.

How do you think Betsy took the discovery of more than a hundred paintings of Helga?

I don't think there was ever a bad feeling between Betsy and Andy. Understand, they had something no one else ever had. You could see that. Andy and Betsy were in love.

Of course the press played the story to the hilt because it sold newspapers and magazines. Andy and Helga were great friends, but they weren't lovers.

Is Tenants Harbor still a pretty good place to live?

I've been all over the world. I don't say that to brag, but when I was in the merchant marine we stopped at seventy-two countries. Of all the places I've been, I still came back here because this is where I wanted to be.

This is where I grew up. This is where I started learning things. This is where I actually found out that girls weren't just soft little boys. I came into being here.

I was at sea eleven years, and after I got tired of being at sea, I still wanted to see it, be on the edge of it. I always said, "I'm going to do three things. I'm going to go to college; I'm going to own a Jaguar; and I'm going to buy a piece of land on the water and live there the rest of my life." And I did.

CHARLES WILDER OAKES
Artist
Port Clyde, St. George
Age 54

Self-portrait of the artist as a young man

I park next to a mountain of firewood. There is no lawn, no walkway, no shrubbery—just a larger version of Henry David Thoreau's cabin on Walden Pond.

Charles Wilder Oakes opens the door and gestures me into the rough-sawn handmade house. Inside there is no entrance foyer, no coat closet, no interior walls at all—just an immense welded-steel stove in the center that looks as if it could heat a Walmart.

I focus on the man in front of me. It is as if Wilder Oakes has grown into his name. There is a wild look about him: in his physical being, in his thick gray mane, in his rough woolen garb, and—most striking of all—in his dark eyes.

But then he speaks, and I am immediately at ease.

My mother gave birth to me up in Rockland, but I was lugged down the road after a couple of days, so I say I was born in Port Clyde.

How I gained entrance into this world was my mother and father got together. He was a fisherman; she was a young woman packing sardines. He was fifty-six and she was going on thirty-five when I came along. He was already married.

I've never made any bones about this. I was the talk of the town before I was even born [laughs]. They ended up making a home in the top of his fish shack.

Wilder's childhood home, top of the fish shack

Grace Metalious' book, *Peyton Place*, came out that summer. It was a best-seller, and the next summer they made the movie in Camden. Port Clyde was its own Peyton Place. Anyway, dad moved out of his family, never divorced, and stayed with my mother about five years. They broke up and she found us a rent, still overlooking the cove and dad's fish house. I realize now alcohol had a lot to do with their parting company.

What do you remember of your father?

He was a good man, kind and well liked. Folks talk about his laugh. I agree, he had a great laugh. He had a good singing voice, a real crooner. We'd walk the path from the shop over to the Dip Net and I'd always get a cheeseburger. Whenever I have one today it's comfort food because of that. He had a tender side to him that I understand and admire today.

He took me halibut trawling, and the ones we landed were bigger than me. I loved being on his boat anytime I could. It was never enough, or enough time. I wish he'd lived longer. I could have learned more. He continued to be my father more or less, as best he could, but he was an alcoholic. That ran in my whole family.

There were six Hussey sisters. They came over from Friendship in the late 1800s and early 1900s. They married the young men of Port Clyde and produced most of the fishing families that survive today. Port Clyde was built pretty much around those Davises, Stones, Andersons, Coffins, and Conants. My dad was a Conant. I'm descended from Roger Conant, who founded Salem, Massachusetts.

But I have Hussey blood, too. My dad's mother was a Hussey. Uncle Robert and Uncle Walt were Andersons. We had to grow up calling everybody "Uncle" and "Aunt" down there because there were so many kin. There wasn't this cousin bullshit, you know. It was considered a sign of respect.

Uncle Walt Anderson: not the Walter Anderson who was the subject of so many of Andrew Wyeth's portraits?

One and the same. He really was my cousin, but I'll always call him "Uncle." That respect remains ingrained. Uncle Walt's mother and my dad's mother were sisters.

So you were raised in the attic of this little fishing shack, where your father built his traps and mended his nets?

Yes. It was unfinished attic and uninsulated. The whole downstairs was his shop. It was unplumbed, no amenities. An adult couldn't stand up, just only in the middle, upstairs. You had to climb a ladder to get to it. We had a Victrola, and I remember nights drifting off to sleep listening to it.

No plumbing at all?

We had a chamber pot. I'll never forget the smell, nor the sound of piss and crap hitting the water or the mudflats in the morning. My dad would take the pot down the ladder and throw the contents into the cove. Back then, it was common, and garbage went over, too. The first painting I did after I quit drinking was my mother throwing the garbage off the wharf.

As a child, that was my job at Dingley Island. I was given a raisin-filled cookie for rowing a paper bag full of garbage out to the middle of the New Meadows River, putting a rock in the bottom, and sinking it. Of course the rock would fall through the bottom of the wet bag, and the garbage would float to the surface, but I had done as instructed. That's what you did because there were no garbage collectors, not even a town dump.

Yes. It was like the social hour. You'd hear them down on the wharf, and you'd hear the bags going splash. "How you doin', chief?" Splash. "Can't complain." Splash.

I can also remember looking out the window of the shack and seeing wharf rats. Man, some of them were HUGE, like Jack Russell terriers and just as frisky.

I used to crawl under the wharves. I was real skinny, so I could slither through the pilings and cribbing. One day I was slithering through there, and I came face- to-face with one of them things, and it scared the bejeezus out of me. Big eyeballs, big yellow teeth, and just looking at me. It was in a whole nest of rats.

As I grew to be a teenager, I started drinking. Part of the whole experience was to take a PBR [Pabst Blue Ribbon], sit down on the wharf among the traps, and take in the whole scene, and just kinda space out.

It was a lot slower pace back then. It was mostly fisher-folk. Everybody knew everybody, and the summer people cleared out on Labor Day and left us alone.

One day I was at Uncle Robert's, and I'd just gotten done mowing a lawn. Uncle Walt fished out a PBR and gave it to me, my first one.

Did it taste good?

It tasted wonderful! Not so much the taste, but the feeling I got off it, that lift. The thing is, the ride can get bumpy pretty quick. I took leave from life, as I had known it, at seventeen. I had some fun, but I paid a price for it. I'm having a hell of a lot more fun now, though. That's a fact! These are far and away my best days.

How did you obtain beer at seventeen?

Through Uncle Walt or wherever I could find it. Older kids. Sometimes I knew where people hid stuff. The "five finger discount." But it was a no-no to come home drunk. I was only 145 pounds, so it wouldn't take more than two or three beers.

Did you develop a craving for it, or did you think it was just a cool thing to do?

I hadn't yet reached the stage of craving. There was this background obsession starting in though. I found out later that's kind of a classic telltale sign something might not be normal, along with wheedling for it, and stealing it.

What are some of the Wyeth paintings Uncle Walt appeared in?

One of the best known is "The Rum Runner." There's another one called "Adrift," where he appears to be either asleep or dead in a dory. "Young Swede," "Watch Cap." Another one is called "Night Hauling," where he's pulling up a wooden lobster trap at night in a dory, and he's flashing a light through it, looking for lobsters, illegally.

Why did Andy Wyeth paint so many pictures of Uncle Walt?

When Andy came to Port Clyde he was a couple years older than Walt. For whatever reason, the two of them fell in together as kids. They just "got" each other, and it never seemed to cease.

Walt Anderson, Cecil Anderson, and Andrew Wyeth [holding paintbrushes]

Was Uncle Walt Andy's passport to the Port Clyde community?

I'd say so. Walt was Andy's first chum here. Pretty inseparable. They went out to the islands together, dug clams, poached lobsters, and from stories I've heard, did their share of drinking and carousing together.

What did people think of Uncle Walt? What was his reputation around Port Clyde?

Pirate, reprobate, drunk, poacher, womanizer. If anything turned up missing, "Uncle Walt did it!"

Alcoholism is in the family, all his brothers and sisters were drunks. His mother, Stella, outlived all of her children. One of the daughters went down to New York. She assumed a false name, and they found her wandering around the streets. She died at Bellevue, and they shipped her back up here.

I researched that as part of a murder case in Port Clyde, back during Prohibition. It involved rum running, and the families, and getting booze for the Wyeths and other wealthy summer people. There were clandestine phone calls and coded messages, where the hooch was going to be dropped off. A young boy, 11 years old, got killed because he saw something he shouldn't have. They say that he drowned, but he didn't. He got whacked in the head and dumped into the pond. Everybody around here knew who did it. It was a sensational case at the time, state-wide, but there was reasonable doubt in court.

Aside from his being your cousin, what was your relationship with Uncle Walt?

I would pay him to get me beer. I never knew how much I was going to get. He'd drink some of it before it ever got to me. Out of a six-pack, I'd get two, sometimes three.

I had mixed feelings about him. I used him to get alcohol, so I had to put up with him. He could be foul mouthed, and I was a sensitive kid. He wasn't a bad guy, but there was definitely an edge to him. At the end he was trashed all the time.

I didn't know then what I know now about alcoholism. I learned the hard way. I had a gut feeling I was taking my chances when I first started flirting with it. All I had to do was look around Port Clyde to see the odds were stacked against me. I thought I could beat it, but then other factors came into play, and I got hooked. It's the first drink that gets you drunk.

Did you ever consider being a fisherman?

My dad died before he could teach me. He tried toward the end, but I was too young, and he was too sick. He'd stopped drinking the last five or six years of his life, but the hard physical life had taken its toll. He took me out in his skiff, and I hauled some traps, so I understood the basics, but I never learned how to deal with the other lobstermen or the dealers.

I did go sternman several summers, so I could find out what my dad had gone through. That was part of my genealogical research, part of my trying to understand where I came from, what I'm made up of. I also wasn't selling many paintings at the time, so I needed the money.

But I understood I was going to be an artist from real young, four or five. I was drawing things at four that you could recognize.

I flunked math, didn't get it, didn't want to get it. My early report cards said, "Charles looks out the window too much, and has cultivated that ability." [laughs]

Actually, I shortchange myself by saying I was a lousy student. That was not entirely true. I won awards for creative writing. I wrote plays in high school and had them performed. In my senior year I submitted a short story to *The New Yorker*. I got a handwritten note back from someone named Sonny. It said, "You're awfully close. Please submit again." I still have that note somewhere. Even my first rejection slip was encouraging!

And I was an avid reader: everything from Thoreau to Ursula K. LeGuin, the science fiction writer. Also Henry Beston, and the Nearings' "Living the Good Life." Here I was fourteen years old, reading this stuff.

I had a fascination with the spiritual. Thoreau, Kahlil Gibran, I had this thing about comparative religion. I was trying to find stuff in the school libraries. The library was my friend. When I found Joseph Campbell, I was in hog heaven!

What did your mother think of you when you were growing up?

We had a death-bed conversation, where you get honest because you just don't know. She went down to Portland and got open-heart surgery. She never came out of it. She stroked out. We had the whole evening together before she went in.

Things got heart-to-heart. I told her about the parts of my life she hadn't known. I told her my very first memory was seeing an angel in front of the fish shack [shows me the old photograph of the shack]. That's the big panel I'm painting right now.

Did you really see an angel?

Absolutely, and I talked with the angel. Not words out loud, but mind-to-mind. Telepathic. I was two and a half. I looked up, and I thought the sun was coming out. Here's this glowing human-like figure, floating above the road. What was really odd was that when I looked around, it was raining everywhere else, but there was this glowing light behind the angel, and the angel was that light, too.

Was the angel male or female?

It looked female. It wore something like a white gown. Shimmery, sparkly. The angel was blonde or reddish blonde. That's why there are a lot of blondes in my paintings. My first true love was a blonde.

At eight I had a near-death experience. I tried to swim across a lobster pound, and I caught a charley horse halfway across. The only thing that saved me was a nurse going to work, and she heard the other kids yelling. By then I had gone down for the third time and given up. I saw a line coming down like this, and another line coming across, like the scope on a gun, four slices. The moment the line came down, I heard a low note that got sweeter and sweeter and higher and higher, and the moment the two lines touched, it produced an arc, and the arc was an incredibly bright light.

Then the upper right hand piece blew away. So I had three pieces and this bright light shining through. Then the lower left peeled back, so I had just two pieces of my final moments in the water. Then the other two pieces stripped away, and I was in the light. I was surrounded by light. I thought, "This is cool."

Then these color bars passed me, and I was going toward an even brighter light. I understood those colored bar things were ancestors, spirits, guides. They definitely were conscious. Then I thought, "Oh, my mother's gonna miss me!" The moment I had that thought, I stopped moving forward. It came to me clearly there was something I was supposed to accomplish back here. I've carried that ever since.

It was peaceful there. I didn't want to leave, but there was an awareness my time was just not up. So back I came. The whole experience shook me to the core. I was just a kid.

I woke up on my side, coughing and puking salt water. I was immediately embarrassed. Number one, I had caught a charley horse. Number two, someone had to save me. Number three, I had to go home and tell my mother. I didn't do number three. I stayed outside until my mother left the house. Then I ran in and got changed, so she never knew I had drowned until I told her as she was lying there in the hospital. She took it all in, and after a long pause she says, "I always knew you were an odd child." [laughs]

Did you go to art school after high school?

There was a woman in the village. Margaret Lewis came here in the 1930s and bought a house on Horse Point Road. She discovered Port Clyde through studying with the painter, Robert Henri. She bought the house just a stone's throw from the Wyeth place, "Eight Bells."

She had money, and she became the town's first woman selectman. Looking back I think she ran for selectman so she could identify the town's hardship cases.

This was back in '67. I was eleven. My mother was on the State [on welfare]. My dad would bring shorts [short, illegal lobsters] every so often and some fish. That was the best he could do.

Margaret changed Port Clyde lives in a karmic way. My life wouldn't have been the same without her, and the lives of lots of other people, too. She bought houses for people knowing there was little chance she would be paid back. She bought men fishing boats. In return she would get fresh fish and maybe a little payment. She bought a number of kids, including me, their first car. She paid for apartments in Port Clyde. She paid for textbooks when people went to school.

This was behind the scenes. The people she took an interest in, she saw through the rest of their lives. She was my first patron. I wouldn't have the same Port Clyde inside of me today without her intervention. It all feels like a novel. A lot of my life does. But yeah, she encouraged me to go to college, and she chipped in here and there. Not a lot, and I wouldn't ask her, either. I had a weird pride thing.

Did she encourage your art?

She did. She bought my first drawings. My first drawings were of wharfs, boats, the Lone Ranger and Tonto, kid stuff. She doted over them. She was like, "You've really got a lot of talent." And when I showed some musical talent, she bought me my first guitar, a 12-string Yamaha, which is a beautiful-sounding guitar [picks up the guitar and plays a chord].

There should be some sort of remembrance or recognition.

I recognize her every time I'm interviewed. Her name was Margaret L. Lewis.

One time I woke up in the middle of a bitter cold winter night, and my wife didn't want me to leave the bed. "Where are you going?" "I've got to write something to Margaret."

I poured my heart out in a letter and went back to bed. The next morning I popped it in the mailbox. Margaret passed away two weeks later.

Her bookkeeper told me Margaret received the letter. I had no idea she was sick. The bookkeeper said she cried and cried when she read it. I was the only person to thank her for all she had done. For whatever reason, I was led to get up in the middle of the cold night to write that letter.

You are spiritual, aren't you?

Well, the angel and the letter …. Because of my birth circumstance, I always felt out of place, yet I knew it was my town, too. I knew I had a lot to say about the town, even though the things I have to say are universal. They are autobiographical to an extent, but Port Clyde is universal.

"I knew I had a lot to say about the town." Do you mean by speaking through your art?

Hmm! Yeah. You're the first to pick that up. Thank you. I never thought that, but yes, you are absolutely right.

I don't know a lot about art, so would you describe yours?

I won't be pigeonholed. "Outsider" artist. That's the latest one. It's my spiritual practice, my joy. But you know what? It's ALL spiritual. This whole trip walking around on this planet.

When I look at your paintings I see, not one scene, but multiple scenes going on at the same time.

One of my wives said, "There are already five paintings on that one canvas! Just sell it and get on with the next one." Yeah, my paintings are a kind of theater unfolding on canvas. [He opens a notebook.] As a painting progresses, I enter notes, my dreams, pieces of poetic interpretation. The notes, the "script" if you will, goes with the finished painting. [He brings over a large painting showing a man chopping wood, a snowy day outside, and a woodstove in a kitchen.] Here is the woodchopper, and the piece of wood he is chopping has a scene within it. The wood is remembering its past life as a tree. You see, it's remembering a rock wall, some other trees, and love. Maybe someone had once wrapped their arms around the tree.

That's wild! Looking at your paintings, I feel like I am inside your head, experiencing your dreams of growing up in Port Clyde. But you are now a recovering alcoholic. What led up to your saying, "Jesus, I've got to stop!"

The party wasn't just winding down; it had been way over for a long time. I'd been married three times. Each one of those marriages ended due to the bottle. Wife number three put it real good, "If I'd known how much you drank, I never would have married you." I felt sick and tired and dead-ended and off-purpose. I drowned and came back, don't forget. I was told I had a purpose I was supposed to accomplish back here. I evidently wanted to live just a little bit more than I wanted to die.

How much were you drinking at your worst?

At the end between eighteen and twenty 16-ounce beers a day, plus whatever else I might come across. I pretty much walked around with a beer in my hand. I don't remember painting a lot of my paintings. I don't even know where a lot of my paintings went.

When I first sobered up, I began to hear what people were saying about me, that I was finished. I was shaking all the time. I couldn't even hold a paintbrush.

I was under tremendous pressure. I still had shows in New York I had to honor. I was dealing with the melee of selling paintings in New York, the loneliness of having loved and broken up with someone really special, and the constant craving and obsession for alcohol. It was nuts, insane! And I was being interviewed by everybody: *Down*

East magazine, the local papers, Salt Institute for Documentary Studies. Salt followed me around everywhere I went for three months. I cringe a little at some of the things I said in those interviews now, I was a dry-drunk. But everything serves a purpose, and I choose to make it a positive one. The silver lining is that those interviews are evidence that it does get better. The mind gets clearer. In the beginning I was scared that sobering up was going to affect my creativity. They don't call alcohol "spirits" for nothing. I'd created under the influence for so long I was afraid to find out. But I was sick and tired of being sick and tired. I made up my mind to set aside any expectations about what might become of me. You've been teaching people how to treat you all your life, and now you're going to change the rules, big time. You learn that what people think of you is none of your damn business.

Has your body come to equilibrium now?

My mind is healing along with my spirit. Life is good. I still have a lot of paintings to do, people to meet. I realize I had this weird fear if I painted the angel, then I would have accomplished my purpose here on earth, so I put off painting the angel.

Painting the angel vision is a real breakthrough for you?

It's huge. It's really about moving beyond old fears.

It's too bad you weren't ready for New York at the time.

I'm going back. A major gallery approached me, I'd like to talk to them again or make whole new connections. That's what it's really about, anyway. That was from just one showing. The guy looks at "The Ex-wives Clambake" and he says, "Have you got any more like that?" I said, "Well, I've got a couple more." Linda Bean [granddaughter of L.L.Bean] just bought the "Ex-Wives Clambake." So it'll reside right here in Port Clyde. Anyway, I'm happy to be clean and sober, grateful to be alive. My art is evolving because it's a reflection of the sober me. I'm finding whole new levels of clarity. I've become wiser I think, happier for sure. I like to think I've become better, and my paintings will, too.

DOWN EAST
Bucksport to Eastport

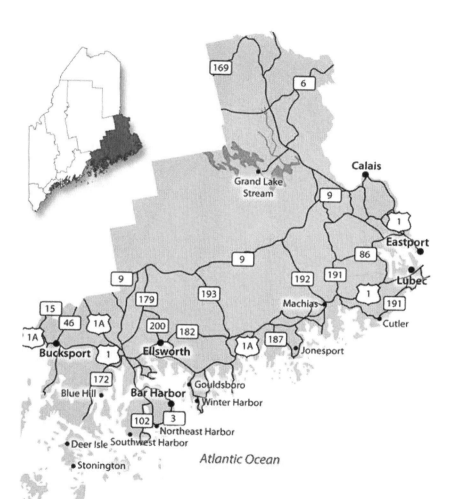

WILLIAM CARPENTER
Professor and Author
Bucksport
Age 74

Bill Carpenter expounding in his College of the Atlantic office

Knowing I was writing a book about the people of the Maine coast, a friend lent me his copy of "The Wooden Nickel." It is the story of Lucas "Lucky" Lunt, a decidedly unlucky fisherman, and his struggles to navigate the too-rapidly changing world. The tale itself is gripping, but what really captured me was the author's total mastery of the Maine fisherman's dialect.

When I discovered the author was actually a prize-winning poet, Yeats scholar, and professor of Literature at College of the Atlantic, I knew I had to meet him.

I came to Maine when I was nine and my dad got a job at Colby College as Chair of the Art History Department. His office was up in the attic with roof insulation hanging down, and his only equipment was an old magic-lantern slide projector. After a couple of years, though, he pulled together some Maine artists and donations from well-heeled neighbors and started a little museum [the Colby College Museum of Art] which has now of course grown into one of the finest in New England.

Dad was also a skilled painter and a truly great watercolorist. My whole family used to have drawing sessions, and they could render anything. All except me, I couldn't even draw a stick figure, and I still can't, despite many attempts. A fault in the replication of family genes deprived me of the 5U4B chromosome, the drawing gene [laughs]. My father's heart was in his own painting, but his museum and his teaching took precious time from his artistic work.

Tell me about your family tree.

My grandmother was a twin. Her progeny have tended to the artistic and literary. Her twin, Bertha's, have excelled in science. Her son Buck Ketchum was a senior biologist at Woods Hole and another son was chair of mechanical engineering at Union College. My cousin Carl Ketchum was our first mathematician at COA. But descendants of the other twin, Beulah, my own grandmother, followed literary and artistic paths. My own siblings all studied art in some form. My sister Jane was an art conservator and my sister Bets is the acting registrar of the Bowdoin museum. Of course there are exceptions. My brother Steve, though he went to grad school in art history, is a legendary computer programmer at BIW. One thing binds us though—we all pursued education outside the state and now we've all come back to Maine.

What do you think it is that draws all of your family members to Maine?

Maine is beautiful ... just beautiful. Dad came here for aesthetic reasons. He had a summer home in Georgetown and painted Maine's rocks and coastline all his life. After his PhD, he was offered jobs at Tulane, in New Orleans, and Colby, in Waterville. I don't think he could envision a subject matter in the bayous, so he came to Maine and built a camp at Indian Point, which had ocean beaches, salt marshes, the rocky coast whose shape and coloration changed every hour with the tide. Indian Point was a place of natural splendor, but also a community of like-minded people. Dad's paintings hung over all their mantelpieces, and we all got together after supper to play mahjong.

After college I went to the University of Minnesota in Minneapolis, a great cultural center because both the capitol and state university were located in the largest city. It was a wonderful environment for studying and teaching literature. The Guthrie Theater had just started up, John Berryman and James Wright were teaching there, and Garrison Keillor was the editor of the campus newspaper. Later, of course, he put Minnesota on the map, which was the quintessence of community for him and all his NPR followers, but it wasn't mine.

You couldn't identify with Lake Wobegon?

It was an urban university and we had no sense of what went on outside the city. One time, though, a bunch of us from the English department drove north to the Lake Superior region and went into a bar and tried to rent snowshoes. Everyone laughed, they'd all gone to snowmobiles long ago. But while we were drinking one of the natives snuck out and returned with five pairs of traditional ash snowshoes so the city folks could tromp off into the woods. It was a "Prairie Home Companion" moment, though Lake Wobegon hadn't been invented yet.

My first teaching job after grad school was at the University of Chicago. Rarified academia, but a troubled campus set in a troubled city. The university was in the South Side, an area of nonstop poverty and crime. We were trying to raise a 5-year-old child, you couldn't breathe the air coming drifting over from the steel mills of Gary, Indiana, and all the trees were dying from pollution. I used to talk about Maine, and people would say, "This is the University of Chicago, no other place exists!" They were convinced of it.

But I knew there was someplace else, and another kind of work. As a literature scholar I had been writing about writers; it hadn't yet occurred to me I could be one myself. I remembered my father's move from Harvard to Maine and how it lifted his spirits. I got a post-doctoral fellowship, and though I could have gone anywhere in the world, I rented a decrepit farmhouse in Rome, Maine. I had to lay linoleum on the floorboards so we wouldn't fall through. I told my colleagues I'd be spending the year in Rome, and they said, "That's the perfect choice." They were thinking of the Coliseum, but I had something else in mind, though I didn't even know what it was.

I bought a 35mm camera and started driving along the coast to take photographs. I had just gotten Eliot Porter's landmark Sierra Club book, *Summer Island*, and I was just knocked out! Maybe I hadn't the drawing gene; but I felt as if my eyes had been reopened and with the camera I could make images of what I saw. When I returned to Chicago, instead of another article on Yeats, I had a photography exhibit. My colleagues couldn't figure it out: "He was so promising. What could have happened to him in Italy?"

The next summer I pitched a tent behind our Indian Point cottage as a study, and I noticed these sow bugs under the floor, and that gave me my first poem, blind crawling insects and other primeval creatures that live their invisible lives beneath what we usually see. The symbolism was obvious. I submitted the poem to Gordon Clark, the *Maine Times* poetry editor, and he published it!

It was the era of Berkeley and Kent State and my university's serene academic atmosphere was ravaged by the student protests. The students were smoking dope in my classroom. I had a guy come to class with a hookah and light it up while I was trying to discuss Aristotle. I thought, "Shit. I can't deal with this!" The students shut the whole campus down. They took over the administration building. The president, Ed Levi, had to move his desk to a tent on the lawn.

The protestors set up an underground university and invited me to be one of the teachers. I was marched into the classroom blindfolded so I couldn't identify any of the guards. When I got to the classroom they took the blindfold off and asked, "What are you going to teach in the Revolutionary Curriculum?" I said, "I'm going to teach Poetry and the Irish Revolution." They said, "That's good; just leave the poetry part out."

I had to get out of there. Then I read in the *Maine Times* that someone was starting a college on Mount Desert Island. It was a chance to start from zero and throw out the old rules and structures and totally reinvent higher education from the ground up. The Vietnam War was still on but the COA founders were way ahead of their time, they already realized the issue of the future would be the environment, and so it is. I asked my department if I could take a leave of absence to help found an experimental school. Chicago was very proud of its history of academic reform, back in the thirties under Robert Hutchins, so they said, "OK, we'll give you a year off." I came to Bar Harbor in the summer of 1972, on loan as the first COA faculty member, not knowing if I'd ever return.

Whose idea was it to start College of the Atlantic?

When the great fire of 1947 destroyed the old prewar mansions of Bar Harbor, many year-round residents lost their livelihood, the caretakers and service providers that supported the affluent layer that we now call the one percent. The town fathers said, "What can we do?" A couple of classmates from Mount Desert High School, one a priest and the other a local businessman, said, "We want a non-polluting industry that would improve the island's year-round cultural life, so why don't we start a college?"

So they assembled a board including summer residents and local citizens, including a couple of scientists from the Jackson Lab who were very influential in the beginning, and they hired Ed Kaelber, who'd been an Assistant Dean at the Harvard Graduate School of Education and had just returned from founding a high school in Africa. Then they starting looking for teachers. I, in the meanwhile, had written them, "Do you want a consultant?" They said, "Yes, and one of the things we want you to do is put together a library." So I went to the university's undergraduate library and started going through the card catalog, piece by piece.

How did you pick the books, by how many times they'd been checked out?

No, I picked the ones I thought every student should read. For a radical startup college, I picked a lot of classics. I already knew the new college would be oriented to the future and I didn't want it to lose sight of the past. I went alphabetically and slowly, so when I finally showed up with my list, it contained only books starting with A through C. When the college opened the library was based on the first letters of the alphabet. We had Aristotle, but we didn't have Plato. I think that had an effect on the philosophy of the college. Plato was very abstract, whereas Aristotle was down to earth, and the education one gets today at COA is still grounded in the material world. We don't believe in Platonic essences, we believe the visible earth is all the reality there is.

Did you ever get beyond C?

Well, that was a bit of an embarrassment, but you'd be surprised what you can learn just from A, B and C. There's a lifetime of reading there. You want to read Aristotle? You want to read Bacon? You want to read Chaucer?

Copernicus?

Copernicus, there you go! Byron, Coleridge. See? Of course we added other books. In 1983 the library burned, so we had to start all over again. And you know what happened? Colleges all over the world sent us books. Trustees and alumni sent their own personal libraries. It was amazing. And my bias toward my own end of the alphabet was repaired.

How many more years do you plan to teach?

This afternoon I am being reviewed for an eight-year contract. We don't have tenure here. Every few years a review committee pokes around campus and asks the students and other faculty members, "Is he senile yet? Is he over the hill? Is he falling asleep in class? Does he use an ear trumpet?" [His contract was renewed.]

So we'll see. I hope to continue teaching a while longer. I love my courses, I love my colleagues, I love my students. I have some of the best young writers imaginable, they're inventive, they're motivated, their eyes are open, and they do good work.

Tell me, is poetry a form of painting, except using words instead of colors?

No, I think each art has a specialty, and it takes all of them together to understand the world. For example, painting, even abstract painting, centers on what you can see, and poetry centers on what you can't.

Thoreau wrote, "The question is not what you look at, but what you see."

And he was a poet. He saw everything, of course, but his focal point was the invisible. He loved the surface of Walden Pond, but his heart was with what was underneath.

Don't a lot, if not most, writers write what they think will sell?

Well, poetry is exempt from that temptation because it doesn't sell no matter what it is, so its quality is uncompromised. And the best fiction writers don't write for the market either, they write from their personal vision and standards. If there's a public interest in what they have to say, their work will be published and sold.

COA had no publish-or-perish requirements so I could write what I wanted. That intellectual freedom has produced some remarkable books from our faculty, not driven from academic structures but from what people want to write. I wanted to write from the inside and not from academic convention. Yeats believed the real writer is not you but your opposite, which you must recognize and discover. In the 70s, when I started writing, I was in the difficult first stages of a divorce, and I realized how little self-knowledge I really had. I found a Jungian therapist over in Winthrop, Maine, Heinz Westman, who had been trained by Jung himself and had come to Maine for his asthma. He was the picture of an eccentric genius. He used to play the stock market based on the revelations of his dreams.

From him I got to know a little about the unconscious, which is the habitation of our demons and our creative life.

Did you suffer this turbulence in isolation?

I was a solo traveler for a while. I went to Yaddo and McDowell; I went to Venice on a fellowship; but all I could write was letters. I learned the hard way that I needed human companionship to work. I find it too distracting to be alone. It's not true for everyone. My longtime companion, Donna, is a writer too. She spent last winter in Oaxaca all by herself, quite contentedly writing nonstop. I won't offer any theories that women are more complete in themselves, but she's twice as productive without me hanging around. I can't get a word on paper unless I know there'll be a shared candlelit dinner at day's end. If she'd been gone another month, the meter reader would have found me dead on the floor. I realize, like many men of my generation, I am only half a person at most, and not the best half either.

When the AIDS epidemic struck in the 80s, I was strangely affected. I wasn't at risk nor was I close to any victims of the disease, but felt a huge unexpected rush of empathy for those afflicted. The theme was too lengthy and complex for a poem, so I found myself writing a novel, *The Keeper of Sheep*, about an AIDS patient and a young college feminist who'd been expelled for setting fire to a fraternity. Writing a novel demanded a different pace, not the intense sprint of a poem that can be begun and ended in the same day, but more of a double-marathon pace with an almost impossibly far-off goal. And it required a more distant relation to the audience. I was used to poetry readings where you can personally witness the crowd's reactions, and the compressed world of poetry where your friends and your audience are the same. When you send a novel into the world it will encounter many more readers than a poem, but the relation is distant and you have no idea who they are.

One day, after *Keeper of Sheep* came out, I got home from work and Donna said, "Good for you. Your book has been reviewed in *The New Yorker*. You got a whole page." With that kind of reaction it was hard to turn back. I don't have the kind of ambidexterity that can produce both fiction and poems; but the skills and habits of poetry are indispensable to a novelist and I always encourage my COA fiction students to study and write poetry as a preparation and proving ground.

Poetry orients you toward the unseen and what goes on in the depths, whereas novel readers need to know the surface of things, how people appear and what they wear and the physical spaces they inhabit. I'm still learning to pay attention to the details of how humans present themselves, what things look like and not just what they symbolize. Sometimes a poet can dive too deeply and needs to put up his periscope and look around.

But you have an ear for dialog. Your book, *The Wooden Nickel*, is a great story, but the thing that impressed me most was how you captured the language, the dialect, of the Maine fisherman. Where did that story come from?

I bought a sailboat the day I moved back to Maine in June of '72 and have been more or less on the water every summer since then. One beautiful morning I was cruising in company with a colleague of mine from COA, two families of adults and kids in two sloops. We were rafted together in Long Cove in Tenants Harbor. I had set up a long table in my cockpit, and eight of us were feasting on a big breakfast with all the trimmings. It was just a great day to be alive.

I heard a deafening engine roar and looked up to see a big Maine lobsterboat coming right at us and not deviating a bit. Instead of slowing down to make less wake, he sped up. He had seen us and must have thought, "There they are, the privileged bastards, while I'm out here working." I had been trying to write a novel about a lawyer who had inherited a boatyard and who got mad when he saw lobstermen shooting seals. I had been struggling a long time on that deadend project, and then these guys came deliberately at us with the intent of wrecking our breakfast, and I thought, "What the fuck!" The wake tore one of my beautiful teak cleats out of the deck. Unbelievable! Little did anyone know they were bringing me a book.

After the cruise I went home and realized I had my character, "Lucky," the frustrated, angry fisherman straight off the boat that had waked us in Long Cove. Lucky, in his entirety, came to me in a moment.

But how did you capture the way Maine fishermen talk? You just nailed it!

I spent my early childhood in Boston so I lack a real Maine accent myself but I have always loved and envied the way Maine people talk, especially the coastal variant. I have three or four acquaintances who have preserved that beautiful way of speech, which is almost an endangered language. Most of these are civilized people, however, and don't swear, so I knew there was still something missing from the way fishermen speak among themselves.

I had a grad student who got a job as the bookkeeper for the Cranberry Island Lobster Coop and knew how the fisherman really talked. He was a Washington intellectual but he said, "I've been working there for a month now, and they're starting to loosen up."

We met twice a week, and every time he'd say, "You just have add 'fucking' to every other phrase." I also would go out, anchor my boat in an area where the lobstermen were hauling, and turn on my VHF radio. In a given area, all of the lobstermen tune into the same channel and carry on a continuous chatter. That's how I got the language and the rhythm. Plus I know a couple of waterfront characters well enough to speak freely and I drink it in.

It seems those words have a different meaning for fishermen.

They are what linguists call "meaningless intensifiers." But the f-word and its companions have a lot of meaning for the fisherman, because those words communicate the urgency of their business and the outlaw community of men at sea. A sentence just isn't quite the same without them. My favorite dialect in the whole world is the Maine lobsterman really letting go.

A big element in my book was the relation of the working class and the summer class in Maine, and another was the cultural differences between many Maine fishermen and their wives. The men will be like pirates while their wives are often very refined. It's an old joke that a bunch of fishermen are sitting around the parlor telling stories, and the wife is knitting. One of the fishermen says, "Well, you know what happened to Frank. He fell off the wharf ladder and landed on a sharp spile. And the spile went right up his asshole." The wife, who to this point hasn't uttered a word, says, "Rectum." "Rectum?" he says, "It damn near killed him!"

One book club member who was a lobsterman's wife said, "My husband's just like Lucky Lunt. I really want him to read this book but he only reads when he's on the toilet. So I've left it right in there where he can't miss it." Sarah Lunt goes upscale and becomes an artist and gets adopted by the summer crowd and Lucky feels lost and betrayed. I think I have both those characters in myself, as I commute every day from working-class Bucksport, where I live, to civilized Bar Harbor where I work. My visible life is more what Sarah aspires to, but I have an inner Lucky and that's who wrote the book. Yeats said, "You create from your opposite." Lucky Lunt was my opposite in every way. He's a redneck, he's a Republican, he shoots seals and whales with a safari gun, and I have a hard time baiting a mousetrap.

But I can tell you like Lucky.

I love him! He is part of me. Not the part that votes, but there is no doubt he's in there. I intended *The Wooden Nickel* as a kind of test. If political correctness blinds you to Lucky's humanity, you may not be fully human yourself.

I don't want to give away the ending, but I couldn't sleep after finishing the book. My heart goes out to Lucky. There he is: his boat gone, his woman in the emergency room probably losing their child, and he is in their trailer putting together a little toy lobsterboat. I turned the page praying I would find another chapter.

The book has been optioned and scripted for film, with a great screenplay written by Cara Haycak, but I see the ending in the screenplay as a little more redemptive and hopeful. That may be a compromise we'll have to make for the American moviegoer, who does not have much of a thirst for ambiguity. I just hope if they are able to make it, it will be shot in Maine. Paul Lepage [Maine's governor] says Maine's open for business, but other states are more film-friendly.

Maybe the story should be presented as universal. Wouldn't it be the same story if it were filmed in Louisiana or Alaska?

A good story should be about the universal human condition. After I finished the book I asked myself, "Is it too local?" But even the universal needs a local habitat, and the Maine coast is as universal as anyplace else, maybe more so, cause it's where we live.

JULIE BROWN EATON
Lobsterman
Deer Isle
Age 47

Julie Brown Eaton on her lobsterboat, Cat Sass

I went to Stonington looking for lobsterboat racers. It didn't take long to find myself in the kitchen of a pair of them, Julie and Sid Eaton. Both race Sid's 28-foot working lobsterboat, Kimberley Belle.

I interviewed both [see page 355 for my chat with Sid]. While interviewing Sid, his wife, Julie, reminded me of a horse in the starting gate at the Kentucky Derby. This filly could hardly wait to break from the gate. At the age of forty-seven, she had the physicality and enthusiasm of a sixteen-year-old gymnast. A better comparison might be one of those aerobics instructors you see on cable television at 6 a.m., except she wasn't acting. We weren't far into her incredible life story before I understood why.

And how old is Julie Eaton?

Old. Forty-seven years old.

I have noticed that women can't wait to get to twenty-one, but once they are, they don't want to get a year older.

When I hit forty-five and undressed to shower, I would notice subtle changes in my body. Now my girls are tucked into the waistband of my sweatpants. I'm hoping this isn't a permanent relocation, but it's not looking too good.

Well, gravity was the subject of my thesis at MIT, and I can tell you that gravity never quits; it's unrelenting. So unless you want to spend the rest of your life standing on your head, I would get rid of your mirrors.

I had a real bad car accident in 1987. I got hit by a cement truck. The reason I bring this up is that, although I'm forty-seven biologically, I am only twenty-five emotionally. I can't remember a thing from before my accident. That works out perfectly because both Sid [sixty-seven] and I [forty-seven] are both twenty-five emotionally.

Where were you born and educated?

They tell me I was born in Surry and attended high school in Blue Hill. I went on to college in Salt Lake City, where I majored in Aeronautical Science and Airport Management. I graduated with a commercial pilot's license. They say I soloed on my fifteenth birthday, got my private ticket on my seventeenth birthday, and my commercial license on my twenty-first birthday. I wanted to fly for the Air Force.

I had time in military aircraft: P37s, P38s, KC135s, and C130s. I joined the Air Force ROTC, but women weren't allowed to compete for the open slots allocated to each ROTC unit. They were only allowed to compete for what the men didn't want. I guess that had pissed me off, because I told the ROTC to shove it.

I had a friend in Utah who flew for Life Flight, so I thought, "Here we go. This is a give-back to help people." We didn't have Life Flight in Maine yet, but I knew it was coming, so I applied to the Maine State Police.

Then I had my accident. I was headed to work. Got caught in the snow, got sideways in the road, and got hit by a loaded cement truck. They had to cut me out of the car. They never thought I'd live to Bangor. It was, by far, the best thing that ever happened to me.

How so?

I was in a coma for months. When I came to I had to learn to walk, and talk, and read, and write, feed myself, cook, everything. It was like I was born the minute I came out of the coma. I'd suffered extensive damage to my brain stem.

So are you operating on half a brain now?

I've been accused of that, but as far as I know, everything is still there and functioning. It's as if my brain were a computer, and the accident wiped my hard drive clean. I had to start from scratch learning colors, numbers, who people were, the works. I had just turned twenty-three, so I was physically twenty-three and mentally one day old.

I say it was the best experience of my life because, all of a sudden, I realized what was truly important.

Which is what?

What really mattered in life wasn't the new outfit I was going to buy for my next date. It was the next breath I could take and not be on a respirator, the next step I could take without somebody holding me up. All of a sudden I got it. It was life-changing.

Tell me about the recovery process.

After rehab, there was this older lobsterman, Bud Kilton, who took me out on his boat. Bud would remind you of the *Old Man and the Sea*. He had this HUGE heart. He knew how good it would be for me.

I no longer knew him, but he had known me from before my accident. I had the mental ability of a three-year-old, so he treated me as if he were my grandfather. I'd run around his boat like a three-year-old.

That winter he worked with two scallop divers, and I went too. I would run around like a little girl with a towel to dry their faces. I thought I was being very helpful. Actually I was being a pest, but they understood and were very kind to me.

At the end of the season I said to one of the divers, "Next year I'm going to dive, too." He laughed because there weren't any women, at least in this area, diving on scallops.

Especially three-year-olds!

That summer I took a SCUBA course. One of the questions on the application was, "Have you ever had a head injury?" Of course I replied, "No, no head injuries here!" I was young, but I wasn't stupid. I just wanted a chance to try it, to prove to myself I could do it. It was the first independent thing I had done since the accident.

If you can dive in Maine waters in the winter, you can do about anything.

That's right. It gave me a huge sense of freedom, and I was able to explore a part of this world that most people never get to see.

Scallop season runs from November 1 until April 15. The water is so cold you have to dive in a dry suit. I took out a bank loan, and one of the divers went down to New Hampshire with me and outfitted me. Naturally I painted my air tanks girly pink.

Before you take that first breath from the regulator, everything in your head is screaming, "I can't breathe under here!" Your lungs don't want to open up to take the air in. But then that first breath is so easy and so sweet. It was like soul food. I was very comfortable under water. Soon I actually preferred being under water to being on land.

Sometimes I dream I am flying, looking down at the ground. Is SCUBA diving like that?

Exactly. You are suspended, totally weightless, and everything is so gentle. Under water, I was always aware that I was a guest in someone else's home. This wasn't my home; this was the fishes' home.

Of course, being a woman, I imagined all the sea creatures were my friends. I wanted to interact with everything. They probably don't see it that way, but I imagined that they did.

Are you still diving?

I dove commercially for fourteen years. I've logged over 10,000 hours under water. That's more than a year living like a fish. But no, I don't dive anymore because Uncle Arthur [arthritis] has moved into my joints. When I realized I couldn't continue diving forever, I immersed myself in learning how to fish from the surface.

The last year I dove for scallops, I was diving on a boat with four other guys. The season ended April 15, and we were in Vinalhaven. I don't come from a fishing family, so I needed to go somewhere and immerse myself in the fishing culture and learn how todo it. So I got off the boat in Carvers Harbor on Vinalhaven.

What was your mental age at that point?

Maybe thirteen. But the guys in Carver's Harbor were good to me, and I got a sternman position. The guy I went to work for was a lobsterboat racer, and of course I was very slow. I'm sure I drove this man crazy.

Did he take you on because he felt sorry for you, or because he liked having a pretty sternman?

Being pretty didn't hurt, I'm sure. There weren't a lot of women sterning, and that was kind of cool. Anyway, this man took a suitcase [24-pack] of beer every day. The only days we came in early were the days he ran out of beer. I didn't know a person could actually swallow that much liquid. He'd drive the boat with one hand and pee over the side with the other.

Did you drink beer, too?

Oh no, I don't drink, and I don't do drugs.

Is that because of your head injury?

Well, I know what it feels like to be out of control and not be able to fix it, so I will never take that chance. That first stern position was eye-opening. It was like, for me, setting up a college syllabus. It was fishing 101. The next year I went with another guy: fishing 201. I tried to go with guys who were the best at what they did.

I went with this older fisherman, Shep, and he was wonderful. He'd sit in the stern and let me drive the boat. He'd say, "Now drive up to that buoy." Of course I didn't know about driving up to a buoy. I'd gaff it, and I'd be going the wrong way. The tide would be going the other way, and I'd be trying to pull this 10,000-pound boat toward the buoy! He's like, "No girl, that will never work."

Why were these fishermen so nice to you? It must have been inefficient for them. You were making mistakes. You were slow.

I think they saw a young woman who obviously had been through a lot, but who wanted this so bad. I was no threat. If they could help me achieve my dream, it made them feel good.

Where were you living all this time?

I lived in a little boat house on Vinalhaven with no heat and no running water.

Through the winter?

For eight years with long underwear and an electric blanket. It was ok unless we lost power. A lot of days it would be colder in the house than it was outdoors. But it was right on the water. The seaweed would wash under the house, which was on posts, and you'd have to rake it out because it would rot and smell. It was like doing Outward Bound for eight years.

I had no neighbors. I did all my laundry by hand and hung it out on a line to dry. One morning I poked my head out and listened—no cars. Then I listened for a boat out front—nothing. All I had on were my white fishing boots. That's it, not a stitch. All my clothes were on the line, so I started hoofin' it in those white boots.

I turned my head toward the ocean and I saw this little flash of red. There are two guys kayaking by, making no noise. So I waved, and they waved back, and I kept goin' for the clothesline. What else do you do when you've been caught naked?

I'll bet it made their day.

Made mine, too! They were kinda cute.

But then the owner sold the boathouse. I moved off island, rented a house in Penobscot, and applied for a job on the Stonington dock. The coop manager, Penny Trundy, gave me a job. His real name was George. I have no idea where the "Penny" came from.

Now, Sid's second wife, Karen, and I were good, good friends. She used to come out to Vinalhaven and spend the weekend in the boat house with me. Karen willed Sid to me when she died. Without my knowing, she called my mother about a week before she died and said, "I'm so worried about Sid." My mom, who knew Karen was dying, said, "Don't worry about Sid. He's going to be fine." "I know that," Karen said, "but he and Julie are awfully close, and I think they'd be good together." Mom laughed hysterically and said, "Karen, that will never happen because he's old enough to be Julie's father." Karen said, in her vast wisdom, "Just promise me you won't stand in the way if it should happen."

Sid had always been my hero. He was everything I wanted to be when I grew up. He was so respected and liked. He has helped so many fishermen, and I wanted to be just like that, but I never thought of him any other way.

After Karen died I called him. I wanted to get him out of his house. I said, "They're gonna have a dance tomorrow night. You wouldn't want to go, would you?" I knew I'd be perfectly safe going with Sid. Nobody's gonna mess with you if you are with Sid Eaton.

He said, "Sure, I'd love to." I'm thinking, "Wow, I am going to a dance with Sid Eaton!" That would be like going to a dance with Mario Andretti, the race-car driver. I had no romantic thoughts. I just thought it would be fun.

Before the dance I said to him, "Uh, er, you wouldn't let me drive your lobsterboat in a race some time, would you?" He said, "Why yes, you can run her, but we're gonna have to practice." The next day I get in from fishing, and he's waiting for me in *Kimberley Belle*.

You had driven boats before, hadn't you?

Yes, but nothing like the *Kimberley Belle*! I was so excited I was literally shaking. I asked Sid, "Should I ease the throttle ahead slowly, or should I gun it?" Sid said, "Gun it!" I slammed the throttle forward, and I ended up right on my ass. The *Kimberley Belle* was doing, like, the "funky monkey" out of the harbor. Sid said, "See, I told you." I said, "Let me try that again." The second time I knew what to expect, I braced myself over the controls. I'm ready.

We did it a couple more times, and I got the feel of it.

What happened at the dance? Did you hear any comments, like, "What's going on there?"

Sort of. The women his age were, like, "Well, who is SHE?" Bent some noses. They don't call him "Sexy Sid" for no reason. All right, they don't call him that. I call him "Sexy Sid." Anyway, I took him home, and I said, "So what time should I come tomorrow?" He said, "Come at seven, and we'll go to breakfast. Then we'll go to the races."

I'm back on the island at 5 a.m., driving around, killing time. I am so excited I can't stand it. He entered me in every race his boat qualified for, and, by God, I won every one! Won every one and won the grand prize, which was a skiff.

And Sid's heart?

And I won my husband's heart.

They had taken the roof off the house I was living in because they were adding a second story. I could lie in bed at night and see the stars. When Sid found out he said, "Pack your stuff. You're comin' down here." I said, "I have a kitty." He said, "Bring the cat." So I went home, packed what I needed, and moved in. A month later he asked me to marry him. It has been a total fairy tale for me. He's my soulmate; he's my teacher; he's my student, my best friend, my lover, my husband. He's the half that makes me whole. He completes me.

If it hadn't been for the ocean, what do you think your life would be today?

I have a feeling my life would be unfulfilled. Being on the water fills me. It's not just fishing; it's not the act of hauling the traps; it's the smell of the air.

I read about people who live in cities, who work in skyscrapers. It's a big deal if they have a window in their office. If they're a big success they have a corner office with two windows. They've worked ten years to get this window. And what do they see? Another building full of people staring back at them.

I have five windows in my boat, and the view is always changing. Every view is like a postcard from Maine.

Do you think most fishermen feel the same way?

I think that, being a woman, I can talk about it more. Men, as a general rule, aren't as emotional about things. They like talking about their engines and their horsepower. I can do that, too, but I can talk about my feelings about the ocean, too.

The author, Isak Dinesen, wrote, "The cure for anything is salt water—sweat, tears, or the sea." Do you think that would include brain injuries and broken spirits?

Oh, absolutely! Last year I took a sweet young woman who'd just had a baby die of a congenital heart defect. I took her out on my boat because all I could offer this girl was the ocean. She was horribly injured. She was devastated, as anyone would be, but all I could offer her, besides the inadequate, "I'm so sorry," was to give her a chance to get on the salt water and hope that what worked for me would work for her. I think it did.

Of course our blood has the same salt composition as the ocean. Do you think it possibly has to do with the fact we came out of the ocean, that the ocean was our original home?

They've done experiments to see if humans could actually live under water. They fill their lungs with salt water, and it doesn't kill them! So who's to say? If someone said, "Julie, you can't fish any more," I don't know what I'd do. I would be totally lost. Even if I worked on the dock, I'd still be wishing I were in my boat out on the water. When I haul my boat out at the end of the year I cry.

I know Sid is very respected among other fishermen. Is it like among the Indians, where Sid is respected as an elder?

Sid is respected because he's been fishing for fifty-five years, and he's proved himself, and he's tough. The respect for Sid is more like in the Mafia.

The Mafia?

Yes, he's a don. The fishermen in any area are a family, and Sid's the don. There's a group that fishes off Head Harbor on Isle au Haut, and they're known as the Head Harbor Mafia. You don't go there. That fishing ground, that bottom, belongs to the Head Harbor "family."

[The don brings me a Klondike Bar.] "I buy these by the case. She don't eat them."

[Julie again] One of the funny things I noticed, when I was sterning, is men's reactions to me having to relieve myself. They get all nervous. They never use the head. They just go over the side. When I go, they don't know quite what to do with themselves.

What do you do when you have to go?

Well, if I have to poop, I go in the bucket. If I have to pee, I just drop my drawers and pee on the deck. It just washes out the scuppers. I don't know why this makes the guys so nervous. So I've come up with a line that makes them more comfortable. I just say, "I have to pee now. If you see something you haven't seen before, shoot it because I probably haven't seen it either." [Sid chortles]. They get used to it. Eventually you become just one of the guys, but it's something you have to work for.

I have a friend who is a Catholic nun from Dallas, Texas. She's retired, and she wanted to go out fishing with me. We're goin' across the bay, and I'm telling her why I fish, where I fish, and why I can't just fish anywhere. I said, "For example, this gray boat we are about to pass belongs to a man named Kevin Clough. He's Sid's nephew.

Well, Kevin Clough is a redhead and right full of shit, and as I go by he moons me. The nun looks at me and says, "How do I respond to that?" And I, of course, say, "Moon him back!" "Oh," she says, "I don't think I can do that!"

Speaking of lobstering territory, I'm fishing where I am now only because I am Sid Eaton's wife.

So you married into Sid's fishing grounds?

Yes, I married into Sid's bottom. And let me tell you, being a female fisherman contemplating marrying another fisherman, it would be very important to know what kind of bottom my prospective husband had. I examined Sid's very carefully. Sid has GOOD bottom.

Do you remember the joke about the fisherman's personal ad? The ad read, "Looking for a good woman with a boat. Send picture of boat." [We all laugh]

I have my own boat, too. I named her *Cat Sass*. Notice that could also be read as *Cat's Ass*. Get it?

Cat Sass has a 210 Cummins, and I've never altered her, so she's stock. I'm in the lowest diesel rating because she's a little diesel, but my little boat does well. She gets up good. The fastest I've clocked was 26.9 mph—not bad for a little old working boat.

There is this guy from Five Islands named Stevie Johnson. He is insane, but so am I. I knew that if he was going to run his boat in the powderpuff [women's] race, he was going to beat me. I was racing Sid's boat at that time, but I knew that year that Stevie Johnson would beat me. Stevie was crazy to win. In his mind taking second makes you the first place loser.

I met Stevie on the dock, and I said, "Stevie!" "Whaaat?" he says. "You gonna race in the Powderpuff?" "Ayah, prob'ly." I grabbed him by both nipples and twisted for all I was worth, and I said, "Stevie, you gonna' run in the Powderpuff?" "Aaaahhh! GOD NO!" he says.

Stonington Harbor in early morning fog

The funny part was, little did I know his son goes to the same gym as my brother. The next day his son saw my brother there, and he said, "My father was at the Stonington races, and some crazy bitch grabbed him by his nipples. You should see him. He's all black and blue!"

I guess it doesn't hurt to have a reputation. People have second thoughts about offending you.

I don't know about nitrous, I don't know about propane, and I don't know about goosing my engine, but I do know something about nipples.

I want to know about your photography. How did you start?

People are always asking me, "What is it that makes you want to fish?" Even my mother said, "You know, Julie, fishing is just a job." I tried to explain to them that it's more than a job. It's a life. Fishing is what I eat, sleep, read about, and dream about. But I'm not eloquent enough to verbalize what it is about the ocean. Taking pictures is my way of conveying my feelings to others.

A good picture can do that. Ordinary pictures can't.

I take a hundred pictures for every one I keep, but I'm lucky because
fishing by myself allows me to stop, and wait for, and compose the
best picture. One of my favorite subjects is my eagle. I just love him.
I've watched him grow up.

Do you feed him?

No, that would be illegal. But he watches for me. When he hears
my boat, he comes in for the old scrap bait I throw away.

Has he ever landed on your boat?

No, and I wouldn't want him to. I don't want him to get hurt. I don't
want him to land on another boat that might not be so friendly.
If you interact with something like this, you have to be responsible. I
don't want to endanger him by making him too tame.

I have another friend, a horse head seal [also known as the grey
seal, weighing up to 700 pounds]. Horse head seals are different
from harbor seals. They come down from Newfoundland, and
they have the body of a walrus.

Frederick [the horse head seal] is probably thirteen feet long,
and his head is as wide as a chair. Most fishermen dislike seals because they eat your bait and steal lobsters out of your traps, but I
know Frederick's head is so big, he can't get into a trap.

Last year Frederick was following me and this black Repco
came up out of North Haven. Frederick took off. The guy came
alongside to discuss lobster and bait prices. We're talking and all
of a sudden, between the two boats, up pops Frederick. There is
no missing him. He is HUGE. I say, "Meet my friend, Frederick." The guy says, "You know him, too? So it seems Frederick
has a fan club.

Does Frederick have a girl friend?

He does! This summer he showed up with a young female and a
baby seal. Frederick prefers my boat, but his girlfriend prefers
Sid's boat. Typical woman! She prefers flirting with my husband.

Do you sell your photographs?

I have a little business, and I make a little money. You only need so much money, but what I experience out here is priceless. I want people to know that fishermen are emotionally invested in the preservation of the ocean. I never thought I'd have one, but the ocean is my mistress.

You consider the ocean to be a woman?

Absolutely. She is unforgiving, but she is also nurturing. When I motor out to my boat in my little skiff, all my worldly concerns are left on shore. It's me and my little boat riding in the palm of God's hand.

SID EATON
Lobsterboat Racer
Deer Isle
Age 67

Among lobsterboat racers, Sid Eaton is a legend. Given his reputation, I expected to meet an enormous man with a salty beard and a gruff voice. What greeted me at the kitchen door were a perky blonde woman with the enthusiasm of a golden retriever puppy and, peeking over her shoulder, a trim and fit older man with a buzz-cut and a grin that stretched ear-to-ear.

Both Sid Eaton and his wife, Julie Brown Eaton, seemed genuinely excited to be interviewed by an actual author. Before I could start my recorder, however, they wanted to hear every detail of my own life, particularly whether I was "from here" or "from away." They were relieved to hear that I was actually born in Maine, and they warmed further as I recounted memories of my lobsterman grandfather. I knew all would be ok, however, after I told them Virginia Goddard, my first cousin, once removed, was married to Lewis Stuart, a well-known lobsterboat racer from Harpswell.

How far back do Eatons go in this country?

My family goes back on Deer Isle, prob'ly two, three hundred years, and the very first Eatons were on the *Mayflower*, 1620. I've seen the Eatons on the *Mayflower* passenger list.

People around here don't move very far, do they? I have found most coastal families have been here for at least six generations.

Oh, yeah. I'm at least sixth-generation. At one time in my family we had five generations still alive on both sides. My mother's and my father's. Most of them were fishermen. I was seventeen when I got married. I was a grandfather before forty.

Well, that's how you get to five generations.

That and workin' a lot late at night [laughs]. I was born on Little Deer Isle, and then we moved to Stonington when I was eleven years old. That's when I started fishing. My dad built me a little rowboat. I set a few traps right in the harbor down here, around Crotch Island.

Did you stand or sit when you rowed?

I stood up. I was standin' most of the time anyway, and I pushed on the oars so's I could see where I was goin'. Oh, I was just a little fellow. Prob'ly weighed sixty pounds.

What did you use for bait?

Cuttin's [heads and tails] because we had a sardine cannery right here in town. Bait didn't cost nothin' compared to today. I had that skiff for a couple of years, then my dad built me a bigger boat, a sixteen-footer, and I put an outboard on it, an Elgin from Sears Roebuck, seven and a half horse. Had that for a couple of years.

When I was fifteen I seen this old twenty-foot lobsterboat that was hauled up. The guy had started to repair it. So I went and got that lobsterboat. Brought it home one winter, put it in the shop. I got that all fixed up

My dad was good on carpentry and taught me all that stuff. I helped him a lot when I was a little kid. I'd hold the clinching iron, stuff like that. If I got off course a little bit, he'd come and steer me back on to the right direction.

Anyway, I took this boat. She had a new keel, but she wasn't finished on the top, and the inside wasn't finished at all. No flooring or nothing. I put a new deck on her. When I got in a mess, I'd go ask my dad a question.

That spring I put her overboard. Had a little four-cylinder gasoline Willis Jeep engine, about fifty, sixty horse. I used that boat three or four years, then I got another one. Finally got a twenty-eight-foot boat I bought off a guy in town.

Did you ever go to the bank for a loan?

Nope, just worked my way up, cash. That's the way we got to where we are today.

Have you ever considered doing anything but fishing?

Maybe a little boatbuilding. I worked in a couple of boatyards. I worked at Billings Diesel, and I worked at Williams Boatyard in Burnt Cove. Oh, I've done other things. I've cut wood, done house repairing, shingled roofs. I shingled roofs 'cause nobody wanted to do it, so there was good money. I used to go right at it and make good money. 'Course I didn't get time to play sports in school. I played ball later on.

You went to school on Deer Isle?

Yep, but not very much. I didn't get much schoolin' in once I started fishin'. Eighth grade I quit. I wasn't learnin' anything anyway. I couldn't read nor write. I couldn't do a damned thing. In fact, Dad said, "Son, you might as well get the hell outa school and go to work. You're gonna have to work all your life, and you're probably gonna learn more after you get out." He was right. I learned more in two years after I got out than I had in eight years in school.

Back then the State of Maine said you had to be in school through the eighth grade or fifteen years of age. I was fourteen, but I'd gotten through the eighth grade. I took right off lobstering. 'Course I had all the gear, the boat, everything I needed.

How many traps did you fish before Maine set the 800-trap limit?

I had 1,200 traps when they set that 800-trap limit. I pulled 400 a day, all in pairs. No one fishes trawls [strings of traps with a buoy at each end] around here 'cause that's the law. That's what the local fishermen voted for, limited to triples. Down to Casco Bay they voted for trawls. From Allen Island east just triples is all, until you get outside. Now I fish singles. Not so dangerous. Now I've had a stroke, now I have to take someone to get me home—just in case.

Were you fishing when you had your stroke?

I was on the boat, but I was in at the wharf when I had the stroke. I knew what was happening. I told the guys, "I think I'm havin' a stroke." They said, "What makes you think that?" I said, "I got no feelin' on this right side at all." Just like I was split in half. I was right numb on that side.

    They picked me up off the boat, called the ambulance, put me right in the ambulance. The ambulance was there in three minutes, and I was right at the Blue Hill Hospital prob'ly twenty minutes from the time I had the stroke.

Do you have a wire cage around your propeller?

No, that slows your boat down. I have a cleanout. It's just a six-inch PVC pipe they glassed over and put a six-inch deck plate over it. I catch a pot [lobster buoy], I just open the deck plate, and I can reach down and free the prop.

That should be standard on all boats in Maine! It sure beats going in the water in January with a knife in your teeth. At seventy-one I no longer want to go overboard to free a pot even in summer.

I don't blame you. It's pretty hard to get back in. I got out of my boat here a year ago. My boat's high-sided and hard as hell to get aboard of. It took me eight tries. What happened was I got caught by a buoy. One of those whale breakaway clips [a clip designed to break free in case of whale entanglement in the line] caught my glove and hauled me right overboard. I was overboard just as quick as that! I didn't know it, but the trap was rocked down on the bottom [stuck under a ledge or another immovable object on the bottom]. The boat was still coastin' ahead, so when that clip caught my glove, it hauled me right overboard.

I was all alone. I always take my boat out of gear for safety, but the wind caught her. I set there in the water for a minute figurin' what the hell I was going to do, then she swung around, so I swam to meet her comin' around. I tried to get aboard over and over, but she was high-sided, and I didn't have nothin' to get aholt of. Finally, I got one foot on the rudder and the other foot in the exhaust pipe. I got me a rope ladder now.

But the rope ladder probably wouldn't have been overboard.

Course not! [laughs]

I understand you are quite the lobsterboat racer. How and when did you get into lobsterboat racing?

Well, I like to get out and back fast. I don't like wastin' time. I never had a boat that didn't do at least thirty, so when I heard there was going to be racin' down to Jonesport, I thought I'd give it a try. I wanted to race Benny Beals and all those guys.

Corliss Holland in the *Red Baron*, I raced against him, too. He went down with me. We some surprised 'em. We cleaned house. All of us who went down won our classes. The boys down there didn't like that at all. [laughs]. We beat 'em, and then we kept on goin' right back to Stonington. Didn't even stop to get our trophies. They were madder than a bunch of hornets! [still laughing]. After that we wasn't welcome too much at Jonesport.

Do you have a lot of trophies?

I had a boatload, but I gave 'em to the Deer Isle School to make over for sports trophies for the kids. I had a whole trailer truck load.

What was the top speed you ever made?

I had my boat goin' over sixty one time, but the fastest I have on record was fifty-seven. That's hiking.

Neck and neck at the Harpswell Lobsterboat Races

Do boats ever flip?

Oh yeah, they flip. My stepson flipped his boat over to Searsport. She hit a wake. She flipped sideways, over and over. Worst part was he had my motor in it! Problem is, there ain't nothin' in the water but the prop and the rudder. Makes it kinda squirrelly to steer.

Do you race in the working boat class?

Working boat, yes. Oh, I built one special for racing once. I named her the *Terminator.* [giggles] After I sold her she was named *Lunacy.* [Sid goes and gets a picture.] This here, the green boat, is the *Terminator.* She goes close to sixty miles an hour.

My great uncle, Lewis Stuart, down in Cundys Harbor, had the *Voop.* He told me he raced her only once because she scared him to death. She looked like a lobsterboat, but was just a shell, and had a 1,000-horsepower engine that burned propane and some other gas. He said that she got right up on just a few square inches of bottom at the stern, and he could hardly steer her in a straight line. He said, "I was damned lucky I didn't kill somebody."

Oh yeah, I know Lewis. That *Voop* was somethin'! [laughs]

We was racin' down in Boothbay one time, me and my nephew, in the *Terminator*. Rudder gear let go while we was goin' full out. My nephew was sittin' on the stern, and when the rudder let go, she flipped over on her side and threw him out. I cranked her down a notch, and when she picked up a tooth or two in her steerin' gear, I give it to her again. *Uncle's UFO* was like to passing me, so I put it to her again! We lost a few teeth in the steerin' gear, but we won the race.

Where do you get your engine work done?

Billings Diesel, right here in Stonington. That's where I got repowered [a new engine]. They've repowered a lot of lobsterboats this last year with this new government program. The government pays half. That's $21,000 for my engine. She don't smoke like the old one. She's all computerized and firin' when she's supposed to. She's some smooth.

How many hours can you get out of a diesel engine?

My boy's got one right now with 26,000 hours, and the one he took out had 29,000 on it. Just give her clean fuel and clean oil, and run her hard. Them are tough engines, tougher than tripe.

Tougher than tripe. I like that. I've never heard that, but I know exactly what it means. Tripe is the one thing I won't eat. Well, that and brains. [Sid chortles and slaps his leg.]

I tried tripe once, just a little piece of it. I'd rather eat my belt. But I'll bet the Japanese would eat it. Them Japanese, they'll eat anything.

I was listening to public radio one time, and the reporter was interviewing a woman in Maine scooping out sea urchins. The reporter said, "Do you mean to tell me that someone would eat that?" The woman replied, "Looks to me like it's already been et!" [Sid breaks up again]

It's been et and throwed back up again! Terrible! And they don't cook nothin' either.

But you don't see any fat Japanese.

No sir, you don't, and I can see why. My god, they eat anything. Why they eat them old sea cucumbers, too. But you know something? Lot of that stuff we catch and send over there, they process it and send it back! You know them egg rolls you get at the Chinese restaurant? They got some of that stuff in them.

I remember going clamming with my father. I asked him, "Why don't we eat mussels?" The ledges were just loaded with mussels, big fat ones. He said, "Only a Frenchman would eat a mussel!" Now of course mussels are all the rage, served in the finest restaurants. They cook them in wine and serve them with garlic butter.

You can eat anything long's it's in garlic butter. You could eat tripe in garlic butter. That and a lot of wine to numb yourself up.

Stonington Harbor, January

When I got down here to Stonington Village, I said to myself, "Jesus, this reminds me of Cundys Harbor fifty years ago. Of course there are a couple of tourist traps, but other than that, do you think things are changing around here?

Not much. This is the biggest fishing village on the coast. We're still a fishing village. We're not a yacht and condo village. A lot of places have been taken over by summer people, Boothbay Harbor, all them places, damn shame. But they'll never take over Stonington 'cause there's too many of us. We rule the roost. There's no room in the harbor for yachts.

What if a yacht anchors right in the middle of the harbor?

We let 'em anchor. You gotta allow a man to set his anchor, but the next day they want to be gone. Or they will be. They'll be floatin' down the bay tied to nothin'. If they own property in town they can have a mooring, just not in the harbor. The harbor's for the fishermen.

Do you run into summer people at the dock?

Sometimes. They're quite somethin', I'll tell ya. They come in here and they buy property. They don't want you on their property, but they'll walk all over yours. But we're not here much in the summer anyway. We're out fishin' most all the time.

So they come in here from Boston and New York and buy property. Do they try to get on town committees right away?

Oh, yes they do, 'cause they got too much time on their hands. Lot of them's retired, you know. But they strike a brick wall. They backwater then in a hurry. You gotta keep an eye on 'em; you gotta keep 'em in line.

Another thing is they've got too much money for their own good. That's how they git ya. They can afford to hire lawyers. Hell, a lot of them ARE lawyers! They're lawyers and retired judges and all kinds of nasty things. Way they're used to operatin' it's who you know; not what you know.

I talked to a fellow in Cundys Harbor who had a problem with an out-of-stater. His land had been in his family for about 300 years. In his deed there was a right-of-way to the water that crossed his neighbor's land. Well, a rich guy from New York bought the property next door, so he figured he'd better reestablish the right-of-way. He was a contractor, so he had a bulldozer. One day he drove the bulldozer down the right-of-way to the water. Of course he knocked a few trees down that had grown up over the years, but they were in his right-of-way.

The next thing he knows, the neighbor from away sues him for $200,000! It went to court, and the native won, but he said, "It cost me $20,000 to beat that asshole down." Now that's just an uncalled for annoyance.

[Sid chortles] That's what it is, that's what it is, just a friggin' pain in the ass. Them people are worse than black flies! Makes you want to take them out on a one-way fishin' trip.

But haven't you met some nice ones, too?

Oh yes, we've met a few really nice people from away. We got people come here and stay to the house to go duck huntin'. They come here for the ducks, not to change things around. They love this place, and they love the people.

They'll sit right here and shoot the shit with us. We bring in a mess of lobsters and give them a feed. They don't know what it's like, where they come from. They say, "We've never had lobsters like that." There was four of them showed up last time. I brought in a dozen or fifteen, and we had a hell of a feed.

Back home when they buy a lobster in a supermarket, it's probably been sitting in a tank for a week or more. Of course it's defecating and urinating like any animal, so it's been recycling its own waste for all that time. No wonder they're not as sweet.

Plus, you don't know where they come from. We've got the best lobsters right here because it's all rocky bottom. No mud. That's the way you get the sweetest lobsters. When you haul a trap out of a mud bottom, you can smell it. It smells just like a turd.

What was it like fishing in the fog before radar and GPS?

Hell, I remember fishin' before there was fathometers [electronic depth indicators]. You didn't know how deep the water was. If you guessed wrong, if you throwed a trap over, it was gone.

I had an old sounding lead. That's all we had. You threw that overboard every so often as you went along. Everything has changed so much in the last twenty or thirty years. It's terrible.

How did you navigate in the fog?

Just a compass and a watch. You'd figure the time it would take to get to a bell or a horn buoy, then you'd steer that compass course for that long. When the time was up, you'd shut your engine down and listen. If you found the buoy you'd take off again.

Do you use nautical charts?

Nope, I don't even take a chart. I could draw the friggin' chart by heart. I've been tendin' traps in these waters fifty-five years.

Have you had any close calls in a boat?

Oh yeah. I've run 'em ashore, smashed one up, stove a hole in her. Down in the kelps, down there back a few years ago. Sixth day of February, 1992, I had two divers down fishin' for whore's eggs [sea urchins]. I was comin' up through a place to the east of Isle au Haut, and I run her ashore.

It was an extreme low tide that night, and I was in a place where I shouldn't a been. I wasn't thinking all that good. I wasn't tired. I just never give it a thought, really, 'til we hit.

Fiberglass boat. Tore a hole right through her, sixteen inches long and eight inches deep. Stopped her right then and fast; threw us up against the bulkhead; dumped all the eggs upside down. We went down fast. By the time I come to, we was on the bottom.

I had a female diver with me and her husband. Broke her hip. I called another boat, and he said, "I can be there in a few minutes, but you've got to tell me how to get in there." I said, "I can tell you how to get here, but there ain't much water in here, I can tell you that right now."

He hauled his divers out of the water, came right straight in where I was. Got us out of the water. My divers had their diver suits on, so they was all right. I was standin' on the ledge with just my head out of water.

How much does a lobsterboat cost?

My boat, twenty-eight foot, is worth $100,000. That's just the boat. A thirty-six foot boat would be $200,000, and that's a cheap one. You start gettin' elaborate, stainless steel this, stainless steel that, big engine, you're talkin' big money. A big engine alone, like a 1,000-horse Cat [Caterpillar diesel] is $100,000, or more. A forty-two Duffy, if you rigged her up, today she'd be $350,000. That's just the basic boat. That's without no shit house [marine toilet] down forward and all that stuff.

How much do lobster traps cost?

An offshore trap will run you $100. A bare four-foot inshore trap with no line and no buoy will cost you $60, but you can get twenty years out of one if you don't lose it. I don't keep them that long. I sell mine at ten years. Sell used, buy new, best way to do it. But a lot of people lose a lot of gear. They put them in tight places or where a lot of boats travel, and they lose 'em.

What do lobstermen think about pleasure boats with those rope-cutting spurs on the shafts?

Not very much, I should think [laughs]. I've hauled the wheels [propellers] outa some of them. I've also hauled the rudders out of their boats, too! [laughs]. I put the line on my pot hauler, and it rips the rudder right out of the boat! Some of them sailboat rudders are plain foolish, stickin' down there, just asking to hit a ledge and get bent. A rudder should always be set up a little above the keel.

Have you ever thought you might drown?

I've never been scared, but then I ain't got brains enough, prob'ly!

But you've been in rough water?

Oh, I been in some wicked rough water, but I know my boat. My dad always said, "A boat will scare you to death before she'll drown you. Always stay with the boat."

I've been out there in some weather, boy, I'll tell you. I used to go draggin' years ago with a guy. Jesus, we used to go all day and all night. Steamin' at night in snow storms, blizzards, a hundred miles offshore. I remember one time we got our gear overboard, and we was towin', and we never took it up for twelve hours. We couldn't get it up. It was blowing eighty-five miles per hour and forty-foot seas. We just got in a trough and towed her back and forth for twelve hours. It was brutal.

I met a fellow who said he caught religion out there. When a wave blew out his windshield, he found Jesus.

Oh yeah, if the waves come in the pilothouse, you are in deep shit.

They say it's like being in a front-loading washing machine with no way to turn it off or get out.

Oh yeah, that's it, it's the same idea. It just washes you to death [laughs]. I was out with Stevie Robbins doin' offshore lobsters once. In six days I lost thirty-six pounds.

You should write a book: *Sid's Six-Day Diet*. Go on Oprah!

That's right! [laughing]. My diet works, I'll guarantee you that.

How long do you think you'll continue fishing?

Long as I can. I'd rather be fishin' than anything else. I just like fishin', that's all. Besides, I've gotta fish. My Social Security won't buy my cigarettes.

What it is you like so much about fishing?

I'm self-employed. I'm independent. Nobody tells me what to do or where to go. I can go when I want to and come in when I want to. And somebody else ain't gettin' the money. The harder I work, the more I get. I figure how much I want to make, and that's how hard I work. When I've made my money I take up my gear. No sense working any more after you've got what you need.

Now I've heard an Eaton raced in one of the *America's* Cups.

Ayah! Uncle Irving skippered the *Ranger* in the 1937 America's
Cup. She was 135 feet, and she was built right down to the Bath
Iron Works. Most of the crew was from Deer Isle. They raced
against quite a few boats in the elimination and done real well.
Skunked the British boat, *Endeavour*, four-nothin' in the final.

Were all of the crew local fishermen?

Oh, no. These were yachtsmen. These were guys got paid to go
yachting for a living. They went to Florida and run boats for rich
guys down in Florida. But they were all from here, Deer Isle.

Uncle Irving was in his fifties by then, but the other guys had
to do all the cranking of the winches. He had a young crew, in
their twenties and thirties. But she was a fast boat, and they was
a good crew. Irving was a smart man when it come to yachting.
He knew yachts from one end to the other.

**So when you see million-dollar yachts from the New York Yacht
Club come up through the Fox Island Thorofare, you're not
terribly impressed?**

Not terribly [laughs].

DIANE DE GRASSE
A Liberal-Minded Woman
Brunswick
Age 68

Diane de Grasse painting en plain air *on Monhegan Island*

Sailing friends told me an interesting couple had shown up at the Unitarian Universalist Church in Brunswick. The gentleman was thought to be well into his eighties, and the couple had just returned from sailing across the Atlantic. Having attempted and failed the same feat in my forties, I was intrigued.

I called and was told to park on the street in front of the house. Why the street was apparent upon arrival: the driveway of the tiny lot was occupied by a thirty-something-foot strip-planked sailboat. The sturdy vessel exemplified the dictate, "Form follows function." This was not a vessel built for racing; this was not an object 'd art to swing from a mooring at the Larchmont Yacht Club; this was a vessel in which to survive an angry sea.

I knocked on the door. The door opened to reveal the bright and genial face of a middle-aged woman. Behind her, ram-rod straight, stood a tall thin man with a full head of coal black hair.

[Diane] It was terrible weather—cold, gray, wet. It was mud season in Maine. I was thinking about being somewhere else, being warm, doing something fun, the Bahamas or something. So I was imagining, well, I'd just love to go sailing. I'd also like to go fishing. I had put ads in the paper before looking for people to take me fishing. And I had gone fishing.

I am an artist. I had an art gallery for a while, and my ex-partner was reopening the gallery in a different venue. So I was waiting for this gallery to open. I had the *Coastal Journal* newspaper with me in my car, and I decided to look through the ads because I was, as they say, between interests. Just for fun I decided to look at the personals, and there was this ad.

> **SEAFARING, SEASONED**
> Mature gentleman, '70s, enjoys sailing, music, nature, healthy cuisine. Seeking liberal-minded, physically fit, gentle woman, 45-60, sense of humor, who loves sailing. Cruise New england, Maritime. Southbound this fall. ☎ 4059

The personal ad that caught Diane de Grasse's eye one dismal day in April, 1990.

So I saw this ad, tucked it away, went to the opening, had a lovely time, said hello to everyone. And then I called the number in the ad, the voice mail box.

Jim tells me he received half a dozen replies. The friends he was staying with listened to all of the recorded messages, and they liked my voice the best, so they suggested that he call me. So he did and we chatted and found out we were the same religion, both born in Boston, a few things like that. We didn't talk about age. He sounded like he was kind of an old guy because, as I later found out, his voice was affected from having polio as a child. I just thought, "Well, he's a nice, nice older man."

We decided to meet. But when the day came, I got cold feet and stood him up. He called that evening and said, "I must have made a mistake, I thought we were going to meet today, and I didn't see you." I said, "Jim, it wasn't a mistake. I really can't do this. I've got a wonderful job. I've got a house. I've got pets. I have a car. And I've got three days of vacation left this year. So forget about it, I can't go with you." But, I said, I wanted him to put his ad in a better place than the *Coastal Journal*. I said, "Good luck, but try the *Maine Times*. You might want to switch a couple of the words." I just wanted to help.

A week later I picked up the *Maine Times* and there was the ad. I was wondering how he was doing, so I called him up. He said he had gone down to hear the Dalai Lama. I had just been messing around with Buddhism so I thought, well, wait a minute, there's something else that we have in common. So I said, "Let's try it again. We'll meet in front of the church after work, and we'll have a cup of coffee, and bring a picture of your boat. I want to see your boat."

That reminds me of the joke about the Maine fisherman who put an ad in the paper, "Fisherman looking for woman with boat. Send picture of boat."

Well, it was almost like that, because I expected him to be a little guy, pot-bellied, maybe even with a cane, balding, whatever. I did not expect this tall, lanky, black-haired man.

I'm waiting in the bakery beside the church, and at 5:30 here comes this handsome fellow with an album of pictures under his arm. So, "Diane, right, Jim, right, okay." Well, the coffee shop was closed, so we went to dinner. He had red wine with fish. I took that as a good sign.

After dinner we started up the hill to where I had parked. He grabbed my hand, and I thought, "Either he doesn't know what he's doing, or he's got some moves." But I thought it was okay. Then, as we approached where he was parked, I could see what he was driving— a VW camper van. I said "YES. He's a rolling stone and I like it!"

That night I wrote in my journal that I had a new friend. I didn't know how far it was going to go, but I certainly liked what I had seen so far. He was gentle and kind and open, and I liked his VW camper bus. It spoke of adventure; it spoke of travel, going places.

So that's how we got together, and it didn't take long. Jim does not mess around. He proposed in two weeks.

How did he propose?

That's a funny story too, because the couple he was staying with had noticed he had come up here for lunch on a Saturday. They also noticed that his toothbrush was gone. Well, he brought his toothbrush and proposed the same day. He told me how much money he had. He said "I've got X dollars."

I liked his openness and his honesty. I had had enough of "not open" and "not honest." I'm thinking, "What I'm seeing is what I'm getting. No hidden stuff going on here. I don't recall everything that was said. I think I said I would think about it.

It took me about ten minutes. I really gave it some thought. I thought it would be a great adventure. I was ready for a change. I had a great job at the paper; I really liked it. I did not like the new computer operating system they were about to install, so I thought, "Well, at least I won't have to deal with that." And this was the sweetest fellow I had ever met—honestly.

So that was it. Then there was a lot of scurrying around. Jim went back to Nova Scotia to finish making a new mast and getting the boat ready and, in the meantime, I prepared everything here. We were married at the Unitarian-Universalist Church. My father walked me down the aisle. Jim's son took the pictures. My daughter did all the flowers. Two weeks later we went off for a year.

He sailed the boat down from Nova Scotia into Portland Harbor. He came marching into the office. It was like the movie, *Officer and a Gentleman*, and Jim was like Richard Gere. I'm sitting in my little cubical. He comes in right off the boat, salty, a mess; he's been going for three days. He was brown and red and all sorts of colors. The other women in the office are saying, "Wow, this is great. He's coming in. It's time to go. You're retiring today."

Home sweet home—Alert, *at anchor*

So he had lunch with my department and me, a little send-off. In the evening we all had cocktails on the waterfront, except Jim couldn't find the place where we were having cocktails. But I could see the boat. I pointed it out to my colleagues. I said, "There's where I'm going to go. I'm going to live on that thing."

Two weeks later we're off on our first cruise. Down the Waterway [the Intracoastal Waterway—a 3,000-mile inland waterway stretching from New Jersey to Florida and around to Brownsville, Texas] to Florida then through the Bahamas over to Cuba.

How did you like Jim's boat?

I thought it heeled too much at first. I thought it would tip over and we would sink. But then we were knocked down off Cuba. I, fortunately harnessed, went into the drink with the boat, but was exhilarated when she popped back up just as Jim had promised.

I was tickled with the way Jim had designed the galley because he had made huge drawers. The storage was unbelievable. The head was right at the foot of the bed. There was a little bit of a partition, but it was not enclosed. I had to get used to that.

I remember a neat incident going down the waterway. Jim had gone below to take a nap; he used to nap every day. I was on the helm, I was just putt-putting along down the waterway, following the markers, and the Coast Guard comes up behind us in a little inflatable with the blue light flashing. I didn't know where anything was; I didn't even know how to stop the boat, so I just kept going. They came alongside, tied up to us and came on board. Meanwhile I'm calling, "Jim, Jim."

Well, the problem was that Jim really wanted to go to Cuba, and laid out in the cabin was this very big *Cruising Guide to Cuba*. We didn't have any drugs or anything like that on board, but I'm trying to wake Jim to get him to come up so they don't go down there. I thought, "Oh God, they're going to find the Cuba book and we'll be in big trouble.

So Jim comes up, and they ask him, "Where is your horn?" And he gets out this big long thing. Then they ask to see his *Rules of the Road*, and Jim said, "Well, I don't really have a *Rules of the Road*. I was in the Coast Guard in World War II. Does that count?" These are all young kids, and they said, "Oh well, you really need to have a little card or something, you know, *Rules of the Road*, you really ought to have that on board."

They looked at our oil discharge placard; that was in the galley. They looked at our birth dates. They got a chuckle out of the fact that our birthdays were back to back; everybody always did, the customs people too.

So they said okay, that was fine, and they said, "Bye, see you later, have a good trip." So we continued going. I don't know whether Jim went back to sleep or not. And then, here they come back again!

I'm thinking, "You know what they said to each other? Did you check out that book down below?" So they came back alongside and came back aboard. They had something with them. They had folded in a triangle an American flag. They said, "Captain Jim, since you were in the Coast Guard in World War II, we're presenting you with this flag that has flown on a Coast Guard vessel."

They were in awe of him. They were just kids.

So on you went to Florida and then to Cuba. How was Cuba?

We saw only one other American boat, an enormous plastic motor boat from Texas, the *XXX White House*, or something. What an ass!

I was quite disturbed when we first got to Cuba. We went into Baracoa, a very, very old city. I think it might have been the first city in Cuba. As we came into the little lagoon, I looked on the shore and was appalled at the poverty. The fishing boats were all rusted, and there were pigs on the beach, chickens, kids, and ponies, and everybody running around. The houses were just shacks.

But then we went ashore and I met an artist. He had a little studio there. We didn't speak Spanish, but he could speak a little bit of English. He invited us to his house for dinner. His house was the size of this living room, the whole thing. Their bed was in the room, and the refrigerator, and their table, and I don't know where their bathroom was.

Did you let him know that you were an artist?

Yes, so I was appreciative of what he did. His wife also made little things which we have; she painted little scenes on shells. They were very, very poor, but they were a delightful little family. Their little boy and I were on the bed doing his homework, because he was studying English. We were playing with words in English and Spanish.

His wife made a meal, a typical Cuban meal which consisted of a lump of something and a lump of something else in gravy. I don't know whether there was any meat in it or not. If there was, it was a tiny little piece. But it was just a bowl, and that was dinner. All of us ate together.

We had a Polaroid camera with us. I took a whole roll of film and gave them all the pictures. They thought that was wonderful. I was so glad to have that camera because we could give pictures to all the Cubans we met.

Mi casa, su casa. Baracoa, Cuba

Did you ever worry about your safety in Cuba?

No worry about safety at all. Not ever. The fishermen on the outlying keys were just friendly and wonderful. The people were wonderful too. Some of the Guarda Frontera [the Cuban Coast Guard] asked if they could have some of our old magazines so they could study English. It was nice. We hated to leave, but we had to get back.

How did you get around the U.S. ban against travel to Cuba?

The Cubans just put a slip of paper in your passport, so there's no record of your having been there when you come back to the States. But Mr. Melcher here, being the honest chap that he is, when we checked into Key West, the customs guy asked, "Where have you been?" Of course Jim said, "We've been to Cuba."

The customs guy is practically drooling. "You came from Cuba? How do you explain that? Did you spend any money?" No. "How did you spend six weeks in Cuba and not spend any money?"

The actual rule is a trade embargo. It's not illegal to go to Cuba; you just can't spend a cent while you are there. So while we are standing there in the customs office, we have to explain in writing how we spent six weeks in Cuba without spending a cent.

I wrote, "We were on a special marine expedition...." I made up a story on the spot, because we were just standing there in the office. They wrote to us a little while later and said, "We'd like a better explanation of why you didn't spend any money in Cuba."

It so happened that when we came into Naranjo, the Cuban port of entry, there was a Canadian boat anchored, an ex-pat from Canada who had been arrested for smuggling. If he were caught again, he'd be in the brig, so he couldn't go near the United States. But he was very happy to help us with some ideas. He gave us his boat card with his name and the name of his boat.

When we wrote back to the government, we said, "Unlikely as it may seem, Joe Blow paid for our visa, and our sailing permit, and some things that we needed ashore, etc. He was so glad to see us because we were English speaking."

They bought that?

They didn't have any choice. However, they had to think of something, so while we were in Spain, we got another letter that said, "Mr. Melcher signed the letter, but Mrs. Melcher didn't, so we want to see you."

We answered, "We'll be back in a year and a half, and we'll get in touch." Then September eleven happened and they had bigger fish to fry than a couple of silly old people who go to Cuba.

[After returning to the states, the Melchers sailed home to Maine for eight months. Diane took a job to fatten the cruising account, and Jim prepared the boat for a two-year cruise in Europe. In May of 2000, they loaded the boat with gear and provisions and sailed it to Halifax, where it would be shipped by freighter to Liverpool.]

[Diane continues:] I remember packing up the boat and saying to myself, "See you in England." We joined it in Liverpool.

Then we had so much fun with festivals. The first one was the Celtic Voyage in Penzance. Lots of fun. Then across to the Brest Festival—absolutely fabulous. We were on French television because we were the only American boat. They met us coming in. We saw the press boat coming and thought, "Oh, isn't this fun. Press boats around. Isn't that great! And look at this, they're filming us, they're taking our picture." They came aboard the next day a couple of times, then followed us ashore.

After the festival we were on our own. We made our way down the coast of France, top of Spain, Atlantic Portugal. We wintered on the Guadiana between Portugal and Spain. Then we went into the Mediterranean, hopped along all the islands: Menorca, Majorca, Formentara. Then to Sardinia, to Tunisia, and Malta and Sicily. Back to Sardinia and then back out of the Mediterranean, across the Atlantic, headed for Martinique and home.

What was it like, crossing the Atlantic, just the two of you?

I was never really, really scared crossing the Atlantic. I had great faith in the boat and in my partner. They both could take it. But often I was pissed, because I got sick of that rolling, rolling, rolling. It's tiring, and it's maddening.

We took turns, standing three or four-hour watches while the other person slept. At night I always checked to see where the Big Dipper was. As long as the Big Dipper was there, I knew I was still on earth.

Being out there, it's all yours, that's the feeling I got. This is all mine, ours. All ours. As far as the eye can see. We saw only one ship in nineteen days, a freighter way off over the horizon.

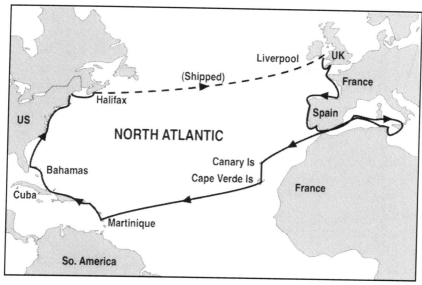

Alert's track, 2000–2002

Being in the cockpit at night you're certainly watchful, but it is boring. You want to know how boring it was? I used to spend hours waiting to see numbers on the GPS line up. If you get three, even two, numbers to line up, it's like pulling the handle on a slot machine and seeing the lemons line up. That's boredom.

Before you took the trip, on a scale of one to ten, how much fun did you think it was going to be?

I didn't think it was going to be very much fun, maybe a four. I didn't expect it to be a lot of fun, and it wasn't.

Then how did it stack up as an adventure?

That's a ten. It was a hell of an adventure. It really was. Because we had incidents. Jim got his skin torn off his face by one of the sheets [lines that control the loose end of the sail] whipping across the cockpit. We had several things like that.

If I had known all the things that could happen I might have had another thought about crossing. It was naivete. I just figured, we're good, okay, we're good. We can go.

So you didn't have a CD player on board. Not an iPod?

Nothing. Correction, we did have a single-sideband receiver. We couldn't transmit, but we could receive. That kept me sane, because there was a radio net that all the boats we had met listened to, and every morning the net controller would come on and say, "Hello *Alert*, wherever you are." We couldn't answer, but it choked me up that they were thinking of us. Then at night there was an evening signoff, "Take-care, *Alert*," and all the other boats were giving their coordinates [latitude and longitude]. I plotted everybody's track on a chart.

We did have a few problems with the boat. We lost a lazy jack [system of ropes that prevent the sail from falling into the water], and the whole sail went in the water. And we had a lot of chafe and broken battens.

When we got to Martinique, we had a just patch of sail left and no engine. After nineteen days at sea, we're seeing land, we're coming into Martinique, the northeast corner of Martinique. Jim knew a little lagoon that we could come into, but to get into the lagoon you've got to go through a whole bunch of reefs. So you're coming in, surf breaking all around you, no engine, tiny little sail, and the wind is dying. You're snaking around these reefs and you just make it.

It was quite a trip across the Atlantic. On day ten, about midway, we opened a bottle of champagne, drank it, put a five-dollar bill in it, corked it up, and threw it overboard with our name and number on it.

But nobody has ever called.

STEVIE ROBBINS, JR.
Fisherman
Stonington
Age 67

Stevie Robbins, Jr., holding court in his fishing shack on a Sunday morning

*Stevie Robbins, Jr., instructed me to meet him at his lobster shack at
9 a.m. on a Sunday morning. "You can't miss it. Right on Main
Street. The only place with traps piled up. There'll be a bunch here, but
I'll chase them out," he said.*

*I navigated through the stacks of lobster traps and pushed open the
door. Amidst piles of rope and buoys, facing half a dozen fishermen,
sat a mountain of a man chewing on a cigar and splicing rope onto a
buoy. Stevie Robbins, Jr., was holding court.*

*"You all have to leave," he said. "I don't know what I done, but
this fella wants to talk with me."*

How did you get started fishing?

Well, I stayed out one year after high school, and I saved up enough money, and I went over to Maine Maritime Academy. Turned out I was about as suited to that as nothin'. All that military, all the marchin' around, I didn't know what I was gettin' into. Somehow I got through the first year, but the second year I found out about liquor. I didn't last too long after that.

"Well," I said to myself, "Now I got to do something." The only reason I went to the Maritime is because everybody told me, "If you don't learn to do somethin' and you go fishin', you're going to be in a mess if fishing collapses." So I said, "I'll learn to do somethin' else. Then I can get some good gear to work with, and I'm goin' fishing. Well, when they kicked me out of the Maritime I said, "Now I've really screwed up."

Of course the draft was on me to go to Vietnam, but I lucked into something. My uncle got a job on a ship going down to the South Pole. There was a number of us went from here. The only thing I was down there for was to save up enough money to buy a boat and go fishing. That's all I wanted to do, to go fishing.

I've seen that documentary about you and your brother and your father, *Salt of the Earth*. Your father never said a word during that whole movie. Just sat there between you and your brother, as if he'd never heard the stories you were telling.

Oh, we said somethin' that was kinda off-color, and he did say to the producer fella, "How often do you fellows make one of these?" I remember him saying that.

Down the bay here, last island out's Isle au Haut, and a lot of the fellows from here fish down around there. My father was havin' his gear poached, and he took a lath on a wooden trap and wrote on the lath, "Whoever hauls this trap is going to be shot." Next time he hauled that trap somebody had added, "Bang!" [laughs]

I understand you were one of the very first offshore lobstermen.

I was the first one from anywhere around here. What happened was I read in the *Reader's Digest* about a fellow, he was studying for the ministry in Massachusetts, and he went lobsterin' summers to make money to go to school. He fished off of Block Island, Cox's Ledge, to the westward I think of Block Island. In the summer everybody used to go inshore more, and he kept going off further. He was the first guy.

I read that story, so I said, "I'd like to do that." I had a regular boat at first, but I kept trying to go off a little bit and a little bit. Then I had a bigger boat, a forty-four foot boat. I had that built for going offshore. Then I went to a fifty-five foot steel boat.

Then, oh my Lord, everybody started doin' it. There was thirty, forty boats. There was boats from Rhode Island, from Massachusetts, from New Hampshire, and all up and down the coast of Maine. They all come off there like a hundred miles. It got so there wasn't enough room for both the draggers and the lobstermen. I lost $43,000 worth of gear [traps] in one night to the draggers. I like to never recovered. That was the beginnin' of the end. I was solvent, but just barely. I had borrowed money that was costin' me 16.5%.

Back in the Carter years?

Yup. I built the forty-four footer in '77. I built the steel one in '81. A lot of people were buildin' boats. They'd give you the money if you could prove you could do anything at all. I think it was $883,000 I paid back on a $250,000 loan.

Then didn't the government buy fishing boats back because of overfishing? I think the government had a program where, if a fisherman could show tax returns for two or three years, they'd pay for him to go to school to be retrained. The program was pretty much a bust because most of the fishermen couldn't show tax returns! Does that surprise you?

Ayah. In the 70s a guy went to a wharf in Boothbay and bought lobsters off a boat, fifteen or twenty lobsters. The guy says to the fella on the boat, "You want a slip?" "No, no," he says, "I don't need no slip." Turns out the guy buyin' the lobsters was an IRS agent.

So the IRS started their lobster project. Thing was, we had treated any crew who went with us as self-employed, so they paid their own taxes. Supposedly. Well, the government was losin' out, see, because nobody was paying any self-employment tax.

I remember there was a store owner in Harpswell who didn't have a cash register. He kept all of his money in a ten-quart pail. When you bought something, he made change out of that bucket, and there was no receipt or anything. I don't know how he ever figured his taxes. Boy, weren't those the good old days!

Well, I found out the IRS is really smart. At least somebody in that outfit is, because I could remember, from 1970, when I come home from shipping, what I grossed the first year, what I cleared. For about seven years I could remember, boom, boom, boom, just like that. Every year I did a little better. When I went to get a loan for that forty-four foot boat, the bank told me I had grossed $63,000 in 1976, and I cleared $33,000. They said, "You are a good manager of money. Any one who clears over half of their gross is doin' all right."

Well, after I paid my income tax, I never had one cent left. Two years later I made a ton of money offshore, before all them other boats come. I had a lot of expenses, but I made a lot of money. Time I got done paying my expenses, and paid my income tax, I never had one cent left, so I figure the IRS is some smart. They've figured out how to get every last cent out of you, no matter how much you make.

Now, to be truthful, I am glad I paid in on the Social Security because now I can get Social Security. Not to be sneezed at because it takes care of your livin' expenses.

Do you mind telling the movie story about the tub of lanolin?

Ha! When we went offshore we switched from our traditional size traps to great big traps because, about the time I started goin' off outside there, a fellow moved here from Massachusetts. He was one of the top highline [successful] fishermen, and he was one of the first offshore lobstermen. He was really interested in what I was doing, and he gave me a lot of information. One was that those big traps, the Anderson traps, would be better suited. They'd hold more, they fished better, and they stayed down better. But they weighed about 200 pounds, and we didn't know how to handle them. You know, there's always a trick to everything.

So we're gettin' the traps up to the side of the boat, and we're fishin' a hundred and somethin' fathom [a fathom equals six feet, so 100 fathom is 600 feet] of water. We'd get the traps up, and we're pulling our guts out. Well, when you pull your guts out for any length of time, over and over, you start gettin' piles. My brother, he had all kind of ruptures.

Well, we had a cook that was a wood cutter, clam digger, apple picker, and he'd gone scallopin' some. He was a good cook, an older fella. Oh, he cooked this fiery hot food: stuffed peppers and such. We was gettin' low on grub. By that time everybody had taken a hand in gettin' that gear aboard, and, Jesus, they was all usin' Preparation H. We went out and got ourselves a big tub of lanolin, probably a gallon. It was down under the stove. They was a cupboard that wasn't bein' used, so we stuck it down there.

Well, this cook come up one mornin', and he had cooked eggs and this and that. I said, "Now just a minute. How're you fryin' them eggs? We haven't got any pork fat; we haven't got any kind of cookin' oil; we're out of everything." Cook says, "Boys, I found somethin' down under the stove." "Oh, Christ!" I said, "That's the ass grease!"

Not only had he used it, but some nasty bastard had applied it to himself and put what he didn't use back in the tub!

Of course that story's a damn lie. We just like to make things up. But you know, if you tell somethin' long enough, sometimes you begin to think it's half true!

I was over to Shop and Save in Ellsworth a few years after they made that movie, and this guy kept lookin' at me. I said, "Can I help you?" He said, "I know you." I says, "No, you don't." He said, "No, you made that movie." "Well," I said, "I was in it."

He was a teacher down to Mt. Desert. He says, "That movie is required viewing for my students." I said, "Are you kidding me? Why?"

He said, "Because I wanted the students to learn, before it was all gone, the old way that people used to be and talk and so forth." He said, "There's not many of you any more." I said, "Did you cut out the ass grease story?" "No," he said, "That's the best part!"

I think that teacher was right. A lot of the coast is changing, but this place is frozen in time.

It's not been very many years these tourist shops been here. Just before the boom, there was a lot of houses runnin' down. Right fallin' into the road. Now there's a couple of places that sell stuff to summer people. Some of the people don't like it, but I believe it's better than havin' the houses fall into the road.

Does Stonington get overrun by tourists in the summer?

Not near as bad as Boothbay. Too remote here. Hell, it takes fifty minutes to get to Ellsworth, up to Route 1.

That's pretty remote, but I see you have a year-round movie theater here [the Stonington Opera House].

That thing's older than the hills. That was taken over by a bunch of people from New York, and they've got it on the Historical Registry. Now they get grants, and they have plays and music.

Is that a good thing?

Sure it is! They have some movies that's just come out. I don't know how they do it, but maybe through that historic association.

I don't go there myself, because one thing they got is the same seats they had when I was a kid, and I can't even get in one! The other thing is they have that same popcorn machine they had back when I was a kid, and they're advertising it as "organic popcorn." Now I ask you, what the hell does that mean?

Maybe that the corn was raised on cow poop?

Cow shit and seaweed! I seen bags of it at a hardware in Ellsworth.

Would you mind repeating the story about the big yacht and the lobsters, the story they got the title of the movie from?

Oh yeah, I can remember that. I was in an outboard, and the guy is anchored out there. Boat was too big to come in to the docks, I

The Stonington Opera House, built in 1912

guess. It was prob'ly eighty, a hundred feet. He beckoned me over there. I had prob'ly twenty-five, thirty pounds of lobster. He said, "Captain, can we buy those lobsters?" I said, "Well, yes, I guess so. I usually sell them into the buying station in there. I don't have any way to weigh them."

I knew it was foolish soon as I said it, but I said, "You don't have a scale, do you?" "No," he said, "but we'll take your word for it." So we did that. He said, "You keep the extra." I said, "No, they cost what they are. That's what I told you, and that's what they are."

He turns to the woman standin' next to him, and he says, "See, I told you, these people are the salt of the earth!" Well, I'd never heard that phrase, but I guess I knew what it meant, so I was kinda tickled, you know, because I was brought up that way.

When you told that story in the movie, you got tears in your eyes.

Well, it made me proud to be called that. [Stevie points to a picture on the wall of himself, his brother, and a bearded musician, all holding guitars] See that guy right there in that picture? He told me and my brother, "I was born and brought up in Hollywood,

California. My mother and father were magicians. All I ever wanted to do was travel and play music." He said, "I can understand why a person would feel like I did, but I can't understand why you people, where you come from, are so fierce to go fishin'. It's hard work and bad weather, and this and that, all kinds of things can happen, and it's dangerous."

He didn't say it, but I know he was also thinkin' to himself there's not too many millionaires around here. I said, "Well, when I was a kid, we'd go on a ride on Sunday. We'd go on the mainland across the bridge, and I can remember ridin' around and thinking, "How do these people make a living? They don't even live near the water!" Fishin' was just what we did. We were proud of it, you know? But that fella couldn't understand that.

Do you remember the fellow's name?

It was John McEuen. I'll never forget it.

You don't mean the leader of the Nitty Gritty Dirt Band? When did that happen?

L to R: John McEuen, Stevie Robbins, Jr., Brian Robbins on stage

We was all up to University of Maine where they was showin' our movie, and my brother and I were playin' our guitars. This guy just come up on stage with his instrument and sat down with us.

It was wicked, one of the highlights of my life. He played four or five notes, and I looked at my brother, and he give me this great big grin, and we knew we were in the big times.

Oh, lord! It was somethin' else to play with that fella. My brother has lived his whole life music, and we always played, and we used to go with the old man 'round to people's weddin' anniversaries and stuff, but nothin' ever like that! That was somethin' else. That McEuen fellow asked me, right on the stage while that thing was goin' on. It wasn't rehearsed. He just come right out and said it.

Wow! That's a memory for the nursing home. Now let's change the subject. Have you ever had close calls at sea?

Well, I been in a lot of fracases. When I came back from the South Pole I ran a boat for a year. The company was in New Jersey, and we were doin' a sand survey for the Army Corps of Engineers. We went from Long Island, right straight around Long Island Sound, up the Connecticut Shore, up to Rhode Island, around the Cape to Plymouth Massachusetts. We done seismic work and took bottom samples. They was going to restore some beaches by pumpin' sand back in to fight erosion.

We was on the outside of Cape Cod, first nor'easter we'd had in three months. We was down in Chatham, and it said right on the chart, "Do not follow the channel markers because the sand shifts." Well, my job was to run that ship in there far as I could and then run back out.

Christ, I got hooked onto one of them sandbars. The owner was on vacation, him and his wife. He turned on the television in the mornin', and there's his boat sinking!

How big a boat?

Sixty-five foot dragger built in 1928. She was worm-eaten from stem to stern so bad they had to put cement down in the bottom of her to hold her together. She just worried right into that sand.

Coast Guard come out and got us in a lifeboat. We had to abandon ship, and the rest of them got off in the lifeboat. I don't swim too good, but they wrapped a line around me and dragged me out over the bow. Jesus, I thought it was over that time!

Then two years ago I run a boat ashore on the eastern side of Isle au Haut coming in in the dark. Ledge broke on me.

You didn't have a GPS?

Yes, I did, but I had the lights on back aft, and I was in a bad place. I saw a wave breakin' right ahead [waves breaking over a submerged ledge], and I looked up at my color machine [chart plotter], and the headin' marker was slow, and I didn't see the compass. I thought it was 'bout northeast, and I was headed north. I pulled her to port and crash!

Lost that boat. They had to send a helicopter to get my son off the island because he had hypothermia, and we like to never got off the boat. She was crashing right into the rocks sideways so hard she'd knock ya. Where we had to jump to she come down so hard you had to get the hell out of there fast or she'd scrunch ya. After the helicopter took my son, other fishermen from Stonington come got us.

What time of year was this?

I think it was December.

Not a good time to go swimming in the North Atlantic!

No, and everything was soaking wet. I got them to put on their survival suits, but when we got on to the island we cut them up and made a fire because we couldn't get anything else to burn.

Do people still go offshore for lobsters?

Well, there's a lot of fellas that's goin' a little offshore, thirty or forty miles. They'll leave two or three in the mornin' to get out there by sunrise and get back way after dark.

Does it pay them to do that? Are lobster prices good enough?

Well, the market went to hell a couple years ago, and that was lean times, but it's a little better now. And the lobster population has held up pretty good. You prob'ly know that. And it ain't just that we're catchin' em. We see 'em; there's a lot of small ones. When I was a kid I never once in my life saw so many little lobsters.

Why is that?

Well, there must be more of them. Jay Crouse worked for the DMR [Department of Marine Resources] for years in that lab over there in Boothbay. He's retired now, but he used to be a great advocate of uppin' the minimum size. They booed him outa their meetin's and all, but I knew it was the right thing to do.

Because the females have an extra year to produce eggs?

Of course they do! When we finally did it, we gave them another year. Plus they cleaned up a lot of this trash that comes down out of the rivers. I know it's still bad in places, but lord, years ago! We didn't know any better. We dumped our oil overboard. It was foolish, but we did it. I did it. Drain the oil outa the engine right into the bottom of the boat, maybe throw some soap into it, and pump it overboard. They've pretty well stopped that. All those things helped.

So you think the government has done some good things?

Oh, of course they did!

Is the government doing anything that's not so good?

Most everything they're doin' now days. My lord, the paperwork alone is enough to keep three other countries goin'. Sendin' us that stuff all the time! And meetings! Ten meetings for every half inch they'll ever move. That politics business don't mix with fishin'.

Lobstermen are pretty good at self-regulation. They came up with V-notching [V-notching is the voluntary practice of cutting a notch in the tail of a lobster bearing eggs. Keeping a notched lobster is illegal, so the practice guarantees more hatched lobsters.] before they was five politicians for every fisherman. The old guys used to say it would regulate itself, and I believe they were right.

Do you have traps out this winter?

Not many. I've got them all up except 180. I didn't go way off this winter because I had a lot of gear that was in disrepair. Boats start goin' off now... I started doin' it in August, September, and that was way early. Sometimes I got a jump on people, sometimes you wouldn't. Now they're startin' in June!

Aren't the lobsters headed back in to shore in June?

We did a taggin' project with Woods Hole [Woods Hole Oceanographic Institution]. They brought the Johnson Sea-Link submarine with them. They released 1,000 tagged lobsters. They were caught and released around 100 miles from here. One year later they caught one lobster off Yarmouth, Nova Scotia, which was a distance of about eighty miles. Another lobster was caught down here off Isle au Haut. One was caught on the west side of this island up here, so that's about 100 miles. One was caught off Long Island, New York. But the majority showed up on the southwest side of Georges Bank, which is about 150 miles from there.

So there are still unknowns about lobster behavior?

Oh Lord, yes! My grandfather went eighty-three years. He said, "I know less about lobsters now than when I started."

And there are a lot of scientists working on it.

Yes, and some of them are smart, but it's a tricky thing. When we did that tagging project we found out, through trial and error, that you couldn't do much on hard bottom. So we would go to mud somewheres near some hard bottom. Spencer Apollonio, the Commissioner of the Department of Marine Resources, wrote a book about the Gulf of Maine, and he theorized that lobsters follow the warm water. Some water would break off from the Labrador Current, get churned up by the Gulf Stream, and come up by Georges Bank into the Gulf of Maine That warmer, salty, heavy water would settle down in them deep places. That's what we found out.

We'd dive in that submarine 120, 130 fathoms. We never saw a lobster in twenty-three dives. I said, "I think they're movin' at night."

Well, the scientists didn't like to dive at night because, if it was choppy, hooking that submarine up was tricky. But they went down pretty close to night, and things started changing. My lord, them slime eels come all alive out of the mud! Fish are going. Everything changed when the daylight changed. But we still didn't see no lobsters in the mud. So I asked them if they'd head over toward the hard bottom. They did, and they said, "Look, we see a lobster!" And before they thought what it would sound like, they said, "That lobster right there is worth $123,000!" That's what they'd spent to get to see that one lobster. I guess the lobsters come off the hard bottom when they get hungry. They go searching around on that mud, and then they go back to the hard bottom. The damned lobsters would fill those traps up and clean the bait in an hour.

They must have a wicked sense of smell.

Wicked! They can smell a trap with bait a mile away.

How do you keep people from away from coming in here and trying to change things? Everywhere I go I hear complaints that retired people come to Maine, having been on Wall Street and presidents of corporations, thinking they know how to run things.

Well, my father-in-law and my wife's uncle owned this buildin', and they leased it to the State as a liquor store. When the state moved out, they said, "Why don't you buy this and use it as your shop? I said, "I can't afford it."

They sold it, eventually, to a couple from upstate New York, Ted and Lil. He was a professor and she was a librarian. This place was just about like it is now [a two-story unpainted shack full of lobster gear]. I had traps outside right up to the top of the stairs.

Well, they come to see me. I said, "Listen, I'll have them traps outa your way in a day or two. They said, "Oh, you don't have to move them traps." "Well," I said, "I'm gonna be takin' my stuff outa here." They said, "You don't have to move." "Why," I said, "you bought the buildin'." "Well, we're not going to do anything to the downstairs. Lord, we got plenty enough to do upstairs."

So I stayed in here. I used to try and take lobsters to 'em, and I'd have to fight to get them in through the door. They didn't want to take them. They'd buy them, but they wouldn't take them.

Then, five, six, seven years, I don't know how many years, I got feelin' guilty 'cause I weren't payin' no rent. So I said, "Listen, I know that insurance is high on this place 'cause they call it a 'fisherman's locker,' so they say they is more chance of a fire. So I'll pay the insurance." They said, "That's good, finest kind." Then I got braver, and I says, "I think I should pay the taxes, too." They said, "What do you want?" I said, "I don't want nothin'!"

Come time, they got old and sickly, and they had a place down in Naples, Florida. We went down there a few times. Took the kids down there. They said, "We're gonna sell." I said, "Ok. I hate to see you go, but." So they did.

Well, people started comin' in here and lookin' around. There was this one old woman with them glasses on a stick, you know? She come in and caught her foot on rope or somethin'. She told the old man with her, she says, "This place is very untidy!" [we both break up laughing].

Well, they sold it to a couple from Bangor. Now maybe I've just lucked out, I don't know, but you asked me a question. I met them, and I said, "You prob'ly want me to get out." They said, "Oh, no. You don't have to move." I said, "Do you understand that I pay the taxes and insurance?" They said, "Well, if that's all right with you."

You couldn't have nobody use you any better. I met her mother. She's about that tall [indicates less than five feet]. She come in here and looked all around. She said, "I know what it's like gettin' up in the mornin'." I says, "I know where you live. You live down around Fulton Fish Market [in New York City], don'tcha?" She said, "We had a fish store down there all my married life. I got up two o'clock in the mornin'. Made the coffee and stuff for everybody." She said, "I like your operation."

Good people. I don't care where they come from. Those are good people.

RALPH STANLEY
Boatbuilder
Southwest Harbor
Age 86

Ralph Stanley rowing to shore—circa 1950

Among wooden boat enthusiasts, the name "Ralph Stanley" evokes reverence. Generally acknowledged as the savior of the famed Friendship sloop, he is equally famous for his lobsterboats.

When I read Ralph had built his last boat and was passing the business on to his son, Richard, I knew I had to hear his story.

After driving past Acadia National Park, catching occasional glimpses of Somes Sound on my left, I entered the town of Southwest Harbor, population 1,764. Like so many fisherman-built homes in the area, Ralph's house is sturdy, compact, and shingled—built to weather any storm. Behind the house is an unmarked boat shed with a marine railway leading down to the water.

Expecting a larger-than-life, burly, bearded figure, I was surprised at the man who opened the door. Ralph W. Stanley turned out to be the gentlest, most soft-spoken, most self-effacing boatbuilder I have ever met.

I was born in Bar Harbor, in the hospital, February 9, 1929.

Where were your father and mother born?

Father on Cranberry Island, mother here in Southwest Harbor.

Is it true that, on these isolated islands and peninsulas of the Maine coast, a high percentage of people can trace their roots to the same few original settlers?

Well, a whole third of the students in my high school graduating class were descendants of Jacob Lurvey, which is the Anglicized version of Loewe.

Loewe? He was Jewish?

Correct. In the early days there were these very tall, straight trees in Archangel, Russia. The British wanted these trees for masts for their navy, but the British and the Russians wouldn't deal with each other. So some Jewish people went up there, bought the trees, and resold them to the British. The British had a special fleet of vessels built to go up around to the north of Norway, into the White Sea to the Russian port of Archangel. They could only get there about a month a year due to the ice. The long tree trunks were loaded through the bow of these vessels and brought back to England.

That went on for hundreds of years, but then the trees were gone. So the Jewish people migrated down across Europe and ended up in Spain. From there some of them went over to England and then to America.

Jacob Lurvey, who may have been an illegitimate child, was bounded out [as an indentured servant] at five to a wealthy farmer, Enoch Boynton, in Byfield, Massachusetts. At fifteen Jacob wanted to fight in the Revolutionary War, but he couldn't go unless an adult went along with him. So Enoch Boynton went with him.

Serving in the war relieved Jacob of his indenture, and he went to sea. When he came home he married Enoch's youngest daughter, Hannah. He built his own vessel in Gloucester or Newburyport and settled here in Southwest Harbor. Jacob and Hannah had ten children.

I am descended from Jacob Lurvey in two ways. His daughter, Hannah, married William Gilley, and another daughter, Mary, married Thomas Stanley of Cranberry Island. I happen to be descended from both William Gilley and Thomas Stanley, so I'm descended from Jacob Lurvey in two ways!

Also, two-thirds of my graduating class were all related to each other in some other way. I can actually trace my roots to twenty of the early settlers of this area.

Have you ever constructed your family tree?

Oh, yes. I've got over 100,000 family names in my computer. It takes about a thousand pages to show all the connections! When I was growin' up I couldn't get away with a thing because I was related to everyone in town and they were all watching me.

Are you related to the Stanley Steamer brothers in Kingfield?

I can't connect them actually, but our ancestors came to Beverly, Massachusetts, about a generation apart. I could be, back in England, but I can't yet connect them.

Now, George Stanley came to Beverly, Massachusetts in 1660, somethin' like that. Some of his sons went south. One son died in Jamaica: he had just been married, and his son was born after he died. Some of his grandsons became Grand Banks fishermen out of Marblehead. In 1754 the French started seizing fishing vessels on the Grand Banks, and I think the Stanley brothers moved up to the Maine coast and stayed off the Grand Banks. They would come up to Cranberry Island, then go back to Marblehead in the winter. In fact, my great, great, great, great grandmother went back around 1790 and died in Marblehead. She had a sister that died up here at Cranberry Island. There were two Stanley brothers, and I am descended from both.

Now there were two Bartlett brothers from Bartletts Island who married two Carter sisters from Blue Hill, and I'm descended from both of them, too [laughs].

[Ralph's wife, Marion] Why don't you just say you are descended from everybody around here?

The Stanleys eventually settled on Cranberry Island. Of course they were squatters to start with. The Cranberry Islands, along with Mount Desert Island, had been granted to Sieur Lamothe Cadillac in 1688 and Governor Francis Bernard of Massachusetts in 1762. After the Revolutionary War, Cadillac's granddaughter sued for possession and received the eastern half of Mount Desert and the Cranberry Islands. She then sold off the land in one hundred acre pieces. The Stanleys bought the land they had squatted on for five pieces of eight per hundred acres.

My great uncle who had this house, he was also from Cranberry Island. He fished the Bay of Fundy and the Grand Banks, mostly codfish. My great grandfather had seven fishing vessels in his lifetime.

Of course the cod run out in the 1890s, but then the summer people came up here, and they hired the fishermen to run their yachts and take care of their places.

In my studying I've learned quite a bit about the summer people. Some of these summer people were characters. The Cabots and the Perkinses had offices in Turkey where they bought opium and shipped it to China. They made fortunes. And they traded in slaves. A lot of them had offices down in the Caribbean, tradin' in slaves, horses, rum, and molasses.

That may have been where the Cabots got their money?

Ayah. Now take the Thorndikes. Israel Thorndike had ships all over the world. In the Indian Ocean there was an island where they could get wild pepper. There was no harbor, and the island was populated by cannibals. They'd anchor off in the ocean, and they'd row ashore to gather this wild pepper. It was quite a dangerous business. The Thorndikes today are still spendin' the money old Israel Thorndike made back in the 1800s.

Well, speaking of history, when did you meet Marion?

Oh, she came down from Hancock in '35. But we didn't get together until I was twenty-five years old.

Your mother was probably wondering if and when you were going to marry!

Well, I had an excuse. I got sick. I had a tooth extracted, and somethin' got down in my lungs, and a lung abscess turned into tuberculosis. I went to the sanatorium for six months, and then I went down to Boston and had a lower lobe removed. When I got back Marion and I got together. She was babysittin' for one of my friends. We got married a couple years later.

[Marion] I used to pal around with his sister. He was a senior in high school, and I was in eighth grade. That was why we didn't get together right away. But we sort of grew on each other.

I guess you might say so. We've been together now for 60 years! After I got out of the sanatarium I went to work for some summer people. I was captain of their schooner, an Alden centerboarder.

The family was wealthy?

Oh yes, oh yes [laughs]! I worked for them for nineteen years on the schooner, and I built boats in the winter.

Were the summer people nice?

They sent me off on the boat one time with seven kids and a nursemaid from Australia. I was thirty years old and she was prob'ly in her early twenties. It was the annual three-day August cruise of the Northeast Harbor fleet.

Well, we got started, and right off the Sister Islands it shut down thick of fog. We were going to Swan's Island and got the sails down and the motor going, and we headed for the buoy off the harbor. Right off we met a sailboat, and he was lost.

From Massachusetts or New York?

Prob'ly. Anyway, we took him in tow, and before we got to the buoy we had two more boats in tow. Seven kids, a nursemaid, and three boats in tow. We got in the harbor and cast the boats off. We anchored, and it wasn't long before a couple young fellows came alongside and picked up the nursemaid. Well, that was fine.

How old were these kids?

Oh, the youngest prob'ly four and the oldest 'bout eleven or twelve. I got their supper for them, and they're playin' cards down in the cabin, and the youngest one went into the toilet, the head. After a while I heard him cryin', so I said, "What's the matter? You all right?" "I'm all right," he says. Well, things quieted down. Bye and bye I hear him wimperin' again, and I said, "You sure you're all right?" "Yes," he says, I'm ok." Well, the third time I said, "I'm comin' in." I opened up the door, and he was cryin'. He was trying to be a man, but he'd never been to the toilet without a nursemaid.

We finally got everybody settled down and to bed, and I heard the nursemaid come back aboard about one o'clock. I don't think the next day she felt very good.

I hope the parents paid you for hazardous duty.

I got $350 a month workin' seven days a week.

[Marion] Another time they sent him off with a bunch of teenagers.

How old were these kids, eighteen?

No, fifteen, sixteen! I had a Coast Guard license for carrying passengers for hire, so I said to myself, "What am I doin' here? I'm paid to be a captain, not a warden!" I decided I'd had enough. I figured I'd better get done while the gettin' is good. So I quit and started building boats full time.

How did you get into boatbuilding?

Well, of course I grew up with boats. I always wanted to build a boat as a boy. I was always building somethin' that would float. Just a natural thing to do, to build a boat. I finally got to start a boat. Took me two years to build it. Thought I'd never build another one. "There, done that!" But two months later a fella came, wanted me to build him a boat, and I couldn't wait to get started [laughs].

So you never had any formal training in boatbuilding?

I read a lot of books on boatbuilding, but I used to go to the boatbuilders' and just sit and watch. I could see what was goin' on.

Seven Girls, *built in 1960 by Ralph for his lobsterman father and named for his seven sisters.*

You know, a fellow could go to art school and never produce anything worth looking at. Likewise, a fellow could go to boat-building school and never build anything special. But someone like you …. I think you have to be born with a feel, an eye for it. In fact, I think boatbuilding is more an art than a science.

You've got to be able to see it in your mind in three dimensions.

How many boats have you built, or have you lost count?

Oh, I think altogether around seventy.

Have you ever built a fiberglass boat?

No, we finished off a couple of fiberglass hulls, but we decided we didn't like that.

What are the advantages and disadvantages of wood over fiberglas?

Well, wood will float. You put fiberglass in the water, and it will sink.

I've thought of that many a time in rough conditions in my fiberglass boat!

And the motion of the boat. A lot of the fishermen have these fiberglas boats, and at the end of the day they're worn out because the boat is moving and throwing you around all the time. It gets to your hips and your knees. It wears them out.

Like the difference between riding an elephant versus a kangaroo?

That's right. And when you build a fiberglas boat, you're kinda stuck with the mold. You can't change the shape of the hull. With every wooden boat I've built, I can see how I changed the hull just a little to make it better. Always tryin' to make it better.

The reason I never bought a wooden boat was I was afraid I wouldn't take care of it, and it would rot. What is the key to maintaining wooden boats?

It's the care you take with the top of the boat. The problem is not underwater where the wood is always in a constant condition. It's the top of the boat, where the wood is exposed to sunlight, water, and air. Water gets in and starts mildew and causes rot. The next thing you know, the boat has rotted from the top down. The cabin top and the decks, where a seam opens up or where a fitting loosens up, water gets in and rot begins.

A lot of fiberglas boats have decks with balsa wood cores. If water gets in there, the balsa rots, and then you have just a soggy mess with no strength.

Are most of your boats lobsterboats or sailboats?

Mostly lobsterboats. I built a number of Friendship sloops, and I built a Herreshoff Rosinante. I modified that, too. Old Mr. Herreshoff'd probably turn over in his grave if he knew it, but it turned out pretty good. I think it was the better for it. The owner just recently sold it down in Long Island Sound, and I guess the owner down there likes it, too.

What kind of wood do you use?

The frames are Maine Oak. It's in the Red Oak family, but here in Maine we call it Gray Oak. You can tell by the inner bark. If the inner bark is orange, it's all right. If the inner bark is yellow, don't use it, because it will rot. Gray oak will last for years. There's a boat I built in '60, and the gray oak frames are still good.

The planking is cedar. I use Maine white cedar, same stuff they make shingles out of. We used to get a lot of white cedar from Down East. They'd cut it long. We put together a 35-footer, and the garboards [first planks, next to the keel] were one piece.

I've heard you are quite the fiddler. When did you start playing the fiddle?

I was about twenty I guess. I was going up to Ricker College in Houlton, and there was a fellow up there played the fiddle.

I said, "Gee, I'd like to do that." My grandmother had an old fiddle, so I got it out, tuned it up, and learned to pick out a couple of tunes. I found some sheet music. Course I'd had a course in music in about the sixth grade, but at that time it just went in one ear and out the other. But I wanted to play the tunes I found on some sheet music, but I couldn't read the notes. Then I happened to look in the "Webster's Collegiate Dictionary," and in the back there was a section on music. So that is how I learned to read music.

I understand you have made your own fiddles.

The first one I made after the sanitorium at about twenty-four. I started another one, then I got busy building boats and didn't have time for the fiddle. After I started playing again, I was playin' up to Northport. I stepped up onto the stage, and there was a loose rug. I wasn't expecting it and fell backward off the stage flat on my back with the fiddle in my hand. Well, I crushed the top of it. So I dug out the one I had started and finished it. That's the one I play now.

[Ralph goes to the closet and pulls out a case containing two fiddles. He pulls one out, tunes it and starts fiddling. The music immediately reminds me of the sound track of Ken Burns' "Civil War." He then places the fiddle carefully back into its velvet-lined case.]

Ralph demonstrating his homemade fiddle.

I like the way you take care of your instruments. Most young people wouldn't take so much care.

Well. I've fixed a number of fiddles, violas and cellos for the school. They brought one to me. The sounding post had come right up through the top. It had a hole in the top 'bout that big. I was able to fix it. I had to make a new sounding post, and the base bar had come loose. In order to get that back together I drilled holes along the base bar and poured glue in those holes. Then I coated screws with wax and used the screws to pull it back together. After the glue set I removed the screws and filled the holes. Then I patched the hole where the post had come up through, and they were able to play it again.

So you have always loved working with wood. It must be a wonderful feeling, the confidence that, if it is wood, you can make it. It is like an artist feeling that, if he can envision something, he can paint it. It's not mathematical. It's not something you can do by following a formula.

Ayah. It's all curves, not straight lines. Boats and fiddles. You have to feel the curves.

Is that why it takes so long to build a wooden boat? If a boat were just a rectangular box, all straight lines and right angles, you could probably build it in one quarter the time. I watched them replanking one of the windjammers. I'd go and check on progress every day, and it seemed like the crew of three were able to fasten just one plank a day! Every plank was curved in several directions and tapered end-to-end. Yet when it was fastened in place, you couldn't fit a credit card into the joints.

Oh, yes. Ayah. That's the fun of it. A wooden boat is all curves and tapers. No two pieces alike. And the wood is a living thing. The whole boat is alive. It's a beautiful thing, a wooden boat.

Now I've read someplace you've been designated a "national treasure." What is that all about?

Well, I was selected by someone, I can't remember who, to get an award from the National Endowment for the Arts.

I had to go to Washington, D.C., and they gave me this thing [shows me a large, metallic, framed certificate]. We didn't go to the White House, but some other fancy place. Mr. Clinton was supposed to present the award. He was busy, so he sent Mrs. Clinton.

[Marion] I was sittin' in the front row in this place, and there was a whole batch of reporters at the back of the room. She finally gets there, and wham, all those reporters come jammin' down to the front with their recorders and lights, and I couldn't see a thing!

Poor Mrs. Clinton was frustrated. She was rushed. They were pushing her here and there. It was a real hard time for her because of the Monica thing. But she decided to stay with him. Both of them were ambitious, and I guess they thought they'd do better together than apart.

[Ralph] I think she'd do better without him.

So you've been to Washington, D.C.. Have you ever been in Florida?

No, I haven't, but Marion has.

[Marion] I went to Florida the year before I married him. I've been there, and I don't like it.

I have friends who go there every winter, and they tell me how wonderful it is. They play golf and shuffleboard and barbecue and go to the 4 p.m. early bird special at the restaurants. Sounds to me like one gigantic retirement home. I tell my wife, "I will never be old enough to live in Florida. If I do get that old, just shoot me!"

I don't know what I'd do down there with all those old people. Old people are boring.

Have you ever been to New York City? Of course you have! You just went through to Washington, D.C., to get your award. But other than that, have you been to New York?

Well, yes. We went down to New York one time. A fellow and I were on the subway. We got to talkin' with this guy sittin' alongside of us. He told us he'd lived in New York City all his life. So I asked him about this place we were going to, uptown. "Why," he said, I don't know. I've never been that far!" And he'd lived there all his life! So I guess it's not just Maine people who stay close to home.

MICHELLE FINN
Island School Teacher
Frenchboro, Long Island
Age 36

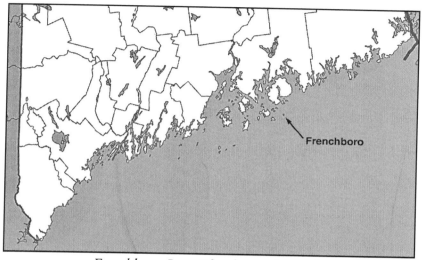

Frenchboro, Long Island, population 61

Twelve Maine islands have K–8 elementary schools. I thought visiting one of the schools would yield views of both island life and island children. I picked the Frenchboro school on Long Island off Acadia, because it was both remote and small.

Three scheduled visits in January were cancelled due to high winds [35-45 knots] and high seas [6-10 feet]. Finally, a scheduled ferry trip coincided with a sunny, calm day. I was the sole passenger on the Captain Henry Lee, *the ferry operated by the State of Maine three days a week between Bass Harbor on the mainland and Frenchboro, Long Island. Because of the limited ferry schedule and lack of an island inn, I was to stay overnight with the young teaching couple, Michelle and Doug Finn.*

Waiting at the dock were two vehicles, both twenty-something-year-old pickup trucks. One contained a weathered fisherman, the other a pretty young woman. I chose the one with the woman.

As Michelle Finn and I introduced ourselves, the fisherman approached Michelle's window. "Who's the stranger?" he asked.

My mother's parents owned a dairy farm in Owl's Head. They didn't have much money, but they had eight children and 200 acres of land.

To keep the family afloat, grandmother also taught school. When grandfather died an untimely death, she was raising children from a newborn infant all the way through college. She never re-married but raised them all herself. All eight of her children went to college, including Harvard and Yale.

Wow! And what were your parents like?

Dad was a bit of a New York City hooligan, into mischief and playing hookie. Grandmother befriended a truancy officer and actu-ally gave the apartment key to this man. He would come and wake up my dad and get him to school. It was drastic, but it worked.

My dad is now an optometrist. His city boy ways have always been in contrast to my mom's farm upbringing. His idea of "roughing it" would be to rent a Winnebago. After forty years in Maine, he's still considered "from away" and takes pride in being a lone Yankees fan in Red Sox territory.

Mom's family were avid outdoorspeople. When I was a child, my uncle used to take my brother and me into the Maine woods to camp and fish. He took us to hike Mount Katahdin when I was only nine years old. Even though Mom has her Master's degree and is a school principal, I still tease her that she's "an old cowhand from way back." She'll always be a real Mainer. If you wanted something fixed in my family, you asked my mom. Once I was working with her in the garden, and there was a tree stump. She just went to the garage and fired up the chain saw.

With eight children to raise, did your grandmother make your mom and her siblings work?

Absolutely. They all had lots of chores around the farm, and they didn't have many of the luxuries that we take for granted, like going out to eat or to the movies.

Do you remember your first impression of the ocean?

The ocean was the backdrop for all of our play. We were allowed to go down to the beach and do anything. We just had to walk through a field to get to the beach. And there was an island in the bay that we'd row out to in our little skiff.

In Down East Maine there are no sandy beaches. It's all stones or clam flats. If you want to swim, you put on old tennis shoes or muck boots. You might dig a few clams while you're at it.

But there was this huge rock in the flats, and when the tide came in it became a little island. That was my spot. I remember I'd go there if I was feeling like I wanted to be alone. One thing I always knew about the ocean was that it would remove all thought. I wouldn't feel sad; I wouldn't feel happy; I would just feel...open. The ocean has a magical effect. I don't know whether it's the sound of the waves, the smell, or....but something about it is mesmerizing.

We spent some time in the woods, but we spent most of our time down by the ocean. I spent the first twelve years of my life there in our big old rambling house. I didn't care that when I woke up the glass of water next to my bed would be frozen. I wore flannel pajamas, and my mother used to fill a milk jug with hot water, and send it with me to bed. When we were really small my dad would hold our blankets in front of the woodstove. Then he'd wrap us up in the warm blanket and put us in bed. It wasn't an issue. That was what everyone did, as far as I knew.

What did you used to dream of becoming when you grew up?

I assumed I would be a teacher. My grandmother was a teacher; and my mom was a teacher; so that was what women did. But I also knew I wanted to travel. I wanted to go to Australia and Alaska. We always had *National Geographics*. I was fascinated by the world, even though I had never been anywhere. Going to Bangor [1975 population: approximately 32,000] once a year was a really big deal. Bangor was the place with all the lights. We'd say, "Are we there yet, are we at the place with all the lights?" Dad, being from the Bronx, would go, "Oh, my God! They think this is a city!"

I was a tomboy. I raked blueberries, I stacked firewood, I saved my money. I never wore skirts or dresses. I wore my brother's hand-me-down shirts and dungarees. It's funny because my dad was a doctor, and my mom was a teacher, so they made good money, but they did not want their children to have everything. They wanted them to work.

I had a job when I was ten. If I wanted something, I bought it with my own money. Education and hard work were the two things my parents valued, and they passed that on to their children. Get good grades, be polite at school, call everyone Mr. and Mrs., and answer the phone a certain way. Their idea was, "We are giving you a set of societal rules so you will fit in." We would not have gotten those rules any other way in that little fishing village.

As you say that, I'm thinking that is exactly what you are doing in the Frenchboro School.

Definitely. Another thing my parents gave me was the right to just be me. I think few kids these days have that right. Everything today is scheduled, controlled, and contrived. You're not allowed outside of your house on your own! We had free rein. We just went out, and we would come home when the sun went down, when it was time to eat. That's why I love Frenchboro. This is how I was raised.

Today you see parents walking or driving their children to school. That never happened when I was a child, even if we had to walk miles.

I call that "helicopter parenting." When I grew up, seat belts were for swinging on. We didn't use them. We used to lie on the seat, looking up at our feet on the roof. I never knew anybody who was injured.

Back in those days you would hear about a dreadful accident once a year. If someone had an accident in Massachusetts, you didn't hear about it. If some child got abducted in Ohio, we didn't hear about it. It sounds so much worse today because the media feed on it. We don't watch the news. I keep up with world events because I use them in my teaching, but I don't, and my students don't, need to know about the latest car pileup in Bangor.

Where did you go to college?

I first went to Syracuse University, but I discovered right away it wasn't for me. I was walking to class and saw a young woman walking toward me. She was really dressed up. I thought that in college you wore whatever, that the important thing was studying. But, no, these girls were, like, done up to the nines! Being from Down East Maine, it was a culture shock. As she walked past, I told her she looked nice. And then the girl spit on me! I said, "You know what? This place is not for me."

I transferred to the University of Maine. It was cheaper and friendlier, and it was the same education as I would have gotten at Syracuse. I didn't think it was any better or worse, but it was smaller, less expensive, and closer to home. I graduated UMaine *summa cum laude* after three years, then I moved into a hole in the ground.

A hole in the ground?

I really went to school just to get the piece of paper for my parents. School was the biggest academic joke of my life. It was not challenging. The only time I learned how to teach was when I watched my mom in her classroom. We did student teaching at school, but, oh man, there was so much theory and so little practice!

Why did I move into a hole in the ground? Because I had been in a relationship, and it had ended very, very badly. I had extricated myself from the situation. But it had made me more open to living in the present and not letting opportunities, no matter how strange, pass me by.

The hole was at a wilderness survival school in the Pine Barrens of New Jersey. The school is run by a man who was taught by his Native American grandfather.

I had a friend I met in Australia. She had gone to this school and really loved it. For some bizarre reason, she thought that it was for me. I said, "Are you kidding me? I want to be Laura Ingalls Wilder, not Tonto!" But it happened that I was doing my last practicum at a Waldorf-inspired school. One day the eighth grade teacher said, "We're going to have this shamanic drumming in our classroom. Would you like to join in? I was like, ok, that sounds great. Let's do shamanic drumming, whatever the hell that is.

Well, it's this guided meditation. She's drumming, and she says, "This is the Eagle meditation. You're going to hear the drumming, you're going to hear my voice;, you're going to go to a high place, and you're going to meet the eagle. I lay down on the floor with the others. She's drumming away and chanting, and I start having a panic attack because I am not seeing anything. I think I'm failing. I don't see any eagle. This is not good, because now she's coming to the climax of the drumming.

All of a sudden I find myself in a cave with this old Indian man. There is a fire between us, and I'm going, "What the hell is this?" I could smell the fire; I could feel the heat; I could feel the coolness and the wetness.

You weren't on any substance, were you?

I swear I was not on anything! But it was bizarre, and it frightened me because it was so real.

It was the grandfather. It was the Indian who'd taught the survivalist teacher, and he has come to me. I had no interest in going to this school at all, and here is this old man. What do I say to him? I say, "So where's the eagle?" [laughs] He takes a stick, and he draws an eagle, and he points to the ground and says, "Here, here is eagle." Then he points the stick at me and says, "You, you are eagle. You will bring freedom to many people." He tells me I'm going to the school, that I'm going to live there.

I called my friend, and she freaked out. She said, "Oh my god, that was Grandfather! What was he wearing? Give me details." I said, "Well, he had this thing tied around his head. It was red." She said, "Oh my god, he was an Apache! You absolutely have to sign up for a class."

The first course was held at an old farmhouse in New Jersey. In the course of the seven-day class I learned how to skin a deer, which horrified me because I was a very strict vegetarian, and how to throw a throwing stick. I almost killed somebody with my throwing stick. I was the only person in my class who couldn't make fire. I was a dismal failure at pretty much everything. I was thinking, "What am I doing here?"

Then I got friendly with one of the helpers. At the end I told him about my vision. He said, "I can't believe that happened to you! That is very powerful. You are going to be a caretaker." The school had this really primitive camp in the Pine Barrens. It had primitive shelters of different styles, and that was where the additional classes would be held. Within two weeks they offered me a job as a caretaker, and I moved into this covered hole in the ground.

Can you describe your new home?

Well, it was five feet deep and ten feet in diameter with a roof of sticks and leaves. The walls of the pit were lined with cedar slabs. The cedar was nice because it was a natural bug repellant, and there were a lot of bugs. Of course it was cold, but New Jersey winters have nothing on Maine.

What did you wear?

Carhartts [insulated, full-body coveralls]. I also made buckskins, but I didn't wear them much. I bathed in the river. In the middle of winter I was breaking through the ice to take a bath, but I didn't think anything of it. That's just how it was!

If the end of the world comes, you and the cockroaches will be the only survivors.

That's what I told my parents. "This is my insurance policy. Anything happens, I'm all set." Given a knife and plastic sheeting, I would do very, very well. If you've ever done any extended camping, you know that after a few days you get into a different place. The first couple of days are a struggle. You are fighting it. All of a sudden you calm down. You get into a different state, your nature state. You are not around other people, and you become a better self.

My parents were horrified. "What? You don't have running water, you don't have electricity, what is wrong with you?"

I came home for Thanksgiving, and I heard about this butcher down the road. It was deer hunting season! I showed up at the butcher's, and I said, "This is awesome! Do you have any deer hides?" He's probably thinking, "What is this chick doin' here askin' for deer hides?" He takes me in the back, and there's a whole stack of deer hides. I was like a kid in a candy store. I took fourteen hides, and deer legs, and bear paws.

My dad was seeing me off, and he looked into the car, and he says, "Jesus Christ, are those deer legs; are those bear paws?" Actually, he had a begrudging respect for me. He said, "I've got to hand it to you, kid. I can't imagine doing what you are doing."

I took fifteen classes, then I was ready to move on. When I moved back to Maine, I was ready to start teaching.

How old were you then?

Twenty-six, but I couldn't get a job teaching. With consolidation, so many school were closing, there were no jobs. Even people who had been teaching for years were getting laid off. The only thing I could get was an ed-tech, but I wasn't willing to settle for that. I ended up traveling around the country, doing rock climbing, having experiences. At the end of the trip I went to a job interview for teaching in Alaska.

I got the job. I already knew I wanted to teach in a remote Eskimo village. I was all about it. I no longer wanted to be a frontier woman. Now I wanted to teach natives. I was a born-again Indian.

They hired me on the spot, and they said, "What grade do you want to teach?" I said, "Fourth grade." That is what my mom taught. It's a tough age. A lot of kids fall behind at that point. Things are getting much more complex in math. They are going from addition and subtraction to multiplication and division. I like that age because they listen to you. They're not yet adults, but they're not so little that you're wiping their...you know. And they don't yet have that junior high attitude. They still like school.

The recruiters said, "There are these islands." I had no idea; I didn't even look at a map! I left the job interview, came outside, and called my parents. I was like, "I GOT THE JOB! WOOHOO!" Dad comes on the phone, and he says, "Where are you going to be teaching? Let me get the atlas." I said "Savoonga, St. Lawrence Island." There's this incredibly long pause. Then, "Jesus Christ, now what have you done? You are closer to Russia than the United States!" [Savoonga has a population of 643, ninety-five percent being Eskimo, and is at 64 degrees north latitude.]

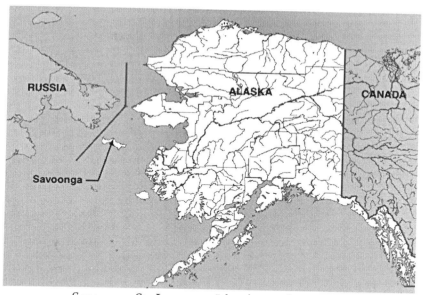

Savoonga, St. Lawrence Island, population 643

This place isn't in the Aleutian Islands?

No, no, farther north, much farther north. It's in the ice pack. It's only thirty-five miles from Siberia. It was really remote. Doug carried a gun, a huge cannon gun, in case a polar bear attacked us. Typical morning announcement: "School will be late because there's a polar bear roaming the village."

The flight from Maine was hellacious. I was on a plane for twenty-four hours. By the time I got to Nome it was already night again. In the morning I flew out to my island, and it was this FROZEN ROCK in the middle of nowhere! I got off the plane, and the little Eskimo children ran up to me, "Teacher, teacher!" These funny little kids are hugging me. Wow!

A few days later I went to the staff training. And there he was, Doug [Doug Finn, from Minnesota, was also in Alaska to teach, but at a different location]. The last thing on my mind was going to Alaska to find a husband. It's not like I didn't look around the room and note people, but I was just in a totally different space.

After my previous horrific breakup, I was totally against any sort of commitment with a man. Love them and leave them. I didn't want to ever go through anything like that again.

Then he started talking about his brother with Down Syndrome. My heart started melting. I'm like, "Geez, he's so great, and what the heck, and so, yeah." I was a goner. I went to visit him in his village, and, you know, we had a kinda romantic interlude. But then I had to go back to my island. As the bush plane was taxiing to leave, he was in his truck. I'm sitting there in the plane, and it was night time, and he started backing up, and I saw his red tail lights. Suddenly I had a sick feeling, and I thought, "Oh, God, I don't want to be without him! Oh no, this is terrible! What am I going to do?"

As soon as I got back I emailed him. I said, "This isn't just a fling, is it? If it is just a fling, then I can't be with you because I don't want to get hurt." I sent the email, and...nothing!

Meanwhile, he has sent me an email. Basically his email said, "I am in love with you." BOTH of our emails were delayed by a whole day. But we finally received them, and we both said, "We can't do this long-distance thing. This is just too hard."

Doug immediately applied for a transfer, and after six months we were together on the frozen rock. We spent three years there.

We got engaged down at the beach, next to a pair of rotting whale carcasses! [laughs] It was memorable. It should have been in *Modern Bride* magazine. It was so cold that I had to wear a face mask, goggles, and a hooded parka. The hood came out so far it was hard to tell if there was really anybody inside. Doug couldn't reach me to give me a kiss.

Do you enjoy teaching together?

We are very compatible teachers. Sometimes he takes the lead; other times I do. Sometimes we co-teach. At the one-room Frenchboro school we are together all the time. We don't compete. It's all about making it the best we can for the kids. Sometimes at school when the kids are working quietly Doug and I text each other love notes across the room [giggles].

Michelle, one-on-one with an island student

Are island children different from mainland children?

The islands require an extreme degree of self-sufficiency. You have to be able to jury-rig your motor because you can't get to the parts store. The buck stops with you and your friends.

It's a different kind of community where everyone is looking out for each other. You also have to be adult so young. Two of our boys have a lobster business they are running. They have all of the expenses of buying bait and fuel and gear. One is in fifth grade. At the age of ten he bought a $7,000 boat, and he already has it more than half paid off.

It was the same in Alaska. The kids had this strange mix of wisdom and naivete. My fourth-graders still believed in Santa Claus, but they had all this other crazy knowledge. They knew how to repair an engine; they knew how to set traps for animals; they were out hunting for seals with rifles; and they were ten years old? Oh my God! It's very similar here on the island.

Frenchboro Harbor. Acadia is in the background.

And these kids have no guile. They are very present, very polite. They are shy, and they are so sweet. I haven't seen that in other places. If a kid were born here and the parents weren't, you'd see it in the child but not in the parents. It's the environment. I hate to say it, but the kids are, in some ways, better than the adults.

They don't even know how to be dishonest. They don't get the concept of dishonesty. In the big cities dishonesty—stealing, lying, cheating—are survival skills. On the island you have to play it straight. Survival here depends on everyone being open and honest. On the island everyone is more aware of each other. Frenchboro is "It takes a village to raise a child" in action. Every adult is a parent of every child.

Nobody on the island locks their doors. In fact, we don't have a key for our house. The fishermen leave their keys right in their trucks! They say, "You never can tell when someone might need to borrow my truck." Most of the islanders leave a car or pickup truck at the ferry terminal on the mainland. It's cheaper to leave a car there than to ferry it back and forth. And they leave the keys in the car there, too! They'll say, "Of course, take my car, and while you're at the store, I need a pound of sugar and a gallon of milk."

Do you find island parents to be competitive?

No, that's another thing that is better than on the mainland, especially in the larger school districts. On the island education is valued, but it's the "other," not the primary thing. Here, education is what the teachers do. There is a little more separation between what is seen as the 'teacher's role' and the 'parent's role', yet we have some of the most supportive parents we've ever had the pleasure of working with. When we have parent/teacher conferences, every parent shows up! Often, when we go on trips, all the parents accompany us.

So you don't want to take over as the parent figures. The teacher and the parent are two different functions.

We feel our job is helping to create the next generation of citizens. When you think about it, that is an incredibly important job. Think about it. If all the children stay on the island, then the kids sitting at these little tables in this room are going to be running the town. That puts our jobs in perspective. There are so few people on this island, we know the skills we are teaching them today will be put to use.

DONALD SOCTOMAH

Tribal Historian, Passamaquoddy Tribe
Pleasant Point, Perry
Age 55

Donald Soctomah and grandson paddling a reproduction
Passamaquoddy birchbark canoe

Many of the Mainers I interviewed can trace their roots back to the 1600s. More remarkable, however, is the fact that several of Maine's Native American tribes are known to have lived along the coast for at least 10,000 years. Thus, when I stumbled across a reference to the Tribal Historian of the Passamaquoddy Tribe, I thought, "Who better?"

I reached Donald Soctomah on his cell phone. Yes, he'd be glad to meet with me. He told me to meet him at the tip of Pleasant Point, overlooking Passamaquoddy Bay.

I arrived early. While waiting I tried to picture what he would look like and how he would arrive. Would he be walking; would he be riding a horse; would he be paddling a birchbark canoe?

A Subaru station wagon pulled up next to me, and a medium sized man with shiny black hair and eyeglasses emerged and smiled.

I understand the Passamaquoddy Tribe lives on the shores of Passamaquoddy Bay. Can you tell me the meaning of the word, Passamaquoddy?

The name Passamaquoddy is an Anglicization of the native word Peskotomuhkati, meaning "People who Spear Pollock." The pollock is a big [up to forty-two inches and forty-five pounds] saltwater fish, and it takes a lot of skill to spear one. But we call ourselves Skigin, which means "People of the Earth."

Passamaquoddys are part of a larger group of northeastern Native Americans called the Wabenaki, which means "People of the Dawnland." The Wabenaki are made up of five tribes: Passamaquoddy, Maliseet, Abenaki, Micmac, and Penobscot.

We are also part of a larger group called the Algonquins, which is a language group stretching from the Atlantic to the Pacific. It is the largest language group in North America.

Everything was different back then. The oceans were warmer three or four thousand years ago. The ocean here had swordfish, and swordfish follow warm water. We know that because we find swordfish bones in native archeological sites.

Tell me about Donald Soctomah. Where were you born?

I was born in the hospital in Eastport, but I was raised here at Pleasant Point [Pleasant Point is a Passamaquoddy community in the Town of Perry, Maine]. I went to school here until I was nine. I was taught by the Sisters of Mercy.

Was English the primary language in the school?

Oh yes, the nuns made sure of that. In school we spoke English, but in church they spoke Latin. I never spoke Latin. I had a hard time enough with English. At home we spoke Passamaquoddy because my mother and my grandmother spoke it.

When my grandmother passed on, my mother had to go away. She picked potatoes up in Aroostook County, she raked blueberries in Columbia Falls, and she worked at the sardine factories and the woolen mill in Eastport. She followed the work.

So who raised you?

When she was away working, my three older sisters. Then my mother was killed picking potatoes, and I and my siblings ended up adopted out. For the first year I lived with relatives on the Penobscot Reservation. My sister got married and had a child. Her husband was in the Navy and was going to Viet Nam. She asked if I wanted to come live with them. At that time the military families stayed in Cherry Point, North Carolina, while the husbands were in Viet Nam. I ended up traveling all over the country. Her husband came back from Viet Nam, and we went to Salina, Kansas; Brunswick, Maine; Medford, Massachusetts; and SanDiego. During that time I attended over thirty schools.

I was never in one school long enough to make friends. The teacher would have me stand up, and she'd say, "Class, this is Donald Soctomah. He's just moved here from..." A month later it would start all over again.

I was in Milwaukee on my eighteenth birthday. I had $100 saved up, bought myself an old '63 Chevy Bel Air, drove across the Trans-Canadian highway, and enrolled in the University of Maine.

There was a program where the University of Maine was trying to recruit Native-American students. A big group went for the summer to get used to the University. Of the big group, three of us stuck it out.

I studied Forestry Management because the Passamaquoddy Tribe had just been federally recognized [1975], and the tribe was pursuing a land claim settlement trying to get back Maine forestlands. I thought there would be job openings in forestry.

When I graduated I couldn't get a forestry job in Maine. I got a job with the U.S. Forest Service in West Virginia. Then an opening came up in the Tribal Forestry Department. By that time the tribe owned 140,000 acres of forestland. The Tribe contacted me; I moved back; and I worked as a forest manager, a silviculturist, for about fifteen years.

Then the urge came upon me for history. I started by researching my family tree. The urge to study history probably came from knowing that my great grandfather was the Tribal Historian, the Wisdom Keeper of the tribe.

Is that a traditional position in the tribe?

Yes. Back then it was called the Wampum Keeper.

What is wampum?

They are sacred shell beads made from quahogs. When the tribes communicated with each other, they carried wampum belts with different bead designs. There was a wampum conference, and great-grandfather would travel all the way to Quebec to meet with the Great Fire Council Tribes, the tribes of the entire Northeast.

Was your great-grandfather's name Soctomah?

Back in the late 1700s and early 1800s, the son would take his father's last name as his first name. It didn't happen all the time, but I've seen it enough to know it was a traditional way.

And what did the son take as his last name?

He took his father's middle name or a nickname, or he could take the name of his uncle or his grandfather. Now we have reverted to the more common practice where the son takes the last name of the father. My family last names have all been Soctomah since 1724.

It's difficult to trace native genealogy back very far because names weren't recorded way back. Long ago, when the tribe signed documents, they drew animals as symbols. I have found documents containing both the Soctomah name and a symbol, so now I know what my family symbol is. Now I can trace the family even further back using just the family symbol.

On some of the treaties with England the Passamaquoddy Tribe used the symbol of a great blue heron. Another time it was a canoe with two people in it and a porpoise in front.

Have you taken any formal courses in history?

No, and at this point I don't have enough time to go back to college. What I did was find out what other tribes do for history and how to create the position of historian within the tribe. I applied for grants and got my position funded. This year I was real lucky. I got two grants. The first one is to teach the community to build the birchbark canoe, to keep that tradition alive. I'm hiring two birchbark canoe builders to hold classes for the kids. The second grant is to create an 18,000-word online audio dictionary for the native language.

How does an online audio dictionary work?

You type "Passamaquoddy Dictionary" in the search field of your browser, and you'll get our dictionary on the computer. Then you click on a word and you hear it pronounced by a native speaker.

The dictionary was completed four years ago by quite a team of tribal language speakers with the help of a couple of linguists. We did have some tribal linguists. David Francis, who is ninety-four, worked on the dictionary for thirty years. He can explain the language up, down, and sideways.

Is anybody teaching the language now?

Oh, yes. They teach it in the school. The school gives them the basics. They can understand the words. They can read it, but not necessarily speak it. To go to the next level, they'd have to start speaking it at home. We are the last tribe on the East Coast, all the way down to Florida, that still speaks its language. About twenty percent of the tribe can speak the language.

And are you doing archeological digs?

Yes. In the last five years we've concentrated on land the tribe owns in Machiasport. There is an old tribal village with are petroglyphs [rock carvings] that are about 5,000 years old. The rising ocean and the toughness of the climate are weathering the ledges with the petroglyphs, so we've been studying and documenting them as fast as we can.

Do you make plaster casts of the petroglyphs?

Some of them, yes. And we've done archeological digs surrounding the land to document the history of the area. We're learning quite a bit about our past.

I just read about the people they think crossed the Bering land bridge to settle the Americas. As I recall, the article said they were thought to be from Eastern Asia, and the migration happened all at once about 12,000 years ago.

The tribes don't agree with the Bering land bridge theory. We feel the historians were faced with an unknown, so they looked at the closest point between the continents and figured it must have happened there. I prefer to look at our tribal legends. We have a lot of legends about this island [Deer Island in Passamaquoddy Bay] and the whirlpool over there [Old Sow, one of the five largest natural whirlpools in the world]. We also have legends about the "great white animal."

The polar bear?

Yes, we have legends about the polar bear. I believe the geologists say Maine was covered by a mile-thick glacier ten to twelve thousand years ago, but if you look at the Gulf of Maine and Georges Bank, you see where all of a sudden the land comes up out of the ocean [the Continental Shelf]. I believe people lived on the fringes of the glacier, and as it receded, people started taking over the land.

So people could have been living here prior to 12,000 years ago?

That's the way I see it, and that's the way our legends tell it. We have a legend about where winter and summer battled. Winter represented the glacier, and summer represented the warmth of the ocean and the sun. According to the legend, after a long struggle, summer pushed winter far, far north. In other words, the glacier receded.

How do these tribal legends get passed down?

The legends are our oral history. My great, great grandfather heard it from his father, who heard it from his father, and so on. The legends weren't written down until about 1880 when a man named Charles Godfrey Leland came and started collecting the legends and history of the tribe. There were a couple of guys before him in 1860 who collected some of the legends, but not as completely as Leland.

What impresses me about legends is how they can be kept intact for thousands of years. I have been at parties where we played a game where a message is passed down a line of six people. By the time the message gets to the end, it is usually quite different from the original.

There was a professor who did studies on the oral history of tribes, and he compared tribal people to non-tribal people. He wanted to see how long a legend could retain its form without being changed. He did it with different racial groups, and he found that Native Americans retained the original details best of all.

Well, it makes sense. Because they had no means of recording the stories the oral history became very important, something to be taken very seriously.

Except for the petroglyphs. Petroglyphs also record the legends.

Then you can read the petroglyphs and see the legends as they existed 5,000 years ago?

Pretty much. We are still learning how to interpret the petroglyphs. Two years ago a fisherman came to us while we were in Machias doing our archeological dig. He said he had found writings on a rock on one of the outer islands. He said it was on a ledge under a giant tree that blew over.

He took us out there, probably three miles off the coast, right to the spot. The tree was twenty-two inches in diameter, and right underneath on the ledge were the carvings. The carvings had star designs. We know that Native Americans used the stars for navigation.

I understand native canoes would go the length of the Maine coast, even down to Cape Cod.

One group of Passamaquoddys paddled all the way to Washington, D.C .and met with President Jackson. That story was in the newspaper. And there are all kinds of stories involving the ocean because our people lived and died on the water.

How large were the canoes that used to go in the open ocean?

Over twenty feet. One of the projects we are doing is recreating an ocean-going sailing canoe. There is an original one in the Maine State Museum in Augusta. We took detailed measurements, and this spring we are going to start gathering the bark and the spruce. It was over twenty feet, because when you are out in the deep ocean, a gale could pick up real fast, and you would want to be in a big boat.

Did the canoes have keels or leeboards?

No, basically they just sailed downwind. The type of sail we are going to recreate was used in the 1800s. One of the first Europeans to sail into Passamaquoddy Bay was Samuel Champlain in 1604, and he kept elaborate details of what he saw. He said, "I see a group of native people, and they have what looks like a sail in their canoe." It was some type of tree with leather skins strung between the branches.

The natives had stories about everything in the environment, stories to help explain it. We have the highest and the lowest tides in the world here. We have the Old Sow whirlpool. The weather changes here are dramatic. It goes from one hundred degrees in summer to minus thirty degrees in winter.

I feel really good when I discover information that hadn't been discovered before. Because there was a person of one language speaking to a person of another language, there is a lot of misinterpretation of the legends The person who first wrote them up may not have understood exactly what the speaker was trying to say. Because I am a Passamaquoddy I can understand the way it was said, so I am trying to straighten them out.

Is it true that the Passamaquoddy Reservation extends on both sides of the Canadian border, and members of the Tribe are allowed to cross the U.S.-Canada border without passports?

We call this our Aboriginal Land, and it extends from the Union River in Ellsworth all the way to Point Lepreau in New Brunswick. That was our aboriginal homeland before the arrival of any Europeans. There is ongoing debate with Homeland Security about our crossing the border, but yes, so far we use our Tribal ID cards.

What is the population of the Passamaquoddy Tribe?

Before the coming of the white man, we were one combined tribe with the Maliceets. Our numbers were approximately 30,000. By 1800, the Passamaquoddys had been reduced to just 250 people. When a ship arrived from Europe, one of the passengers might have chicken pox or small pox. The natives had never built up an immunity to such diseases. Seventy-five percent of the Passamaquoddy villages along the Maine coast disappeared. Wars were a factor, too, but disease claimed more.

Reading some of the ships' journals, they said people in the native villages were laid low left and right. The tribes that survived went inland to get away from the white man's diseases. We've been dealing with war and European diseases for 400 years. The tribes out West have had to deal with European diseases for only about 100 years.

Slowly, our population began recovering. Today the Passamaquoddy census population is 3,300, and there are another 10,000 who have some percentage of Passamaquoddy blood.

What qualifies one to be called Passamaquoddy?

You have to have at least twenty-five percent Passamaquoddy blood. If you have less than twenty-five percent you are a descendant. We have the strictest requirement of all the tribes in the Northeast.

Are the Passamaquoddys trying to get a gambling casino on their land?

We had a lot of support in 1990. A major casino group was going to invest millions of dollars to help us, and the surrounding towns supported it, but when it went to statewide referendum, the people voted for no gambling anywhere in the state.

I think the reason was that it competed with the State Lottery and with bingo, and the voters were hearing from all of those people. Meanwhile, unemployment has skyrocketed in Washington County. We have fifty-percent unemployment on the reservation. It's one of the highest rates in the country.

First we lost the sardine canneries and the woolen mill, then the blueberry and potato harvests were both mechanized. We used to be able to fish right off this point here [we are sitting on Pleasant Point, jutting out into Passamaquoddy Bay] and catch a bucket of flounder in a couple hours. Today you could spend all day and catch one or two. The flounder are gone.

Except for lobstering, the fishing industry is in rough shape now. Lobstering, scalloping, and wrinkling are providing a little work.

Wrinkling? I've lived in Maine all my life and never heard the term.

Periwinkles. They pick large periwinkles for food. [Periwinkles are marine snails that probably arrived in North America from Europe on rocks used as ship's ballast. They were first observed in Maine in 1840.]

Speaking of eating "wrinkles," are there any dishes that are unique to the native culture?

One food I remember is muskrat. Muskrat is a delicacy. It's twice the size of a squirrel and half the size of a beaver. The hide is worth money because it's used in crafts, so the muskrat is first skun and gutted, then broiled with potatoes. What you as a white person might not like is that they cook it with the head and eyes intact.

Yuck! You are right. And do you eat beaver?

Yes, that, too. It's a little greasy, but it's good. We utilized all animals, either spiritually or for food. All vegetation: trees, grass, roots. There was a use for everything: for medicine, for teas, for food.

Did the Passamaquoddys grow corn?

That is one of the big debates. From what I understand, the Passamaquoddy had a lot of game: deer, moose, caribou. They'd trade game meat with the tribes in southern Maine because that's where they grew the corn. Because of the different soils, we were hunters, while they were farmers.

We have a place in Calais called the Magurrewock Marsh at the 34,000-acre Moosehorn National Wildlife Refuge. In the tribal language, "Magurrewock" means "the place of the caribou," so caribou was a staple. When you have to survive, you learn to live off everything from the land and the sea.

Another delicacy was porpoise. The tribe is really known for its skill at hunting porpoise from a birchbark canoe.

I understand a porpoise is not a fish. It's a mammal, like a whale, so its meat is red.

Right. A darkish red meat, like beef.

There was a story of a New York reporter who wanted to go on a caribou hunt. He hired two tribal guides, and he wrote down all the details of what they taught him. Now we are able to collect the wisdom of those native guides from the reporter's writings to teach our children.

He also went on a porpoise hunt. After 1900 they used #6 pellets, like a shotgun, to shoot the porpoise when it came up for air. The porpoise would sink, so they had to paddle quickly and then use a long lance to spear it as it sank.

I heard you wrote a book.

I wrote a book called *Remember Me*. It's a story that took place in the 1900s between the Chief of the Passamaquoddy Tribe and the President of the United States. The tribe had a little hunting village on Campobello Island, and Roosevelt spent summers there as a young boy. The Tribal Chief was friends with his father. He sold baskets to him, and took him out canoeing. If you ever go to the International Park in Campobello, you will see the canoe the Tribal Chief made for Roosevelt.

When I heard about that I said, "Gee, that's a good story."

Why is the title, *Remember Me*?

The Chief's name was Tomah Joseph, and he was a famous tribal artist. He carved scenes into birch bark: hunting scenes, fishing scenes, family scenes. Every time he did a nice scene he signed it with the message, "Always remember me."

Nice. Have you written any more books?

I have seven books: *Remember Me, Jean and Titiylus, Hard Times at Passamaquoddy 1921 - 1950, Passamaquoddy at the Turn of the*

Century 1890-1920: Tribal life and times in Maine and New Brunswick, A Visit to Our Ancestors' Place, and a series of four books covering the period 1800 to 1950. *Remember Me* was published by Tilbury House; the rest I self-published.

Are you optimistic about the survival of the tribe's traditions?

We have survived the last 10,000 years, including the white man for 400 years. Who knows what the future will bring, but I feel we will always be here on our tribal land.

You are preserving the language and the culture through the schools and your writings. Is there a tribal consensus that the culture should be preserved?

Yes, I think if you talk to any Passamaquoddy you will find that they are proud of their culture. That's why we alone have retained our language after 400 years of being surrounded by English-speaking communities.

The present generation has to work a little harder because the people in the community who are completely fluent are dying off. We are trying to utilize things like Facebook and the computer to get the young people interested in their language. We are going to be here forever. I feel part of the ocean and part of the earth is in my veins. When you talk about Maine, Maine is embedded in me because the Passamaquoddy have been living with and consuming the fish and the wildlife.

You have travelled all over the United States. When you were in Kansas City, or wherever, did you long to get back here.

I think every child yearns to get back to the their childhood place. For me, I had a hard time speaking English. I'd stutter, and people made fun of me. I knew I was different. I even lived in Washington, D.C., and I knew I was different there.

Did you feel pride or shame in being different?

I was always proud of who I was, but it was an awareness that I wasn't like the others. I felt different, and I thought different. Traveling around really opened my eyes because I saw other cultures. You go to the airport, and you hear five or six different languages, and those people are all proud of what they speak. That makes me want to return and do more work so the young people from here will have that opportunity to share the language. We always tell the kids, "Culture and language are one. If you lose your language, you lose an important part of your culture."

How long has this reservation been here?

The tribe never stayed long in one spot. They followed the game. They went to Calais when the salmon were running; they went to New River, New Brunswick, when the caribou were herding up; they went further north when the deer were in rut; they just followed the game.

But then the settlers started arriving after the American Revolution. This was part of Massachusetts, and Massachusetts set aside just ten acres for the Passamaquoddy.

They gave you ten acres of your own land! How generous!

Massachusetts gave anyone who served in the Revolutionary War a 200-acre parcel. Pleasant Point was a small part of one 200-acre parcel. A few years later they gave us another ninety acres, and the other 100 acres was owned by a non-native family. But then that family married into the tribe, so now the Passamaquoddy own the whole 200 acres. Later we bought land from the Town of Perry, so now the Pleasant Point settlement totals about 1,000 acres.

Pleasant Point wasn't part of the 1975 land claim settlement?

No, the land claim settlement gave us money, with a certain amount set aside for land, and another amount set aside to set up businesses. Now we have land. Prior to our owning land, we had to sneak like criminals onto land we didn't own to get birch bark and other materials we needed for our crafts.

I found a story in a local newspaper where a craftsman from the tribe wanted to make a birchbark basket, so he went to Perry.

He was in the middle of the forest, and the owner, a farmer, came and said, "You are stealing my bark." The tribal member said, "The Great Spirit made this tree. The Great Spirit gave this land to the tribe. All I'm doing is taking the outer bark, and I'm not going to hurt the tree."

Native Americans are said to be very spiritual. Do you consider yourself spiritual?

Um, I was raised a Catholic, an altar boy, and I go to church, but I believe every group has a way to communicate with a higher power. It could be God, it could be Buddha, it could be the Great Spirit.

So you are a little off the straight and narrow Catholic track?

The church has had a rough past, especially in the native community where there have been some problems. The Catholic Church had some bad apples, and unfortunately they got rid of a lot of the bad apples by sending them as far away as they could—like up here. It has lost a lot of followers, but the majority of native people still have a good relationship with the church.

I'm surprised. I never thought of the spiritualism of Native Americans in terms of Catholicism.

Well, our Catholic Church incorporates a lot of our native language, and inside the church are a lot of native decorations. It's sort of a marriage between Catholicism and native culture.

But I go to church mostly for funerals. My personal church is Nature. I go out in the woods and sit on a stump and just become part of Nature. That is my religion.

You, Wisdom Keeper of the Passamaquoddy Tribe, remind me of lines by J. R. R. Tolkien: "All that is gold does not glitter, no all those who wander are lost; the old that is strong does not wither, deep roots are not reached by the frost."
Your roots are clearly very deep in this earth.

JUDY MCGARVEY
Sardine Packer turned Diner Waitress
Eastport
Age 60

Morning news hour at the Waco Diner—established in 1924

I asked a friend from Eastport to suggest the name of a talkative local. One of the names he gave me was Judy McGarvey, a waitress at the Waco Diner. "Judy," he said, "is information central." Later, at my B&B, I asked the owner whether he knew of Judy. "You mean Radio Free Eastport?" he asked.

With fresh batteries in my recorder, I headed out in a cold rain. Judy's house, typical of most in Eastport, was small, sided in white clapboards, and looked as if it had settled in for the next few hundred years.

I was met at the kitchen door by a short woman and a large enthusiastic dog. Inside, I could see what could have served as the command center for a NASA space shot. Wearing earphones and a cockatoo on his shoulder, Judy's husband, Skip, was communicating with the world.

Judy pointed to the kitchen table and placed half a loaf of freshly-baked banana bread and a steaming cup of coffee in front of me.

Where were you born?

I was afraid you was gonna ask me that. I was born in Calais [gives me a defiant look]. Not my fault! I was gonna be born in Eastport, but no, Momma was shopping up to Calais [27 miles to the north]. Oh, God, it was just disgraceful!

Eastporters never let you live it down, being actually born outside the city limits?

Never, never! I have a friend from Massachusetts rubs me 'bout it all the time.

Well, Calais is not as bad as Massachusetts.

Oh, God, no! I would never tell anybody I was from Massachusetts. The way they act, those people still think they own the State of Maine! [Maine was part of Massachusetts until 1820.] But they can have southern Maine back if they want it. They might's well. They've about ruined it.

Where did your mother come from?

She came from Lark Harbor, Bay of Islands, Newfoundland. She was a "Goofy Newfie."

My Aunt Rebecca came down to stay with my mom while she was passing away. Mom had a physical therapist, Jamie, that would come to the house. He was British, so when Aunt Rebecca and Jamie got together, I never understood a single word they said.

And where did your father come from?

Dad came from up to Robbinston. He worked at the woolen mill. After forty years at the mill, he died of non-Hodgkins lymphoma. You would not believe how many people in Eastport died from that. It was because they all worked at the mill, breathing in those wool fibers. Dad wouldn't let any of his daughters work at the mill.

Where did you attend school?

Right here! I went to Eastport Elementary School, Eastport Grammar School, and Shead Memorial High School.

Were there more people in Eastport back then?

Oh my God, there was tons more people back then! [Eastport's present population is about 1,600.] It peaked in 1900 at 5,300 when there were thirteen sardine canneries in operation].

Lots of people had to leave when the sardine factories closed?

I had to leave! I went to South Carolina for twelve years.

I'll bet that was a shock to your system.

Oh, my God! I never saw a four-lane highway until I graduated high school. When I went down to Charleston, we're talkin' eight lanes. I'm scared to death! I was in an apartment building with 400 units. You could of stuffed everyone in Eastport into that one building!

Why did you go to Charleston?

Skip was in the Navy.

I have never been in a town with as much spirit and pride as Eastport. It seems everyone who left would really rather live here if they could afford to.

That is correct. My sister lives in St. Louis. She comes home for the Fourth. When she lived in England, she'd fly home for the Fourth. When we lived in Charleston I told Skip, "If I die you'd better ship me home and bury me up in the cemetery with Mom and Dad. I'm not going to be dead in Charleston.

I'm staying at a B&B in Eastport, and I asked the owner if I could book a room for July Fourth. He said, "I'm sorry, but we book solid for the next Fourth of July on July sixth."

Skip and I have a little house down on the water, and it's already booked. We've had people calling us since December. When Skip's mom died, someone asked if they could buy her house at her funeral. We hadn't even buried her yet!

Let me guess: the person who asked was from away.

Of course they were.

You can hardly blame them. God made only so much Eastport.

That's right. It's the smallest city in the United States, and it's the easternmost city in the United States. Lubec is the easternmost town in the United States. That's why we keep Eastport a city. Now that the sardine factories are gone, we wouldn't be famous for anything if it wasn't a city.

I'll tell you, it is so much fun to be here when the tourists arrive. My dad was **so** bad! Oh my God! Dad would go down on the breakwater, and he'd say, "Oh my God, England is some close today." And the tourists are going, "That's England over there?" Of course what they're seein' is Campobello Island! [Judy giggles]

I used to run a tour boat down in Phippsburg, and you wouldn't believe the number of tourists who asked me, "What do all these colored buoys mean?" They are pointing to the hundreds and thousands of lobster buoys, and they ask, "How do you know which side to pass them on?" So I tell them they mark the lobster traps. They say, "They don't catch lobsters with a hook?"

I know! You never know what they're going to say.

So you went to Shead Memorial High School. How many were in your graduating class?

Forty-two.

Did you have a basketball team?

Yes, but we sucked, we so sucked! We were so bad! We never made it to any of the tournaments, and everybody gets to go to the tournaments. We had a girl's team, but we couldn't play full court. They didn't think it was good for girls to run. Now the girls play like boys, and they are brutal. Oh, I tell you, they are brutal! I like playin' hockey, and let me tell you, I play boy's hockey. Boy's hockey is safer.

Do you body check?

Check? I guess I check! God yes. I'm built for hockey: short and fast. They can't upend me because they can't get under me, plus I'm wicked fast.

We used to skate where the IGA parking lot is now. The Rotary built the little warming shack and kept a fire goin' for us. The fire department would come and flood it on calm, cold nights. Those guys were big drinkers. Whenever the fire department was going to flood the rink, everybody would go down and watch and get drunk with the firemen.

Was it a volunteer fire department?

'Course it was. We couldn't afford a fire department.

Does Eastport have a police department?

Less as of last night. The City Council fired the Chief. They said he wasn't a good enough boss. I know him, and it's just because he's too nice to be a boss [tears well up in tough little Judy's eyes].

When you were a kid, did you have to work?

Money-making work? I started that when I was eleven. You want to go to the movies? You'd better have your own money.

My parents didn't drink, but my best friend Carol's father was a drinker. Before I was eleven, if we wanted to go to the movies, we knew where to find his bottles. We got five cents for a bottle, and there was plenty of bottles because he REALLY liked to drink.

When did you get your first regular salaried job?

When I went to the fish factory. I was sixteen. That was the youngest you could be, and you had to show them your birth certificate.

That's when I found out I wasn't born in Eastport. That was a bad day! I cried for a week when I found out I wasn't born in Eastport. For a while I didn't think life was worth goin' on.

I thought being born in Maine was the big thing, but I guess around here Eastport trumps even Maine. Kind of like being an Eagle Scout instead of a Tenderfoot.

Skip and I are Wood Badgers [the Wood Badge is the most advanced training for adult Scout leaders.]

I was an Eagle Scout. I still have my medal and ribbon.

ARE an Eagle Scout! [Judy acts indignant. I'm afraid she's going to take back the banana bread she just placed in front of me.] You are ALWAYS an Eagle Scout! Don't you ever tell anyone you WERE an Eagle Scout! And don't you ever lose that medal!

Ok, ok! [sheepishly] So what was your job at the fish factory?

Packin' fish. Slowest damned packer you ever seen!

You were slow? I can't believe it!

Oh, my God, was I slow! And I gotta' tell you something. This here is awful. My grandmother would roll over in her grave. You know there are two ways of packing fish, correct? When my grandmother packed fish, the fish were cooked. When I packed, they were raw.

Do you know how they got the term "herring choker?" My grandmother was a herring choker. She never used scissors 'cause the fish were cooked. She just twisted their heads off.

I have to tell you another story. I'm sixteen, so I'm not allowed to do government pack. For government pack you had to be eighteen. That was for the military.

Navy guys would come in there all the time. My heart would be beatin! [Skip yells from the other room, "You married ME!"] I married Skip because he was a Navy guy. Oh, didn't they look good in their uniforms!

Anyways, government pack is thirty-six fish to a can, and the cans are oval. I am only old enough to do fours and fives and eights and nines, dependin' on the size of the fish.

They were all the same size, weren't they?

Oh, no, they were all mixed up, plus there was some mackerel in with 'em. Jimmy Brown was my boss. Big guy! Oh my, he was big. He used to pat me on my head 'cause I was so short. I was like "Step-and-a-Half Stella." There was this girl we called "Step-and-a-Half Stella." The reason was they had these little steps you could stand on to reach the table if you were short. Well I needed one step; Stella needed a step and a half.

Packing sardines in Eastport in 1973

You say you were slow. How fast were the other women?

Well, my aunt was the fastest packer in the state. She did raw. My grandmother was also the fastest packer in the State of Maine. She did cooked. How fast were they? You couldn't see their hands.

My uncle would keep my aunt's scissors sharp. They was sharp as a razor. They always taped our fingers. Even with the tape, we'd still cut ourselves. When you cut a finger, you'd hold up the finger and yell "tape!" and a man would come runnin' with the adhesive tape. Johnson and Johnson musta felt some awful when them factories closed. That tape was on so good, you had to grind it off when you went home at night. But the salt healed your cuts. You never saw anybody with sores on their hands because the salt healed them right up fast.

How many small cans could one packer fill in an hour?

The cans had to go on a flake, and there was twenty-four cans on a flake. There was eight to twelve fish in a can, and my aunt would do ten cans a minute.

So she would cut off a tail and a head and place the fish in a can at the rate of almost two fish every second?

Oh yes! Plus she was talkin' a blue streak at the same time. She didn't even look at the fish! She said she did it by feel.

Oh, wasn't it fun! We talked, we whistled, we sang. We all looked forward to goin' to work.

But I gotta' tell you another story. Remember, my grandmother did cooked fish; I did raw. My table was one of the first you come to when you come into the packin' room because I was slow, and I was on the end of the line.

Well, this guy comes in. He's from away, and he says, "I know all about sardines." He picks up one of my raw fish, and the next thing I know he pops it in his mouth. See, he knew about cooked sardines, and he thought the fish were cooked. Well, you wanted to see my table. I had to clean up his throwup. We laughed our fool heads off all day.

After the sardine factory closed, what did you do for work?

I went to work for Hathaway's. I used to make shirts for the military, not in Eastport, over in Calais. By that time I had my driver's license. We made only officer's shirts. I was a final inspector.

I almost had my sister fired. She's a wonderful sewer, makes all her own clothes, but she could not work at Hathaway's. Their shirts only went to admirals and generals. That's how good Hathaway shirts were.

She finally quit. She says to me, "If I can't sew for them, I'm gonna' join them." She did. She joined the Air Force. Stayed in twenty-two years. You'll never guess her last job. She closed bases!

She retired from the Air Force, but now she works for a private military contractor. You ever hear of the companies in Iraq who train the Iraqis and the Afghans? She works for DynCorp. She made really big bucks working for them!

I guess she won't be back to Eastport!

She'll be back. She could move to the moon, but she never misses the Fourth of July.

How did you meet Skip?

Now there's a story! Skip, and I, and Vina—my sister Vina—we were downtown. Skip says we met in front of the liquor store, but I say we met in front of the post office. I said to Skip, "Walk us home." He said, "Ok." See, Vina knew him. Vina lived with my Aunt Gladys all summer long, and Skip's grandfather and grand-mother lived right next door.

I said, "Vina, are you holdin' Skip's hand?" She says, "Well, yeah." I goes, "You let go of him 'cause I'm gonna' marry him." Four years later we got married. Poor Skip didn't have anything to say about it!

He could have run away.

He coulda' tried, but I'da tracked him down.

[Skip] Our sons were twelve and fourteen, and one day they asked me, "Why did you marry mom?" I said, "Well, I was out trying to get laid, but things just kind of snowballed." [We all laugh].

You went to Charleston when Skip joined the Navy, but came back to Eastport when Skip got injured. What did you do when you got home?

Worked in a whorehouse! [A long silence ensues while I try to re-cover my wits.] I cleaned whore's eggs. Some people call them sea urchins. Around here they're whore's eggs.

So you cleaned sea urchins.

If you insist, but I prefer whorehouse. Anyway, you ever seen an urchin? You never, ever touch a sea urchin with your bare hand. They have spines, and they are so infectious. Some people have died. So we wore these real heavy gloves. We'd pick them off the table, turn them upside down, and poke them in the eye. I hated doing that. I'm not strong enough to crack them open, but I had a friend who would crack them for me. Then you took this teeny, tiny spoon with a long handle and scooped out the eggs. You did not want to ever break a single egg. There was probably a tablespoon of eggs in each one.

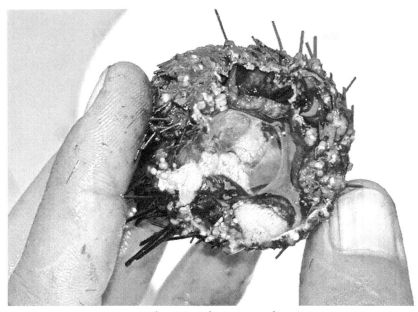

What's inside a sea urchin

Would you believe the Japanese pay $500 a pound for that stuff?

Are you crazy? I wouldn't pay five cents a pound.

After they fished out all the urchins, where did you work?

The Waco Diner. Did you know the Waco is the oldest diner in Maine? Opened in 1924. The tourists say it like Waco, Texas, but it's pronounced "whack-o." The owners lived right next door to me when I was a kid. The name came from their two boys, Watts and Coldwell.

I did the mornin' shift. I had to be there at five in the morning. The first thing you did—you didn't even turn the lights on—you turned the coffee pot on. By five-fifteen the place was packed. That's when you got your "Waco News."

The Waco News?

What happened the day before, what happened overnight, what happened five minutes ago and you missed it. The police station was right next door to the diner, so you got everything bad that had happened overnight.

Kids were not allowed in the diner because they served beer at five in the morning. I was never in the diner until I started working there!

Beer at five in the morning? Those are pretty hardcore drinkers

But you have to realize, people had been working all night. What tastes better after work, even if it is five in the morning?

Once it became a family restaurant, everybody, including kids, came there. There was a jukebox. You never knew when the juke box was gonna' come on. You didn't have to put in a quarter. You didn't have to put anything in. There was a ghost. We called it the "Walter Calder ghost," 'cause Walter always played the juke box when he was drinkin'. You could tell when Walter was in the diner drinking because you could hear the juke box all the way down the street.

Did anybody ever try to get the juke box repaired?

We had it replaced fifteen times, and the new one would do the same thing! And it never played the same song! We knew it was Walter because he never played the same songs, and we couldn't get rid of his ghost, even by replacing the damned thing!

Why did you quit working at the Waco?

New owner. It closed because the old owner, Betty, was not well. Betty was the best damn boss I had in my life.

Now I'm gonna tell you about the night we closed the diner. Let's see: there was the other waitress, Rita, Dickie Flagg, the undertaker, Marie Tinker, and I can't remember who the fifth person was. We'd been havin' a lovely time all evenin'. They'd been drinkin' and singin'. Before they started drinkin' I took their keys because I knew there was gonna be trouble. See, I don't drink. I had one of those drinks with orange juice in it one time, but I don't drink anymore 'cause I don't want to miss anything. I'd rather be the designated driver.

I had a van, so I put Dickie in the van, and I go in and get Rita and put her in the van. I come back and get Marie. When we get back to the van Dickie was gone, and Rita was gone. They were back in the diner havin' another drink. So I go get Rita and put her back in the van. I go looking for Dickie, but I can't find him for a while. Finally I get Dickie and the other person whose name I can't remember. I come back to the van and everybody's gone. This went on for two friggin' hours! I didn't get home until four in the morning.

Marie lived over in Perry. Dickie and everybody else lived in town. So I said to Dickie, "Dickie, you want me to take you home first, or do you want to wait?" He said, "Take Marie home first." We get to Perry, and Marie lived upstairs. It took me an hour to get her up the stairs.

Dickie says, "I guess it's my turn to go home." Dickie lives in this house that, the only way you can get in the house is push these buttons, and he couldn't remember the buttons. He says, "Judy, what's my button numbers?" I said, "Dickie, "How the hell am I supposed to know?" Then Rita says, "I know them!"

How did Rita know Dickie's numbers?

'Cause Rita used to go in the hot tub with Dickie when Dickie's wife was in England. Things were happenin' at the diner, let me tell you.

Dickie was the undertaker, so it's a good thing nobody died that night! Rita said she knew the numbers, but she was so drunk she couldn't remember them. Finally, Dickie got it in his head that he had a key. I said, "Dickie, what does the key go to?" He goes, "Crawl up here, put the key in, and put in these numbers." Well, that actually did work.

Why was Dickie's wife in England?

Screwin' around on Dickie!

Did Dickie's wife ever find out about Rita knowing Dickie's numbers?

Everybody at the diner knew Dickie's numbers—except Dickie!

Why did everybody at the diner know Dickie's numbers?

'Cause Dickie had a hot tub! Oh, it was a swell time!

Dickie was a riot, but Dickie died. I was takin' an exercise class down at the gym, and Dickie was doin' basketball. Dickie had a heart attack and died.

Eastport lost a great resource when Dickie died?

Oh, he was such a great guy. He was so much fun. He was my next-door neighbor.

I've just got to tell you another story. Remember, Dickie was the undertaker. So was his dad. There's been a running joke in my family for over fifty years. My mother always told Dickie's dad that she was not going to pay transportation charges to the funeral home. She said, "You open your back door and my front door, and roll me across the yard." This was goin' on forever, and Dickie knew that was the deal.

When Momma died, Dickie come in. We had Momma wrapped up in a sheet. He looks at Momma and he goes, "I'm not gonna charge transportation fees, but can I keep the sheet?"

Do you have any more diner stories?

Are you kiddin'? The very first day I go to work at the diner, a guy knocks over the salt shaker in his lap. I'm a mom, so I've got no brain. I'm lookin' all over down there under the table for the salt shaker. Of course I finally find it right in his lap. The man left me a $20 tip. He said, "That was the best damned time I had in my whole life!"

CAPTAIN ROBERT PEACOCK

Eastport
Age 61

Captain Peacock's ship at the age of twenty-nine

Eastport was my easternmost destination. After checking into one of the two open B&Bs, I headed downtown in search of something to eat.

It was a cold, windy, rainy night, and Water Street was dark and devoid of life. It wasn't looking good for fish and chips and a beer. Then, at the very end of the street, I saw neon lights and parked cars. The "Happy Crab" was open for business.

The front dining room was hosting several large family gatherings, so I threaded my way among the tables toward a back area illuminated by numerous beer signs and flat screen TVs. The only patron was a lone man of my age fondling a martini. Although there were plenty of empty stools, I took one next to him.

Call it muse, fate, or serendipity, I found myself seated next to Eastport's self-appointed public-relations department. The martini lover, a transplanted Irishman from Boston, had invested his life and savings in building Motel East a few doors down. As the evening progressed, from the best haddock fish and chips of my life, to a pint of Dogfish Head Ale, to another pint of Dogfish, it emerged that the Happy Crab was not only the local watering hole, but news central and the local seat of government. By 9 p.m., the bar was standing-room only. The City Manager, the Police Chief, the Harbor Pilot, and the owner of a boat-yard were all exchanging news and conducting business.

As each VIP entered the bar, he was collared by my new friend to meet the author from out of town. By the time the bar closed I had several interviews lined up, including dinner at the home of Captain Peacock the following evening.

I was born in Bangor, and I didn't get to Lubec until I was two days old. They still remind me of that.

Why were you born in Bangor? Was that the nearest good hospital to Lubec?

My mother was shopping in Bangor.

That's a woman for you!

It wasn't as bad as it sounds. Both my father and mother were going to the University of Maine. They lived in student housing. In the apartment on one side was Fred Hutchinson, who became President of the University, and on the other side was the girlfriend of Bill Haggett, who became President of the Bath Iron Works.

Maine, in spite of its geographic size, is a really small community!

Yeah. Senator Margaret Chase Smith used our family's camp at Indian Lake. She was there every summer for at least two weeks. All alone, no phone, no nothing. We were allowed to go up on Sundays while she was there to go swimming. We kids called her "Aunt Margaret." I got to know Margaret, Ed Muskie, Bill Hathaway, Joe Brennan, John Reed, Bill Cohen, all those people.

Did you attend the local schools?

Yeah. I was scheduled to attend Milton Academy for high school. My great uncle was head of the English Department there, but my brother got Hodgkins disease, and the money went to his treatment. It devastated my family, it really did. My brother was tall, good-looking, an athlete, and smarter than I was.

Ten years later, my father got the same thing, but by then they had improved the chemo. That gave me real insight into life and death. I was on the ambulance here for twenty five years. We'd pick up bodies and work on people, and people would say, "How can you do that?" People thought I was a cold-hearted bastard, but they don't understand. My brother's dying for four years was great training for that sort of thing.

Did your dad work at Peacock Canning?

He purchased it from his father, but his true passions were emergency ambulance work and teaching.

How could he do those things and run the cannery at the same time?

He owned the company. He could take off any time he needed to.

So what do you do for work?

That's hard to describe because I am into so many things. I'm a ship pilot, but I also run a fish business that morphed from the sardine business into an international operation importing and distributing salmon, shrimp, and tuna.

I started out as the processor and production manager, but now I do the government affairs work, the importing, and the distribution.

We have four different companies under one umbrella: Maine Freeze, Nordic Delight Foods, Peacock Canning, and Trufresh. When the local Maine production went down we went to Chile and then Norway for the salmon, to Mexico and the Philippines for the tuna, and to Guatemala for the shrimp. My job was to go to those places, live there, and get the production up and running. So in the past eleven years, I have spent a year in Chile, nearly a year in Norway, and six months between Guatemala and Mexico. Two years ago I did 160 flight segments.

Are you still doing that kind of travel?

No, the production is up and running. Now it takes just one trip a year to Norway and one trip to Guatemala. Now I just commute by sea from Eastport to the office in Lubec. It's less than two miles by water.

Our partners have 300 employees in Norway and before that another 300 in Chile. All of our fish are produced by aquaculture, even the tuna. The tuna are caught wild, then raised in pens. Our partners run 1,500 ton a year of tuna. The bluefin go fresh to Japan for sushi, and the yellowfin gets frozen and sold to Sysco. Distribution is run from here.

You are also a ship pilot?

Yes, there are two kinds of ship pilot: harbor pilots, who bring a ship into the harbor, and docking pilots, who maneuver the ship into its berth. Here, in Eastport, one pilot performs both functions.

I think most people would consider being a pilot a full-time job.

Well, Eastport used to have so few ships. A few years back we were doing only forty ships a year. I also used to do the big cruise ships down in Bar Harbor, but with all my travel for the fish business I just kept Eastport. Now it has changed. Now we are shipping cows, and there is a ship in port nearly every day.

Shipping live cows?

Pregnant live cows. Turkey had to destroy all of its dairy cows due to mad cow disease, so it's importing 12,000 pregnant cows from the United States. Eastport is the closest U.S. port to Turkey, so we're getting the ships.

So what do you do in your "spare" time?

A few things. I am chairman of the City Council, and on the Port Authority, and the Board of Trustees of the Maine Maritime Academy, which is a fabulous school. It's the best.

I have met people in corporations who say they would hire a Maine Maritime Graduate before a graduate of MIT or Harvard because of their work ethic.

That's the key. That's the difference. If you graduate from MMA you are already a proven worker. You may not be the brightest guy or girl in the world, but you will get the job done, and you will still be there working when everyone else has gone to bed.

I sailed twenty years on merchant ships, fourteen as Captain. I made Captain at twenty-five and sailed Captain at twenty-six. I was Captain of a 400,000-ton supertanker when I was twenty-nine

Wow! How long was that thing?

1,198 feet. It was the largest ship ever to fly the U.S. flag.

Captain Peacock—the one in T-shirt, shorts, and flip-flops

That's a quarter of a mile! How long is the *Queen Mary II*?

I believe it is 1,132 feet. Anyway, shorter than my ship.

So, at twenty-nine you were the captain of a ship larger than the QM2.

I shipped hard. Here is a picture of me as Captain. [He shows me a photograph of a bearded young man in shorts and flip-flops leaning nonchalantly against a ship's bulkhead. I kept looking for another figure in the photograph because the "boy" in the center looked more like a college student on spring break than the Captain of the monster ship.]

That guy in shorts sure doesn't look like a captain of a supertanker.

The crew knew who was captain. I ran a tight ship.

How old are you now?

I'm sixty-one.

Really? Well, all those years at sea didn't turn you into an ancient mariner. I don't see a wrinkle.

I've always employed a good crew. I made sure at least three-quarters of my officers were from Maine. My chief engineer was a Native American from the Passamaquoddy Reservation. That good-looking girl at the bar last night? She's a Maine Maritime grad, too.

Really? She doesn't look tough enough.

Oof! She's one tough girl, and she's smart as they come. She has her 500-ton license. She works on tugs.

When I shipped [went to sea] I worked six months on, six months off. In the six months I was ashore I ran Peacock Canning.

A real deadbeat, weren't you! [we both laugh] You must have crammed some studying in there at the same time because those Coast Guard Mariner Licenses are not easy to get!

Yeah, I just renewed my Master of All Oceans, unlimited tonnage license in November. I had to go to three schools: one in North Carolina for a helicopter dunking school, one in Virginia for ship security school, and then to Maine Maritime for anti-piracy. The anti-piracy wasn't required. I think it's going to be by the IMO [International Maritime Organization] this year, for sure.

I understand the National Maritime Center, the agency that issues mariner licenses and vessel documentation, has been moved from Washington, D.C. to West Virginia.

That move to West Virginia was very problematic.

I also write books about boating, I used to be able to call the Coast Guard in Boston or Washington and get a person to answer my questions. Now I can't reach a human being, never mind one who can answer questions.

I got to talk to people, but only because I go in the back door. I was called to testify before Congress, and they had to list the names and telephone numbers of the officers in West Virginia. So I called the new Captain. I talked to him twice.

Those people were disconnected from reality in West Virginia. Nice people, but none of the civilians have ever been to sea. In fact there were just six Coast Guard people there. Every other person was a civilian.

What the hell was that move all about? I mean, West Virginia isn't even close to the ocean! Don't tell me it was some Congressman's order of pork for his state!

Bingo! Robert Byrd, there you go! He was the Senior Senator. He could get anything he wanted, and he wanted everything for West Virginia.

When something is that disorganized, people get frustrated and quit. We're going to lose a lot of our merchant marine. There are at least five people I sailed with, people in their fifties and sixties who are just what we need, and they've all said to the Coast Guard, "It is not worth the aggravation to renew my papers." But the USCG did listen, and the system at NMC has slowly improved and has become more customer friendly.

How many hours a night do you sleep?

Right now, not very many because of all the ships coming into Eastport. But I love everything maritime. To me it's all just one big job. I try to be the best pilot in the United States. I have a big ego. Of course every pilot in the U.S. thinks the same thing. But for a small port, we've been told by too many ship captains that Eastport is the sharpest operation they've ever seen.

It appears the Peacock family carries a "hard-work gene."

That's probably true. You either enjoy working, or you don't. I truly enjoy the maritime business.

I've been working hard with the Maine Marine Patrol, on finding the sunken boats up here. We've found a few.

We've had five draggers flip and kill a whole whack of people. We've lost seventeen people within a fourteen mile radius of here. Two were tourists, and two got caught by the tide working the flats.

Working the flats?

One was clamming, and one was wrinkling [harvesting periwinkles]. The tide in Lubec can drain out two miles. On a dark night with no moon, overcast, no stars, no nothing, the tide can surprise them, and they can't outrun it. You can't run in a clamflat because you sink into the mud half a foot. Even if you could move fast enough, the exertion would give you a heart attack. The twenty-foot tide just rises over them, and they drown.

One guy was twenty-seven and fit as a fiddle. The other guy they think had a heart attack.

Draggers flip when the tidal current is running hard and their net gets caught on the bottom. They flip in about two seconds, so the crew doesn't have time to even find their life jackets.

Senator Collins and Senator Snowe got NOAA to do a detailed depth survey of the whole area. In the process they used a side-scan sonar to find the sunken boats. We have to find these wrecks because they are just another hazard waiting to hook another net.

I imagine this is a difficult area to dive in.

It's impossible. We finally got the State Police Dive Team to dive and identify the boats. Even though they did it at slack water [time of minimum current at high and low tide], of the six divers, only two were even able to get to the bottom. In the process, however, we got the world's best charts.

With these tides and currents, it must be nearly impossible to maneuver large ships into the dock! [Captain Peacock pulls out a plotting sheet showing the track of the 700-foot ship he maneuvered to the Eastport Pier the previous night.]

This is our track berthing a ship last night. We know where we are every ten seconds. We plot the ship's position every ten seconds off the ship's GPS. The blue line is where I want to go; the red line shows the actual track of the ship. There are many reasons why the two lines may deviate: the current may set us, the wind may blow us, or there may be another vessel in the way.

Here I was coming across the current, then when we got here I turned because the wind was setting us. Then I stopped here, and I just let the wind set us backwards alongside the pier.

You backed a 700-foot-long ship into the pier?

Yes.

I can't back my 30-foot sailboat into a slip. I guess that's why you are a pilot and I'm not! Did you use any tugboats?

Normally with ships having thrusters I don't, but last night we had 35-knot winds. I thought we'd better just in case she got away from us. See this other plot? That's real-time wind speed and direction at the dock, so we can somewhat predict what the wind will do to the ship.

You have been both captain and pilot, so which is more difficult?

Being a ship captain is extremely difficult now because of the regulations and paperwork. But the crews today are much better than they were in the past. They are professionals. Also, dealing with the government agencies in so many countries is mind-boggling. So operationally it is more difficult to be a captain.

But Maine waters are notoriously difficult. When you are piloting in Maine, everybody leaves you alone. Everyone—fishermen, recreational boaters, the Coast Guard, all want the pilot to do a great job.

When you are piloting, the captain is also on the bridge, right?

Right.

But basically the captain says, "Take it?"

Coming into a harbor I give steering instructions to the helmsman, but once we are coming alongside the pier I take over the engine and the thrusters. It's all on me. That way there can be no miscommunication.

How about some stories about the old sardine-canning business?

Ok. My family's company was the R.J. Peacock Canning Company in Lubec. The second or third day after I took the company over from my father we got a load of herring in and the phone rings. A woman on the other end says, "You gonna come get us?" I said, "Who are you, and why should I come get you?" "Edith, to pack sardines." I said, "Where are you?" She said, "The nursing home." I said, "Well, how long do you want to pack for?" "Two or three hours," she says. "Till we get tired. Don't worry, we'll do ok." So I said, "Can you make minimum wage?" [The workers got paid by the can, and if they couldn't pack fast enough to make the minimum wage they were let go.] "You try to keep up with me, Sonny!" she says.

So I went up and got her. Her younger sister was sick that day, so she didn't come. I walked Edith up to the packing line. My God, she was fast!

How old was she?

At that time she was in her eighties. She and her sister had their own table. Nobody else would ever use their table. I could never figure it out because it was in a good position, near the head of the line. None of the other women, as long as the sisters were alive, were going to touch it because that would be bad luck, very bad luck. So I walked her up to the packing room.

The forelady came up about three hours later and said, "Edith's ready to go home." So I took her back, and I said, "I expect you back tomorrow." She said, "I'll be there, don't you worry. My sister will be there, too, if she's feelin' any better." The next day her sister was there, too

They did that for four years—until Edith was ninety—and every day I had to go up and get them personally. She said to me, "Your great grandfather promised us when we came to work here that as long as the name "Peacock" was over the door, we'd have a job. That's a contract as far as I'm concerned, and you'd damn well better honor it!"

Neither of the sisters were married. The older one started working in the factory at seventeen, so she packed sardines for seventy-three years.

Here's a story about Senator Ed Muskie.

Two older women were sitting in the factory cutting fish. Everyone knew that if my grandfather took politicians around, he was endorsing them. The women would look up and say, "Oh, the boss is endorsing this guy." He welcomed all politicians to come in because it was good for the business. He was on the Governor's Council with Ed Muskie for years and years. They were friends socially; politically they had different views.

So grandfather comes to me—I'm maybe eighteen—and he says, "Mr. Muskie is running again for U.S. Senate. Now you take him around and introduce him to all the ladies." "Yes sir, I will." So I was taking Senator Muskie along. He had his brochures, and he'd slip one into each woman's pocket, because she wasn't stopping from cuttin' sardines.

I introduced him to Effie and Mabel and Gladys and Rachel, and we get down to Paula—and these women are all in their seventies and eighties up at the head of the line—and Muskie says, "Gee, Bob, you know every one of these lady's names." I said, "Well, a lot of them were my babysitters, and it's a sign of respect in the plant that you know everyone's name. That's what my grandfather taught me." So Muskie says, "You must be from here." I said, "Yes, sir, I am." Paula says, "Gov'nr', that's a damned lie! He didn't git here until he was two days old!"

Well, Muskie remembers this. I'm on this ship, the largest ship ever under U.S. flag, and we go into Saudi Arabia. Muskie's there visiting the King because he's now the Secretary of State.

He comes out with the King of Saudi Arabia. We're throwing a reception on the ship for 200 people. The two of them come up to the bridge. I look pretty young. I had a beard. I got fixed up the best I could. The Secretary introduces me to the King. He said, "This is Captain Peacock. I happen to know his family very well, and I remember him as a young man bouncing on my knee in the Governor's office in Maine." The King says, "How do you do? And where are you from?" I says, "I'm from Lubec, Maine, sir."

Muskie says, "That's a damned lie! He was born in Bangor, and he didn't move to Lubec until he was two days old."

Salt in Their Veins is built on the personal stories of eighty-eight Mainers who let me into their kitchens, their workshops, and their lives. Without their trust and willingness to share, *Salt* wouldn't exist. It also wouldn't exist without the patience and encouragement of my life partner, Barbara Fairfield. More than once during *Salt's* eight-year gestation she said, "It's not about you. These stories just have to be told."

At the final stage of publication I was faced with the difficult task of selecting thirty-five of the eighty-eight stories to fit into a 480-page volume. To my rescue came my literate little sister Sue Beach, sailing buddy Ralph Pears, old friends David and Jane Inman, and new friend Dan Cupido. They read and rated the entire collection of stories, making my onerous task bearable. "Onerous," I say, because I loved each and every one of the original eighty-eight. If ever there is a volume 2, you will see why they all deserve to be in print.

CREDITS

Page 11   Map: courtesy of Maine Tourism Association

Page 29   Photo: Library of Congress

Page 60   Photo: Dale Holmes.

Page 67   Photo: Gabriela Bradt, UNH Sea Grant and Blue Ocean Society for Marine Conservation

Page 95   *View with Jaquish Island:* courtesy of Frost Gully Gallery

Page 109   Map: courtesy of Maine Tourism Association

Page 135   Photo: Robert Anderson

Page 159   Photo from movie *Around Alone:* the New Film Company

Page 183   Photo: Don Hinckley

Page 205   Photo: Wikimedia

Page 227   *Vigil:* ©Will Barnet Foundation, courtesy Alexandre Gallery, New York

Page 249   Photo: Jenny Mackenzie Films

Page 327   Map: courtesy of Maine Tourism Association

Page 341   Photo: Julie Brown Eaton

Page 352   Photo: Julie Brown Eaton

Page 355   Photo: Julie Brown Eaton

Page 369   Photo: Molly O'Rourke

Page 388   Photo: Randy Olson Productions

Page 395   Photo: Millard Joseph Herrick. The Southwest Harbor Public Library Digital Archive, Number 11670

Page 401   Photo: Charlotte R. Morrill. The Southwest Harbor Public Library Digital Archive, Number 10737

Page 435   Photo: Jason Pike